THE STORY TELLERS

PUBLISHED AND AUTHORED BY
RICHARD E. DAVIS

WITH SPECIAL THANKS TO
JANICE S. DAVIS
WIFE AND PROOFREADER

THE ART OF GOOD STORY TELLING HAS BEEN PASSED DOWN FOR GENERATIONS AND IS STILL VERY MUCH ALIVE AND WELL TODAY. IMAGINE YOU ARE JOINING WITH US IN THE EVENING AS WE'RE SITTING AROUND THE CAMPFIRE OR WOODSTOVE. YOU WILL GET TO SHARE IN SOME OF THE BEST STORIES EVER TOLD. PERHAPS YOU WILL BECOME A STORY TELLER TOO.

ISBN: 0-9721526-0-1

FIRST PRINTING - JULY 2002

Additional copies of this book are available by mail.
Send $22.00 (includes tax and postage) to:

RICHARD E. DAVIS
P.O. BOX 317
HOMER, NY 13077-0317
(607) 423-5063

Printed in the United States by Morris Publishing
3212 East Highway 30
Kearney, NE 68847

1-800-650-7888

TABLE OF CONTENTS

Note: Photos are at end of book pages I thru VII – book written using interview style.

CHAPTER 1   RICHARD E. DAVIS

Janice, my wife, and I were invited to attend the 80th birthday party of the eldest member of the Knobel deer camp last May, 2001. The moment we showed up, Howard Henry, the birthday boy and host said, "you gotta write another book." My first book was entitled, "Deer Camp, Oswegatchie River And Other Places" and was published by ourselves thru Morris Publishing, a company that caters to writers who cannot get their books published by any commercial publisher, and allows you to Self-publish to your heart's content. As long as you are willing to spend the money, you can publish whatever you write. However, the main drawback to this method is that you also need to distribute your books once published, and that is the hard part. Imagine taking a few dozen books and your wife, if you're married, and heading for the north country with the intent of presenting your creation to a number of strange bookstores or any kind of a store, for that matter, that will sell books. I soon found that about every store includes an area where they sell books and a number of self-publishers are included. One drug store I checked for interest indicated that the only deer hunters they had in their town were the drunks that hung out at the local bar. They were interested in things other than books, or so the clerk said. The owner was out that day and I didn't bother to return. However, I found that most were very interested and would take time to at least thumb thru the book and look at some photos and maybe even read a portion of a paragraph – and usually wound up ordering three or a half dozen books.

The owner of the hardware store in Old Forge, New York took a copy of my book, looked at the front cover which included a photo of my father and some friends on a deer camp vacation back in 1937, said "wait here" and took off on a trot to tend to something important, no doubt. A few minutes later, my wife noticed him talking to some customer about an item he was trying to sell – but he had the book opened to about half way and clutched to his chest. Again, he disappeared. However, five minutes later he returned to us and said he would take six. Their book department in that famous store is unusually large for a north country store of any type and has a large section of children's books as well as a good variety of typical outdoor books such as historical, novels and outdoor types – the usual assortment for hunting, fishing, camping, hiking, etc.

A couple of months later, I received a phone call from a young friend, the son of one of the members of my Dad's hunting camp, who said he and his wife needed some R&R so went up north and stopped at the hardware store in Old Forge. He said he recognized my Dad from the picture on the cover of the book. Then, when he got to looking thru the other photos in the book, he found a picture of his own father. He said they only had three copies left and he bought all three. A few weeks later we went back on another trip to follow up on our first one and when we checked again with the owner of the Hardware Store in Old Forge, he had taken a trip up the Oswegatchie River once shortly after moving into the area and the thing that interested him so much was the photo included of High Rock, a main landmark part way up the River. I can understand the nostalgia as the view from the top of that rock is awesome – especially after paddling around several hundred bends in the River. At least from the top of that rock, you get to see over the top of the tag alder swamp the outline of the spruce and hardwood forest in the background that at least hints there might be an end to the swamp in sight.

Well, Howard's birthday party was held at his grandson's home. By the time we arrived most of the other guests were already there. They had a large tent set up and numerous tables loaded with a huge variety of food. In response to Howard's question about the possibility of another book, my first question was to ask "why." Howard said, "I'm getting old – and if something happens to me, there go all my stories too. I think we all ought to have a chance to get our stories down in writing. We've already lost several members of this camp and without any kind of a written record of their stories, they'll soon be forgotten." Well, this all made real good sense – so, here goes.

Howard said, "come on inside – I'd like you and your wife to see my grandson's collection of heads and antlers that he has displayed on his living room wall." Wow – what a beautiful collection. Howard had helped him put together a beautiful hardwood display board against one wall and it provided a safe and very secure place to attach heads and antlers. About then somebody rang the dinner bell and we all gravitated to the tables loaded with food. It was a real celebration of appreciation and love for this individual who had given unselfishly so much of himself to friends and family over his lifetime.

In reflecting about all this, it seems to me that the general focus of many deer camps is different from what it was in the past. None of the change is bad – just different. The present Knobel deer camp is basically the family retreat that they use year around. The grandchildren have all experienced growing up in the woods at a place that affords privacy and protection. Being situated in the Adirondack mountains on North Lake, swimming, fishing, scuba diving, sailing, canoeing, hiking, trail marking, firewood gathering, etc. are all an important part of the activities available and shared from time to time. Woods crafts such as drawing scenes on bracket fungus, sketching and painting, both from scratch and paint by number are also enjoyed. The use of map and compass has just been a natural in this environment and a great way to introduce this aspect of woods lore to the younger folks.

Deer camp in the past was an almost exclusive experience available to men only. The thought of sharing deer camp with a woman – wife or otherwise – was not even to be considered, at least not during the hunting season. Now days, however, many women enjoy hunting and genuinely share the joys of the experience with their husbands and friends. I believe this has come about due to the fact that women have been included in every aspect of the sport – from practice sessions with firearms to talking over menus and methods of cooking that would be appropriate at camp. I have previously invited my wife to visit my tent camp after getting it all set up and greatly enjoyed receiving her approval.

The Knobel deer camp really began to take shape shortly after World War II. Bob and his father, Hank Knobel loaded up their Thompson boat at the launch facility at Lewey Lake about ten miles north of Speculator, New York located in the central Adirondack mountains. They were both primed for adventure and definitely weren't disappointed. The time of this event was the second week of November. They took their chance on location of their campsite – in fact, I don't think it would have been possible to "reserve" any specific campsite back then – you just had to look around and take what was not occupied by someone else. Well, they found a delightful spot on the east side of Indian Lake near a trail that hunters had used for a number of years while hunting in the vicinity of Owl Pond, about two and a half miles east of the campsite. Midway into their vacation, Bob killed a beautiful, heavy ten-point buck on the little ridge just south of the pond. They soon noticed while dragging the deer to their camp that the weather was beginning to turn cold. That night it dipped down into the single digits and lacking any wind, the lake froze over solid with about an inch of ice. The next morning, after an early breakfast, they broke camp, loaded the boat and began their very difficult trip to the launch site. It took them the whole day. They had to break ice all the way and took turns sitting astraddle the bow of the wooden boat and chopping the ice with an axe. Both men were about totally exhausted but also were relieved and delighted to finally make it to the launch area and get the gear stashed into their vehicle, the boat onto the trailer and head home. They loved to hunt deer and had a really great adventure together – but decided they needed to look up a spot where the chances of being frozen in again would be minimal.

Previously, Hank had been introduced by a friend to the North Lake area and in fact had killed a non-typical buck several years prior to their Indian Lake trip. In the process, he became acquainted with Otto Koenig. Otto resided with his family at the State House at North Lake. Hank and Bob checked things out one summer in the hopes of finding a suitable place to hunt deer. They were hoping for a spot where they could set up their rather large wall tent during the hunting season each fall. In making their desires known to Otto, they acted upon his suggestion that they check out a spot over at South Lake where Otto knew some other hunters had used a campsite for a number of years, but just the previous fall had decided to go elsewhere. They took a run over there in July and decided the spot lived up to their expectations of what an ideal deer camp location might look like.

Near the lake itself, most of the land was cutover black spruce, balsam and hemlock. Much of the area near the lake had been clear-cut and that left thousands of small spruce trees sprouting up. It wasn't much of an area to attract whitetail deer. However, in back of the old abandoned lumber camp there were several hardwood ridges. This area was only about one and a-half miles from the campsite so would be well within reach of the camp. Also there was a considerable stream nearby the logging camp. This was the outlet to Little Salmon Pond and it was always handy to have a nice creek in the area to use as a landmark for hunting – especially when many of the guests to the camp were unfamiliar with the territory. Even though the logging had been done in the area at the turn of the century, the basic trails were still very much in evidence and made ideal places to still-hunt. Bob was uncanny in his use of names for about every spot used as a landmark in the woods. For instance, there was the bottle trail – the nearest one to the logging camp. A gallon wine bottle was very much in evidence – probably had sat there fifty years or so. Twin Bridges was another area he named. He also made it a real point to advise anyone who would hunt that far from camp that he ought to remove the shells from his rifle so that he wouldn't even be tempted to kill a deer so far from camp.

Each fall the camp had to be set up as nothing could be left in the woods from one year to the next. Several times I received an invitation to go to camp with Bob and some of his old Army buddies and help set up the camp. This entailed loading all the gear into the boat at the landing at South Lake. It was only about a two-mile boat ride to the campsite location. Everyone pitched in and soon all the gear was hauled up the bank to the campsite. The next item would be to erect the huge Army type wall tent. Stove, pipe and tables came next. Someone would string a line between the uprights that would serve as the clothes line for the duration. Bob planned to use the place each weekend during the hunting season and usually a different bunch mostly made up the camp each trip. Bob's Father-in-law, Blanchard Wilson, known as Willy, was a regular each weekend. Willy really loved the woods and enjoyed the hunting and also easily became acquainted with Bob's many guests. Several each year had previous hunting experience only in the southern tier and so their trip to the big north woods was definitely a new experience.

After a good supply of seasoned firewood was cut, split and stacked back at camp, it was dinner time. Bob loved to cook and was truly good at it. He always furnished steak to the bunch that helped set up the camp. I recall one day helping him gather a good supply of hardwood sticks that were well-seasoned. Bob started a small cooking fire down on the beach and when he had a large quantity of coals, then he would place a couple of rocks in strategic spots to support a beautiful

3

stainless steel cooking grille – then came the steaks. Oh, what an incredible odor wafted thru the woods. In no time, the whole gang would gather to watch the expert chef at work. Others had a good fire going in the wood burning heating and cooking stove and heated up a couple of cans of veggies, crafted a toss salad, set the table and made a huge steaming pot of coffee. The coffee pot was an oversized affair with no guts. The coffee was added after the water began to boil. The grounds would be settled by adding a cup of ice-cold water from the lake.

After enjoying the delightful meal, we did the dishes, dried them and carefully put them away in containers that would keep the mice from fouling them. Next came the card game. Being mostly Army buddies, the game was always dealer choice poker. Penny ante was fun. After a season of good conversation, before we knew it the time would be midnight or after. Sleep seemed to come easily and was very satisfying with the odor of spruce and balsam filling the night air.

Right from the get-go Bob would get everyone off to an early start by setting the alarm for about 4:30 a.m. This way everyone would have ample time to wake up, freshen up, brush teeth, enjoy breakfast and could leave the tent for the day's hunting before daylight. Almost everyone would concoct a lunch, usually consisting of a couple of hot dogs on a couple slices of bread that had been buttered, maybe a piece of cheese, a candy bar and an apple. Back then, everyone carried a small drinking cup intending to use raw water found in one of the numerous small clear streams. No one ever seemed to contact giardia or any other problem from drinking the water. However, recently, almost all will carry a half bottle of water in their day-pack to be on the safe side – which is a very good idea. If you ever suffer from a bout with giardia, you will make a similar decision.

One day while working in my general insurance office, the phone rang and it was Bob. He said that a black bear had ripped the tent and he was going to take a couple days off from work and needed someone to help run the speedy stitcher and would I be interested? You bet I was! We left for camp that evening – and for dinner I was treated to my first experience with chicken wings. It is funny how some of us seem to miss out on some really nice things for so long. Don't tell me it was just the woods appetite taking control either. They truly were delicious. Bob's mother-in-law had furnished him and Ginny with a large mince pie and we absconded with half of it for that emergency trip. This reminded me of my own mother's mince pies. That night a deer mouse just wouldn't quit climbing up the crates and chewing on the pie keeping us awake until we placed the pie inside a plastic carrier on the tent floor. The sewing job proved to be a real challenge as the man that had to be outside to pull the thread thru the loop with each stitch had to endure the rain. But we got the job done and it certainly was good to have a secure tent again. Not only did the bear enter by ripping up the tent flap in the front, when he departed he must have done it in a hurry as there was another rip in the rear of the tent near the table that held the pots, pans and containers of silverware. We picked up plates, cups, the coffee pot and silverware over an area of about ten feet behind the tent. I imagine all the racket made the bear pick up speed in his very hasty departure!

One weekend Bob and I were hunting south of the old lumber camp and after separating, worked our way slowly up the ridge. A little later I heard Bob's gun go off. A half hour later I spotted Bob appearing to be on a blood trail. He saw me and came over to my watch. He asked me if I'd help him track his deer that he wounded. Apparently when he fired his rifle, the deer stepped up on a little rise in the terrain. He figured his bullet hit the deer too far forward, probably in the brisket. We separated slightly with one of us taking turns following the blood trail and tracks. The deer had run quite a ways and only slowed down to a walk when coming upon Little Salmon outlet. The blood trail seemed to disappear totally. The deer actually crossed the creek on a little beaver dam and we followed one at a time. There was about two inches of snow on the ground and it was still coming down regularly.

After following the trail for a ways Bob decided his wasn't a very good hit and we should give up as it was getting late in the afternoon and we had a good two and a half miles to go to get to camp before dark. Just
as we were about to turn around and head back to our beaver dam crossing, I spotted a large ruffed grouse sitting on a hummock. I told Bob, "shoot his head off." He pulled up his rifle and, bang! The bird still had his head and didn't even fly. Bob didn't seem to be interested in shooting again, so I pulled up and, bang! This was more of the same. I injected another shell in my .35 Remington, took more careful aim and this time the bird was sans head. I was amazed at the size of the bird. We had him for dinner that night along with burgers, so everyone had an opportunity to enjoy some. It was delicious. Over the years I would imagine that probably a couple of dozen partridges have succumbed to this routine.

In all the years that I hunted with Bob, I don't ever recall taking part in a single drive. Everyone in his camp seemed much to prefer to still-hunt. Just having numerous men in the woods tends to put deer on the move. Sometimes, I am certain, we would cause a deer to move and sometimes that turned out to be to the benefit of another member of our party but it would be rare indeed that we would ever move deer to someone else on purpose. Many hunting camp parties utilize a combination of putting about three members on a watch at a place they know deer are apt to travel. Then about two members will still-hunt in the general direction of the watchers and this has been a very effective method to collect deer. However, for the camps that utilize the still-hunting method – good still-hunters can be extremely effective in putting game on the pole. The method of still-hunting that seems to work best for those that wish to try it is simply to work your way slowly into the wind or at least cross wind. By slowly, I mean really slowly. Specifically, take only two or three steps at a time. Then pause for at least a couple minutes. That time will pass swiftly as you will be very busy. You will be using your eyes. Begin to scan the area close by and gradually increase the size of the area of your vision until gradually you are scanning as far ahead and to the left and to the right of your position as possible. Check the path directly ahead for sticks or stones or other uneven items and then carefully take an additional two or three steps in the general direction you are heading. Then stop again and repeat the scanning procedure. If you begin to tire, and I don't mean tire of the method - if you genuinely begin to feel stressed or fatigued begin at once to spot a downed log or stump at the right height or a rock or something which you can sit upon and proceed to take a rest. While resting, try to sit as quietly as possible without making a motion. It is okay to turn your eyes and also okay to turn your head in order to sweep the area with your vision in a very real sense continuing what you are doing when standing. However as you turn your head, do it very slowly. Remember, deer or other animals for that matter, will detect motion very quickly – that is a dead give away. Hunters that are accustomed to covering a lot of ground while hunting will find a great difference and a real challenge to use this method. However, after spotting a deer a time or two before that animal has reacted to your presence will tend to give you much encouragement in the use of this method. Also after you are able to surprise yourself and come upon a buck within twenty-five or thirty yards of your position and get a good shot - not at a running deer but perhaps one standing still while feeding or even perhaps while lying in its bed will give you such a moment of pride in your accomplishment that you no doubt will become another hunter that will prefer the still-hunting method. After giving this a fair try you still prefer doing something else, by all means go for it. Many hunters use this method as they prefer to be in the woods and able to see all forms of wildlife in their natural habitat and doing their natural activities. Check out the stories of the members of your camp. Does your group always put on drives? Or do a few members spend at least a part of their time still-hunting. Which hunters, according to the stories shared and the game put on the pole seem to have the most fun? I don't want to appear to be dogmatic. It is just that the method of still-hunting is such a drastic departure from the method or behavior followed by most hunters that it will take a definite mind set in order to make the transition – even for a brief trial period. If you don't believe me, try it – you'll like it!

When still-hunting, suddenly a deer may "just appear" where none were observed previously. It is not at all unusual to come upon a deer that is feeding close to the ground – may have its head down while feeding on beechnuts or perhaps upon fern roots. Years when there is no beech mast crop, the deer will feed extensively on fern roots. They don't seem to eat the actual fern leaves much but will dig up the fern roots with their front feet. They put on about as much fat from feeding on fern roots as on beechnuts. If you should spot the body of a deer that is standing but you can't see its head, consider it to be feeding and count on the head coming up soon. You had better not be making any movement when it does. Also if the animal doesn't appear to have spotted you, just relax –the head will shortly go back down and it will resume its feeding ritual. You may even see the animal digging with its front hoof and of course you will see it chewing what it has gathered into its mouth. Immediately after the animal puts its head down to feed is when you should make your move. Merely raise your rifle and position your gun so you can see plainly thru your sights – whether using a scope or open sights. Next time the head comes up, you have your chance to merely adjust your sights and squeeze the trigger. Several times I have been able to make neck shots that have struck the backbone. That brings the animal down and causes the death instantly. You haven't even spoiled any meat. Also you don't have a nasty tracking job on your hands. It is truly wonderful when you can dispatch an animal in such a quick and easy fashion. I never hesitate to take a traditional heart-lung shot when a deer is some distance away and providing a broadside opportunity. Hold just behind the front shoulder and you probably will double-lung the animal. I hate it when I have blown apart the heart. At the end of this book somewhere near the very last page I will include the only recipe included in this book. It will give instructions for pickling a deer's heart. The same deal works equally well for black bear. This comes with a guarantee. Once you have tried it you will always pickle your heart after my recipe. If your doctor has told you not to eat organ meats, then give the product away to another hunter after you have followed my recipe. Another word about fern roots. Deer actually gain about as much protein from feeding on fern roots as they do feeding upon beechnuts. I personally feel a deer that has fed extensively on a heavy beech mast crop will be sweet and tender in the extreme. I have also hunted extensively in the southern tier where the deer herd has ready access to growing crops such as corn, apples and soy. I would prefer the flavor of a north-country deer every time if given the choice.

The years that the tent camp experience was enjoyed proved to be some of the most memorable of all in my hunting career. I have developed a feeling about the men I have hunted with that I don't have about my non-hunting friends. It is a good and confident and satisfying feeling. I guess this is very natural. Of course the same close feeling exists among friends of any hunting camp – whether it consists of a family retreat cabin that is also used as a hunting camp during the season or a tent camp where the living quarters are set up each and every year or whether the "camp" consists of someone's farmhouse. In some areas the only opportunity the men have to bond is early in the morning while they share breakfast at the local diner. All of these types will qualify as deer camp. Speaking of a local diner – one of the first times my wife Jani shared deer hunting with me we set the alarm clock for about 4:30 My wife is definitely not a morning person – she doesn't even drink coffee. We were going to spend the day within ten miles of our home hunting in some State land. We had packed a nice lunch to carry into the woods with us in my day-pack. For some reason we decided that we ought to go to the diner to get breakfast. So far so good. We arrived and found the only two seats left at the counter and gladly occupied them. We had enjoyed eating lunch at this local diner for several years – seemed like a good way to break up a busy day. It gave us a chance to get away from the telephone and all other causes of stress for a while. Well, normally there is so much conversation and noise by the patrons that you can hardly hear yourself think. After our orders were served, my wife mentioned – "my, it sure is quiet here." You could have heard a pin drop. I think everyone was so stressed out and tired out that no one was making any conversation.

There's a saying – "It's not what you know but who you know that really counts in getting some things done or accomplished." Well, I suppose this holds true for purchasing property. I suspect that friend Otto had something to do with making the availability of the camp at North Lake known to Bob and his family. I think all the while Bob was really interested in making a purchase and the tent camp at South Lake was sort of a temporary approach to what he really had in the back of his mind – to own a seasonal residence where the family could enjoy the summer weather and also that the camp would be used in the fall deer season for a hunting camp. The present owners of the North Lake Camp were getting older now and finding that normal maintenance and upkeep was more than they could handle. Bob needed some help with the financing and a friend came to his aid – in fact for several years the property was jointly owned. The opportunity came along for Bob and his family to become sole owners of the camp and he was able to handle this change and felt it to be a valued accomplishment in his life.

In taking over someone else's property you buy their problems as well as their advantages and it takes time to sort out the difference. For instance, there was an old time kitchen heater that ran on kerosene and the cooking range of course ran on propane. Bob had several propane tanks and could change from an empty to the next full one by the mere flick of a switch as I recall. Later on, they changed from kerosene to propane for both the heating stove and lighting. They soon discovered how efficient propane gaslights were and so were glad to discontinue the use of the electric generator that came with the place. The generator required quite a bit of annual maintenance and parts were getting nearly impossible to find. Also several changes were made in the location of appliances until finally the cooking range and kitchen sink and cupboards were moved to the opposite end of the camp which made it easier and more enjoyable to sit around and watch the wood burning unit. At first they used a Franklin Stove but the fall of 2001 changed to a new airtight wood burning unit – similar in many ways to the Franklin but even larger in size and easier to control with the airtight features of the new stove. One of the special benefits of deer camp is when we can just sit near the fireplace and spend time sharing.

I received the usual invitation to visit the camp to hunt for a weekend the fall of 2000 but had to back out at the last minute as I came down with a hard cold or the flu.

The fall of 2001 my wife insisted I take a few days to enjoy camp however I was reluctant to leave her alone. Just ten days previous, she had surgery for a hernia and wasn't supposed to lift anything weighing over about thirteen ounces. That means even heavy dishes were out of bounds. Also at the last minute, the battery on our generator died so I spent Friday getting a charge on it and reattaching it to the generator and hoped it would start when she needed to pump up our water pressure tank. And of course, she definitely could not pull the starter cord on the generator. In spite of my concern for the welfare of my wife, I really enjoyed the weekend at camp that fall. We had a full house in both the main camp and also in John's A-frame cabin across the road. This unit acted as a facility for the overflow crowd for weekends when the number visiting camp would be more than usual. For instance, Saturday night we served dinner to seventeen in the main camp. What a unique time of fellowship and friendship we all experienced. As John commented, it was really great to get to see and spend some time with special friends that we hadn't seen in months or in some cases several years.

Perhaps one of the greatest contributions every hunter today could make to the sport would be to take a youngster under his wing and share his love of the woods and the outdoors and eventually, hunting. Otherwise, the sport will disappear for lack of interest. Eventually all the mature hunters will die off and if there isn't a new crop of hunters coming along, the antis will take over and you won't be able to hunt small game or deer and bear. This past summer a friend took me on a three-day canoe trip up the Oswegatchie River – it was an adventure into nostalgia for both of us. Gerry Hines had taken a week of his vacation time for the past seventeen years and taken the youth group from our church on a canoe trip. They went up the Oswegatchie River a few times but the Conservation Department adopted a rule where the number of participants would be limited to ten people. The average number that signed up each year was sixteen or eighteen. That sounds like a lot of young people to be responsible for and it was – however they usually included as a leader someone who was willing to dedicate a week of their vacation to the group and also had a background in medicine. It wasn't easy to find a person in this category but most times, they did. In all the years of tripping, there never were, thankfully, any dire emergencies. A couple of times they ran into fiercely inclement weather meaning it rained about the entire trip. Can you imagine crawling into a wet sleeping bag inside a wet tent and waking up in the morning to the sound of more rain? Usually though the weather was great. If it rained one night out of the trip after the tents were set up, normally anything that got damp could be dried out when the sun shone again.

The new limitation rule as to the number of people you could include on a trip meant they had to search out regions that didn't enforce that rule. There were several sections of the woods that were more lenient. One of their favorites was the Cedar River Flow area. After setting up the permanent campsite, they would do day exploring trips with their canoes or perhaps hike one of the surrounding mountains so there were always plenty of options for a variety of activities available.

Then of course there are always the popular summer camp programs – but the danger always exists in these being led by people that have their own agenda regarding hunting. I don't believe very many young people become hunters who have an early influence that is against hunting or trapping.

What it all boils down to I believe is that most hunters are hunters because either their fathers or other relatives were hunters and took the time to instill valuable insights and attitudes regards the out-of-doors, conservation and hunting. My Dad was a hunter and most of his personal friends that he was really close to were also hunters and fishermen. One of my first memories as a child consists of my Father carrying me from our car to a picnic area somewhere in the Adirondacks. In the other hand he carried a Coleman gas stove. My Mother and two sisters carried all the other food, dishes and stuff. We had a marvelous meal and I also can recall that I enjoyed hearing the wind making its delightful noise in the branches of a nearby white pine tree. As I got older, we took frequent hikes into the local woods and in my early teen years, we did a lot of plinking with .22 caliber pistol.

I have a friend whose own son didn't seem to have any interest in the out-of-doors or especially in hunting. He invested himself in the life of a young teen that just couldn't get enough of the woods or stream. They went on day trips frequently and soon the young man was trusted to carry a shotgun and they hunted grouse, squirrel and pheasants. The upcoming deer season seemed like a long way off – but they made plans to go and spent time sighting and zeroing in the shotguns. However, a week before the opening day the young man was killed in an automobile accident. The trauma was about as much as if it had been his very own son that had been killed. He hasn't taken any other young friends hunting to my knowledge.

Since our retirement, my wife and I reside in our log home that we built with help around 1994. We actually moved in full time in 1998. One thing I have noticed is that living in a hardwood patch of woods, we tend to enjoy changes more. It is fun to watch the progress from summer to fall. Suddenly, when all is ready, the trees lost their leaves and only a few are left on the oak and beech brush. We enjoy experiencing the changes in the seasons. My wife has remarked I have helped her appreciate the winter woods. This simply means what the woods look like after the leaves have come off. My present wife has problems with a variety of allergies including leaf mold. So, we really rejoice when the first few heavy frosts occur and both notice how much easier it is to breathe.

We have noticed more vividly the changes that occur in the wildlife such as deer and turkey. After the bucks lose the velvet from their antlers they almost totally discontinue running with other bucks and become loners in preparation for the breeding season. The turkeys seem to retain their habit of following the leader in single file – I suspect they will give that up after they have been shot at a few times or after predators such as coyote or fox scatter them. The rigors of a long winter also have a profound effect on the habits of turkey. We have counted as many as forty jakes all together traveling thru our woods at the first signs of spring in late March. After a few sunny days, the gobblers tend to part from the flock and will roost by themselves apart from the other hens and young of the flock. I much prefer to hunt wild turkey in the spring when you can actually call in a gobbler to kill.

I would hate to face a fall and not be able to hunt. And the "hunt" might only consist of sitting out on a beech flat waiting for a grouse or squirrel or deer to come along. Just "being there" with a gun in my hands provides a feeling of completion and satisfaction.

CHAPTER 2   HOWARD HENRY

I called Howard Henry on the phone around the middle of July, 2001 and told him I had thought it over and decided we could put together a compilation of stories in one form or another and would he like to be the first person that I was to interview? He said, "yes, but my contribution will be on the light side." Well, that made sense as many times, Howard was the life of the party in camp. So, in a few days Howard accepted an invitation to visit us at our log home up in Scott and after dinner we got out the tape recorder and began to talk about deer camp. The following is much of what we talked about.

Rich: Howard, I bet if you were up in the woods now you could carry a rifle and tromp around.

Howard: I could – but I don't – because my family worries about me too much.

Rich: But they don't worry about you when you are swinging an axe or running a saw or working on firewood!

Howard: Yeah, they worry, but it doesn't do them any good.

Rich: Outdoor exercise is wonderful, isn't it?

Howard: Yeah. I really enjoy being up in camp – they're a nice bunch of guys, every one of them.

Rich: You and I both remember Bob Knobel very fondly. He was a unique personal friend and individual and he was an easy fellow to admire and appreciate. What are some of the things you remember about Bob that you might want to share?

Howard: As I said, mine will be on the light side. Probably the one that crops up in my mind first is that everybody used to take something to eat up to camp when they would go. My sister used to bake bread. She'd bring the bread over to my house – and one Friday night it was still warm right out of the oven. I removed it from her car to mine and covered it up with my sleeping bag and clothes and stuff and when I got up to camp, I drove right up there and carried my things into camp and Norm Bahnsen said, "hey, this is still warm – I'm going to have a heel." He took out a loaf of bread and started to cut the heel off – and Bob Knobel took the knife from him and says, "you don't know how to cut the heel off from a loaf of long bread" and he turned the loaf around and cut it right down lengthways and he handed Norm the other half and said, "now, that's the way you cut the heel off a loaf of bread."

Rich: Did he eat it all?

Howard: Yeah, every bit of it!

Rich: Your birthday party was at your grandson, Bobby's house. Was he the one that was invited up to Knobel's camp and spent the night in the woods that time?

Howard: No, that was his brother. He was, I think, sixteen at the time.

Rich: I didn't recall meeting him at the party – was he there?

Howard: No. He works on a farm over in McDonough and he couldn't get time off to come over. He works on a farm that raises racehorses. They got over a hundred head of them – they race all over – the Kentucky Derby and other races. They're worse than tending cows – they take up just as much time.

Rich: How did you happen to get involved in hunting at the Knobel camp?

Howard: Well, I worked at the boat company and both Bob Knobel and Ted Thompson worked there and they knew I hunted up in the Adirondacks and they asked me if I'd like to hunt up at their camp. I had hunted out of Old Forge in a camp that some friends had for over twenty-five years before then.

Rich: They probably figured you'd have a few stories to share. One I'd like to hear is about the one that involved Norm Bahnsen and his hunt up on Sugarloaf Mountain that time.

Howard: He was up on the rim watch in back of Knobel's camp and Norm was settin' up there and a four-point buck walked out and stopped in front of him. Norm pulled right up and shot at it – he didn't see a beech tree right in front of the buck and he hit it dead center. He came back down to camp and told about it. I went back up there and I had one of them saws you carry in your pack. I cut a chunk out of that beech tree and took it down to camp and hung it on the buck pole. Norm took it home and had a brass plate put on it. One time Norm was hunting with several of our group over across the lake. He was on watch and saw what he described as the big feet and legs of a large furry animal walking along thru some nearby spruce. He couldn't see the body because it was so thick there. There's no doubt he saw a bear all right. Another time Norm was coming down off the mountain late in the afternoon heading for camp and he met a bear coming up the trail right toward him. He pulled up to shoot at it and he was looking right in the kitchen window of the camp – so he didn't shoot! Norm had a lot of chances but very few shots.

Rich: How did Norm get started at the Knobel camp?

Howard: He was a salesman for XL – sold fiberglass to the boat factory. Bob Schoenfeld went to school with Ted Thompson out in Peshtigo, Wisconsin. He should be up this fall – he is a dedicated hunter. He usually gets a deer about every year he comes up here.

Rich: Are you at all acquainted with the brook trout they have found in South Lake recently?

Howard: No.

Rich: A couple of years ago Jani and I read a story in the Cortland Standard paper about the DEC putting in some gill nets in the deep parts of the lake, to see what they could catch. Apparently this is the way they check to see what species of fish that any body of water holds. The lake had been identified as one of the most heavily impacted by acid rain of any in the Adirondacks at that time. I think they primarily thought there were no brook trout left in the lake at all and if they were lucky, might come up with a lake trout. They did catch some lakers that were pretty good-sized fish but the

11

thing that surprised them was they did catch several good-sized brook trout. I think sixteen to eighteen inches long. I don't believe they said anything about how the brookies were colored and they didn't say anything about whether the lake had ever been stocked in the past – but they have stocked it to some extent recently – probably with natives. They were amazed to find any trout there at all. The lake has a fairly decent inlet stream at the east end – that might have a bearing on the matter, I don't know.

I think if anyone wanted to shoot a lot of deer he wouldn't bother to go up north at all. Would probably hunt down in the southern tier where the deer are plentiful. The thing that attracts us to the north- country is what – tell us all about it.

Howard: You go up there and get a look at a good buck and you've done the same as getting a trophy down here. I've had several chances. I remember the first year – 1965 – I didn't have a rifle so carried my Smith & Wesson .357 revolver. Ted and I were coming back one afternoon to camp – there were five to six inches of wet, sloppy snow on everything. Ted went down under the bank and as we were heading back to camp I was walking along and I saw a real fresh track where the deer ran up over the bank – apparently I had kicked it out. I was just moving along and I came to a bank that went down into a little ravine. I slid down on that slippery snow and when I got to the bottom I stopped and stood there for a minute – when all of a sudden, the biggest buck deer I ever saw in all my life jumped up behind a pile of brush and landed right on top of it making a heck of a racket – and walked out on solid ground and stood there. I had a pair of brown cotton gloves on and I took my revolver and drew down on the top of his neck – he wasn't over one hundred feet away – drew very carefully down on his neck and shot – and the deer started walking. I shot again and my glove caught under the trigger so I put the revolver back in the holster, took my glove off, then drew the revolver again and fired three more times at him – and he never did anything but walk. I figured if I had shot at him all those times and couldn't hit him I wouldn't try again – so I put the revolver back in my holster and hollered to Ted. The deer walked straight away from me – then he got down on his knees and I think he said a prayer, I don't know. But he just walked away. Ted came up to where I was and we went down to where the deer had knelt – each side of his knee prints was a little spot of blood where it had ran down each side of his neck. I must have creased the top of his neck. We followed that deer over into the Lewis Paper Company property where he got into a bunch of other deer and we lost him. There didn't appear to be anything wrong with him. It just wasn't his day.

Rich: What would you say the rack would have amounted to?

Howard: At least a big eight-point. He was a big deer – had a huge rack. It might have been the same one they told about the week before that they saw when they were dragging out somebody's deer. This buck came down as they were strung out on the trail and ran right thru them. Nobody got a shot at him.

Rich: Probably someone was carrying all the rifles – the rest of the group was helping to drag the deer. Well, we don't get them all – sometimes they get away.

Howard: Then one time – I never could sit and watch for deer – I had to always be moving. Bob told me, he says, "if you take a magazine up with you and find a good place to sit and read the magazine, that will pass the time away – keep you occupied." So, I did – chose a Playboy magazine and the article I started to read was some political thing and the driest story I ever tried to read. I sat

12

there on this boulder with my rifle laying on the ground there beside me and reading that story – I guess I must have dozed off – 'cause all of a sudden, I heard a buck snort. It scared me – the magazine flew and I jumped and I looked and there was a buck standing about fifty yards from me and looking right straight at me – no cover whatsoever. I very carefully reached down for the rifle, and while I was reaching for the rifle, the deer was walking on by and he stopped behind a little spruce tree there and I couldn't see him very good but I figured, this was the only chance I would have. I shot and missed and the gun jammed so I didn't get another shot – and he got away. I called him the Playboy buck. All the deer I saw up there that were of any size always got away. The only ones I got were small – kettle meat.

The only deer I got while hunting out of Knobel's camp was a spike-horn. I got a nice eight-point at Third Lake Creek when I was hunting up there one time – a small one.

Rich: I guess they had quite a project a couple of summers ago when they had to dig out underneath the camp to replace some of the sills there. The originals had rotted out and that let things settle quite a bit. They did a nice job – everything is in good shape now. I remember the first time I visited the camp with Bob. It was in the middle of the winter and we found a huge raccoon had built his winter nest underneath the camp. We figured he'd find his way out in the spring so didn't disturb him. We heard a lot of noise from under the camp and were curious what the cause was. When they replaced the sills, Martin got to do most of the digging, I recall. He said that it was right in the black fly season and it was very tiring work.

Howard: Ted and I were trout fishing one summer during the fly season and I tried Skin-so-soft – I put it on the backs of my hands and around my face and it seemed to work fine. However, a little later on I looked down at my legs and when I pulled my pant legs up, my hide was just covered with black flies. I had forgot to put the Skin-so-soft down there. Apparently it doesn't work for everybody. Bob Schoenfeld, Bob Knobel and Darrell Cottom have all had good luck hunting over towards Mud Lake Ridge. There have been several good bucks killed over there. You got a bear over in that area one year. That was another lucky point for me – I went to camp the weekend after you got your bear.

Rich: One of the men that visited camp that weekend was a timber cruiser that worked for Gutchess Lumber. He was a big, strong fellow – used to hard outdoor work. He claims that I owe him a day's wages.

Howard: I wish I could walk like he could.

Rich: I guess he had the right kind of job for his legs – his stride was almost twice my normal one. I think the highlight at Knobel's camp is in the evening after dinner and the dishes are done. We all gather around in a comfortable chair in by the fire and tell stories of the day's events. It seems everyone has something interesting or exciting to share.

Howard: I think the easiest deer we ever got while hunting out of that camp was the one Harry got beyond Mud Lake Ridge. He went up to camp early with Ted and I think he killed the deer on a Thursday. They hung him up and waited for the gang to arrive Friday night so that Saturday they could help drag him in. Well, it got cold – well below freezing – and when we all got up there to drag him out, we found that the deer was froze stiff – so we took turns carrying him over our shoulder.

Rich: You wouldn't dare to try such a thing hunting in the southern tier – somebody would get shot for sure. I wouldn't try that trick even up north if I were alone, either. Bob had a unique way of marking trail. He would saw off a sapling about belt high. There wouldn't be any blaze on it or anything – but you could follow a hunting trail easily by watching for his type of blazes.

Howard: From time to time, we have all enjoyed hunting the area over by Sand Lake Road. It is quite thick in places but the deer seem to hang out in that area. Ted has killed several nice bucks in that general area. There are several streams that course thru the section. These tend to attract the deer. That's where Skeeter, my Grandson, got tangled up that time. He shot at a buck near Mud Lake Ridge on the League Line. He didn't hit him but there was a good tracking snow, so he followed him. It was raining at the time and he kept following the tracks and eventually got another shot at the buck. When he came to the Sand Lake Road he didn't know where he was. He thought he was on the other side of the line over on the Lewis Company property. So when he hit this road he turned to his right thinking it would take him back to the lake – but he was on the Sand Lake Road. Going in this direction, it just took him back farther. He followed that road until well after dark and came to a lean-to. He said the Lord must have had hold of his hand as the lean-to was quite a ways off the road. He found it and built a fire and it started snowing. It snowed three or four inches that night. His fire went out about two-thirty in the morning and when he woke up the moon was shining bright so he went back down into the road and kept walking. About seven o'clock in the morning, a couple of loggers came along in a pickup truck and wanted to know where he was from. He told them, "Knobel's camp." They said, "you sure have come a long ways to get here." They took him up to that cemetery just inside Forestport and contacted the Troopers – he was lucky.

Rich: How did you hear that he had been located by the authorities?

Howard: Well, a couple of us were told to stay in camp that day. Pretty soon, about eight-thirty, a State Trooper showed up. We invited him in and asked if he'd like a cup of coffee. He said, "sure, I'll have a cup of coffee." So we sat there drinking coffee and eating donuts – he was there at least a half an hour – finally, someone says, "any word on the lost boy?" The Trooper said, "oh, yes, they found him – he's at the diner over at Forestport." An hour or so later, they brought him back.

Rich: That was good news! Let's see, right about then, Martin Knobel and one of the Rangers must have been out in the woods laying out that string trail. Martin said "the Ranger kept saying, are we there yet?" They were looking for Sand Lake Road. The whole idea was to establish a demarcation line – I suppose in the event he didn't show up by the end of the first day of the search, the next project would have involved many more men and a much closer search. The Ranger carried a big spool of string that unwound itself as they walked along. Martin led the way, knowing the woods in that area pretty well. The Ranger would catch the string on top of a piece of bark on a spruce tree or over a limb or something. The idea was to keep the string a couple of feet above the ground level so that if it snowed, the searchers could still readily see the string. After what seemed like a long time, they finally reached the road.

Most deer camps in wilderness areas have one or more "lost" stories either about their own members or perhaps involving strangers they are able to help. One thing I believe we accomplished with the Brigade boys group that we worked with several years was to give each one a working knowledge of how to use map and compass.

14

When they got done laying the string trail, eventually I bet the birds and squirrels and other things had quite a time using the string for nest material. Maybe it's biodegradable or something.

Howard: Must be because two or three years later you never could find a trace of it. All that deep snow would have put in on the ground – then the leaves would have covered it up. If anything like this ever does happen to me, I don't want you to come up there looking for me – just go up there and say, "happy hunting" and leave me there.

Rich: Now, you got how many grandkids?

Howard: Fourteen. They all live within thirty miles of where I do. Several of the boys in the group all hunt. One of the youngest turns eighteen. He got his first deer two years ago – a twelve-pointer – it had a huge rack. I says "boy, you made a mistake." He says "what do you mean?" I says "you got to do an awful lot of hunting to better that one!"

Rich: Well, I was told something like that – let's see - I must have been about age twenty. A couple of years before that fall they had a real bad windstorm in our area near the headwaters of the Oswegatchie River where my Dad's deer camp was. It blew down a large number of huge pine trees and many others and in just a short time a lot of berry bushes and other brush grew up. This just made the deer herd expand. When you bought your deer license that fall the department gave each one an extra free license for shooting a doe. Their whole idea was – we better harvest some deer – if we didn't the next hard winter would get them. Well, about all winters up in that country are "hard." That's pretty much the way it worked out. I happened to be in the right place at the right time and killed a beautiful eight point with a very pretty rack. He dressed out at one hundred seventy-three pounds - that was nice for Adirondack. A friend of my father said, "if you ever plan to have one mounted, this would make a good one – it could be a long while before you ever kill one that is any more pretty." So, I took his advice. The mount has held up quite well – I still have it hanging outside in my shop in the barn. The head has started to age a little - but is still very beautiful. I shot at a few that would have been better than that one – but I never managed to harvest a bigger one.

Howard: The first deer I shot had an eight-point rack but it was just a little thing. It wasn't very wide and not very high. At the time I thought it was huge – but since I've seen a lot of them that were much better than that one.

Rich: Your Grandson, Bobby has really got a beautiful display on his living room wall – you helped build that, didn't you? I don't know that I ever saw a display of mounted heads or racks that look any nicer.

Howard: I think I made all the plaques they were mounted on. He got his muzzle loader eight-point back this past weekend from the taxidermist. He took that over to my Granddaughters just a few days ago to her birthday party. It had a nice rack. They did a nice job of mounting it for him. I don't think anybody could do up a deer as nice as old Hardendorf in Apulia. I don't know how he does it – you look at a head he has mounted – he's got the eyelashes all there – it looks like that deer could blink any time. So far as I know, the old man is gone now – but his son, Jack, is still in the business. He's got his price up to where he doesn't have to work too hard, it seems to me.

Rich: Well, it all costs plenty these days. That mink I got mounted recently – he did that for me – in fact that may have been the very last mount that Hardendorf Senior ever did. A friend had his dog out for a session of training towards spring one year. The dog went on point and he felt sure a partridge would fly up at any moment. When it didn't he walked ahead of the dog and then saw a black object on top of the snow by a creek. He went forward and found a beautiful buck mink that had died. There was only a little spot of blood on his nose. He felt that the mink got struck by a car and had crawled off towards the creek and died. He didn't want the animal so gave it to me to have mounted. I had trapped several years ago but had never gotten around to having one mounted. Hardendorf sure did a beautiful job for me – it's a treasure.

Howard: A taxidermist gets $65.00 apiece for the plaques they mount a deer head on today. I offered to make the one for my Grandson. His taxidermist said "if he's going to make the one he might as well make both of them" and he sent me the patterns for both the muzzle loader deer and his regular one. It was fun making them.

Rich: How do you figure the turkeys being in the Adirondacks these days? John Knobel told me just before your birthday party last May he went up to camp to look things over after the winter and saw eight turkeys right on the beach in front of his A-frame cabin down by the lake. I can't figure how they can survive up north. The snow usually gets over eight feet deep.

Howard: I don't know how they ever got started up in that north-country. The groceries are pretty scarce out in the woods – especially when the heavy snow comes on.

Rich: several years ago, his brother Larry was just out for a hike and was up on top of Sugarloaf Mountain. He flushed a big hen right off the top of the mountain and he was really surprised to see it back in there. It wasn't long after that and they began seeing groups of three or four turkeys at a time down by the lakeshore.

Howard: Just five or six years ago I believe – I was traveling down the road near Koenig's Sawmill and there were a dozen or more turkeys that just crossed the road beyond the mill a little ways. It was a surprise and a thrill to see them!

Rich: One summer about that same time Jani and I were traveling that same road and we saw a large bunch of them climbing up a steep bank from the roadway. There was a huge gobbler that at first stood right in the middle of the road. I had to hit the brakes pretty good to keep from running over him. We watched him climb the bank in pursuit no doubt of the large group of hens and the whole bunch disappeared into a group of pine trees. I finally grabbed my camera and got out of the car and climbed up the bank hoping I could be there in time to get at least one photo of that group of birds. By the time I arrived under the pines the birds had dispersed pretty good – I was able to catch a glimpse once in awhile of one or two here and there running across the patches of snow that remained on the ground under the extra shade provided by that group of pine trees. I didn't spot that gobbler – he was a beauty! His beard was at least twelve inches long and my wife marveled at the color of that bird. The sun was shining and when he was standing in the middle of our road we could easily observe how beautiful a bird they really are. Once when we were hiking around in a thick pine plantation during the middle of the day, we flushed a large group of turkeys out of the treetops. We had no idea they were anywhere around. The initial racket they made when they all took off out of there was quite a shock to our nervous system. In the process of flying out of there, they broke branches off some of the trees and made a terrible racket. A moment after the shock and surprise wore off we were awesomely delighted to have had that neat experience. They truly are a magnificent bird.

Howard: Last year must have been a tough year for the young birds – I didn't see any.

Rich: Yeah, last year it was unusually wet, it seems, and I guess from what I have heard, a young turkey is pretty apt to get pneumonia. It's about two weeks before the poults are able to fly. During that stage of their life the predation must be very severe from owls, coyotes, foxes and others.

Howard: Did you hear about the deal five or six years ago – Syracuse University purchased a bunch of lynx from up in Alaska and brought them up to the Adirondacks and turned them loose.

Rich: Nope, I didn't hear about it.

Howard: They turned forty-nine of them loose up near the high peaks area. They let them loose in an area where there were a lot of snowshoe rabbits and they thought they'd be happy to stay around there due to the available food. About the only ones that showed up after awhile were the ones that got killed in the road. So far as I know, none of them stayed around – the ones that didn't wind up as road kill must have swam the River and gone back to Canada or somewhere. I enjoy still-hunting for red fox. I'd rather hunt a red fox than a deer or turkey. They are smart – and they like to show you they are smart. They are more of a challenge.

Rich: Did you ever have one bark at you?

Howard: Yes, I have.

Rich: So have I. I was still-hunting deer one nice mild sunny day – just after a storm. I got a glimpse of a large red fox uphill from me and he goes, "bark - - bark- bark." That was the last I heard or saw of him but he left nice tracks.

Howard: One year when I was a young fellow, we had a lot of snow that winter – I mean, a lot of snow. When you strapped on your skis, you could go anywhere – you could ski right over the fence. So I decided I'd go fox hunting. I was going along on this side hill by a neighbor's pasture and up ahead of me three or four hundred yards I saw this red fox come out of the woods. He came right towards me and I stood still but he saw me and he turned and went right down the hill. I said, "hah I'll fool you." I turned and started skiing down over the hill just as fast as I could go. All of a sudden the bottom dropped out and I went right down – snow in my shirt, snow in my face and snow in my gun barrel – snow up to here – there was a spring there and it had drifted right over and left a big hole. Out of a hundred and fifty acres of pasture that was the only place I could go. I finally climbed out and got the snow out of my clothes and got the snow out of my gun barrel and I said, "I guess I didn't scare him any. I'll follow him and maybe I'll get a shot." So I followed his tracks down over the hill and he turned and went thru the woods and then he made another turn and went back up the hill and I could see where he went back about where I first saw him and I could see where he sat down and from there I could look right down and see that hole in the snow where I had fallen in – it seemed like he was sitting there watching me when I was cleaning the snow out of my gun.

Rich: My Dad wasn't much of a church attender. When I was small he and a few friends owned a black and tan fox hound named Slim. How they loved to get together and go fox hunting on a Sunday and I got to go with them a few times. Ray Williams would go with the dog to make sure he was following the track in the right direction and kind of put on a drive at the same time. Once in awhile he would see and get to shoot the fox as sometimes it would double back on its track. But usually they would line right out. There were several of us that were on watch much like you'd do when hunting deer. Well, one of our favorite watches was up the Health Camp Road – in fact we climbed the fire escape on the south side of that building and would wrap an old horse blanket around us and hope the fox would come down our trail – which he did many times. My feet about froze – all I had to wear at the time were shoes and overshoes. I recall several times being with my father when the fox would come out that trail – that was usually several minutes after we would begin to hear the hound baying on the trail. I don't know how many he killed from that spot but I guess at least six over the years. I was with Ray one time and the fox doubled back like I mentioned above and he shot him. I watched as he skinned the animal on the spot and I got to carry the hide. They are a beautiful animal. It's fun to watch a fox while he is hunting for mice. They jump up in the air and pounce down with their front feet to pin the mouse they have heard scurrying around in the leaves. I can hear in my mind and memory to this day the sound of old Slim baying on the trail – that was marvelous. Dad never had a chance to go coon hunting but we sure enjoyed the fox hunting together. One morning after a hunt we got a phone call from a farmer saying that he and his wife were out for the evening and when they got home, old Slim had taken up residence in their living room – right in the baby's crib. When hunting that day, they lost track of the hound and when it got dark they gave up. They left a shirt near where the vehicle was parked and sometimes they could go by the next day early in the morning and find old Slim snoozing away on the shirt. They had a nameplate on his collar with his name and the owner's name and phone number included. Over the years they received several calls of this nature.

Howard: One time we were hunting deer up on Brake Hill. We had quite a group with us. Elon Preston was along and being older, we'd put him on watch each time. There's a patch of woods, then an open spot, and so forth in that area. The first drive we spread the watchers out and two or three of us came thru the woods patch. After it was over Elon said he saw a nice red fox – but no deer. The second patch of hardwoods was about the same. A red fox came thru in front of Elon – but no deer. Finally we put on the third drive – I was down under the hill but heard a shot about the time the drive was finished. Elon had taken the slug out of his gun and figuring there were no deer, he put in birdshot in the hopes of seeing the fox again. This time, however, a nice four-point buck came thru – he forgot he had the birdshot in and fired. So, we didn't get the fox or the deer either.

Rich: Did you ever hear the story of Dutch Casterline – he was hunting rabbits up in Bear Swamp. He was going along on snowshoes and suddenly fell down into an abandoned well. Fortunately part way down into the well, the snowshoes stuck so it didn't let him way down to the bottom but he was stuck and couldn't get out. He could just about reach the top of that well with his hands. Fortunately he was hunting with some friends – I don't know who they were - they heard him hollering and they found where he was and came and finally got him out of there.

Howard: One time when I was a kid – just sixteen years old – I was fox hunting with a bunch from McGraw Sportsmen. They were driving that ridge from McGraw out toward Solon. They drove it out thru and I was watching on the Stillwell Road. I had a little .22 rifle my Dad owned though at the time I didn't have any license. They saw several foxes but they didn't go anywhere near any of the watchers, so they decided to drive it back. We watchers said we'd drive and let the ones that drove before go down and get on watch. A game warden came along and started checking for licenses. I didn't have a license and he says, "you aren't supposed to be even driving – but go ahead this time – but you got to leave your gun in the car." So we started out and I hadn't gone very far and I got into a real mess of blackberry briars. I was trying to thrash my way thru them and I looked over and about thirty feet from me was a red fox trying to do the same thing. He was hung up too. There wasn't a thing I could do about it – I didn't have any gun. Nobody ever did get him – he got out before I did. On TV recently they were advertising one of the outdoor shows and they had a section that showed a red fox that dove down into the snow for a mouse or something and his hind feet stuck right up in the air.

Rich: One of the most incredible films I had ever seen was one of a goshawk catching a partridge. I always thought that a partridge was a pretty fast flier – at least when I was hunting them they usually managed to avoid being shot by me. The film I saw must have been one by Marty Stauffer – it showed the partridge taking off and then it showed the goshawk catching that grouse in midair. It was just like the partridge wasn't moving hardly at all.

The Canada goose mates for life according to what I have read and observed. The goshawk is another bird that mates for life. I was helping Darrell Cottom haul out his buck one time – he had killed the animal way over by Mud Lake Ridge. When we got to the top of the hill near camp, we put the deer down and we were taking a much-needed rest. We were sitting down resting and we heard this noise – we looked up and noticed a pair of goshawks coming – flying just above the tree top level and sometimes they would fly together real close – then sometimes they would fly maybe fifteen feet apart but all the while they would be muttering and talking back and forth constantly and we said, "what in the world are they?" Larry Knobel looked up and said "they are goshawks." The female was mottled in coloration just like a partridge and the male, which was considerably larger, was solid black. My, what a beautiful pair they were. Larry said back at the camp there's a large bird book and there is a full-page color picture and quite a write up on them. When we got back, we looked it up and it told about the fact that they mate for life. In fact, if something happens to one of them, the other spends the rest of its life just mourning. It makes the most mournful sound and constantly – day in and day out. Jani and I were up on the South Branch onetime fishing and we saw this goshawk flying and it was making the most mournful sound you could imagine all the time while it was flying. It's the most heartrending thing you can imagine. Day after day you could hear this thing coming and it was making this mournful sound and it was all alone - still calling for its mate.

Another thing we learned to identify that trip was the sound that a loon makes when it is flying from one body of water to another. We actually saw one in flight so were able to identify the sound. I think it is a marvel – on another trip we were hauling our canoe thru the woods on our wheels and I heard that sound and was able to identify it as a loon. That kind of woods lore is really fun and very satisfying

Howard: The other day I ran into some of my mother's things that were included in her diary. There was a little poem on a slip of paper that I thought was kind of cute. It goes something like this – "Between the drawer or pantry shelf, I always argue with myself, for if I throw a thing away, I know I'll live to rue the day. But should I choose to use it still, I know, of course, I never will. Whereupon I now beseech, some modern college please to teach, along with all their other bunk, a course in analyzing junk."

I think the best deer hunting story I have personally heard this fall was the one my Nephew's son told me. He has a neighbor that is an eighty-two year old gentleman who resides right next door. They got to talking before the deer season opened. The boy is an avid deer hunter and the old guy had hunted deer all of his life and the boy tried to talk him into going hunting. He said he was too old and he didn't want to get out there and cause any problems for anybody. The boy finally talked him into it. All he had to do was go out in his backyard there just a little ways from the house. So, the first morning he went out there and got probably a hundred yards or so from his house and he came to a hedgerow. It looked like a pretty good spot. He thought he had gone far enough, anyhow. So he got sat down and started to settle in and he just took out a cigar to light it and heard something coming. He looked up and the biggest buck he had ever seen in his life was walking right to him. He dropped the cigar and shot the deer. He then went up and got my Nephew's boy to come down and drag it home for him. The deer scored one hundred thirty-seven. I talked to Bruce the other day and asked him what it scored. I think he said the width of the rack was twenty-three inches.

Rich: I think that the present Quality Deer Management program has resulted in a number of deer living long enough to be able to grow nice racks and a few of these deer are being harvested every year now.

Howard: We had a lot of fun this last summer moving that dock down by the lake. Apparently it was a little over on the neighbor's property so we had to move it.

Rich: How did you do it?

Howard: Piece by piece. We moved the deck off the top of it and then unloaded the stones from the cribbing. We loaded them onto Todd's truck and then he drove up to the opening by Ted's camp where he would back up and then slam on the brakes and the stones would unload themselves. Soon we got all the stones out of the cribbing. So then, we hooked onto it with the tractor and pulled it over – got it about where we wanted, squared it up, scooped the stones up and put them back in it. We floated the deck over to the cribbing and dragged it up on the beach and picked up one side of it with the bucket loader and shoved it up on. Nobody had to strain themselves at all. The stones were a little heavy to handle but we took our time and were careful when we lifted them and managed to stay out of trouble. The cribbing has got a bottom built out of two by six material. You fill that up with stones and the thing isn't going anywhere. Martin Knobel figures it isn't the ice breakup that damages docks and stuff – it's the freeze up that sometimes causes the damage. Once the ice freezes and then it gets colder, the ice expands and pushes everything out.

They're figuring on putting a new roof on the boathouse and a new sill under the woodshed this year. We're supposed to be up there the end of August to do one or the other – and get the job done and still have time to go to the logger's convention at Boonville. It's the weekend before Labor Day. I always wanted to go to that event all my life and I haven't been there yet. I've been to Forestport and Old Forge and North Lake that weekend and nobody but me was interested in going to the logger's convention. On TV lately they have a half hour show about every week showing some of the competition events. It looks like the show would be fun.

Rich: Jani and I went for our first time about five years ago and enjoyed the program. We hope you get to go too. Howard, we really thank you for sharing and also we thank you for your suggestion that we write this book.

CHAPTER 3   MARTIN KNOBEL

Rich: Robert and Ginny Knobel had four sons – Larry, John, Martin and Todd.   My next interview will be with Martin. How old were you when your folks purchased the camp at North Lake?

Martin: I was just two.

Rich: Must be you didn't have a lot to do with the decision making process, then did you?

Martin: No, I guess not – I just went along.

Rich: How old were you when you can recall being aware of the camp and going to visit the place?

Martin: Probably four or five – I can remember going with my Grandfather for walks. He died shortly after that.

Rich: How old were you when you started to hunt up there?

Martin: Fourteen, I think. I hunted with my other Grandfather, Blanchard Wilson (Willy). We just went down the draw and back – that was as far as he could go back then. I know I didn't have a gun so I must have been around fourteen.

Rich: I recall Willy telling about making it up to the first level – that was about where spike rock watch was located. He always felt if he made it that far he was really doing something. Boy, how he loved and enjoyed the woods. He was an important part of the South Lake camp – that was where Bob first had his tent camp set up each fall – before purchasing the present place at North Lake. He really had a heart for some of the friends Bob would invite up to hunt in the fall. One weekend Bob invited Chuck Haraveth, a neighbor. I don't believe Chuck had ever been deer hunting before, and he told Bob, "I don't even have any clothes that would be warm for deer hunting." Bob said, "oh, don't worry, you're about Willy's size – he'll fix you up." So they checked with Willy, and he outfitted him with wool pants, shirt and jacket. Willy says "you got long underwear, don't you?" He says, "oh sure, I'm all set there." I think he let him have a hat – borrow one, you know. So they went – and I don't think he saw anything to shoot at – but that was not all that unusual – most of the rest of us didn't shoot at anything either. We sure had a lot of fun. Chuck saw a fisher when he was on watch one morning. I don't think he had any idea of what it was but from his description of the shape and size of the animal, its gait and everything, we figured what he saw was definitely a large male fisher. It was not exactly a common thing to see one of those animals in the woods either – in all the years I have hunted, I only saw one myself – and that was over on the stovepipe watch.

Martin: I don't think I ever saw one.

Rich: Your Dad told one time of seeing a fisher. He was sitting on the usual spot at that stovepipe watch where there's a rock there at the base of a large beech tree just at a convenient height to sit on and you can get real comfortable resting your back against the tree. It's possible to look quite a ways down the draw from that spot though it used to be a lot more open than it is now. He spotted the fisher coming along towards him on the left side of the draw and it came up to him – in fact, it came right up beside him not any further away than the length of his gun barrel. The fisher stopped, stood right up on his hind legs and looked right at him. Bob said he didn't know what to do – he was in hopes he wouldn't jump on him or something. Apparently, after looking him over real close, he was satisfied so he dropped down and just kept loping away with that strange gait they have. Being a member of the mink family, they jump along about like a mink does only the fisher is a larger animal – about the size of a red fox. The one I saw, I was sitting in exactly the same place – in fact, it might even have been the same fisher. It was just the following fall that I saw mine. This time he came up the right side of the little draw and only about twenty yards away. There was a big tree that had blown down and it was lying on the ground parallel to the draw. That fisher came along my side of that tree so that I got a real good look at him. In fact, I followed his path while looking thru the scope on my rifle. This one didn't stop but kept jumping along with that strange gait they have – they seem to go thru a lot of motions while doing their running. It sure was fun to see that animal.

Over the years you and your brothers have helped a lot of hunters drag in their game. I'm sure you have a story or two to tell.

Martin: One time, early on, just Dad, Larry and I were up there. Dad was still in camp puttering around with something that had to be taken care of. Larry and I were on the other side of the swamp, up on top. I was sitting on a blown down tree – half asleep. I heard a noise and looked and coming around the tree I was on were three bears – a mother and two yearling cubs. I remember sitting there and trying to decide if I was supposed to shoot one or not. Finally, the mother and one of the other bears went on. The other one lagged behind so I thought I would shoot at that one. When I fired my gun, the bear took off. I fired the signal and Larry came over. It took awhile to find where the animal was when I shot at it. We discovered my bullet had struck a one-inch beech sapling – almost cut the tree off.

Rich: That would tend to deflect the bullet for sure.

Martin: We discovered that it did hit the bear. We tracked it about half way to the Sand Lake road. By then the bear had stopped bleeding entirely. We figured by the time the bullet reached the bear there just wasn't much left of it. There were patches of snow so the tracking job was fairly easy. I'll never forget the time we were up the hill in back of camp hunting and Dad was back in camp working on something underneath. At one point he looked up and saw a nice buck standing right behind the camp. By the time he got into the camp and got his rifle, the buck was long gone.

Rich: Probably the deer was surprised to see him come out from under the camp.

Martin: Several times over the years we have come down the hill in back of camp and after hunting all day and seeing no deer, there would be some that we would see right in back of camp on our way down the hill. There have been several bear killed by hunters out of our camp over the years. That one hanging on the wall there was killed by Russ Pringle. The mice have been chewing on it pretty good but there's still some left – enough so we can recognize it as a bear. Mother keeps threatening to move it – we keep telling her it belongs there. Sheldon Johnson got one after that – his first one. Then you got your big one and Sheldon got another one after that. I was sitting on top of spike rock at the time and pretty soon, he comes down the hill dragging his bear. I couldn't tell at first what he did have – the leaves were curling up over it as he dragged it. But when he got down by my watch he picked it up in the air and said, "see what I got." I said, "yep, and if you can do that, I guess you don't need my help in dragging it into camp."

Last fall I had a friend that came up to camp to hunt – his name was Doug Bloodgood. This was the second time he came up to camp to hunt. The second day in camp, we went down to the end of the lake hunting. We parked the truck and were walking off down the log road. I think Frank Underwood had seen a big deer there the day before. We split up some and began to hunt up one of the log roads in the area. After about twenty minutes I heard Doug shoot. I waited awhile and then walked over to where I thought Doug would be. I found him and he said, "I shot one." So, I went over there and said, "well where is it?" He said, "well it took off." Oh, ok. The way he said it, it sounded like he shot and it dropped in its tracks. He hadn't collected it yet. Just about then Frank Underwood caught up with us. We tracked that deer up and down over several hills and we must have monkeyed around over three hours trying to find the deer. Finally, we gave up. Frank went his own way and Doug and I headed back towards where he had shot it. We split up again to cover more territory. I hadn't gone very far and he shot again. I went over there and said, "what are you shooting at this time?" He said, "the same one." It was lying on the other side of the creek right next to the road. We had walked right by it. When Doug crossed the creek he was able to spot the deer. I guess in his excitement he didn't take very careful aim as he missed the deer. The animal took off. He had told his wife, "if I ever do get one with a big beautiful rack, I'll quit hunting." He said, "that one would have done it." He had never seen one that big. We like hunting that area because there are several old log roads we can follow and go along quietly. It's fairly open in a lot of places.

Rich: Up the hill in back of your camp you can usually locate one of your old hunting trails and you can move along on one of them thru the woods and not make a sound.

Martin: Last year when we were hunting, we never saw another hunter outside our own party all week. Even the guys from Cortland that go across the lake into that big tent camp didn't show up.

Rich: So there's a bunch that go over across the lake and hunt that Jock's Brook area. Do they usually do pretty good over there?

Martin: They usually get one or two from what I hear. One year that bunch was in there and it got cold early and the lake froze over. They finally came out and dragged their loaded boat right across the ice. There was a heavy snowfall too so they couldn't get the trailer up the road to get their boat out. They towed their eighteen-foot boat up the road behind the truck. I was down by the road at the time and I heard something coming and looked up and here comes this pickup truck with the boat right behind it and a guy sitting in the boat. It was an aluminum Starcraft so it didn't hurt the boat any.

Rich: Would you be able to tell us something about your father. We all thought an awful lot of him. He was a good friend and wonderful companion.

Martin: The years I hunted while he was alive, he didn't do any hunting then. He would maintain the trails – he cut them out and marked them. He was mostly done hunting by then. He would come up the hill around lunchtime and meet us in the woods at a predetermined spot and join us. Then he would go down to camp and prepare dinner. I remember as a kid when I first started to come up to camp to hunt we'd have eighteen or nineteen for dinner sometimes. I remember sleeping downstairs on a cot as we were out of beds. My brother, John, is in food preparation in the Service.

He's a weekend warrior – belongs to the National Guard. He served a stint in the Gulf War and just a few days ago got called up again and shipped out overseas somewhere. He also has a degree from college in Restaurant Management.

Rich: I guess he takes pretty good care of his bunch down by the lake in his A-frame log cabin. I recall one fall John came up to the main camp to borrow some vegetables for making a stew that night. I don't know anywhere on earth that food tastes so good or the fellowship and camaraderie is so sweet as in deer camp.

Martin: Sometimes John would be in the kitchen when I'd be preparing dinner. He'd make some comments on my cooking and sometimes I'd hand him the spatula and say, "here, you think you can do better than I can, you go ahead and cook."

Rich: I think both you boys kind of take right after your Dad in that department – it's a labor of love, I always thought.

Martin: I usually start planning the menu a week at a time. I try to spread it out over two weeks. Usually ahead of time I know who's coming and when, so that helps in the planning. I plot it on a calendar for the days of each trip in order to know how many there will actually be in camp at one time. It's a little easier now – some of the members have gotten older and don't eat as much as they used to. I have had to learn to cut back somewhat – I buy too much now. It takes awhile to realize that everyone doesn't eat like I do.

Rich: There are two things I remember especially about your Dad's cooking. The first one is chili. I don't remember why I was in camp mid-afternoon one time. Probably I didn't feel good or had leg cramps or something. It was fun watching Bob chop the stuff up and put it all together. The other thing Bob fixed – and I have watched you do this too – would be to put together a large venison roast in the oven. Howard Henry would be there and after we sprinkled a package of that onion soup mix on the meat he would cover it with aluminum foil. Then we'd stick that thing in that slow cook oven for all day. Boy, that would come out so juicy and tender.

Martin: Yeah, and I also found out I could do something similar with a turkey. We'd put that in the oven for all day and it would come out nice and juicy and tender and beautiful – not all dried out. It would be totally done. The last hour or so, I would pull the foil off of it so I could brown it a little and make it look pretty. Frank Underwood and Frank Buerkle – one of the first questions they will always ask when they get up there is, "we having turkey?" I can recall a couple of years when we didn't have any venison – Dad got a sheep one year and tried that but it didn't go over too good.

Rich: I remember a couple of years when Bob would stop in to Coe Dexter's meat market in Cortland. He had a way of fixing lamb patties – nice and lean. Bob always thought that tasted remarkably like venison. I guess when you graduate up to a larger leg of lamb, you can't help but get some of the mutton taste that is sometimes strong – I guess that is why they always serve mint jelly with the meal when you buy lamb or mutton in a restaurant. The flavor of those lamb patties was about as close as you could come to venison – it wasn't greasy or strong or anything – it was just plain delicious.

Martin: Another item that didn't go over too good was the time he tried canned Spam.

Rich: I recall using Spam several times on backpack trips. We'd get a little hardwood fire going and toast our Spam sandwiches over the coals – that always went over good on the trail.

Martin: When I first started hunting we always used to have peanut butter and cheese sandwiches to toast over the coals – but we soon tried hotdogs. The peanut butter and jelly sandwiches used to get burnt on one side and were usually cold on the other. With a hotdog you can put that on a stick and hold it over the coals and it turns out nice. If you get the hotdog hot – then lay the bread over the top of it and carefully get that warm just a little bit and it goes good.

Rich: Your Dad had a way of taking a small limb from some green beech and twisted it around and made a grille out of it. One of those beech grille items would often last an entire season. After using it each time, they would prop it up against a tree and it would be ready for the next weekend. The bunch tended to eat lunch in about the same place each time depending upon where they were hunting.

Martin: One difference I have noticed in the woods just since I began coming is that you used to be able to see some other hunters from your watch. For example, I can remember standing by the cannon and seeing Sheldon Johnson standing way up by the initial tree on his watch. Also by looking over to the north towards ladder rock I could spot the hunter on that watch – you sure can't see around that way now. You're lucky if you can make out the stand when you get there. Some of the woods are beginning to open up now because some of the young brush is grown up – but it sure isn't like it was. We're trying to keep most of the old original trails opened up just for convenience. In the event brother John or Todd's kids decide to take up hunting at least they could somewhat find their way around.

Rich: I'll make a comment about my Dad. The times we spent together going up the river to our camp and hunting in the woods and spending time together on the trap line over the years – those were very special times that I'll never forget. As my father got along in years I began to realize it got progressively more difficult for him to make that trip. I was glad to be able to help out and payback as it were the many times he had run the motor on the canoe, helped erect the tent – and Dad almost always did all the cooking in camp. Having come from a dairy farm background, he was used to hard work. One summer I took my Dad and his friend, Ray Williams up there in our aluminum boat. I tied my loaded pack basket to a center seat and I had a motor extension handle so I could stand-up to run the motor. I had a good grip on the handle at the top of the pack basket with one hand and ran the motor with the other. That worked pretty good as from the standing position in the back of the boat you could look down into the river and see the rocks, logs, snags, beaver dams and whatever else there was. You could tell when to lift the motor so you wouldn't wreck the propeller. We had good water for traveling and Ray made the comment when we got up to camp, "well, I have traveled this river many times but I never had it any easier."

The two of them sat side by side up in the front seat – I think it was a special experience for them – also as I recall, probably their last trip. They both just loved that river area and had enjoyed many years of hunting experience and it was a privilege for me to be a part of that. My Dad and his friends were men that I really looked up to and admired and they set the example of a lot of aspects of my growing and learning years. I am certain that many of the life decisions that I made and the kind of life I wanted to live were molded as a result of having a group of trusted peers to emulate.

Martin: Yep. We had definite good times – not just hunting but the summers and other times we spent at camp when Dad was alive. During the summer he religiously went to camp every other weekend. There were no ifs or buts about it – nothing else got in the way. Come hunting season, he was gone – every weekend. The biggest thing then was Mother would let us kids stay up Sunday night to see when he got home if he had anything on the car. It was good – companionship and everything, you know. With our help he still got to hunt his last year – he was in the wheel chair but he got to go to camp.

Rich: It was a heartbreaker in a way. I remember getting a phone call and it was Bob saying, "you want to go to camp?" I knew instantly who it was and I said, "you bet I want to go to camp." I happened to be awake that first morning and remember whoever it was that was supposed to stir around and get breakfast – four-thirty it was, was supposed to hit the floor running – I heard him – let's see, I think it was you who was sleeping downstairs with him – I think I heard him call you. He was the alarm clock. I heard him wake you up – not that you needed waking up – maybe you did, I don't know – but he was awake and he was going to see to it that whoever wanted to get out early – could.

Martin: I recall that the first year I hunted too. I was sure I just went to bed and the alarm clock went off. What are we getting up for? That's something that has changed over the years – hardly anybody gets up that early anymore. Bob Schoenfeld likes to get an early start but even he doesn't get going quite as early as he used to. I can recall Art and Ted and him going up the hill behind camp with their flashlights early in the morning.

Rich: Up the river, after breakfast, my Dad and generally the two Ernies, Hammond and Bennett, if they were up there –they would head out to where they would take their watches out near the hogsback and Nick Pond. Ray and Dick would be the ones that would hang back in camp – they would do up the breakfast dishes, for something to do to take up time because they wanted the other hunters to have a chance to get on their watches and get settled down in the woods before they came thru on their silent drive. They actually would still hunt in the direction toward where the watchers would be posted. Well, I'll tell you, that method paid off – it really worked. If there were deer in that vicinity of those knolls and woods, in most cases Ray and Dick would move them on to the watchers. Of course, over the years they discovered the best place for a man to take a watch – just like they do up to your place. The deer don't seem to change their habits too much and the lay of the land has got a lot to do with it.

Martin: Yep – and most of the spots up behind camp were originally set up to take advantage of the fact that other people hunting near the road would unknowingly drive the deer up toward us. It has changed somewhat recently. Recently the area by the road has gotten more public and the deer don't hang down there that much. This fall though, we have seen several deer right down by camp.

Rich: One year they were doing the dishes and Dick happened to look out the tent flap and he spotted a nice little four-point buck. He whispered to Ray, he says, "Ray, get your gun – there's a buck out here." So he slipped back where he had his rifle and put a couple of shells in it and then Dick said, "right over there." It couldn't have been more than ten or twelve yards from the tent. Dick held the tent flap open and Ray shot and ejected the empty shell into the dishpan. I don't think the guys out on watch heard anything. If they heard the shot they didn't hook it up with them and shooting from inside the tent it wouldn't have made as much noise as normal anyway. They had no inkling that they

26

had a deer all hung up on the meat pole back in camp. If anything, they may have wondered why they were a little extra long coming thru on their drive but they were pretty surprised when they got back to camp and here was this buck all dressed and hanging. Tell us about the time your Grandfather shot the buck thru the kitchen window.

Martin: Willy wasn't able to make it up the hill that fall. Someone spotted the buck and said, "Willy, there's a deer out here – get your gun." So he did, and shot it. Dad was taking a nap upstairs at the time. It must have woke him right up. We got to remember, he had gotten up at four-thirty in the morning to get breakfast for this bunch and was entitled to a nap. By the time he got downstairs he must have smelled the gunpowder.

Rich: What do you recall about Art Rutan?

Martin: Well, he used to put mustard on his pancakes – on the ones left over from breakfast – he took them up the hill for his lunch. One of the best pictures we got of Art was back when the cast iron stove used to be out in the kitchen and he's sitting there in his chair right next to it – sound asleep. He was one that didn't want to give up hunting, that's for sure. I remember the last few years, his hands were so crippled up with arthritis I don't know how he was carrying his gun, let alone how he might fire it. He still got himself up on the hill. We put that tent up the hill on his watch. Sheldon Johnson and his wife, Judy, Mom and Dad and I think Todd and I dragged that thing all the way up the hill and then set it up on his stand. That fall when Art showed up at his favorite spot, he must have been totally confused to see that thing on his watch. They said he just kind of stood off to one side waiting for somebody to show up or something. He wanted to go deer hunting – had killed several nice bucks at that spot over the years, and here's this tent! Later on that fall when he was up there one time it started raining so he was kind of glad it was there.

Rich: I'm surprised he didn't wind up shooting a deer from that thing. Something about the rocks there and the lay of the land right by the edge of that spruce swamp – it was a good place to see a buck.

Martin: Boy, did he have the stories to tell about back when he was young and hunting.

Rich: One year Bob let us take the Brigade kids up to your camp in the middle of February for a weekend. Bob went along to help with the cooking and for the outing. On the way in, we discovered about nine bobcats hanging on the pole on the porch of the State House there at North Lake. I had never seen any before and could hardly believe how big they could get. Some of these had great big paws and they would stretch out to four or five feet – from their heads to where their hind paws hung. Some local fellows had some top-notch cat dogs and the Koenig boys got to hunt with them some. They would carry a hound on their lap on a snowmobile and head over to South Lake and the trail beyond on the way over to Nobleboro and would go as far as they needed to in order to strike a fresh bobcat track and when they did, they would let the dogs go. They'd take off baying on the track and the first thing you know, everything would get quiet. They couldn't hear a thing. The cat would dive down thru the deep snow where apparently he knew there was a down treetop or something and figured he was safe. Well, the dogs would disappear into the snow after the cat. You couldn't hear them bark under all that snow. They had one man with a gun and the rest of the party used their shovels that they took along. They would dig down and pretty soon they could hear the ruckus of where the cat was – holding off the dogs. At an opportune time the cat would bust up out of there and if the guy holding the gun had any kind of luck, they had the cat. That's how they got them. I think they seriously depleted the cat population. It was a number of years before the bobcats came back in the area.

Martin: I think Ernestine Koenig has a picture of them hanging there. She's got it in her house. She and Otto moved and she does the books for the sawmill and she's got a lot of the old outdoor pictures in her office.

Rich: When they lived in the State House were the boys home-schooled?

Martin: No, they went to school in Forestport. When Mom and Dad bought the camp, Bruce was in high school.

Rich: I recall one winter hiking into your camp with your Dad – we were on snowshoes and we heard a roar and he said, "we'd better step off the trail." I said "what do you mean?" He said, "you'll find out." All at once here came the two Koenig boys on their snowmobiles and they came around a bend and they were right up on the snowbanks. They were logging it back in the woods and they plowed the road with a bulldozer or something and they had quite high snowbanks. They came around a curve with their snowmobiles and then they would hit the straight on the road for a ways to pick up speed and head for the next curve – they were having fun. I'm glad we got out of the road though as they had no idea we were there. I don't know if they would have missed us if we were still in the road when they came along. It appeared like they were doing at least forty miles per hour.

Martin: I can remember back when Otto was the dam controller. Every Sunday when we went home we had to go over there and tell him we were leaving. No matter what the weather was or how bad the bugs were he would be sitting on that porch about every time.

Rich: He loved that country, didn't he?

Martin: I see Bruce and his wife while I am snowmobiling in the winter. You can really cover the ground while snowmobiling. I recall thinking, "let's see, during hunting season it would take me about three hours to get here." With the snowmobile you can get there in about twenty minutes.

Rich: We always used to drink freely from those beautiful streams that would come tumbling down off the mountain. I think we need to be very careful now. In fact I carry some drinking water with me. I'd take a chance in a minute if I was without water and lost or something but otherwise I don't take a chance. Those beavers will build their dam in the most unusual places. You see a little bitty stream and follow it a ways and the first thing you know, you come right on to a beaver dam – many times with a house and the whole works. That's all it takes to get right into the giardia.

Martin: One year they dammed up the little creek that goes near our hunting trail right by the swamp. It must be two miles from nowhere and the creek isn't over two feet wide anyplace.

Rich: Did they have a pond big enough to build a house on?

Martin: Oh, yeah.

Rich: I know it pleased Bob immensely to be able to share what he knew about the woods with you kids. I know that was one of the high points of his life.

Martin: Yep.

Rich: I really appreciate the example you boys set when your Dad became ill. The way you supported him and encouraged him – it was marvelous and I appreciate it. And you might say "what's so great about that? Who doesn't want to take care of their father?" But I'll tell you, it doesn't always happen. And you can love somebody and still not feel you got the capability to do all you guys did for him and I take my hat off to you and I know he appreciated it and I admire you for it.

Martin: I know we have been lucky too that since he's passed away to have all you guys still be able to come up and hunt with us. And have that companionship. Hunting is just an excuse to go. The companionship is the important part.

Rich: Well, that's what makes deer camp so interesting and intriguing and such a blessing really, because boy, I'll tell you, in this day and age in which we live and the rat race that it is that we all have to contend with, or I used to have to when in the insurance business, oh boy – and it can't be any easier now. I don't care what the business is and with this computer stuff – you guys had it in school and for you its second nature. It's anything but second nature for us.

Martin: I think even with us – like my generation you know, the kids nowdays put us to shame. Eight and nine year olds can whip thru that computer faster than I can even think of it. They were showing me something on the internet one day and I said, "would you slow down – I can't watch it that fast."

Rich: Well, Jani and I are struggling. She's got an E-mail address now and we get to play with that up to my sister's – she has a computer that she lets us use. Usually she can get her E-mail and do what has to be done but it still is pretty much of a mystery. You'd think after awhile we'd learn something but we don't own a computer ourselves now. We don't have electric or telephone service at our home presently. We keep going down to the high school or at the Community Technology Center at the J.M.Murray Center – they have somebody there that can help us out and answer our questions. The last time we went down to the high school they had a filter on so that the kids couldn't get into the internet. While we were there I asked if I could use the printer. She said, "yes you can do six copies." I said, " that is real generous but the report I am trying to get has eight pages." "Ok," she says, "you can do eight." So by the time I got the deal going there, somehow I pressed the "print" button twice so I got two copies of my report – so I gave the extra one to her. It was a nice report and had to do with some investments we were following – we could get the report we were looking for about two weeks earlier than if we were to wait until the thing comes in the mail. With the market pretty much in a downswing, we really wanted the update information as soon as it was available.

Martin: I know, I get my report on my IRA and it's about back down where it was when I started. It gets discouraging.

Rich: Yes, and just think – you will retire on that, some day. I appreciate this Fabian plan that we have been following – it doesn't get us in at the very bottom or out at the very top but we come close enough to both following this plan that we make out quite well. Remember the fall that Frank

Underwood dragged in those iron runners from the old lumber camp so he could make a sleigh? What a surprise it was seeing him drag those things into camp one day – boy, those things are heavy. Well, thank you very much for sharing.

CHAPTER 4   VIRGINIA KNOBEL

Rich: I'd like to introduce you to Virginia (Ginny) Knobel – the Mom of the Knobel boys we have been interviewing. On any story about a family deer camp I believe we ought to include the Mother of the bunch. I can well imagine there would have to be some extra concerns about safety for your children. After all, this is a real wilderness and there are things like coyotes and black bears around and cliffs and rocks and of course – water.

Let's see, the year you bought the camp was about when?

Ginny: 1961.

Rich: How old was Larry, your oldest son at the time?

Ginny: He was born in 1950, so he would have been just eleven.

Rich: I was just kind of curious what your thoughts were regards purchasing a camp in the North Woods

Ginny: Oh, well, I always enjoyed the outdoors – camping and everything. Bob came home once after being up there with Ted, I guess. He said, "we saw a camp – Otto told us about it, and we thought we'd like to buy it." I was pregnant with Todd and I couldn't go in the car anyplace so I didn't see it until after they bought it. He came home and told me all about it. All the dishes were still there and they left hunting clothes and everything – a lot of extra stuff came with the camp. They even left furniture, bedding and blankets.

Rich: I always used to admire that antique armoire that was where the living room used to be. This fall when I was up there I mentioned that item and Howard Henry said, "yeah, and it is still here – they moved it next to the stove in the living room." What do you think of Howard's cupboards that he built this last summer?

Ginny: I like them – they match pretty good.

Rich: The thing I like about them is they are so deep – you can get a lot of stuff in there – and they are deep enough so they hold the large pots and pans which the boys need when preparing meals for the large group. This last weekend when I was up there hunting with the bunch, Bob Schoenfeld was there and he remarked to Martin how he appreciated his cooking ability and in fact said, "all you boys know how to cook pretty well – how did that happen?" John was there and Todd – Larry didn't go up there that weekend. John said, "well, Mom went back to work and she didn't get home until quite late and we were hungry." You told him, "well, that's okay, I'll just open the recipe book and leave it on the counter for you – go ahead and read the recipe and fix it yourself, if you want to eat earlier."

Ginny: It wasn't quite that way – I used to plan the meals and they would start them before I got home. Martin used to mix up a meatloaf. I would get something ready for them to put in the oven.

Rich: It wasn't quite as raw as they described?

Ginny: No.

Rich: John had to tell us about the time he was going to do chicken something or other – he read the directions and it said, put the oven on 450 degrees for a few minutes and then put it down to simmer. Well, he stuck the chicken in and put the oven right up to the 450 degrees and then he thought of something he wanted to do so took off. He said, "Mother got home and she could smell it way out in the driveway – and that chicken was well cooked and the house was full of smoke. In fact, we even put in a claim on the insurance."

Ginny: I don't remember that.

Rich: You don't remember that? I'm glad I got that story.

Ginny: Bob always used to do breakfast up at camp. John went to college and took food service. He does this in the military and that's his regular job also at the Recovery Center where he works. He plans and shops and helps the residents cook.

Rich: I imagine you have a story or two to tell about adventures you were involved in up at camp.

Ginny: Well, Matthew, Larry's son, when he was seven or eight was playing down by the creek and he came crying into camp and said "I fell in the creek" and he was all wet, you know. I said "do you hurt anywhere?" He said "oh, yeah, my arm hurts a little bit." Well he pulled up his sleeve and he had a great big gash in his arm – we knew it needed stitches so they wrapped him up and took him out to Forestport to a doctor and he stitched him up. He didn't realize he was hurt – just wet. When you fall in a place like that, there's pretty apt to be glass.

Rich: Did you ever have any concern for the safety of the kids playing around up to camp – there were bears in the area – or about the kids wandering off and getting lost?

Ginny: I remember letting two or three of them together go down to the lake by themselves to go swimming. I was kind of uneasy with them down there alone but Bob said, "they got to grow up." One time he heard one of the kids holler, "help! help!" Bob was up on the porch and he went tearing down the hill and he got down there to the lake and there was nothing wrong. So, they got kind of chewed out. After that he explained "do not holler help – unless you really need it."

Rich: Recently I read an article – two, actually, telling about fly fishermen, in both cases. The first fellow happened to notice an otter in the area which is not so unusual – but I guess it was unusual as otters normally don't put up with people being in their space and the three times I have observed otters in the woods, each time as soon as they realized I was there, they disappeared. This article told about the otter approaching the fisherman and he bit him. He beat him off with his fish pole. They were afraid of rabies so they gave him the series – he didn't have anything with him to kill the animal. He was just glad to be able to get out of the water as the animal kept attacking him – bit him several times on the leg and also on his wrist once. The other guy suffered something similar but in a different State. This otter swam over to him, took a look at him and came right after him – and he kept it up.

The fisherman happened to have a .22 pistol and he shot the thing. He presented the animal to somebody to check it for rabies and sure enough, it was rabid so they had to give him the shots.

Howard Henry was telling about a friend of his who had a nice pond and he stocked it with brook trout, and he loved to fish. Well, the State introduced some otters to the region and a pair got into his pond. I think if he could, he would have shot them as they proceeded to eat up his fish. As a kid I had a little 9/10th of a horse Elto Pall outboard motor. I put that on our canoe and would go along close to shore up at Skaneateles Lake where my parent's cottage was. Beaver would jump off the bank into the water, and I'd see mink families, shore birds and a whole bunch of stuff – it was a lot of fun. Another mink family I saw, the little ones were about four inches long, nose to tail. The thing that was so pronounced about them was they had a bright pink nose. I suppose that was nature's way of helping the mother keep track of them. There was a large flat rock that was tipped up with one end up on the beach. The mother mink had caught a rock bass about four inches long. The little ones were right around her when she let that fish go. It flopped down the face of that flat rock and the babies would pounce on it and be practically knocked off as the fish flopped its way back down the rock and into the water where it would begin to swim away. The mother then would re-catch it and the whole episode would be repeated, quite a sight.

Ginny: About every time I had been up to camp, we would see and hear loons. We love to hear them. Onetime a bear came into our camp – while we were there – all upstairs in bed. My Mother was there with us at that time – she was about eighty then. Of course we heard the bear trying to break in so Bob said, "well, I'll go down" and took the gun. So I went into the bedroom and woke my Mother up and said, "Mother, there's a bear breaking into the camp, but Bob's gone down to take care of it." "Oh, all right," she says, and she went right back to sleep. How's that for trust. Well, he went down there and shot at it as it was coming thru a window in the living room. He hit the thing in the jaw and fortunately, it backed out onto the porch. It's not that Bob is a bad shot – he had just been wakened and had to hold a flashlight near his gun barrel in order to see to shoot. The bear ripped around on the porch a bit then busted out thru the screened porch. In the morning Bob teamed up with the local Daniel Boone and they tracked it as far as they could but the bear got away. We felt bad about the animal being injured like that but would have felt even worse if he had managed to enter the camp – which he almost did!

This was one of those rare times when it was really hot and muggy up there that morning. Well, Bob was cooking breakfast. Bacon and eggs, and oooh, I don't think I am very hungry. The smell of all that blood was not conducive to my having a real good appetite. I said, "I guess I don't want my egg." Mother says, "well, put it over here – I'll eat it." It didn't bother her at all. After breakfast, we got pails of water and the broom and tried to wash off all that blood. What a mess.

Rich: Over on South Lake – when Bob had his tent camp set up – did you ever go over to where the old lumber camp used to be?

Ginny: Yeah, we went over there several times. The buildings were still there at that time.

Rich: That made a nice hike. The buildings are all gone now. There are saplings two inches in diameter growing up all over the area now.

33

Ginny: We were up there the weekend after they got the tent set up one time. A bear had gone right thru the tent - in one side and out the other.

Rich: I got a call from Bob the following Monday saying he needed help to operate the speedy stitcher to repair the tent and would I go up with him the next day? I went with him and we had a great time fixing things up. I got to work the stitcher from the outside – in the rain. When the bear busted thru the back of the tent he scattered dishes and silverware all over the woods. That was the first time I had ever had chicken wings – they were delicious. I was telling Jani, I never got to eat spaghetti until my senior year in high school – my folks just never had it at all. What do you remember about that sailboat that Bob built?

Ginny: That was our rinky-dink. He and the boys used to have a lot of fun with that. It was really hard to get that boat thru the narrows. The wind always blew it seemed, in a contrary direction. You've seen the photo album, haven't you, that I put together – it's on the bookshelf up at camp.

Rich: No – I was just up there and didn't notice it – no one said anything about that. I'd like to see it.

Ginny: That will give you a reason to go back.

Rich: I won't need much of a reason – all I'll need is the opportunity. Oh, it's a wonderful place.

Ginny: All the snapshots I had of camp, I put in there. I've got some to add to it now. When Todd and Martin were ages seven and nine we bought them each a motorized boat to play in the water with – I think it had a strong rubber band to wind up and this one night when they went up to bed they each put their boats under their bed. I went up to tuck them in and I arrived at Todd's bed first. I managed to get my foot a little too far under his bed and I hit that boat and it went RRRRrrrr, RRRRrrrr, RRRRrrrr and I just about jumped out of my skin – I guess I thought it was a bear under the bed or something!

Rich: One thing that is just super about a place like this – if you have kids – is just to help them appreciate the things about the out-of-doors.

Ginny: I think their Father did that.

Rich: He sure did. You and Bob had four boys. Normally you might expect that maybe one or two out of that group would be interested in the out-of-doors – but as in your case, to have all four that are keenly interested really says something I think about the type of sharing that was done – it meant so much to them. You know, it isn't just that your boys all enjoy the woods – most of their close personal friends enjoy it too. There were seventeen they fed for dinner Saturday night and again for breakfast Sunday morning. I could hardly believe there was such a group of young men. There were only three of us at that time that were "old timers" – guys over sixty. The rest of them were young people the age of your boys and that is unique, it really is.

Well, Ginny, we appreciate your input towards our new book. Howard Henry said we just had to do this – needed to capture some good stories from some of us older fellows before we kick-off. I guess he's got a point. He suggested the best time to do this would be for me to bring my tape recorder up to camp this fall the weekend when everybody is up there. Well, this past weekend I tried that. I discovered however you got all these guys that are excited to see each other and they are all talking at once and you're trying to interview somebody and you can't hear for shouting and it was just awfully awkward. But Martin has been here and Howard and now you.

One thing I have discovered is that I have got a good story and you have got a good story but just about everybody knows somebody else that has got an even better story. I'm hoping to include background, history and stories from a variety of deer camps with a variety of subjects to try to make this book of interest to everyone. Thanks again for your part in this.

CHAPTER 5   JOHN AND ROBERT KNOBEL

Rich: John Knobel – how old were you when your folks bought the camp up north?

John: I was just age ten. The year before they bought the camp, Dad and my older brother Larry and I stayed at the last campsite on North Lake road just before you arrive at the gate. There was a big fireplace there at that location and we pitched a tent and stayed there over a week. We went up and down the lake fishing. The trout fishing was really good back then and we could catch bullheads at night.

Rich: What do you recall about trolling for lake trout over on South Lake?

John: I recall going with my Dad and Larry one time. We didn't have any downriggers so we just threw out our lines and trolled behind the boat. Mostly we just got snagged on the stumps and stuff on the bottom although I do recall Dad caught one lake trout. We'd always stop by the old tent site and cook our hotdogs and have lunch there. The blueberries were huge at that spot.

Rich: Yeah, that place was quite open back then. The spruce trees were all less than a foot high and the area got a lot of sun. You killed a nice buck one year up behind the camp at North Lake, I understand.

John: That was up the ridge near what they call seven-point. Mid-afternoon one day I went up behind the camp and crossed the creek and climbed the ridge and found what looked like a good spot and sat down on a big log. I sat there quite awhile but then it started to get late – I decided I'd stick it out for a little longer. All of a sudden, this nice buck came out and stood out there in front of me. I had Dad's old 8 mm Mauser and I took a shot. The deer took off running but with a good tracking snow on, I soon found his tracks where he had been hit and there was a lot of blood. Earlier that afternoon my Dad had climbed the hill and was still-hunting somewhere in the general area – so I fired the signal and soon he came over – he had been on watch up by the cannon. We started trailing the deer and soon he headed over towards nine-point and then suddenly turned down hill and not far from there, we found him. By then it was really starting to get dark. We dressed the deer and with the snow on the ground there was still plenty of light so we could see to drag him around the rocks and over the logs.

Rich: I bet it was just great to have your Dad nearby and for him to be able to join you and help track it and for the two of you to drag it out together – that must have been fun.

John: That was my first deer – we were both celebrating.

Rich: How did it come about that you were able to get that beautiful little log cabin that you have across the road down by the lake?

John: The Lyons Paper Company had made a deal with the State to trade some land. The cabin was on that property about two miles down the road from our camp and would have to be burned down along with several other much newer and nicer pieces of property. I had talked with the supervisor about the possibility of my buying that little cabin as I thought it would make a great place for the bunch that usually hunts with me for us to stay together. The group at the main camp was getting so

large by then that we needed some extra space. Well, I called that guy every week for over a year –
and finally, he said, "okay, take it." So I lined up some friends for the next weekend to help dismantle
the place so we could get it ready to move. There was Darrell Cottom, John Miller, Norm Sherman
and a friend of his that happened to want to come along that weekend to help with the project. We
brought a sawsall, hammers, crowbars and all that stuff plus a generator to run our tools with. We
were supposed to meet with the supervisor Saturday evening at the site but I had something I had to do
so couldn't leave with the bunch Friday night but planned to drive up there on Saturday. After the
group left Friday night to head up there, I got a phone call from the supervisor that was coordinating
the whole thing and somehow he found out that I didn't own my own company and said that I needed a
hundred thousand dollar liability insurance. I called you about that and you advised what with the
minimum premium that would be charged by the insurance company, the insurance would cost more
than the whole place would be worth. When he found out that I didn't have insurance, he said I
couldn't touch the place. He says, "what if you cut yourself or a log falls on you and you get hurt –
you'll be suing us." I told him we wouldn't be suing him but he wanted us to stay off the property or
we'd have to hire somebody else to do the work. Well, there's no phone up there – and at the time I
didn't try too hard to get in touch with them. The next day one of his men came up and saw the guys
taking the place apart and stopped to visit and said, "how you doing – everything's looking good -
you're doing a fine job" and he didn't know that his boss said we weren't supposed to touch the place.
So, when I got up there, in two days we took the roof off and took all the windows and doors out, took
off both floors' flooring so that all that was left was just the shell. The log walls had been just put
together with wooden pegs. The nails they used around the windows were the old square cast nails and
the sawsall wouldn't touch those things so after going thru about three blades, we decided the only
thing to do would be just rip that old framing out and put in new – but we managed to save all the
windows.

The next Monday, the guy calls me up and he was kind of yelling at me on the phone and said,
"I told you to stay away from there." I said, "there was no telephone – I could have driven a hundred
and fifty miles to stop them but I couldn't get away." Then he said, "I don't want you on the property
any more – you'll have to hire somebody to move those logs." They had hired this company to do the
demolition of all the other camps and so he gave me his name and then he said, "if he'll do it, he'll do
it and if not, you're out of luck." So I called him up and he said he'd do it. He wasn't normally in the
business of salvage – he was in the business of construction. Lyons Falls were paying a flat fee so the
sooner he got the job done, the more money he made. So, to do the job for me, he wanted $300.00 an
hour. I thought, "oh boy, but it can't take him more than two hours to do the job and it would still be
cheaper than buying all the wood to build my own camp," so I said, "all right." Then he said, "well, be
here on such a day – up there – at nine o'clock in the morning. If you're not there to pay me and take
possession of the wood and stuff, we're going to bulldoze it." So, I get up there and I wait, and wait –
and he doesn't show up. I had Darrell and John and all those guys with me. The next day when I got
home I called him up and he said, "we had a death in the family and I couldn't make it." So, I said,
"when is the next date?" So, he gave me the next date and it was the same deal – "be there." I got up
there with my brother Larry and his son, Matthew. Darrell and John and those other guys couldn't get
off another day from work. So, we got there with our flatbed trailer – and waited. They were
supposed to be there at nine o'clock and they didn't show up, and I'm thinking, "oh, no, not again."
We drove back to our main camp and hung around there for over an hour and then decided maybe we
ought to head out if they're not going to show. We started out and met a pickup truck coming in – and
it was him. It was amazing how they got that big eighteen-wheeler flatbed trailer in with a big
bulldozer and stuff. I figured the log picker they would use would be a small rig like what the

Koenig's have at their sawmill – but because they were destroying stuff, they came in with this huge machine and the jaws were really big and when they picked up logs it made it look like they had toothpicks. The jaws were so huge they couldn't wrap them around the logs – they had to pick them up using their tips. All the big long logs, he removed with his picker and the short logs Larry, Matthew and I were able to pick off by hand – we didn't have to use a hammer or anything, they just lifted right off. He loaded them all on that truck in one hour. He said that it was the first time he had ever picked up logs. Those jaws could have snapped the logs easy but he never busted a single one. He laid them all in a ten wheel dump truck and drove them over to our campsite. The week before I contacted the Koenig boys at the sawmill and they came in with their bulldozer and removed all the trees we had cut in preparation for the new site and pushed them all over into that big hole there behind the boathouse. They charged me $75.00 is all to do that job and we really appreciated their help. He was up there that week anyway doing some work on Ernestine's camp and doing some landscaping over there and he said, "I'll just drive around the lake and do your place."

It took us about nine weekends to put it back together. We put on an all-new roof – made it of one by sixes. All the original roof rafters were rough sawn four by fours. We used one by eights for the bucks for the doors and windows - the frames were quite wide due to the size of the logs. That's all the material I had to buy. We were able to reuse the flooring, windows and doors. The lumber bill came to about one thousand dollars. I was able to move and rebuild the place for about fifteen hundred dollars. That made it livable. We had the stove installed but had to chink up some cracks and apply some stain and fix the railing and items like that – but we were in it that hunting season. We never broke a single pane of glass – we saved and reused it all. It was the old fashioned poured, leaded type, and you could see the ripples when you'd look out a window – yet it was amazingly clear. If you're looking out a window – and move your head, it seems to get a little bend to it but that just goes with the place, we believe. In a pinch, we can sleep seven there.

Rich: Well, that's quite a story, I think. It came awful close to not happening, didn't it? Those logs are holding up real well, aren't they?

John: It was amazing. The roof hardly leaked at all – it was made out of cedar shake shingle. There was very little signs of leakage but you could look up and see daylight in several places so it wouldn't have been very long and the roof would have been gone, and when that happens, the rest soon follows suit. When we took it apart, the roof came off in, like, a half an hour. You could just push it off. They had stuffed newspapers in between some of the cracks and when we tried to unroll them, they just disintegrated. The one we did finally manage to unroll was dated 1887. The outside of the logs showed some signs of age – cracking and stuff. The inside of the log walls, I just used some soap and water and washed them off and then I rinsed them with just plain water and let them dry and then painted them with a water based polyurithane and that restored them to where they all look like brand new. They were pretty black from over a hundred years of wood stove smoke, mold and stuff but they cleaned right up.

Rich: That's an heirloom – you hate to call it an antique – but it is that too.

John: The first deed we have a record of for the main camp goes back to 1865. Apparently that was when the original portion of that camp was built. It was just a log cabin with the logs squared off inside – that makes up the living room in our present main camp. Originally the camp was owned by the Adirondack League. This place was what they called a guide camp and they arranged to take "sports" hunting and fishing from that location. Back when it was a part of the League, they owned that land but as the membership started to dwindle, they had to sell off some land. A number of paper companies and logging companies purchased land in that area back then. Some of the names were Pratt, Lewis and then Lyons Falls.

Rich: I'd like to hear about that trip you and your son Robert took last fall. You got your map and compass going there – where'd you go? You went to some place where neither one of you had ever been before.

John: We went to Stone Lake Dam. In a straight line on the map, it said it was four miles. That trail weaved thru the woods – and it went thru an area where there were some of the biggest hemlock and white pine I have ever seen. It showed on the map a little spot where there used to be a camp at the lake so we thought we'd go there and check it out. When we arrived we couldn't find any trace of their ever having been a camp. We talked to Ed Bink since and he said there never was a hunting camp– but that a woman used to live in that area and stayed in there alone with her German shepherd dog. Ed and a friend used to hike back in for something to do. After working all day, they would sometimes hike back in after dark. It would take them over three hours. They'd stay there as the camp was still in good shape then. The woman and her dog were long gone – I don't know that they knew what ever happened to her. When they went out there, they would sometimes hunt or if it was during the season, they would fish in the lake – he said there used to be pretty good trout fishing. I told him there were no signs that there was ever a camp of any kind. He said, "it's been gone for over twenty years now." There were some of the biggest tree trunks I have ever seen. We ran across an old trunk of a white pine that must have been over five feet in diameter. Ed said he knew the trunk I was referring to and it had been dead as long as he could remember. The tree must have been blown over by the wind, long before he first saw the place. There were deer trails all over the area and one huge scrape. It took us about three and a-half hours to walk in and we were moving right along. If it had been any warmer, we'd have really worked up a sweat. It was a real nice day for a walk in the woods.

Rich: Well, there are a lot of places like that in the woods that have a lot of history connected with them. We all know about the old-time lumber camps that are all gone now, but you can sometimes still find the iron tips of the tools they used. The wooden handles have long since rotted away. What have you heard about Frank Underwood's situation?

John: I called my brother the other day and told him I just got my orders to report to the base this Thursday to start out processing and he said, "did you hear about Frank? He got feeling poorly one way and another and he went to a doctor and he got some kind of tests - X-rays and CAT scan or something and they said he's got cancer in his brain and in his lungs and its tough. He must be going on seventy-five."

Rich: He sure doesn't look it – the last time I saw him up there he looked more to me like a man about age fifty-five.

John: He's at least in his late seventies – and he can walk up that hill with the best of them. One day we were out hunting and he'd never been to the top of Ice Cave Mountain and he said, "how would it be if we were to hike over there?" I said, "it'll take us most of the day." He said, "I'm for it if you're for it" so I said, "let's go." It was a nice day and there was snow on the ground. We never cut a fresh track all the way from camp clear over to the mountain. His friend, Frank Buerkle went with us. We got clear up to the top of that mountain and we saw where somebody had carved into the granite rock way back in 1918 that they had been there.

Rich: Killroy was there.

John: Yeah, something like that.

Rich: How long did it take you to get there?

John: If you step right along about two hours. Frank Buerkle could move right along when we were walking down the road – but when we came to that hill, he has a little trouble with asthma. It took us about twice as long to climb the hill – but Frank Underwood is up there on top of that mountain waiting for me. I was kind of hanging back as I didn't want to leave the other Frank behind. Finally he said "please go on ahead and when you get to the top, wait for me." So we sat up there quite awhile and finally we thought we ought to go back down and look for him. There was good tracking snow on the ground and the State had put good markings on that trail – there were ribbons and they had cleared the brush and made it easy to walk up there. The first year we climbed that mountain was the first year they had opened it up to the public. Nobody had been there – no trail – nothing. Probably nobody had set foot up there in years. It felt kind of neat to be the first one to go up. The only ones that had been there were loggers and that had to be a long time ago – about 1920. Down at the foot of Ice Cave was Camp 7 – no buildings – nothing was left. There's a beautiful view from that spot – it sets right at the foot of Ice Cave and looks right up the mountain. There were huge blackberries and raspberries and Ice Cave creek runs right past.

Rich: Those loggers had an eye out for where to put their camp, didn't they? They had all the water they needed and if there was a way to include a piece of scenery, they didn't turn that down either.

John: The closer you get to that base the steeper and bigger it looks. We used to walk the road to get into that area and then hunt on the old skidder paths. There were always deer back in there but it was such a long walk, it didn't seem too practical to spend much time hunting the area. Years ago, a Lewis Paper Company person or someone had built a tree stand and we used to go just to hunt out of that. Darrell Cottom said he found an old dug well one time. Ice Cave Creek runs into North Lake. In the early days we used to take both the canoe and little rowboat and my Dad and my brothers and I would all go fishing. Back then, usually we would all catch our limit. We even used to catch trout right off our dock at camp.

Rich: Well, things change, don't they?

John: I was up to camp with my son Robert this last weekend. We saw several people ice fishing. Sometime ago the DEC put tiger muskies into the lake. I think they introduced the muskies to get rid of the perch.

Rich: That will do it. Those fish have got a big appetite. Did you ever catch any of those big fish?

John: Well, last summer Robert and I rowed our boat back into a cove and used a rather large Daredevil spoon. The whole purpose was I wanted to catch one of those tiger muskies. I never thought to bring a net – we never needed a net. We were casting and about every second cast, I'd have to pull a wad of seaweed off. I made a cast up into that bay and I thought I'd hit a snag. There was no strike – it just stopped moving. I thought, "oh, darn, I got a snag" – but then, it started to move. I must be hauling a stick. I could just visualize a stick about six inches around and about three feet long, you know. I got that mess toward the boat and the water was fairly clear and all of a sudden I saw this fish and he turned onto his side and it was like he was looking up at me and then he started to thrash. I thought, "oh no, I don't have a net" and I told Robert "please row us to shore and maybe I can jump out and drag him up.

Rich: You could use the boat as a net, you know. Of course you'd get wet – how big do you figure the fish was?

John: He was over three feet long and well over twenty pounds I would guess. So, Robert is rowing us toward shore – and the boat almost touched the shore and I'm getting ready to jump out – and he took the lure and all. He was gone. Probably he bit the line thru. The following year John Miller was fishing right off the beach. I've heard those big fish patrol the shorelines at dusk and at dawn while feeding – and then they spend the day resting. Well, he hooked one and dragged it right up on shore and it flipped off and he was wrestling with it trying to keep it from getting back into the water but it got back in and it was a big one. Just this last weekend I was up snowmobiling - heading towards the north end of the lake towards the last narrows and there were these three guys out there ice fishing and I slowed down because they got all these little tip-up things and there were holes all over the place and I thought, "I hope they don't get upset about me coming thru here."

So I slow down and start to go thru there and this one guy starts waving his arm, come here, come here, you know – so I pulled over and stopped and he came over and said, "here, take this camera, take our picture" – and then he bent down and picked up this tiger musky that was way over three feet long. I was in hopes he would tell me what he had caught him on – I didn't think to ask him. The musky must have been just coming by and hit whatever he had on. It was just eleven o'clock – a beautiful sunny day. We were going tubing.

Rich: Do you pull the tube on the ice – behind the snowmobile?

John: We were going to go up to the north end where Canachagala is located. For some reason they had bulldozed all that big hillside off years back and there's not a rock on it – nice and smooth and we go up there and he snowboards and I tube and we go down that hill.

Rich: Robert, you haven't said much so far. How's that snowboarding – is that kind of fun?

Robert: Yes – but it's dangerous.

Rich: I bet. It's amazing what they do in the Olympics – you get to see some of this stuff – absolutely awesome. My wife says, "crazy" and I agree.

John: Yeah, the board is over a foot wide and it has grooves on the bottom. Your feet are strapped onto that thing. I tried it – and if you fall, your feet stay on there and I don't like that feature. I tried it out and the first time I fell, I kind of shook my head so that I had a headache. The next time I wore a snowmobile helmet. If I fall again and my head hits the ground, it won't matter.

Rich: Did you get to go a ways on it?

John: About half way down the hill I fell, so then I got up and went the rest of the way down.

Rich: It's amazing that there are fish like that in the lake. Those guys all got into the picture?

John: There were three of them in the group and they all crowded together so I could take their picture of them holding up that fish.

Rich: What you should have done was given them your name and address and asked them to mail you a copy of that photo.

John: I didn't think that fast.

Rich: They really get huge. We were camping over on Otsego Lake one time and my daughter and I were out in our canoe and we happened to look down into the water and here was this huge fish. It must have been a tiger musky – it was well over five feet long and looked like it would have weighed around 45 pounds, at least. It had vertical stripes coming down on the sides. I'm not sure I would want to go swimming in that lake.

John: Two years ago, they dumped in some more but this time they also put in some little tiger muskies. We were fishing out of the canoe for perch one day and right by our dock I looked down and what I saw reminded me of a baby crocodile with no legs. When they're small, the heads are huge and they had those stripes. I thought, these things aren't supposed to reproduce – they're a hybrid – a cross between a musky and a northern pike. It turned out, Ed said they dumped in those baby ones. Two years before they dumped in the bigger ones – all about a foot long. Before they dumped them in the lake, I used to be able to catch quality perch right off my dock. The following year, after they dumped them in, I couldn't catch any perch. I thought, "these muskies have eaten a lot of fish."

Rich: It's something that they can get that big – they got a good appetite. I'm sure they wouldn't hesitate to eat a duck or muskrat or anything that swims that they think they can get down their maw – they would grab it, that's for sure.

John: I hope they don't get any of the baby loons. They come in pretty close to shore as they travel along. There are more loons than there ever used to be – they're doing pretty good. They'll eat the small perch and other minnows – if the loons are there, the fish are there also. The fishing is real funny up north – some days you make a killing and some days you can't catch anything.

Rich: That's typical north-country – whether it's lake, pond or stream. Sometimes they bite and sometimes they don't, according to our experience.

John: One year my Father, Grandfather Knobel and I began fishing off the dirt dam at North Lake. I only got to fish with my Grandfather Knobel twice. Once we fished the Black River and the other time we went over to the South Branch. If you fish all day, you normally will get a few fish.

Rich: He loved fishing. He was an electrician. He worked hard – up and down ladders and pulling those wires all day, he kept in good shape. He had that place up in Grout Brook – you probably remember that.

John: You bet. Every April 1st, my brother Larry and I stayed there over night at that camp and fished for the rainbows the next morning. That was an annual tradition. That began when I was about seven years old. My Father taught me how to fly fish. My Grandfather handed down an extra fly rod he had so I came up with the equipment at an early age and we'd go fly-fishing. There was a large back yard at the place near the brook and he'd show me how to get that fly line going.

Rich: Well, your Grandfather certainly was a lot of fun and he was one of my Dad's special friends. Every spring Dad would get together with the Legion bunch and they'd go up to the camp at Skaneateles. They'd stay there overnight and they had some great meals, play some real exciting penny ante poker and they never caught a great quantity of fish but they almost always would pick up one or more nice lake trout. That made it a lot of fun. What a wonderful way to welcome spring each year. Sometimes the ice would only have just gone out and there'd be huge chunks up on the beach where the waves had washed them up on shore. As long as the ice was out, they could fish and if the ice wasn't off the lake yet they just played cards and kept a good fire going in the woodstove.

John: One time I recall being up there fishing with you. There was my Dad, brother Larry and myself – all in that aluminum boat you had. I recall seeing a huge falling star that kept coming down and down – it looked just like it was going to fall into the lake. Of course, it was a long ways away but it looked like it could have.

Rich: There's a time each August when we see a lot of falling stars. We'll take blankets and boat cushions down on the shore and just lay there on a clear night counting them – sometimes it is quite a display. My older sisters would be in college and they'd have the date when you could expect that meteor shower. One February Bob let us take the Brigade kids up to your camp. One of our leaders worked at   the college and he was able to borrow a telescope with a tripod. After dinner that Saturday night we all went out on the ice. It was cold – only about five degrees above zero as I recall – but there was no moon and it was clear and bright and he set that thing up and would get it pointed at a planet or something and we'd all take turns looking thru that thing. It was so clear – you almost didn't need a telescope to enjoy it – but that was a new experience for most of us – and it was awesome.

John: I got a deer one time on Cool Mountain. That's just south of where you cross the big dirt dam at the Lake. I walked up there one day during black-powder season. I got about a third of the way up the hill and noticed a piece of land that jutted out into a point so I walked out there and I could see down below pretty good. As I got out toward the end of that point, here was this buck coming right up toward the top of the hill right towards me. So I took a couple of steps backwards and then I was standing perfectly still and the deer just walked right past me. He was within good range so I shot him. He went right down – I was using a fifty caliber round ball. It went just under his backbone – didn't break his back but must have shocked him pretty good. He just walked by me and BOOM –

well, I flinched and then looked and didn't see him run so then looked down – and there he was, lying right there. As I started to walk over there, his head pops up – he was trying to get up and I've got black-powder so here I am with an empty gun. So, I jumped behind a fir tree and I figured the less he saw of me, the better – so I'm trying to reload as speedily as possible. I get it all loaded and I keep watching him and he keeps trying to get up – and he can't get up. I figured I'd give him a minute and he'd die naturally – but he didn't. So I lay down on that hogsback and waited until his head came up again and shot him in the back of his head – and that took care of him. It put him out of his misery and he wasn't going anywhere and I didn't ruin any more meat. I dragged him down the mountain by myself. I got him down to what we call the gravel bed, went and got my truck and drove right up to where I had left the deer. I had all I could do to get him up on the tailgate. I was tired. Finally I got the front end up on there and just got it to stay, so I grabbed his hind quarters and tried to lift that up and the front end would fall off. I finally got him up in the truck. The following year the beavers had built their dam right across that road. There was a large culvert at that location with a little stream running thru it and their dam went across the whole road so you can't drive there anymore. Eddie Bink has always asked me – in all my travels in the woods, if I came onto any fresh beaver dams to please let him know. He lives right near the lake so when I saw him, I said, "you probably know about the new dam on that little creek on Cool Mountain, don't you?" He said, "no, I didn't know about that." He enjoys beaver trapping in the spring when the pelts will be prime.

Rich: I've been experimenting some with that new doe in heat bleat type of call – it looks like a little round tin can – has holes in both ends. You put your thumb over the single hole in the bottom and tip it over and then when you tip it back upright it goes – blaaaatt – and sounds just like a doe in heat making its little bleat. Well, I managed to call in a nice buck this past fall using that item, so I'm sold.

John: Yeah, I had one and tried it a couple years ago. I was heading home early one day from camp and planned to stop on the way out to check over a little area where I had observed deer crossing fairly regularly about each time I would drive into camp. I had worked my way down into that area and pretty soon came to a beautiful little hogsback ridge and worked my way back into the woods and it looked so inviting and deery that I sat down just to watch for a while. Well, I thought of that little call I had been carrying in my pocket, so I got it out and tipped it over and made that neat sounding little blaaatt. About twenty seconds after I made that sound, I heard what I thought might be a buck grunting. So, after a few minutes, I tried again. This time I didn't have to wait so long to hear a reply. I couldn't see anything so got up and very carefully began to still-hunt hunt towards where I thought that grunting sound was coming from – then I spotted another deer hunter – and he saw me at the same time – he was stalking too – and we both got a good laugh over that – but you know, that exercise could be dangerous. Especially during the turkey season, when you're wearing camouflage – they definitely warn against stalking turkey.

Rich: Your right. A friend of mine makes turkey box calls to sell. The way that his calls are constructed it is not possible to make a gobble sound. This is unusual for a box call. When I asked him about that he said it was too dangerous. Robert, I've got a question for you. Are you planning to become a member of deer camp?

Robert: Oh, yes – I will be sixteen and plan to hunt for deer my first time this next fall.

Rich: Many other camps have had a definite problem with a lack of younger members to come along and take the place of aging members of the camp. I think this is not something that just happens automatically. Fathers need to take the time to show interest and encourage their sons to take an active part in camp. Then they will become future members and the tradition will continue. My Nephew and his partner were talking about this matter back about twenty years ago when they first joined their Adirondack Deer Camp. They thought, my goodness, we have fourteen members and each one of these guys are at an age where they are raising their families. Pretty soon there will be so many kids that will want to join that there won't be room enough in the camp to hold everybody. Well, you know, this just hasn't happened. I think that's kind of too bad – and for it to happen, somebody has got to make some investment in the young person, you know – do something like what your Dad did with you the other day when you went on that hike. Are you doing any target shooting?

Robert: Yeah. I started out with a BB gun one magical Christmas. We set up a target range in our basement. On my birthday, I got a shotgun and then after that, we went up to camp and started trap shooting.

Rich: Can you hit one – once in awhile?

Robert: One time I was hitting about every one. Then my friend, Darrell came up and when I'd miss one he would go, quack, quack, quack – sounding like a duck flying and I just fell apart after that.

Rich: I don't wonder.

John: He's got an excellent duck call that he makes with his voice. Robert does a lot of playing with Nintendo – their duck hunting game – he was doing real good I think for his first time shooting. At one point we were neck and neck – he was hitting about as many as I was getting and I thought, "he's going to beat me his first time shooting" – but I beat him.

When he was fourteen, we started going around on all the deer trails up behind camp so he would become familiar with the lay of the land and get acquainted with our woods. I showed him how to use the compass and at the end of the day I had him take me back to camp. At that time we weren't on any trail so I suggested, "just take me south-east and we'll end up on the North Lake road somewhere." I followed him out and he took me down to the road and we came out by Spellicy's camp. I recently discovered its not legal for me to be in the woods and have him accompany me while deer hunting and for him to carry a shotgun loaded with bird shot so he could be hunting partridge while I am deer hunting. The year before, I didn't know that. I'd be hunting with my .44 magnum revolver or black-powder rifle or regular rifle and he would carry his shotgun and one day, Darrell said, "you know, that's illegal." Well I didn't know so I didn't have him carry a gun this fall but next year, we'll go deer hunting as he will be old enough to have his own license.

Robert: We had some great hikes and saw some wonderful country and deer signs and everything.

Rich: When will you be sixteen?

Robert: It already happened – on February 12th.

John: Next fall, we'll both be able to carry rifles and begin to hunt real serious.

Rich: Look out, deer!

John: In the past I always got a little grief, you know, from the wife – "well, you're taking off again this weekend." I'd reply, "it's only six weekends out of the year and pretty soon, it's over with." Starting next fall, I want to teach the son the ropes – so, it's deer hunting every weekend.

Rich: There's really something very special about deer camp – you don't understand unless you take part in it. There's plenty of sports and stuff that people do but I just don't. It isn't just, you know, killing a deer. Bob Schoenfeld says, "if you're lucky enough to kill a deer, that's frosting on the cake." But it's just the love of the woods and being able to be out and enjoy the experience and of course the real fun is around camp at night. That's when the stories start. We're all amazed at what can occur in the woods in just one day's time. It's fun to share these stories – it's more than entertainment, though, that it is! It's a way of life.

In real life today, when we're all so busy and operating these computers, doing all this junk, dealing with the public, putting up with stress and everything else – it's really healing to get up in the woods and forget all of that for awhile. It's pretty important.

I was really impressed one night at camp recently. I had this tape recorder stuck in Bob Schoenfeld's face and I was trying to get a story and everybody's talking all at once, and I thought, "oh my, how am I ever going to make any sense out of all this racket when I play back this tape. How will I ever be able to sort it all out?" Robert is sitting over there in a chair looking real serious at me once in awhile and I thought, "I wonder what this kid is up to?" All of a sudden, he picks up this large pad and goes, rrrripppp - and holds up this picture of me – a portrait that he had drawn of me with his pencil. That was fun – I couldn't believe it. Do you like to draw, quite a bit?

Robert: Yes.

Rich: Well, that's quite a talent, I think.

Robert: I have a long ways to go before I'm like my sister, Lisa, though.

Rich: Is she really good at it?

Robert: Oh! She can draw a picture in just a few seconds that I couldn't do justice to in about twenty-five minutes.

Rich: My wife is real good about drawing plans for cupboards or plans for construction, like a building or something. I can hardly believe it. Some of this stuff we have done here while building our home, I would say, "dear, how do I put this together?" She would give it a little thought and come right up with the plans, you know, and it would help a lot. She laid out these kitchen cupboards – showed them to the carpenter and then told him "this is what we want." She did the same thing when we lived in town. Her Dad was a real talented guy – he worked with metal and did a lot of welding and also worked at the boat company and worked as a carpenter for a few years with his Dad. In fact, during the Second World War he and a partner helped develop the nose cone for the first atomic bomb – all out of their little, totally unknown shop here in Homer. When he saw the results of that thing, his partner got pretty disturbed.

John: You mentioned about remodeling the kitchen at your house in town. I came over to pay on my insurance one day and you had all that debris piled out in your front yard and I was doing the cabin right then and I said, "what are you doing with all that old kitchen counter top there, that kind of a burnt orange stuff?" You said, "throwing it away – we're waiting for the trash guy to come pick it up and haul it away – why?" I said "well, that piece there, I think it will fit in the cabin," and you said, "take it away."

Rich: Are you using it?

John: Yeah, it's in there.

Rich: All right.

John: You had a piece big enough that we were able to cut holes in it to fit that double sink and that burnt orange counter top is still right there. It came from your house. We had a lot of little things donated here and there. Darrell was working on a plumbing project over at Cornell and they threw away all these cabinets. A friend of my wife bought his house years earlier and in the backroom was a Timberline wood stove. He says, "I want to get this removed. Do you have any use for it?" At the time I hadn't decided what to do so I said, "yeah, I'll take it – I'll put it in my garage and it might come in handy someday." So, when I built the cabin I took that wood stove up to camp and that's where that came from. The kitchen table used to belong to my brother, Larry – that was their first kitchen table. Darrell gave me the old chair that used to be in his parent's house years ago. My first couch came out of the cellar of Bob Young's house – he had a spare couch down there and for years we put up with the musty smell of that thing and when my Great Aunt, Cathy had to leave her house – she had a love seat sized sleeper-sofa. The place isn't big enough for a huge full-sized couch, so we put that in the camp.

Rich: Let's see, I think it's Darrell that sleeps downstairs and keeps the fire going – he's not very tall so he must fit on that item pretty good.

John: Actually, he takes the outdoor couch cushion and lays that across the item and that works okay for him. I first met him when I was in fourth grade and when we got into the fifth grade, he began to come up to camp with me and my family. We became good friends and have hunted together every year since we were old enough to hunt.

My Grandfather Willy had an old .35 Marlin lever action rifle. One day I had borrowed that gun and had gone up past the stovepipe and headed into the swamp and I got into the swamp a ways and I looked at my ball compass I had pinned on my shirt and I said, "okay, I'm going to go north." I'm walking along and I picked out a tree and I headed north toward it and looked down at my compass and it wasn't north, anymore. So, I thought, "oh, no." The little round ball on the bottom had become disconnected from the compass thing, so I'm down in that swamp all twisted up and I thought, "I have no idea which way is out of here." So I took my best guess at which way to go and I'm beginning to work my way out of that swamp and suddenly I heard this click, click, click, click – thru the brush and I looked and here is this buck coming across and he had this huge rack, so I raised up the rifle – he's not running, he's just moving along pretty good, like bucks do, and he's headed into the swamp. I thought, "if I squeeze this off and I don't get him good – he's going down into that swamp and I'll never find him" – so I didn't take the shot and I got myself out of there.

Darrell got a nice eight-point that weekend with my 8 mm. I really thought if I had a scope I could have gotten that deer I saw by the swamp that day, so I took the gun down to Hank's Gun Shop that next Monday and asked if he could put a scope on the rifle for me. He looked at it and said, "you sure you want me to put a scope on this?" I said, "why not?" He said "your gun was built the way guns used to be built – the correct way. I'll give you a brand new Marlin lever action for yours." I asked "what's the difference?" He just stepped over and grabbed one off the rack and handed it to me – and I said "it's half the weight." Then he said, "this gun is all stamped out metal – yours is made of real machined steel parts – they don't make them like this anymore – I'll trade you a brand new one." Well, it's not mine to trade – my brother said to go ahead and put a scope on it. Then he said "once I drill and tap it, the gun will lose it's value." So I told him I want a scope on it. So, he said he'd do it.

A few days later, he called me up and said, "your scope is ready." When I got there he said "when is the last time you fired this rifle?" I told him I hadn't fired it in years and I was sure my brother hadn't – probably my Grandfather was the last one that fired it – years ago. "Well," he said, "I put a cartridge in there, aimed at the target and pulled the trigger. The hammer dropped and nothing happened. I waited awhile and then ejected the cartridge and took a look and there was just a tiny dimple on the primer of that cartridge – the hammer didn't hit it hard enough to fire the primer. I thought it might have just been the cartridge – so I stuck another one in, aimed down range, pulled the trigger – nothing. It had a broken firing pin."

Rich: That was a good time to find that out.

John: If I'd had a nice shot at a big buck it would have gone, click - and then I would have been angry.

Rich: I bet he fixed it okay, didn't he?

John: Oh yes, he did a good job. I took it up to the Homer Rod & Gun Club and sighted it in for about a hundred yards and I could shoot a quarter with it, so I figured that was as good as I could get. Awhile back I got a Traditions .54 caliber black-powder rifle and this year I put a scope on it. I took that up to the Gun Club and I had one of those square boxes that wine comes in and the vent thing had a little rubber cap on it so I took that off the box and put a nail thru it and stuck that right into the center of the box. I set that onto a stick and drove that into the ground just a little over fifty yards. I put on one of these quick release scopes as during the black-powder season, you can't use a scope. During the regular rifle season, you can. I figured I'd use it for both and believed that rifle to be very accurate. I put the cross hairs on that cap at fifty yards and squeezed the trigger, and when I looked up, the cap was gone. When I checked the target, there it was – with a hole right at 3 o'clock in that cap – almost cut it in half. I thought that was good enough.

Rich: It's amazing how accurate they are. Yours is a percussion cap rifle, isn't it?

John: Yes – it has the lightning fire system – it has a musket cap instead of that little teeny thing. When you pull the trigger it's instant – I can hardly tell the difference between a center fire and my new black-powder rifle.

Rich: They're deadly – in every respect.

John: Mine is a .54 caliber.

Rich: I think that's better for hunting. You got more oomph and use a little more powder, probably.

John: This year I used a .340 grain bullet – or it might have been a .430 grain – big enough, anyway.

Rich: That was about like they used back in the Civil War days probably. If you got hit by one of those things, you didn't think it was very "civil" – it could take your leg right off.

John: I killed a deer on my brother's property with a .54 caliber round ball – it did the same thing – it hit the back bone by the front shoulder and the deer went down instantly – but then tried to get back up so it took another round to finish him off. That round ball just doesn't cut it – it goes in with a hole so big and comes out with a hole the same size – it just doesn't expand like the Sabot slugs we all use now in our shotguns. I didn't get a deer this year – I had stuff going on and just didn't get as much time for hunting as I wanted.

Rich: It was unusually warm, too.

John: It was difficult to hunt in that warm weather. Opening day on my brother's land, they just built a new house across the road where the deer came up across the lot but the year before I saw all kinds of deer and I got a nice deer. This year I didn't see a single deer on that property. My brother didn't get one either.

Rich: It doesn't take much to change their patterns, does it?

John: We're looking for a good place to go turkey hunting – we both got one of those calls you put in your mouth, a diaphragm call.

Rich: I can't use that kind – I'm afraid I'll swallow it.

John: One summer I was fishing on the Black River using our canoe. We were just floating slowly downstream, fishing as we'd go. All of a sudden I noticed this deer – swimming upstream. I picked up my camera and just sat there and when the deer got within about five feet of the canoe, we looked at each other for an instant – and the deer came right by the canoe – I could have petted him on the head – but then it must have caught our scent as it climbed right up out of the river, and disappeared into the brush. Another time we were sitting down on our beach by the lake and noticed this doe swimming up the lake. We don't know what spooked her into the water. She appeared to be tiring so we got our rowboat out and kind of forced her to shore. She got out of the water but as soon as we went away, she got back into the water.

Rich: She had her own mind made up. Maybe the coyotes chased her into the water. The other day we were hiking out on our property on some of the woods roads and there was a nice fresh tracking snow about two inches deep. We came across a really large coyote track – bigger than any I'd ever seen before. We are pretty apt to hear them howling and carrying on at night.

John: I've just been recalled by Uncle Sam to get involved in our present war – I expect to ship out in a few days. I'll do my tour and come home – hopefully, in time for the deer season this fall.

Rich: How many years ago was it that you were over in Desert Storm?

John: Eleven – Robert was age five when I was away – I missed his birthday party. I figured I'd only have to do one war in my career – now I got to do another one.

Rich: We're glad they got thru the Olympics with no major problem.

John: I was in bed asleep when my wife called me – she called me from work. She said, "turn on the TV – a plane has just crashed into the World Trade Center." I thought, "no way – who could run into those towers – they stick way up there." So, I turn on TV and I'm watching – the building is on fire and the helicopters are taking pictures and the camera people from other buildings are taking pictures and just right live on TV I see the other tower getting hit – and I thought, "oh, my God" – and then I never expected to see them coming down.

Rich: Really – I don't think the enemy did either.

Robert: I was in school when it happened – I went in and called my Dad, just in case he wasn't watching.

John: My cousin Tom's wife died in the tower.

Rich: I'm sorry to hear that, my God.

John: She was on her second day back to work from being out on maternity leave.

Rich: My cousins Art and Jackie Tucker live in New Jersey. Their son-in-law works for Morgan Stanley and on average, he would spend two days a week working in one of the towers. Well, it just happened to be his day to work in their Philadelphia office, so he missed it. Last week we were looking at a Business Week magazine that my sister lets us take after she gets thru reading them – and they had just started hauling cars out of the parking garage from underneath one of the towers. They recommend that they don't use these vehicles because of all the poisonous ash and stuff that has accumulated on and in them. They're trying to get them all condemned so that the people don't get sick. I'll tell you, we sure got some dandies out there, don't we?

John: Yeah – it's too bad about that reporter.

Rich: Wasn't that terrible. Its hard to imagine why these people think the way they do – I guess it is the way they are trained – brought up and taught. We're not perfect, that is for sure – but

50

man, we don't have a license to go kill anybody. You probably have seen the movie, Forest Gump, haven't you?

John: Yes.

Rich: It was funny – probably wasn't true, but where they showed the break-in that turned out to be the Watergate deal – he called up in the middle of the night and complained "those lights – they are keeping me awake." We certainly appreciate our military. It seems like some of the leaders in government – some of this childish way they carry on – honestly, it just seems so unnecessary. I'm thankful we have the leadership we've got. We're thankful for every serviceman and servicewoman that gets involved.

It was good to see how the firemen and others rallied in the area of the towers – it seemed to bring the people together in many ways. I was invited to attend a sportsman's dinner a while ago that was held in some little church out near Cazenovia. I hadn't heard about this group previously. That church had just built on an addition, it was their gymnasium and fellowship hall so it was a good sized room. They had been local sponsors of this sportsman's group for several years previous to this event so they were aware that members and guests would like to bring their trophies and mounted heads and display them for the evening. So when they built this gym, they made it so you could drive in a spike or screw in a fastener to hang your mount on and that feature existed all the way around that large room. For example, a full head mount of a bull elk is a rather huge mount and very heavy. Well, that was no problem. There must have been over fifty racks and mounts, bear rugs, wolf hides and everything you could imagine beautifully displayed.

There must have been about three hundred in attendance for this event. At our table I noticed this guy across from me – he was wearing a cap that said N.Y.F.D. on it. I thought, wow, I don't know who told these guys about this event, but here they are – about four or five of them that just came for this dinner and for the evening program. Somebody must have sent them an invitation saying if there's anybody interested in a game dinner, you're welcome, so these guys showed up.

John: Have you ever been to the game dinner in Syracuse – I think it is at the Spinning Wheel Restaurant. They have bear and elk and moose, rabbit and squirrel – and all kinds of fish and of course, venison.

Rich: No, I haven't heard about that. Well John, I certainly have enjoyed our time of sharing. I have contacted your brothers Larry and Todd about our getting together to get their stories. I got Martin's story several months ago. This book project is beginning to come together now. It's been a real struggle to learn to use the computer but I'm making some good progress. Thanks again, to both you and Robert for this time you were willing to set aside so we could do this. We wish you the very best with your upcoming stint in the military.

CHAPTER 6   ROBERT SCHOENFELD

Rich: Bob Schoenfeld – it's great to see you. How did you get involved in coming to this camp?

Bob: Ted Thompson and I were lifelong friends in Wisconsin. When I moved to Syracuse in 1972, he invited me to visit this camp and see what this Adirondack hunting was all about. I hadn't hunted deer in about fifteen years and I fell in love with mountain hunting and the charm of it and peacefulness – you could spend time here in God's creation – and I've been coming back here ever since. I've been carrying my Father's old .30-30 carbine model 94. There's a lot of history behind that old rifle.

Rich: Are the woods in Wisconsin similar to the Adirondacks or are they quite different.

Bob: They're very different. They are flatter – some hill country but not the mountainous terrain that we have here. It's not nearly as dense as the country around here.

Rich: Is there spruce and pine or is it predominantly hardwood?

Bob: There is a mixture of hardwoods with some spruce and pine scattered throughout – not nearly as much wild country as we seem to have here. The men in the legislature that set aside this country for the most part as a wilderness area have my vote of confidence and thanks – they were really wise men – they had a lot of foresight – and I'm thankful for them.

Rich: The State is still involved on a limited basis in making trades of land with some of the paper and lumber companies. After taking the timber they desire they can sometimes make a trade with the State and get to utilize and harvest timber on other more productive plots of land.

Bob: Near this camp a paper company recently traded over ten thousand acres with the State. That is a lot of hunting ground that recently has been opened up to the public. When they first opened that up I recall seeing a lot of new hunters in the area but the numbers declined in recent years. Maybe that has happened due to the wild terrain and the fact that they aren't able to see as many deer as they have been accustomed to seeing in the southern tier. Up here, it is a different type of hunting – I think it is a lot more challenging. If you bag a buck here, you've really earned it and it's frosting on the cake – but that's not the main reason most of us come here. We appreciate the tranquility of the mountains and the fellowship in the hunting camp and being able to enjoy God's creation without seeing a horde of other hunters.

Rich: I'm aware that you have killed several very nice bucks while hunting out of this camp over the years. Please share some of these experiences with us.

Bob: I have been very fortunate in that I have bagged eleven bucks in the twenty-nine years I have been coming up here. Most of these I got with my Father's old .30-30 rifle. Again, that's just the frosting on the cake. The real enjoyment I have had in wilderness hunting is seeing a large variety of wildlife, very interesting terrain, wild rivers and streams running into beautiful lakes – also the opportunity to climb to the top of a beautiful mountain and read God's Word and thank Him for the privilege of enjoying His great creation. This is certainly a beautiful area He has made. I have had a unique experience with each of the bucks I have trailed or that I have seen and I have some beautiful memories. There's a different story with each one, as you know. From what I have seen in this area, there do not appear to be any well defined runways – like there are in other parts of the country. So, you have to stalk the animals or find an area where they are quite active thru the sign that you discover. It is really a challenge to hunt – more of a challenge than hunting in other types of the country. It's a different type of deer hunting and I'm thankful for that.

Rich: Do you welcome years when there is a heavy beech mast crop or doesn't that matter as far as you're concerned? Would you just as soon not have a lot of beechnuts?

Bob: I like to see a lot of beechnuts so the deer will have more food. Then they become very active and you can certainly see where they have been and will be apt to be congregated. How do you feel about it?

Rich: I enjoy the beech too – but a friend that hunts up at my Nephew's camp has a whole different slant on it than I have ever heard before. He hates years when there are a lot of beechnuts because the deer can be just anyplace. There's beech all over the woods. For example, this is not a good beechnut year – I didn't locate a single tree that had any crop at all. He'd much rather still-hunt in an area where there are ferns because the deer will utilize the fern roots and get fat on them just about as well as they do on the beechnuts. He'd much rather hunt years when there are no beechnuts.

Bob: That's interesting. I've seen a lot of ferns – a lot of lowlands that would take you to that situation – but I guess we're all different in the way we approach things. I recall one year back in 1977 when I was tracking a good buck. I must have tracked him about two miles or so thru some rugged terrain and on top of a ridge. It had snowed throughout the day but then it started snowing very hard. I stayed on the track but that deer must have become confused as he turned and ran thru a thicket of small beech directly at me. He really surprised me – you would have needed to have been a really bad shot to have missed that deer. I got that one.

Rich: How far away was it?

Bob: Not more than twenty-five or thirty yards. After I had shot, I knew I had hit the deer. He made a big jump and then ran about a hundred yards and suddenly collapsed. I trailed that deer and it was dead when I got to him. When I field dressed him I discovered that my bullet had penetrated his heart – had just blown his heart apart. I was really amazed that the deer could run so far after having had its heart blown apart.

Rich: I have had several experiences similar to that one myself. I know exactly what you are talking about.

Bob: On another occasion I was hunting across the lake on that mountain range with Ted Thompson, my dear friend from Wisconsin. I took the boat across the lake and started working my way up the mountain. Ted drove his vehicle around to the other side and he was hunting towards the lake and figured one or the other of us might jump a deer. He's a very good mountain hunter. He travels very quietly – very slow – and as I approached the top of the mountain, I jumped two doe. It was snowing that day and I just stood still for about ten minutes. Suddenly I heard this snapping of the brush and crashing sounds and I thought at first it was Ted – but then I realized he would never make that much noise in the woods. I looked up and the very next thing I saw was a big rack - right where those two does had been. The buck had apparently been following them. I shot that buck and then discovered he had been heart shot too. He traveled about a hundred yards before he died. It amazes me again how determined these deer are. The whitetail deer are certainly beautiful, aren't they?

Rich: Yes, they are. If a turkey could smell like a deer can, we'd never kill one. What they can't smell their eyes make up for.

Bob: Isn't it nice to come back after a long day in the woods to a warm camp? We all enjoy the wood fire going in the stove – it's really good to compare the stories with the other hunters and sit down to good fellowship and be thankful that you have the opportunity to do what we do.

Rich: You bet it is. I was thinking on my way up here, in European Countries the Royalty own the land and they are the only ones with hunting privileges. If you get caught poaching, it could cost you your life.

Bob: How many years have you been coming up here?

Rich: About forty years now, to this camp. Originally I started coming up here with Bob Knobel at his tent camp over on South Lake. That was about fifty years ago. Presently you can't see that campsite from the lake. When we first started going over there, the spruce trees by the tent were only about a foot high.

Bob: Did you have to use a boat to get over there?

Rich: Yes – that was a unique spot.

Bob: I remember one fall I was out all day and it had been snowing hard. I hadn't seen any deer and was on my way back to camp. I came upon a small ravine and was crossing it when I noticed a grouse sitting in a spruce tree. It sure looked like a delicious bird so I shot at it with my .30-30 rifle and I hit it and it fell out of the tree. We had that bird for dinner that night. It was delicious.

Rich: Did you know those birds grow snowshoes?

Bob: I guess I don't know what you are talking about.

Rich: In the wintertime they grow feathers between their toes – you can see the imprint of them when you look at the bird's tracks in the snow. The feathers act like snowshoes and help the bird keep up on top of the snow. Then, in the summertime, those feathers disappear.

Bob: I enjoy watching the woodpeckers up here – especially the pileated woodpecker. They're a beautiful and huge bird. One year as I was sitting on watch hoping a big buck would come along, I heard this pounding noise and I spotted a pileated woodpecker and I watched that bird work for an hour in a dead tree cutting a big rectangular hole into the tree to apparently have its lunch. It was fascinating to be able to watch that bird work. You could actually see the chips fly out of the tree.

Rich: Have you ever heard one cackle?

Bob: Yes.

Rich: Have you had any experiences with a coyote?

Bob: I did shoot a coyote about eight years ago. At first I thought it was a small deer – I was sitting in a swamp area. There was snow on the ground and I saw it approaching from maybe a couple hundred yards away. I just sat tight and as it approached me I realized it was not a small deer, it was a coyote. I waited until it turned broadside and then fired. It went down and as I approached it, I was maybe within ten yards of the animal. I thought it was dead but it wasn't dead yet. It turned on me and showed its fangs and it made growls and it made one final leap and tried to get me. So, be prepared. Don't just presume an animal is dead – and that goes for bucks too. They can play dead and they can turn on you so you have to be careful. It's not just their antlers but also their hooves that are weapons. I have seen black bear in the woods but I never shot one. I did have some bear stew one time and thought that was very good. Two years ago I shot an eight-point buck in the afternoon. I was hunting the Golden Stair Mountain area. I dressed the deer and tried to hang it up in a tree to protect against the coyotes – but I couldn't do it. I'm getting old, I guess. I spread the opening with a stick and let it drain and left it on the side of the hill. I wasn't certain where I was.

I thought I should go northeast in order to get to the trail - I didn't have any fluorescent ribbon so I marked the trees with my knife. By this time, the snow started coming down even harder. When I got back to the car it was about four thirty and I thought if it would stop snowing we could probably find the buck the next day. Back at camp, some others had arrived early due to the stormy weather. They persuaded me to go back and that was a good decision because although it was about dark by then, we were able to follow my footprints. The heavy snowfall hadn't let up a bit and it took us over an hour to walk back there with steady walking. These young guys were complaining because I was pushing them too hard. I was two years younger then than I am now. We had flashlights and my tracks still weren't quite yet totally covered up so we were able to get back to the ridge but the deer was just about completely covered with snow. If we hadn't gone that night to get it – and the guys really pressed to do that – we might not have found the deer at all. After resting a bit, we began to drag the deer out. On the way out, it stopped snowing and the stars came out so brilliant – we had a wonderful time. We had Jim and Todd and Mike – and the old man.

Rich: Now, who is that?

Bob: Me.

Rich: What would you guess the deer weighed, dressed?

Bob: Oh, probably three hundred seventy-five pounds. Oh, it was about a one hundred forty pound deer. It was a nice one. Howard took the rack and he mounted it for me. He did a beautiful job. Another memory. Another story to tell – to my Grandchildren – and some day, Great Grandchildren.

Rich: Yes, and that time will be here before you know it.

Bob: I hope.

Rich: That's wonderful. Thank you for sharing that story. That's a good tale.

Bob: Jeff, my son – can tell you a story. He doesn't hunt but every time he comes up here, somebody either shoots a bear or a deer and he's got to go back in and help drag it out.

Jeff: I'll never forget that bear. There wasn't any snow on the ground – that makes it a lot of work. Ted shot the bear. It was just off that logging road a ways back in the woods. That was a long time ago – that was about when I developed back problems. Actually, it was eighteen years ago. It was after dark when we arrived in camp. Ted met us and said "come on – let's go drag in that bear." I was so sorry I came that day. Rich, you put a stick in the bear's mouth on the one you got, didn't you?

Rich: Yes – we tied a short stick in his mouth and that gave us something to grab hold of when we dragged him.

Jeff: I don't think we had any kind of a stick involved – we just pulled from the paws.

Rich: I don't see how you could do that. How were you able to hang on to the thing at all? I wouldn't have had a notion of how to go about it but one of the guys that helped with the project had previous experience – he suggested the stick in the mouth method. We tied the stick in his mouth with a light-weight line. Two men could grab that stick and then when they stood up in position to drag, they would have some of the weight of the bear off the ground. Snow on the ground always helps - but even so, it's a lot of work.

Jeff: I heard something about deer having a disease.

Rich: Maybe what you are referring to is the fact that sometimes a deer may contract rabies. If deer live in an area where there has been a rabies outbreak among the small game like coons, skunks and foxes, it is possible for deer to get that – but it is rare. About ten years ago there was a major rabies outbreak in our area back home and we all bought gauntlets to wear while field dressing any deer that we had killed. I still carry a pair in my daypack but don't bother to wear them in most cases now.

Bob: How did you make out on your hunt today?

Rich: I enjoyed being in the woods but I didn't happen to see any game at all – not even a chipmunk.

Bob: A couple of years ago I was hunting on a ridge not too far from camp. It was a rather high ridge and I was still at the base. There was snow on the ground at the time and I saw three animals coming down the mountain. They were coming at a pretty good rate of speed but I couldn't tell what they were. They kept coming closer and closer to me. As they came zipping by I could see that they were three big otters. They were sliding along and having a great time. I had never seen any otters in the woods before. They were having fun. They must have been going cross-country from one lake or pond to another. I just said, "hi guys" as they went zipping by.

Howard: They travel all over.

Rich: I went to a spot last spring hoping to do some trout fishing. I noticed some signs and when I read one was surprised to discover that the DEC had released a pair of river otters in the area. The sign said no trapping for the next couple of years. Normally I could catch a few nice brookies in that creek but couldn't even get a nibble. I guess the otters had helped themselves to the trout ahead of my arriving on the scene.

Bob: Another thing I saw today on my travels thru the woods was four partridge.

Rich: Did you see them all in one place?

Bob: No, two were together and the other two flushed out separately in another area. I really always enjoy seeing and hearing them.

Rich: Howard, this is just about the best chocolate cake I ever had in my life.

Bob: Barb and I took a trip this last summer. We flew to Portland, Oregon. We rented a car and drove down the Oregon coast. That is something I have really wanted to do for a long time. We purchased a couple of coolers, some cold cuts, fresh vegetables, fruits and soft drinks and whenever we saw a beautiful spot around lunchtime we'd just stop and enjoy looking at the ocean. We'd try to pick a place where we could get to the beach and walk along for a mile or so. When we got to the California border we drove thru a redwood forest. This was the first time I had ever had that opportunity – I think it was at Crescent Beach. We would call one day ahead to get a motel and we'd just enjoy stopping at any interesting place we found and spend some time and I'd never been on a vacation like that. Usually we had everything scheduled in advance. From there we drove inland to Idaho and visited some relatives there and then we went to our favorite State, Montana. We did some trout fishing and then circled around and came back thru Washington and Oregon – made a complete circle. We dropped the car off and came home.

CHAPTER 7   JOHN DAVIS

Since Jani and I retired from the general insurance business April 1st, 1997 we have entered into a small book store business working out of our home – but most of the sales are generated at our book table during the Holiday In Homer event each July on the green, downtown Homer, New York. The first year we were involved in this was July of l997 and the only book we had at our table that year was the first one I had written entitled, "Deer Camp, Oswegatchie River And Other Places." We sold about eighteen books as I recall and autographed them when requested and sometimes when not. We had so much fun we thought we'd try that another year and add some titles to our book table that we felt were good books to recommend to friends. Our books were almost exclusively about the out-of-doors and especially about deer hunting. We had a few titles that were historical such as "Adirondack French Louie" by Harvey L. Dunham, published by North Country Books of Utica, New York.

The summer of l999, a man by the name of John Davis, no relation, visited our table, saw the outdoor titles and struck up a conversation. I think he purchased one of my remaining books on "Deer Camp" as well. The following July he made it a point to look us up just to show us a color photo of himself posing beside a beautiful eight point buck which he bagged while hunting out of an Adirondack camp that he was a part of. This past summer, he looked us up again and this time showed us a color photo of four of the other members of his hunting camp and they had collected three large Adirondack bucks. Actually, he had two photos – the second one showed the same club members and deer but this time the men were holding their rifles they used to bag their deer. It turned out that John made each one of those rifles. I thought that anyone as enthusiastic about deer hunting as he and his friends seemed to be, deserved a chapter in our new book. I hope you enjoy reading our interview as much as we enjoyed doing it.

Rich: I'd like you to meet John Davis – we met at Holiday in Homer. Mr. Davis is a deer hunter. He has had some interesting experiences that he'd like to share. What was that story you were starting to tell me?

John: Well, that was about the four deer and four bear that were taken in the fall of l926. Three of the bear were sold to Mr. Forshee that owned the hotel in Marathon and he had the hides set up, made into rugs and hung them on the front porch and called it, "Three Bear Inn." It has become an established landmark in the area ever since. Dad's party consisted of seven hunters from the surrounding area. They camped up in the Adirondack Mountains in a tent in a place called Smith's Clearing, four and a half miles back in from Route 8 above Griffin. Forty years later, Cousin John and I were hunting in the same area. I put him on watch within forty yards of where he shot the three bears, ran another one by him, and he killed that one. And in the years in between, he had killed four other bears. He managed to kill a bear while hunting in the north woods about every forth year. I've taken thirteen Adirondack deer and two bear and have killed most of them while hunting out of Smith's Clearing. Of course, we didn't kill them in the clearing – that's where we camped. We killed the deer and bear back in the woods quite a ways from there.

My dad died in 1954 and Cousin John and I went off and on as circumstances allowed for quite a number of years. The last year he was able to go with me was 1969. I have hunted in that area three or four times since. There's a snowmobile trail going from Route 8 over thru just above Wells about eight miles. A couple of years I took some fellows and we went over on the other end of that trail – to a place known as Pine Orchard and took a tent back in the woods about two miles and made camp and hunted but we didn't have much luck. In 1993 a group of us hunted up at Raquette Lake – the camp was owned by one of the members – on North Point Road about seven miles from where you turn off the Route to Long Lake. He has a nice cabin. I like to rough it there. He has everything, including dishwashers so I go along and cook for the fellows. Dick got the first buck in 1993 and it was in 1997 I got my first buck out of that camp. I made a rifle for a fellow and he wanted to know if he used it, would I guarantee success? He had never gotten a north woods deer. He got a buck – his first deer. Then his Dad got excited about it – wanted me to make him one so I did – in 2000. I told him, "I can't guarantee a thing." Dick's Grandson got the first one and the son got the next one and then he shot his new rifle and got a nice buck.

Rich: I'm looking at a picture of the camp you're describing and on that trip there were five hunters and you got three incredible Adirondack bucks – all within a five-day hunt. The antlers are beautiful and the deer appear to be good sized. One of them looks like an older deer – like he's been around for some time.

John: Look at how dark that deer appears – that is the darkest deer I ever saw. Jeff got his at ten o'clock in the morning – he shot it right across the Raquette River. He waded the river to get over there and then he came to get us to help him drag it out – it was raining some at the time. Then in the afternoon, we hunted over near Forked Lake and about a quarter past four we got another buck. That was two bucks the same day for our party and we got pretty excited about that.

Rich: Now you say the grandson's name was Jeff – when did he get his deer?

John: He got his Thursday morning and we got these other two on Friday.

Rich: How long was your trip – was it planned for a week or longer?

John: We came on election day and went home the following Sunday – we only had five days to hunt.

Rich: I assume the family uses this camp in the summertime?

John: There's good fishing in the area – they use it a lot. Dick lives over here in Union Valley. The Grandson was born and raised just down the road from here but I don't know where he lives now – he just got married this past summer and moved away.

Rich: When you hunt out of this camp, what basic method do you use? Were you still-hunting or putting on drives or what did you mostly do?

John: Our method primarily is for two or three fellows to go out and take what we have discovered to be likely areas for a stand. The other fellows will go and hunt toward them. Now, to call it a drive is a stretch of the imagination – and you can't drive a deer anyway, especially in woods of that size. So far as I know any deer that we have gotten has not been "driven" or spooked to the watchers. The deer come along on their own.

Rich: Now your drivers, so called, are the other hunters in the party that are moving in the general direction of the watchers – they are not barking like dogs or making all kinds of racket. They are still-hunting. However, they actually are driving if the wind is such that it is moving towards the watchers – there's a good chance – you don't have to call it driving – but there is an excellent chance of moving deer. That was a method my Dad's bunch used while hunting many years at the headwaters of the Oswegatchie River in Herkimer County. Up at the Knobel camp in all that wild country I don't know how you'd ever put on a "drive" so everyone pretty much does his own thing. We all enjoy still-hunting. I suppose there's always a chance that a hunter could move deer which would benefit someone else in the party but mostly that happens by accident rather than by design up there.

Since you showed me that picture of those three beautiful bucks and the three hunters with their rifles (I didn't know at that time you had made the rifles) at Holiday in Homer, I haven't been able to get this out of my mind. I think that was an incredible experience. The only thing that even comes close in my mind was the very last time I was up the Oswegatchie River hunting out of the old camp. We could still use outboard motors at that time. We had completed our hunting vacation and were on our way out and just below High Falls we passed a pair of hunters paddling their canoe. They were also on their way out from their trip. They had camped just below the falls. The first morning they went out from their little camp and worked their way along the side of a little stream. They split up and one went one side and the other hunted the other side and way back in, they killed this beautiful buck very late in the day. They didn't want to lose their deer and I didn't blame them – so they camped right beside their deer that night and they had a little lunch left over and they built a nice fire and they took some liver and broiled that on a stick. They didn't happen to have any onions with it – but so what. They sure didn't go hungry.

The next morning when daylight came, they dragged their deer back to the river and they figured they had their fun and they both were on a real tight schedule with their work anyway, so they broke camp and here they were – paddling out. We got to see their deer and enjoy their story and share a little bit in their reverie by congratulating them. The buck had a very pretty head and a beautiful rack – at least a big eight-point – it was lovely. For a pair of guys to come into a strange area, pick a spot – they used a map to locate a little stream – to camp there for a couple of days and to have success like that – was incredible. Hunting from your camp, however, is pretty much based upon experience. It's based on a basic knowledge of the terrain and you have hunted there previously.

John: Yes – to some extent. We spread out and covered quite a bit of territory – more than usual that fall. Over the whole trip that year we only saw two other deer – other than the ones we killed – I didn't kill anything that fall but I was greatly pleased with the outcome. I had the satisfaction of having made the custom rifles. This fall I made a .270 for a man that went hunting out in Oregon. I haven't had a chance to get the whole story yet but I did hear that he got a nice deer out there with that rifle, so the success goes on. I assume he got a mule deer but I'll hear from him shortly.

Rich: When you make a gun, do you rebuild or start from scratch or what do you do?

John: Some of the rifles I have made – you begin with an old Military from the DCM. You get just the barrel and you have to have the bolt forged to bend it to work with the scope and get a scope safety. Then I would polish – and back in those days, in 1958 I'd have my own ability to do blueing – had my own tanks and stuff. Well, when I worked for thirty years as a carpenter, I didn't have time for much in the gun business. So lately when I have gotten back into it, I have a fellow down in the Binghamton area that will take an action and put on a new barrel, forge the bolt and do all that sort of work but not polish up nor blue. So I have been polishing them and I put on a cold blue but I'm not satisfied with it. A good blue job runs $75.00 to $100.00.

Rich: To do it correctly.

John: Yes. So I'm able to build what I call a custom rifle. One of those stocks is a walnut. The two I made back in 1958 – one is cherry and the other curly maple and I've got some walnut drying now – I used up the last of the curly maple – my Dad chopped that with an axe back in 1955 – so I guess that would be dry by now. I put the last one from that on a .22. I've got two or three blanks left of cherry that I've had since around 1955, so I am sure it is dry enough. That .22 I'll show you later – it's out in my shop.

Rich: It must give you a great deal of satisfaction to be able to build a rifle and have the stock so beautiful and everything and then present it to somebody and have them get all excited about killing a deer with it. I imagine this is considerably more involved than making a fly rod although similar in a way.

John: That .270 rifle – I had a lady come and set up her video camera and take pictures of me doing the checkering. At that point the rifle didn't even have a scope or anything – I just handed it to him and he was going to work up a load for it, you know, by trying this and that and I heard that everything he tried shot in there just right and he didn't have to do a thing with it. He had another rifle so he said, "if you don't get this done, I'll be all right." He was going the 27th of September. He said he had a backup rifle – a .30-06 that he could use. It was open shooting out there in Oregon where he was going and he wanted something that would reach out a little flatter, you know.

Rich: Now, this is curly maple, right? It looks like it.

John: Yes, that is a stock he furnished – that blank. He had it for some years. I told him, "you're going out there and this is probably a once in a lifetime experience and it adds to it if you have a rifle made purpose for it and take it to see if it will perform." Apparently it did, from what I heard, so that made me feel pretty good.

Rich: Did you make all the rifles in this picture?

John: Yes – that one was a shotgun but I made all the rifles. I've made over sixty of them over the years.

Rich: Wow!

John: I've had fellows go moose hunting and elk hunting and I used to charge them so many dollars – and so much meat. Jokingly, of course – but I did get a little meat once in awhile. Back in 1997 was when I got that buck in the picture.

Rich: Yes, I remember you showing it to me during Holiday in Homer that time. How old were you then?

John: Sixty-nine.

Rich: Tell me about how that happened, if you would.

John: I think I mentioned that the trail behind the cabin goes right down toward Forked Lake. There's a good place to watch just up from the water a bit – a little opening and you can see not over fifty yards in any direction. We got ready to go that morning and Dick Smith, the owner of the camp, said "where do you want to go?" I said, "I'll go down to the lake." So they went off in the woods and swung around after awhile and hunted toward me. They hadn't gotten to where they would have moved the deer. My method is standing a watch – not sitting. When you sit, there's a spot right behind you, unless you put forth twice the effort, you're not covering. When you're on a trail, if you pause for just a few seconds, they will go by you so you can't see them. So, my method is to stand by a tree and get all obstructions out of the way – then I swing an arc. I start at a point and I rotate right around – right back to the starting point and then I go right back around again.

Rich: Are you turning your head or moving your whole body?

John: Well, a little bit. But I have gotten the stuff out of the way so I can move a little and not make a sound. I lean the gun right up against the tree. I lean it up where I can grab it quick. I had a problem one time with a scope that would fog – if I laid it across my lap. So now, I lean it against the tree. If you have your hands in your pocket you keep them warm – instead of having gloves on. You can grab that gun and shoot quick. I'd been there maybe a half an hour. I was looking down the trail in one direction, and then I made my swing around and when I came back around again, I could see a deer standing broadside near the trail. I could see that it was a large deer but I couldn't see the head – it was behind some thick brush near the trail. The deer moved a little then so I could see the head and I saw a nice rack so whipped up my rifle and fired. I had the feeling as he started to turn, just one jump and I wouldn't be able to even see him any more. He started off on a run. In our old age and many years of experience, we'd like to think we don't get excited any more.

Rich: Ha, ha – says who?

John: I went up that trail there – and there was something pounding – I think I was putting my pacemaker to the test. I went up thru there looking for him, looking for him – I thought I should be able to see him if he's still going. I went over thru the woods a ways where I last saw him, and there he was.

Rich: Wonderful!

John: Thank the Lord.

Rich: Amen, you bet!

John: It had been quite a few years since I had shot a deer. I gave up hunting deer back in 1986.

Rich: Why?

John: No one to hunt with – and I would go right up in back of my house about a mile – there is a nice ridge up there. After five years of standing right there and shooting them – with a shotgun – I'm a rifleman. I have an accurate shotgun and still there are times it doesn't work to suit me and I wasn't able to kill them about right – right then, you know, and it always bothered me, and I thought "hey, what for? Why continue? I won't do this again." I took my scope off my shotgun and I won't have it back on.

Rich: I don't blame you – I understand.

John: As you get older, you have more appreciation for life, no matter what it is, who's or what animal – and so, I don't enjoy the shooting and killing like I used to. And yet, we have deer right around this house – does that ought to be shot. The cars get a lot of them. I have a neighbor who likes to hunt – he'll take care of quite a few of them but – ok, so be it. What would be the results if we put a ban on hunting. It's hardly safe to drive a car along these roads now – what would happen then?

Rich: What would you guess that deer dressed?

John: I thought at the time, about 175. These deer here were big and we thought they were heavy – especially after we had dragged that one thru the brush – one of them, after dark. Up to Long Lake at the Adirondack Hotel, there's a scales right there and they'll take them and weigh them and one dressed 168 and the others just a little over 160.

Rich: Well, those are nice bucks – nice deer.

John: Actually all three of them weighed all about the same. We learned to cut the deer right in half and put it on a pack. The bigger the deer the more you have to cut toward the front to get some ribs too – to make the loads about even in weight. They pack nicely by doing it that way. Put a red jacket or shirt over them. You don't dare take a chance. Even with a bear – put something red over them when dragging them out.

Rich: You'd have somebody spot a bear and they'd think he was trying to climb a tree or something and, oh boy.

John: I think it is an interesting story of the first year I went with my Dad and his bunch back into Smith Clearing. There were two other camps set up when we got back there. I was age eighteen and had just graduated from high school. I was pretty excited – I think both feet were off the trail at once some of the time. One of the men of one of the other camps – that fellow went in there for the first time the same year my Dad did – 1917. This was in 1946. There were also a man and his wife – they loved camping – he wasn't much of a hunter – in fact, he was well known for getting lost if left to his own devices. If he were hunting with a group he would get along all right. We packed in there and set up our camp. Then we went down to visit the two old fellows – they painted a vast picture about the amount of game. They had been there several days and hadn't been encouraged at all. Cousin John was an optimist and going back to our camp, he says, "we'll show them tomorrow."

Well, the first day it rained and we had to make some tables and stuff and kind of set up our camp. Right behind our camp was this steep little mountain. There also was a little brook that went right down by our camp. The two old fellows were in the habit of going down the little creek – it was called Billy Creek – to a couple of watches they had down there. It looked to them like a good place to be if the deer were moving. They liked to be there around 9 o'clock. We talked it up that night – they would go down on their watch and that would give us time to drive what we called Little Smith Mountain. So, John and I went right up Billy Creek and took a watch on Little Smith and Big Smith and Dad would go up the trail and come right over the mountain, coming right towards us. There's not much area on the top and the bucks like to go up there and lay down. I was just a kid – fresh out of high school – and I was following Cousin John and had my .30-30 lever action Marlin and he had his Craig.

We were walking right along and I was looking up the side of the mountain and he shot – I practically ran right into the back end of him. I looked right over his shoulder and saw this nice eight-point buck jump up out of his bed and just stood right there – looking at us. I was standing behind him so I decided I would just wait and see what he would do – see how it was done, you know. Well, that buck took off in great big jumps – not running – but jumping these great big jumps and went right across Billy Creek. John finally shot at him – he couldn't think for a few seconds where the safe was on that Craig and he shot twice and he was still going. By then, he was beginning to run in a circle and went behind some cradle knolls and so I thought, "if all he's going to do is make noise, I can help him with that." I pulled up on an opening ahead of him. I figured he might come thru that opening and just as I pulled up, he went thru it – and I whipped my rifle up the rest of the way and fired. I reloaded and pulled up on the next opening. He didn't come thru! Cousin John came along then and says, "you stand right here and keep your eyes open – I'll trail him." He went only a little ways, and said, "come over here – he's right here." I broke his back – he was almost thru the opening before I was on to him. He shot him in the head to finish him off and then he said, "your Dad is coming right up over the top with another deer – we better get up there." We weren't that far from camp at that point – the married couple hadn't even been encouraged enough to go hunting. It surprised him right out of bed with all the shooting. John left me beside the creek and he went on up to his favorite watch on a ridge that went right down over to the other mountain. I thought, "well, that was pretty good." It hadn't yet sunk in the fact that it was my buck – we had been shooting together on it and in all the excitement, I really hadn't sorted it out yet. Pretty soon, we heard Dad shooting twice, and I thought, "well, this is pretty good for squirrel hunting." Then I heard John shoot twice. I knew I should stay on my watch until somebody came for me. It was very steep up there and Dad came out into an opening and hollered for me to come on up. I went up there and here was another nice big eight-pointer. When John got up there, Dad said, "what's going on?" "Well," he said, "we got a buck down by the creek." Dad said, "I got another one – he's right there." If I'd made my shot originally, we'd all would have had one. When I got up there and heard the story, I picked up his head and looked, and there was a bullet crease right in back of his ear. So if Dad had made his shot just a little lower, he wouldn't have made it over to John. We dressed that one out and then took him down the trail toward camp and hung him up and then took the trail back to meet the boys. We still had another buck to go up and get.

One of the guys from the other camps came along and said, "what's going on – you boys have got blood all over your hands." I think he figured we had shot a doe for camp meat. "Yep," John says, "two down and one to go." We went up and got it and dragged it right down by their camp and hung it up.

When we got ready to go out again, Herb, the married guy, was ready. He was dressed and had his rifle and he went with us. They put on some drives – the day turned cold and it was windy. I was on watch and it seemed like forever and a day – and finally the guys came and got me. We'd hunted

Big Smith and now we were going up on Bear Mountain. They left me on watch by a draw that went right up to the top of that mountain. I could see Herb over across and there was a green ridge that went right up and they were going to hunt that too. Dad went up to the top. Then I saw Herb coming along and he said, "come on up to the top." They had already had their lunch and I hadn't had mine so I got into a little cave to get out of the wind and I was enjoying the restful spot – eating my sandwich. Pretty quick, up at the top, PUNK – PUNK – I thought, "what in the world?" – sounded like somebody shooting right into the ground. I looked over at Herb – he had started right up there – so I went right up. Up above me was a batch of ledges with evergreens on them – and then another batch of ledges with evergreens. I got up there and the other fellows were all there – I had quite a little climb. I could see them all lined up on a ledge – looking at something – but with the evergreens, I couldn't see what they were looking at.

I came right around the edge of those evergreens and came right up to within about four feet of a big bear sitting right on his haunches. I stepped right over around out of the way and we talked about how to finish him off. Dad said, "I tried to finish him off." He had only a .32 Remington and the cartridges weren't very heavy and while we were talking, the bear dragged himself down to the next ledge. Dad shot again, and when he did, that bear took his paw and rubbed it, like you and I would, just back of his ear. Cousin John said, "that's enough of that" – and shot him in the head with his Craig – flattened him out. So we all stood there looking at him and talking about the circumstances and Herb says, "boy, what a beautiful trophy. What will he look like hanging out on the porch at the Hotel in Griffin?" Dad says, "yeah, but I don't know what you fellows will look like when you get him there." This was another two miles from camp and it was very steep. Dad says, "we'll skin him right here." Herb says, "oh – we'll see about getting him out of here." He went and cut a couple of short sticks so you could put a rope between two men – so four men could drag. Elder Newman and Dad took the rifles and the four of us fellows started dragging him. Well, when we got down to a level where it wasn't so steep, Herb looked around some and says, "there's a nice tree over there where we could hang him up to skin him." Fortunately, we did – we would have spoiled the hide if we had continued to drag him – but I don't think we could have done it. We figured the bear weighed 450 to 500. One of the men got right around his back legs to see if he could pick him up – and he couldn't do it. So, we skinned him right there.

Rich: The head and hide must have weighed 150 pounds.

John: I carried that out – made a pack of it. The next day, we went hunting with those fellows and we tried to drive them some deer. They hadn't had any luck. We went with the packing equipment and an axe and cut that bear down and of course, they were entitled to half of him. So we took our meat and left some of the fat - and he sure was fat – just like a pig, you know. We took it into camp and we gave the two old fellows a couple of steaks that night. They said, "bear – they weren't going to mess with a bear." The next morning when we were getting ready to go hunting, I heard voices down at the other tents. I looked down there and Herb Spencer was heading out and the two of them had their packs on their back and I said, "well, what's going on, boys?" They said, "we're going up after the rest of that bear – boy, was that good!" They went up and brought down every bit of it. Herb's wife tried it out for baking and cooking fat, you know.

Rich: Good stuff.

John: Mother made doughnuts and whatnot with it. It was good. Since then, we've always eaten the bear that we got. That was a good one. The hide we took to the taxidermist in Whitney Point and sold it for $15.00 He made that hide up into a rug and sold it to somebody in New Mexico. Dad said he didn't have any wall or floor big enough to display it and somebody ought to have it that could enjoy it. When I got my first bear in 1951 I had the head mounted – not with the mouth open and them teeth – that's not normal. When I got thru selling hides and so forth to the taxidermist, I had $11.00 into the head – was all it cost me.

Rich: I had mine mounted with the mouth closed, too. The taxidermist made a couple of little ivory teeth for the outside and they hang down very natural looking – very pretty – I'm pleased with it. I think it is just beautiful.

John: When John got one in 1958 he had the head mounted too. It was a large male bear. That was a pretty interesting day for an eighteen-year-old boy with his first experience hunting in the Adirondacks – I got all excited and I have been going ever since. That was in an area where supposedly there wasn't much game – that was the other party's opinion. We hunted another week with those fellows and we never saw another thing. I guess we cleaned it out.

Rich: Conditions can change overnight.

John: I figure there's a lot of acreage there. It would take four or six hunters to get things to move in an area that size – those are big woods.

Rich: Here's a place where putting on a drive makes sense.

John: In 1962 John and I packed in to that same area and there was four inches of snow on the ground. We would leave the stove and cooking equipment right in there – we had a place where we could kind of store it. The stove would last four or five years and then you'd have to take in another one. By the time we had gotten back to camp we had seen four or five deer tracks. Right where we set up the tent was a buck track. We knew for sure because he went right down toward the Billy Creek where we got our drinking water and he rubbed a tree – so we knew it was a buck. It wasn't long and we had camp all set up nice and comfortable and a good fire going in our wood stove. The next morning we were going to go hunting and see if we could get one of those deer.

Rich: Talk about memories!

John: Well, John used to say, "if you don't do something when you are younger, you haven't got any memories for when you get older."

Rich: Say, that's profound.

John: He was a country philosopher. He said one time, "you know, you might better be ready and not go than go and not be ready."

Rich: Amen to that – that's for sure.

John: He carried that on to spiritual realms. One year we had done a lot of packing to get camp ready, you know. He sat right down to rest his pack and himself a bit after he had lugged and lugged and he sat right there and says, "you know, it sure is great to be a sportsman. All this work – you couldn't hire us to do all this. No way – but in the interest of fun and sport, we do it."

We were up there, I was starting to tell you, in 1962 in all that snow. So, we started out hunting and thought we'd get a deer because we had seen so many tracks on the way in and around camp when we got there. We drove Little Smith's and John went up on his favorite watch and I went around, like Dad did in the old days. I didn't see a fresh track or a thing. I got over to John – he was quite excited. He said, "if you hadn't of come along when you did, I might have been decimated by a bear." I said, "what do you mean?" He said, "come on over here." We went out to that sharp point and he said, "look right down there – at that pawing patch right over there – and another one, right over there. There are several of them all in a row and they appear to go right down towards camp." It was where a bear had been feeding on beechnuts. I said, "well, we don't have any good dry wood in camp and we don't have anything with us to eat for lunch – we'd better go right down to camp, cut a little wood, eat something and then we'll come right back and I'll drive the green ridge to you." That was where he got the bear years ago. He said, "that sounds like a good idea." We went back to camp and it didn't take us too long to get ready to go hunting. If we had stayed right where we were talking, we would have gotten a bear. When I came back up thru, one had been right down thru that same area. I hunted very carefully over between the two mountains. The snow was soft so I could go quietly. As I approached a small hogsback I noticed some downed trees on the side of it and when I stopped, I could hear a bear pawing. I took it ever so careful and soon found where a bear had been pawing. The whole area was disturbed so that I couldn't tell where he had gone or anything. I went along a little further and right on the edge of that hogsback, there was a bear.

I sat right down in the snow. I tried to take careful aim but he was working behind some beech trees and I couldn't get a good shot. I thought "well, just wait." I'm sitting there – waiting – and all of a sudden, he just threw up his head and started running – right towards me – and appeared he would go by me on my right side. That's a difficult place to get a shot. There I was – sitting – which was no good. He came running right along, pretty as could be – and on the hogsback right next to me there was a down spruce or something all grown up with little evergreens – he went behind that. I swung up on my knees to be ready and he came out right there. I just saw his head at about thirty yards. I thought, "you know, I have heard of fellows shooting them in the head and they didn't get them. Their brain is only about the size of a fifty-cent piece. I'll wait – maybe he'll step out and I'll have a body shot right there." I just waited – right at the ready – that head just pulled back – and I haven't seen him since. He didn't smell me – the wind was from him to me – so I jumped right up and thought maybe he would run up the mountain. However, he went around the corner so I didn't get to see him. Well, I at least got him started and he appeared to be heading right towards where John was supposed to be. Maybe I can push him thru – what a time I had. The snow was slippery – my boots weren't very good. I followed his track and saw where he got to within about a hundred yards of where John was on his watch and the bear just turned left and went on his way.

The afternoon was getting well spent and so was I. If John got the last bear, it was my turn – then I'd get one and it would be his turn. I said, "I had my chance and blew it – so it's your turn now." He said, "that don't count." There's a side of the mountain there that we call Shag Hill. Camp is right down to the base of it. He said, "you go down and pick a spot and I'll go out here to Fall Brook and come over along the side." Ok. I went down there and this time I was sweaty and hot and tired and everything so I just sort of melted down at the end of the hogsback and thought, "I'd better check on the area." So I swung back on the other side of that mountain and there was a bear right there. I thought I'd wait for a better shot and something said, "you did that on the last one." So, I took what I thought was a pretty good shot and he disappeared – I didn't know where he went.

I reached in my pocket to get some more ammunition. Those rifles only have three shots – not a regular magazine. I had the bolt back to slide in another round and all of a sudden he turned and started running right up the mountain. I closed the bolt and took another shot at him and the bear turned and ran right towards where I expected John to be. He was loping right down thru there and I couldn't get another shot at him – no use shooting at a running bear. I just waited. When John came down, he got up there about where I last saw the bear. He said "hey, come up here – bear wounded bad." It was getting toward dark. On the way up to where John was, I saw where the bear had laid down and then got up. We had no choice but to take up the trail in the morning and when we did, we found the bear. I suggested, "you go up on a watch and I'll cross the creek and hunt up to you." There were tracks of bear going up or down all over that side hill. Normally the bear are nocturnal – they just go nights. That was the second time we had seen where they had been actively feeding during the day.

Rich: When there's a good crop of beechnuts, they just rip up thru the snow and utilize them – they love them.

John: John shot another bear in 1958. I was hunting toward his watch. I told him where to go – I was hunting deer and would work my way up the mountain to him. In the fifties we had a blow that knocked down quite a lot of trees.

Rich: I know all about it.

John: There was a strip of timber I had to go thru that was down. I was paying attention to how I might be able to work my way thru the tangle – then noticed a large beech tree that was down and thought if I could make my way thru that, I'd be in the clear. I was down on my hands and knees and right ahead of me – about thirty yards ahead of me – was a bear. He said, "woof" and took off – not leaping, just running. I worked my way clear of the brush as soon as I could and was able to get a shot at him just as he reached the top of a little knoll. I got up there and could see that I had hit the bear – he was leaping then. Just then, John shot. A bear will be pretty apt to run straight. John got that bear. He had been in Arizona for two or three years and hadn't been out to hunt. Circumstances came so I could go so he came out on purpose so we could get back at it again. That was on Thursday – on Saturday, I shot a nice buck. The two of us did pretty well that year too. A bear story is always unique.

Rich: You bet it is. That is fun. It is good to have the experience and always fun to tell about too. Thank you John for sharing these wonderful stories. It must be really special for you to have all these wonderful adventures to recall and share.

CHAPTER 8   SAM MROSZ

January 3rd, 2002 Jani and I pulled into the driveway of a friend whom I had not seen since about April 1963. We camped at the deer camp at the head of the Oswegatchie River during the kids' Easter vacation. The ice had just gone out of the River and we were able to make the campsite in very good time as the water, of course, was very high. The spring rains and ice and snow melt swelled every small stream and tributary of that huge watershed. We were using my Dad's twelve foot aluminum boat with our six horse Evinrude kicker and that provided plenty of power to propel our heavily loaded boat not only around all the bends in the river but up thru all the rapids below High Falls. The water was so high we even motored up over several large beaver dams. We never had to get out of the boat once in that whole trip. In fact, we couldn't go underneath the footbridge at Cage Spring Hole but actually motored around the left end of the bridge right up thru the tag alders.

The first time I met Sam was just as we arrived at High Falls and began to unload our boat for the carry. Sam and his trapping companion had arrived at the falls just ahead of us and practically had their load all carried around. I was impressed by the size of the man. I think they both were a little surprised to see a family on what appeared to be a camping trip that time of the year. It was obvious to them however by the size of the load in our boat that we were intending to stay several days.

We didn't catch much in our traps that trip – but we had an enjoyable camping trip. It was relatively easy to establish our camp at Dad's deer hunting location. There was still about three inches of solid ice on the floor and even after a week of having a heavy fire in the wood stove, all the ice hadn't melted even by the time we broke camp and headed out. My wife and I both got laryngitis out of that deal but the two girls – Sally, age nine and Peggy, age five thought it was a lark. Before we even got the tent set up they both went to work and made a snow fort – at least they were going to have some place to stay back there in the big North Woods.

The next time we saw Sam was the very next day of our vacation. He stopped by mid-morning just to check us out and be sure we were all right, I suppose. I appreciated that. We put out a few beaver traps along the river not far from camp and checked our traps every day – mostly for something to do. The kids really seemed to enjoy the boat ride and the scenery was lovely along the bank of the river. There were some alders close to the riverbanks but for the most part, the woods came right down to the river so it was not unusual for us to see deer and other wildlife while we were traveling in the boat.

The day we broke camp and started to head down river we were pulled over into a small stream that emptied into the river and had pulled our final set when Sam came along in his boat. He shut off his outboard and politely asked if I thought I had plenty of gas to get us down river. Apparently he had stopped by the campsite just to check us out and seen by the sign that we had just packed up and left the area. Actually, I hadn't given the level of fuel in our six-gallon tank any thought – we were having too much fun just running up and down the river. I lifted the gas tank and there wasn't hardly any gas left in it at all. Sam said, "get that cap off your tank" – and then he gave us a good quantity of gas that proved to be more than enough to get us out. If it weren't for his consideration and help, I am certain we would have had a very long and uncomfortable row on the way out.

I mentioned in the last chapter how John Davis and I became acquainted at our book table at the Holiday In Homer event. When he stopped by July of 2001 he mentioned, "you and I have got a couple of things in common – sorry I haven't mentioned this before." I could hardly wait to hear what those things might be. "First of all," – he said, "I used to be involved in the Brigade program for boys in our church – you mentioned your involvement in that program in your book, "Deer Camp" – the other thing is you and I have a common friend." Well, I couldn't imagine who that might possibly be. I said "who is that?" He said, "Sam Mrosz." Well, I hadn't heard that name in almost forty years. I had thought of Sam many times since that chance meeting up the river that spring. It was much more than the fact he had been friendly and helpful and given us some much needed gas. He spotted my trap that I had pulled as I tossed it into our boat. He said "what kind of trap do you use?" I said, "Blake & Lamb, number 44 double under-spring." He asked "how do you set it?" I told him "well, I find a firm spot of ground and step on the springs." Then he said, "I usually set mine with my hands." Then he asked "may I see that trap?" I handed it to him and fully expected he would crack it across his knee but was totally amazed – he merely extended both arms and with his bare hands compressed both springs and using his fingers, flipped the jaws open and set the pan. If you don't think that is some feat of strength, try it. I never in all my life saw a pair of hands so large. Then John said that Sam Mrosz and his wife were practically his neighbors – they lived about eight miles from his place in McDonough. Jani and I decided at once we would contact Sam and if possible, go pay him a visit and catch up on each other's outdoor activities and if possible, maybe include some of Sam's outdoor adventures in this book.

Rich: Sam was standing at his front entrance shortly after we pulled into his driveway that January day. When Jani and I walked up the path to his front door, he greeted us warmly and said "come on in and meet my wife, Ruth." John Davis had told us, "he's as sharp as a tack – you've got to go see him – he'll give you some stories for your book." We were invited to make ourselves comfortable in their living room. I got out the tape recorder and had already explained over the phone what it was we were looking for. Sam's trapping was more than just a pastime – it had been a major part of his income over the years. We could see from his living room over across the road – a lovely wooded area where a fairly large stream ran by and he still had a small mink line out. In fact, the day before our visit, he had shipped off a package of furs to the buyer.

Sam: On the twenty-eighth day of March 1959, my friend Charlie Frair and I pulled into the little Village of Wanakena. We had heard about the great Oswegatchie River region and decided to look the area over and perhaps do some beaver and otter trapping there. As we entered the Village, we noticed a man by his house with a German Shepherd dog attached to a run. I didn't realize it at the time, but the man was Herbert Keith. We pulled over to the side of the road and Mr. Keith came over to our vehicle and we talked for a while. Keith was very helpful and told us how to get into the Inlet area where Riley and Rose Smith had their home with their son, Ernie. He said that they also rented boats and outboard motors for use on the river and that Mrs. Smith had a small cabin that they would rent and also that she was a marvelous cook. She seemed to receive special enjoyment from preparing meals for anyone who came to the Inlet landing after having had a trip up the river.

Rich: I own a copy of Keith's "Man Of The Woods." It's a favorite of mine – he tells about the old time guides on the Oswegatchie that operated back in the days when it was common to catch native brook trout out of the river that would run up to five pounds.

Sam: Two years ago I had some health problems and spent some time in a local hospital. I got acquainted with a nurse that had been tending to Herbert Keith about two hours before he died. She had been born and raised in the Wanakena area. In about twenty-six years of trapping the

Adirondacks, I believe the Oswegatchie region was some of the very best trapping we ever had. The roughest country we had trapped was Metcalf Lake. We flew in there – Clyde Elliott was the pilot from Speculator. He told us right from the start, "we can fly in there only when the wind is just right – otherwise, it will blow us into the trees because the lake is so narrow." The Indian River in that area dumps into the West Canada and the whole region is full of small ponds, lakes and streams. The beaver had spread out and dammed up every stream or river they could find provided the food was there. An old friend of mine built a camp just where the Indian dumps into the West Canada. He was age 96 this last fall.

That Oswegatchie was enjoyable all the way. The Smiths were there at Inlet and anybody that went up there got their orders. "There may be other people in the area – you don't touch anything that doesn't belong to you." One year we took up 45 gallons of gasoline. It took a lot of fuel to run the outboard up and down the river while we checked our trapline. We just set the gas cans by the river – nobody bothered anything. A couple of fellows came in one time from Potsdam – we didn't know their names – they didn't stay long as we had the area pretty well covered with our traps. Then, there was Skip Lansing that you have mentioned. He had a Grandson. We came down the river one day – we didn't know anybody was anywhere around. We heard this chop, chop, chop. We knew it was somebody chopping on a tree – right opposite of where the Robinson River came in. Up there on a little ridge, he was chopping one of those big pine trees. We walked over there and got him to stop that activity. The Grandson's young friend was chopping on a monster white pine – but we put an end to it. You know, kids got a lot of energy – they just got to do something like that. One time we came down river and met Skip Lansing – he was on the way out after having trapped for several weeks that spring. He had an awful heavy load – it looked dangerous to us so we helped him out – we took some of his traps and wolf lure. He used to trap wolves in there. He collected a bounty on some of the wolves he had trapped.

Rich: I've heard wolves howling and seen their pictures on TV. The last night in my Sand Creek hunting camp we definitely heard a gray wolf – it was no coyote that we heard howling.

Sam: One day out on the trapline I saw two large animals running together – they were way to big to be coyotes – they definitely were gray wolves. I was born on December 23rd, 1910 in the State of Washington. My interest in the out-of-doors began then – I was age 6 when we made our first move. The bears came right in our backyard. Our house was near the coast. One day the wind blew so hard it wouldn't let the tide go out. The water backed up and came in under our house – it had been built up on stilts. There were three sawmills in the area – they were built up on blocks. One of the guys that worked there had a whole bunch of bear. One of them got loose and went in under the mill. I was one of the kids that went in there and flushed him out. It seemed the bears were as thick as rabbits. The black bear were a real problem for the lumber companies. They would peel the bark off the trees in the springtime when they first came out of their hibernation. A single bear could ruin as many as 164 trees in a day – at that rate they were a real problem.

Rich: Ralph Flowers has written a wonderful book entitled "The Education of a Bear Hunter." It tells of his adventures as a professional bear hunter and trapper in the State of Washington. He used snares in the early spring to catch the bear. They would enter a cubby that had been baited with a beef head and when they tripped the snare, the action would begin. The snare would be attached to a drag that was a fourteen inch diameter log about sixteen feet long. Usually this affair would leave a trail where it had been dragged by the bear. It was Ralph's job to track the bear down and finish him off

71

with his rifle. The book is 277 pages of real excitement and at $14.95 makes a nice gift for yourself or someone else.

Sam: Our first move landed us in Bartlesville, Oklahoma. Dad worked in a smelter there and about the only thing I recall about that place is that the sidewalks were cinders. Going barefooted, you couldn't stand still out there in the middle of the day. You had to keep going. One day we saw a train wreck. There was an engine switching in the yard there and a freight going thru and somebody didn't throw the switch. The freight went right into the yard and the engines hit nose to nose. Us kids were over there real quick. They had a lot of grain in one of the cars and that buckled and the grain was coming out and we climbed into the boxcar and then jumped in the grain. We thought that was a lot of fun. I remember they picked a fireman up. There's a steel grate between the tender and the locomotive – it got buckled up someway and caught him and when they picked him up, both legs were cut off about by the ankles. He died of his injuries eventually. From there we landed in Donora, Pennsylvania. Then in 1919 we moved to McKeesport but then later in 1919 we moved to Chenango County in New York State where we ran a dairy farm. We milked about 40 head – we were a little bigger than the average back in those days. We didn't have any electricity. In the wintertime one of my chores was to light the lanterns, and each one of us had their own cows to milk. The folks attended a wedding and were gone a couple of days. I had to milk all 40 cows by myself – it took a long while.

Charlie and I were trapping one year out of Otter Lake – that's on Route 28 before you get to Old Forge. There was a whole week when there was fog. It didn't freeze or anything. Charlie had some traps set way back in and he was waiting for a day when it froze. Soon he went in beautiful in the morning on the crust but it thawed up during the day. I didn't think I'd see him that night but he came out. It was an awful struggle – he was traveling on showshoes. When it's soft you load up with each step. He carried a stout stick and would have to bang the snow off. Sometimes when we ran our traplines up the Oswegatchie area, we'd have to start out on the line to check our traps about 2 a.m. in order to have heavy crust that would hold us on top. So long as we returned to camp before the sun had a chance to thaw the snowpack we made out fine. It was normal to catch seven or eight or more beaver on a trip. With all that weight, you had to rough skin the animals at the area of the set. It got so that black bears were following us around cleaning up the carcasses after us. These bears were fresh out of their den and no doubt acquired a taste for meat!

One time Charlie and I got up to the falls and there was a live beaver in a trap that apparently the Ranger had caught. We shot the beaver and of course left it in the trap. He could drive to the falls at that time. Recently, however, the old railroad trestle has rotted where it crosses the outlet of Bassout Pond that drains into the river. Vehicles can no longer travel to High Falls. Over the years the Rangers could drive in on the railroad grade to the falls and so could an ambulance in the event a rescue operation in the area was required.

The first time we went up into that area there were a whole bunch of logs down near the river. This was a result of the big blow of 1954. The State allowed at least two logging companies to attempt to salvage some of the huge white pine logs. We found a post marking St.Lawrence County right in the river. There was a beaver house nearby and one of the pike poles the loggers used with a big long handle, the beavers had put that right into their house. I brought it home and my wife Ruth uses it out back when she burns papers. It came out of the beaver house right on the border there. Another time on top of the County Line Ridge I found a post with a bronze plaque on it. St.Lawrence County Line

72

goes straight thru and Herkimer and Hamilton comes right up against it. The farthest I got up the Robinson River was almost up to sliding falls.

One time we were camped by the Wolf where the Five Ponds outlet hits the river. Years ago the loggers were in the area and cut a bunch of pine trees and left the stumps in the ground. I cut some of them out to use for firewood. Charlie wasn't acquainted with burning white pine and filled the woodstove right full. I woke up sometime during the night and the thermometer registered over 200 degrees in that tent. I had a beaver stick I had been carrying and I broke that to use it for a pair of tongs and opened the flap – the creek was right there and I started pitching those chunks out. I thought Charlie was dead. I went over and shook him up and he was all right – that was a close call.

When we first started going up the river the beaver season opened up the 28th day of March and the season closed the last day of April so we were in the woods a little over a month. One time we were on our way out and when we got to Griffin Rapids, a bunch was camped there from Eastman Kodak. They wondered if we wouldn't run up and down the river a few times by their campsite so they could take our picture. We were a rugged looking sight – with a month worth of whiskers, stacks of beaver pelts and all the rest. We must have looked like something out of the wild West. We really had a ball up there. One day we brought in nineteen beaver – that was the most we ever caught in one day. We always quick skinned – we had to do that as we couldn't carry 500 to 600 pounds of beaver. One thing we did discover was it didn't work to put the hides in a bag and then put it into the snow. They started to spoil. What did work was we would find a cool place underneath the evergreens and lay the first hide down on the snow – flesh side down and then throw snow on it and another one on top and keep going like that and they kept beautiful.

In 1935 we were hunting deer around the Blue Mountain area. We came out to the Village and talked to a storekeeper. We had been hunting back in the Salmon Pond area. We came out on a Sunday and asked if anyone had killed a bear in the area. He said 26 years ago someone killed a bear. The very next day we went back into the area and I was hunting up on Tongue Mountain. I always preferred to hunt alone. I was coming down the mountain – could come down a ways and then it would level off. On one of those level spots I caught sight of a movement and noticed as nice black bear – pretty soon, I was dressing him out. I had a .35 Remington pump gun and I carried a shell belt with shells in it. He was about 120 yards away standing by a log. He started sniffing almost broadside to me – I held for his shoulder and touched one off and the bear went over in back of a log and he started kicking. I shot nine times. The first shot killed him I found out later when I was dressing him out. He was hit at least seven times. That night in camp I told the boys, "I think I killed a bear up on Tongue Mountain." The boys said, "it couldn't have been you – no one guy could shoot that fast." The next day the boys went up with me. We dragged the bear out. I shot my first buck that afternoon. I've killed three bear in all in the Adirondacks. The last two I got were near the dump. The first one was on Rt. 8, Oxbow Lake area. The bear dressed out 606 pounds. The bear was about a half mile from the road. I knew a logger friend up in Speculator. I went up to get him to drag the bear out. When I got there I found out he was down in Wells doing some cutting or something. While we were gone a bunch of guys were over there looking at the bear. If we'd only stayed there and had ropes enough they would have pulled the bear out. A year or two later I killed one at Limekiln. You jump off Rt. 28 at Sixth Lake. This one weighed 434 pounds. The two weighed over a half ton. I shot two in Alaska and I shot one in Newfoundland.

One day on the Kenai Peninsula in Alaska I sat on this log – there was a mountain range right in front of me. I counted over eighty sheep and nine bears. They were all black bears except one big brown. Shortly I could see this mother black and a little cub and a yearling bear. It was unique to see the mother run the yearling bear off. The very next day I was looking for a brown bear and I had a two year old think I was his mother. He was running down to me. I hollered at him thinking he would run but instead he came running down to where I was on a hill – the mountain was so steep I could hardly stand there. I thought I would scare him so I shot over his head but he kept coming so when he got about thirty yards away I shot him back of the shoulder. He rolled a half-mile on down the mountain. I got down there and dressed him out. His stomach was full of blue berries and there wasn't even a stem on them. All the bears I killed were males – if you shot a lone bear, it's quite apt to be a male.

Over the years I have had a pretty good hunting experience. I killed ten bull moose – I don't want to kill another one. I shot one in Alaska and the rest were in Newfoundland. If you want to hunt moose, go to Newfoundland. However, it isn't cheap anymore. A friend of mine went a couple of years ago and it cost him over $2,000.00   When I started going out there it was $35.00 and you got a bonus bear permit thrown in. You must have a guide lined up before you go now. Back when we went we found somebody to guide us locally after we got there. We met a Game Warden out there who was real friendly and helped us quite a lot. Even back then, the legal requirement was one guide could handle two hunters. Well, there were three of us in the party. I told the boys "you go ahead – I'll stay here and do up the camp chores and then maybe take a stroll outside the tent." I did – and left my gun in camp. I saw a nice cow moose and thought maybe one of the boys would want to shoot that – but we didn't meet up with her again in the woods. Anyway, we all got back to the tent and the game warden was there. He wanted to know if we had seen any ptarmigan – he called them partridge – but they were the ones that changed color with the seasons. I told him I didn't see any but one of the other boys spoke up and said "yeah, we saw two bunches of them." Jack, the Warden, was real polite. He said "could they all fly away?" Rather than asking, "did you shoot any?" It got to be the last day of our trip and one of our gang said, " I'd like a couple of those birds to take home." Well, I didn't know anything about the season on them. We hiked up the mountain – and I saw one of the birds and drew down on it. When I fired with my .270, the bird about disappeared in a cloud of feathers. There was nothing left. We went on a bit and after awhile I saw two more and waited until they got close together and took both their heads off with one shot. Well, it came time to leave. Our guide had put the birds in the pocket of his jacket. When we loaded up the boat at the dock to leave the last thing we did was to toss the jacket into the boat. The birds fell out of the jacket pocket right at Jack's feet. That was on a Saturday – and Jack looked down at them – then looked over at me and said "well, the season opens Monday." We gave him some meat and everything – he was good to us. But, the poor fellow was a chain smoker and it finally got him. Our meat was in a locker plant that was only open certain times. He pulled some strings for us and came up with a key so we could get our meat – he was nice to us.

A friend of mine is a collector of turkey calls – he has over 3500 of them. He was just here the other day to pay me a visit and brought along a copy of the "Turkey Book." When you look in there, you'll see there are sixteen pages of calls, all in color near the center section of his book. There's even a picture or two of a wingbone call. You don't blow on it – you suck on it to make the sound. I make calls myself – my call is the only one that comes with a case. I use a lot of butternut to make the reeds. The bottom and sides are made out of cherry. The top or striker can be anything. The case has got a camouflage finish on it. The story about my calls is on page 162. I'll go get one and show you. On each call I sell I include the year, the last name of the owner, the Town and the serial number. Underneath is the chalk and the sandpaper to keep your reeds in shape. This one is the three-feather model. It's got a spur on it that serves two purposes. It keeps it from squawking while you're walking thru the woods. Also, it gives you something to strike against. This is all original – I have never seen anyone else make any like it. I've got orders for over twenty now. I'll put your order in line and you can pay me the $25.00 when you pick the call up. Before you go, I'd like to have you take a little trip out to my shop to see where I do my work. Also when a turkey gets in real close, you can make a light cluck or sound which won't spook the bird. Here's a couple of ducks I carved. The fellow I made these for is half Apache. His mother is Irish and his father is full-blooded Apache.

I've trapped since 1920. Many years the catch was an important part of our income. There's three guys I have taught some about trapping. I am a firm believer that if you get too many people involved in anything you may just spoil it for everybody. One of them that I taught was a logger. His family were all trappers – but he was so busy with his logging business he never had time or paid attention to learn how to trap. I taught him and showed him the real stuff. Anyway, I still trap a little bit – in fact I sent in a package of raw furs to the buyer in the mail just yesterday. It's been a great life, you know. A lot of people look down at a trapper – they just don't understand. There are people that think a trapper is mentally retarded – for starters. They think he just goes out into the woods to make animals suffer. Nothing could be further from the truth. The worst of these is the ALF – stands for Animal Liberation Front. They did $500.00 worth of damage in a McDonald's Restaurant in Arizona. They're the group who don't want you to wear furs – they don't want you to eat meat and they do the darnedest things – for instance, they go to a mink farm in the dead of winter and turn the mink out. Maybe burn and steal – and get away with it. Now we're half way around the world chasing terrorists – we've got them right here. This terrorist thing – over the years we've seen them be active over in Israel or some place and sat back and said, "oh, that's too bad," don't you know. Now at long last we have reason to consider what they have been going thru and can really understand their plight – now that we have one too.

John Davis and I are friends – we have worked together some on various jobs at church and others. I call him, John the Baptist. Now, my wife belongs to the Episcopal church and I was born a Catholic. I take a dim view of the Catholic church – so if I go to church it's the Baptist church.

Rich: That's where Jani and I go too.

Sam: Every morning before I get away from the table I read a little portion from "the Daily Bread." And I thank the Lord for another day and ask Him to be with me today – and he always has. Maybe you think I'm just a rough old guy but I'm a believer.

Rich: So are we – praise God – I can't imagine going thru life without having a relationship with the Father thru the Son – He makes it available. Jani and I have learned something recently. We've had concern and still do – and probably always will for as long as we live for different folks. Some of them are our own children and grandchildren and friends that we know who just don't seem to have interest in the things of the Lord. We have discovered recently a good way to pray for people that we are concerned about. "Dear Lord, please grant them the gift of faith so that they may have the ability to receive your salvation." We believe there is power in that and we're trusting the Lord to use that for their benefit and blessing. We think that is something positive we can do. We can pray that for our enemies also.

Sam: I tell folks I'm on a direct hook-up and he's been good to me.

Rich: Sam, you're my kind of guy!

Sam: I had rheumatic when I was a kid. I think it damaged the valve of my heart. But I know my limits – is one thing, when I'm alone. Anyway, I was 91 the 23rd of December 2001 and we had our 60th Wedding Anniversary this last week – the 28th. I just ask the Lord to be with me every day – and that takes care of it. I've known John Davis for many years – he's a good friend of mine. I met him on the beaver trapline one day.

The out-of-doors is great – we have had more fun. One fall, we were out west – supposedly hunting elk – and we got after the jackrabbits with our pistols. I even killed squirrels with my .22 Colt Woodsman. Also, I killed five ducks on the wing.

Rich: would you believe, I killed three partridge up in the woods one fall at the Sand Creek camp. They were all roosted up on the limbs of a huge dead white pine stub. The closest bird was about 40 feet up the stub. The first two dropped like a rock – however, the third set his wings and glided to the ground and disappeared. I searched for 20 minutes and couldn't find it. I felt sure the bird was dead. I just stood there after awhile, feeling sad, as I didn't want to lose that bird. Suddenly, I heard flutter, flutter – and looked down. The tail of the bird showed where he had struck just under a decaying log on the ground. I was real happy to be able to go over there and pick up that bird and add him to my take. That evening, we had fried grouse for supper and that was really good.

Sam: One fall we were hunting out west and we had sandwich meat from grouse. They had three kinds of grouse out there in Montana. There was the ruffed grouse, a Franklin grouse, we called them a fool hen, and I was sitting on a log one day and one of them came and lit right on my log and walked right over to where I was sitting – I could have reached out with my hand and touched him. Then they had a sage hen that would fly up into a tree. Those Woodsman pistols were nice when you got used to shooting them.

Rich: My Dad had one and we had fun shooting together – target shooting at tin cans and stuff.

Sam: Mine had hunting sights on it.

Rich: So did mine. Then we graduated to hunting squirrels and frogs.

Sam: There was a time I wouldn't go afield without one. I wore out two holsters with my handgun. Anyway, those were the days.

Rich: I'd really like to get a picture of the two of you – that's it – just sit on the couch together.

Sam: In 1929 I bought a Montgomery Ward pump gun made by Stevens. It had a full choke barrel. Back in those days I wanted extra power and the thirty-inch barrel helped. I wanted something that would reach out there. A friend and I were partridge hunting near a local pond one day and we came out of a piece of woods to where it was brushy. This was back about 1932. There were lots of briars there and a lone pine tree – with branches right down to the ground. When I got over a wire fence and got straightened up, a partridge went out from under that tree. I fired my gun and missed it clean. However, I took the next five straight. They kept going out – ones and twos – there probably

76

were thirty birds under that tree. I bagged five of them. Another time I was down hill from my partner who put the birds out – they came my way and that time I took three straight. That's what partridge hunting used to be. I think the morning I caught my 20th mink – I shot my 50th partridge. It dumped into the creek right close to where I had my mink in my set, over in the Town of German.

Rich: Sam has had so many and varied experiences in the Adirondacks and other places he offered to let me borrow some papers he had typed some stories on over the years. However, his pages weren't numbered and kind of got out of order. I would get in the middle of an exciting story and get to the bottom of the page – where it said "continued." However, look as I might, I never could find the page that the story was continued on. Anyway, I will share bits and pieces of woods lore and portions of various trips Sam and his friends were involved in.

Sam: This story is about how Raquette Lake got its name. During the Revolutionary War, a group of French and Indians were going back to Canada by this large lake in the Adirondacks when the warm weather of spring overtook them making their snowshoes useless. So, they piled all of the shoes in a pile and went on. Years later, some trappers found them. In the French language, snowshoes are called racquettes so the early trappers named this lake Raquette Lake. The lake is a big one having a shoreline of 99 miles. The outlet is known as the Raquette River that flows north to Long Lake and eventually empties into the mighty Saint Lawrence River.

Years ago when our group used to hunt at Blue Mountain, Raquette Lake was one checkpoint along the way. We knew it was only 13 more miles to Blue Mountain. Several miles up the road, there was a straight stretch of road where we could glimpse the mountain. Our hunting area lay behind old Blue in the Salmon Pond section of Hamilton County. Also close by was Tirell Pond. The last time we hunted in that area was in the Tirell Pond section. The previous winter was very severe and it killed off most of the deer. There were about 28 hunters in the area that season. Deer were very scarce. As a matter of fact, the eight-pointer I bagged was the only deer killed that fall in the immediate area that had any kind of a rack. I will always believe the only reason I got that one was the fact that Ray Aldrich and Arthur Stiles got lost the day before and spent the night on the mountain.

Now, you might say, what has two hunters got to do about me getting a buck deer – especially when they were lost the day before. Here's what happened. Ray and Arthur began to chase a black bear until late in the afternoon. It was getting dark and they didn't know which way to go to get back to camp. So, they decided to build a fire to get as comfortable as possible and then see if they could figure out the way back to camp in the morning. When we decided the boys were lost and wouldn't be in camp, we touched off a few rounds to see if we could get any response. At that time other hunters in the area started shooting. Later the boys said that the echoes were rolling from hill to hill and they had no idea where they were coming from so they decided to stay put. I vividly recall the echoes that night. They rolled from hill to hill until they finally died out. The next morning the remaining three of us in our party started out looking for them. A hunter we met in the woods said he saw the boys over back of Dun Brook Mountain. So, we headed over that way to see if we could cut any tracks. We didn't find anything. While on the trail, a deer flushed out running up the ridge. Thinking it had antlers we touched off a shot bringing the deer down. We dressed out the animal, hung him up, and continued our hunt. Not finding any trace of the lost boys, we decided to go back to camp hoping the boys would be in.

They were in their bunks – none the worse for the hairy experience. After hearing the whole story the two of us went out hunting again. Later in the afternoon, Carol and I went back in to bring out the deer we killed that morning when we ran into the eight-pointer mentioned earlier. Members on that hunt were Mike Talutus, Ray Aldrich, Carol Yarnes, Arthur Stiles and myself. Those were the only deer bagged on that hunt. A few years later I went back to trap beaver but found that someone had trapped earlier in the winter even though the season was not open, so I didn't find much. I never will forget that scouting trip. The snowshoeing was good early in the morning but later when the sun hit the slopes, the shoes would load up with snow so I had a rough time of it. I got tired out about 8 miles back in the woods. However, I did manage to get out to the road and car. We were staying in one of Bert Wells' camps. At that time, the beaver were scarce so the price was high. The pelts brought $1.00 an inch. A 65 inch beaver fetched $65.00 which was a far cry from what they bring today. Since that trip I have been back to trap the Adirondacks many times but never again in the Blue Mountain area.

One spring, we trapped at the head of the Oswegatchie River area. The boys trapped at Nick, Clear, Tamarack, Big Deer and Slender Ponds and also in some water that flowed into the Bog River. It was quite a big area to cover. I stayed closer to the river. After a few days we moved up river where a ridge extended to an area that we called the Mud Flats. At this place there are some of the largest white pine trees I have ever seen. One day I got out of the boat to check one out – it was about 14 feet around the base. These giants will tower well over 100 feet tall. The tops of these trees are bent way over from the effects of the prevailing winds. You can look at the tops to tell the direction the wind blows from most of the time. One night, there was a heavy snowfall. When I went outside the tent in the morning and looked around, I immediately let out a yell for the boys to get outside on the double and not to ask any questions. So, when they came out and asked me what the problem was, I said, "look at that pine tree." It was about 12 inches in diameter and loaded with snow. This tree was bent right over the tent only inches above it. I expected it to break any moment – crushing everything in its path. We chopped the tree down even though the Department has a rule against cutting green timber on State lands. This area of the Mud Flats was fairly low ground where all of the creeks came together that made up the head of the Oswegatchie River. From this location, we ran our trap lines in several directions. Dick ran a line up the Partlow Mill Dam Brook while Charlie went over the hills to Toad Pond and several others. I used the boat to trap the water closer to the river. My line took in Cracker Pond, Gal Pond and some streams connecting some other ponds nearby. I also trapped Tomar Mountain. At this place there was a beaver pond where a black bear tried to claw into the beaver house to get the beaver out. He gave it a good try but finally gave up as the house was froze real solid. I never did catch any beaver in this pond. They just didn't move at all. At a pond further down the mountain, I did catch a really big pair and also a nice family there.

From the above-mentioned locations that spring, we caught about 48 beaver. Meanwhile the weather was warming up with a resultant increase of volume of water everywhere. Finally, one morning, as I lowered my feet to the ground from my cot, they landed in water – so I said to the boys, "now is the time to go." We pulled all the traps, packed up and moved back down the river to where we had left our other tent all set up. That tent was still dry but the water was just about ready to flood it. The day was warm so one of the first things we did was strip down and take a much-needed bath. The total catch on that trip was 75 beaver, several otter and also a few muskrats.

An interesting thing happened on the way down river on the first bend below High Falls. At this spot there was a pile of flood trash across the river so the boys, who had been taking the lead, waited for me to come along to see how I would navigate the spot. I noticed quite a bunch of alders along the river bank that were well covered with water, so without so much as slowing down, I roared right thru them and was gone. I had found out that while trapping up in the headwaters – if there was plenty of water around the alders, the boat would part the brush and go right on. Further down the river below the falls is some fast water known as Chicken Rapids. I had already gotten thru them and as I watched the boys come along, suddenly Dick jumped into the river. Fortunately, the water wasn't very deep at that spot so he didn't get very wet. The problem was that Charlie's motor caught on fire! They soon had the fire out and we continued on to Smith's Landing. That completed the trapping for that year. Of all the areas that we trapped, I liked the Oswegatchie River the best. It was real handy to get around in as you could run a boat way up to the very end. However, there was one little problem. Sometimes the ice was late in going out in the spring so we couldn't get started as soon as we would have liked. As I recall, our catch for the total trips amounted to 335 beaver and about 20 otter.

Rich: Now, for you who might be interested in some big game hunting up in Alaska, I would like to include a couple of Sam's stories.

Sam: August 30, 1961. One of the first things that I wanted to do when I got to Alaska was to go after a Dall sheep. The next was to hunt caribou – then a goat. After all that, I would hunt whatever would show up. I had dreamed of going to Alaska to hunt big game for a long time and my dream was finally going to come true! My wife, Ruth, agreed to go along for the ride but she didn't hunt and I wasn't really sure where she would stay but we were confident we could work something out. I had hoped to make the trip one that would be enjoyable for her and appreciated her willingness to accompany me, even though we knew up front no doubt we would be separated some of the time.

We stopped at a place called Cathedral Rocks to get some gas for the car. There I met a native that asked me what I was doing in Alaska. I told him I was looking for a dependable guide to see about a sheep hunt. I then told him about the guide that a Customs Officer told me about the day before. I talked to him, but didn't like the way he was operating as he said that he had two sheep hunters back in the mountains. He had flown them in by plane and he was supposed to have gotten back to check in on them the day before. Now, this didn't sound very good to me as the guys could have gotten into some kind of trouble and needed help. He also said something about moving some horses in the Yukon. One of the broomtales jumped out of the truck, escaping into the woods that resulted in a long chase before the animal was finally caught. This whole debacle didn't sound like anything I wanted to get mixed up with so I said, "I'll be back later to go over it again." I drove down to a gas station to get the oil changed in the car and there I talked to an Indian boy that knew this guide well. He said, "don't have anything to do with that fellow – for all you will have is problems." That was enough for me, so I went back to tell the guy that I would go looking around some more.

We drove back to Cathedral Rocks and it was then we found out about a guide by the name of Bob Buzby located at Mile 47 on the road to Fairbanks. When I got to Bob's place I found out that Bob was at his camp in the Alaska Range but would be out before dark. I decided to wait for him. It didn't take very long for me to make up my mind – here was a man that would do what he claimed, for sure. He said to me, "the only reason you won't get a sheep is because you can't hit one." I knew we didn't have a problem here as I had been hunting woodchucks all summer with excellent results and sheep were an awful lot larger. We next talked prices for the hunt and finally settled for $110.00 a day for 5 days. Bob tried to get me to have Ruth go along with me on this trip – there would be plenty of room for her at the sheep camp but at $50.00 a day, I couldn't quite afford that. However, she probably would have had a good time at the camp as there were two other women there. Bob's wife and mother-in-law were there. I finally made arrangements at a local Motel for about $30.00 as I recall.

That night we stayed with Bob. For supper he served moose steaks that were real good. The next morning, it was sourdough pancakes – now, they were definitely tops. We were to have them several more times during our stay in Alaska. After settling Ruth at the motel, I thought it would be a good idea to sight in the .270. Bob said to use his airstrip as that would be long enough. So, while he was gassing up and otherwise getting the plane ready for the flight to camp, I took a few shots at 300 yards. The rifle was dead on. In an hour or so, we were airborne and on the way to the Little Wood area of the Alaska Range, where Bob's camp was located.

On the way in, we saw several moose and a black bear. Just before getting to the airstrip, we flew over a salt area that had some moose and caribou. When we sat down, Bob said, "you can wait here until I come back with my son, Eddy and my brother. Then, we will take the John Deere Crawler with the wagon – or you can follow the tracks to camp." I said, "I would walk in as it was a really nice day." I had dreamed of being in Alaska country for too long a time to be just sitting around waiting. Then Bob said, "when you cross a stream that has milky white water, you are in Dall sheep country – but be careful what you shoot at because you just might bag a ram that might be too small."

As it turned out I didn't see any big game. Finally, I could see the camp but I had to cross a large stream to get there. I took off the sixteen inch packs, rolled up my pant legs and waded across. On the other side a short distance from the main camp was this fellow laying in a pup tent. Always having a sense of humor, I said to him, "am I going right for Chicago?" Well, he looked me over and then says, "yeah, you probably could get to Chicago, but it is a long way off." I proceeded to the camp and introduced myself to Mrs. Buzby. She said, "you are probably hungry so come in and get something to eat." The time now was about 3:30 and I had not eaten since 6 o'clock that morning. Mrs. Buzby set a huge platter of sheep steaks on the table along with other goodies. I want to tell you, the platter shrank down considerable before I finished. The sheep was the best wild meat available. It beat any wild game, at least in my estimation.

After eating, it was still time enough to do a little looking around so taking the .270 and binoculars, I headed upstream from camp. A short distance from camp, I caught some movement across the river in a cave on the side of the mountain. Using the binoculars, I could see it was a Dall sheep digging for salt. There were several others further on up the mountain. This was interesting as these were the first sheep that I had ever seen. There were no large rams in the group. Possibly a young one, but I believe they were all ewes. Next, I looked over the river and saw numerous grayling trout. They look a lot like brook trout but have an extra large dorsal fin. Later I was to find out how shy they are to catch. A little time later I heard the John Deere arrive so knew that the boys had gotten to camp. We told stories for a while – then turned in for the night. Tomorrow was to be the day that I had been waiting for – for a long while.

The next morning, we saddled up two horses and headed into the sheep country. My mount was called Spider – he was a very nice horse and easy to get along with. A short distance from camp we noticed a group of 5 caribou that came in close to get a better look at us. Bob said that they are curious animals and will sometimes come quite close, which these did. They lined up side by side for a while – then, turned and ran away. Their hooves made a loud clicking noise. As we sat on the horses, Bob said, "they will be right back for another look." Sure enough, here they came again –

lining up just like they did before. They went through this routine for a total of 4 times – and then left with a loud clicking of their hooves. Their hooves are extra large and when the animals are running, they will spread their hooves. When they raise their hooves while running, they will snap together making a noise that can be heard for at least 75 yards.

One of the bulls out of that group had a real nice rack of antlers that I would have settled for but Bob said "don't shoot – as we are after sheep today and there is a possibility there will be a better caribou in the area." So, we rode on following the river a short distance – then we turned in toward the mountains. Several miles further, we saw a group of Dall sheep walking along on the mountaintop. I will never forget the sight of the rams as they were moving along – with the white clouds behind them. What a sight it was. Bob had a spotting scope and took a look at them saying, "there are several real nice rams in the bunch." Then he handed the scope to me so I could take a look. He asked me what I thought of the one with the full curl. I said, "it looks good to me – let's try for him."

We rode a little further to get out of sight of the rams – in case they had seen us. We dismounted, tied up the horses, and began to climb on foot. Midway on the climb up the mountain, we ran into a large group of sheep that could have numbered at least 60 animals. These were ewes and lambs mostly with several small rams that had visible horns. The lambs were so curious that several came up within a few feet of us for a better look. We worked our way on up the mountain on a ridge that would bring us to a place where we were hoping to see the rams. It all worked out just perfect. Bob moved on ahead until he got to the top. For the last few yards, he removed his hat to hopefully be less conspicuous. Then, he cautiously raised up for a look. He immediately eased back down and motioned for me to crawl up beside him. This was the big moment I will never forget as long as I live. There were 6 rams – all of them legal, lying down within range. I asked Bob, "how far are they?" He said, "about 250 yards." We were whispering as there was a possibility the rams could hear us. Bob said "take the one facing us – but wait until he raises his head up," as he lay with the head resting on the end of one horn. Finally, he changed positions to rest his head on the other horn. All this time my thoughts were to keep cool and not blow the whole hunt that I had dreamed of for many years. Suddenly, here I was, with 6 legal rams within range. I knew the .270 would deliver if I did my part. The rifle was loaded with 130 grain Sierra bullets ahead of 57 grains of 4350 powder. Fortunately, I was just as cool as though I was about to shoot at a woodchuck.

The rams were down below us about 200 feet or so – I wadded up my hat and used that as a protection against the stones. I rested my hand on it and held at the base of the ram's neck and squeezed the trigger. We heard the bullet hit so believed we had a good hit. Even though the ram died instantly, he managed to give a mighty kick and that was enough to start him rolling down the mountain. I groaned every time he hit the bigger rocks – expecting the horns could be broken – but they came thru in good shape with only a few small nicks. There was a bigger ram in the group than the one I killed – but the ends of his horns were broomed off for about 5 or 6 inches. We noticed this before I shot, so I took the best one of the group. The other rams in the group just stood up and looked around like they didn't know what to do – and finally, moved around the edge of the ridge and out of sight.

This was Bob's way of making a living – he only harvested so many rams in a season leaving plenty for future years. That day, I had a problem with my knees. They both hurt like never before. Going up hill was bad but coming back down was pure torture. After getting back to the horses, we tied the ram on Bob's horse while I rode Spider back to camp. That was the hunt for that day, so I stayed around camp giving the knees a chance to improve, which they did. I believe what caused the trouble was wading the river the day before as the water was ice cold. Maybe my legs were a little sweaty and the cold water caused the condition. The following day they were back to normal. One down – the next hunt would be for caribou.

The next morning we found out the horses had opened the gate and headed out. While Eddy went looking for them, we were watching a hunter by the name of Wheat cape out a ram's head when Bob said, "look up there." Here came a huge bull caribou going into a piece of woods bordering the river. Bob said, "how does he look to you for antlers?" I said, "very good, and he is close by." Then Bob said, "grab the rifle and walk out to the river and the bull will appear shortly." It was no longer than several minutes when he came trotting out intending to cross over to the other side. Well, he never did make it for the 150 grain bullet hit him behind the left shoulder dropping the bull in his tracks. Another easy shot at 200 yards or less. Bob got the Caterpillar and drove it to the kill where we dressed out the animal and buried the insides so not to attract the grizzly bears that were in the area. The four quarters were hauled in with the tractor. Bob said the bull was an Osbourne caribou – a real nice trophy. He was shedding the velvet off the antlers with only a little left on. All of this took place by 10 o'clock. Number two trophy was in the bag with a lot of time left of the day – so I took my rifle and fishing rod – along with some trout flies – to try to catch a few of the Arctic grayling that I had seen in the river several days before.

I soon found out I had to keep out of sight in order to be able to get any strikes. They bit just about like trout do. It was fun for a while but I quit after catching about a dozen as I thought that would be plenty for the cooks to use for a meal. I then decided to head up the mountain to see if I could find a bear or some other game. I soon ran into a bull caribou that was smaller than the one I had shot that morning. He came running up to me like the ones did when we went sheep hunting. After looking me over, he ran away with his hooves clicking only to come back two more times. After that encounter, I went up the mountain and spent most of the afternoon but didn't see anything so returned to camp just before dark.

The fellow that I mentioned that was staying in the pup tent was a photographer staying with Bob to take some pictures. That night in camp I told him that I had one more day to spend there and would like to take Bob's .410 shotgun and do a little scouting with the hopes of finding some ptarmigan. He asked if he could go along. The next morning, with lunches, camera and all the attachments – including the tripod, we headed for the mountain. Before we left, he said we had better take his .30-06 just in case. His gun was the lightest of that caliber I had ever seen. On the way up the mountain he told me about the time he went on a similar scouting trip with another hunter – similar to what we were doing now – and they ran into a grizzly sow with two cubs. The mother charged them so they had to shoot her. After climbing about two hours, we came to a deep ravine that the melting snow had torn up over the years. It extended about two miles up the mountain to finally disappear behind a huge outcropping. At this time, my companion, we'll call him Joe, wanted to rest and smoke for a while. As he was enjoying his smoke, I was looking around with the binoculars. A long way up the mountain in a snow slide, I saw an animal of some kind. At first, I thought it was a marmot – an animal similar to a woodchuck, but larger. However a closer look told me it was a grizzly sow and sure enough, out came the cubs into sight. They moved down the slide for a while until the mother stopped to dig out a ground squirrel. She was digging with both paws. The stones were flying a steady stream. It reminded me of an ensilage blower going full blast. Then I said to Joe, "let's go up to get a few pictures of the bears." So, away we went – to get closer. After climbing up to where we expected to see them, they were not in sight. We decided to climb out of the slide to a nearby ridge. We lucked out, for the cubs stood about 100 yards away on a ridge while the mother was only 40 yards from us. At this point I snapped a picture of the cubs – then started to move a little closer to the sow for a better picture of her. Joe grabbed me by the shirttail to hold me back – which was a good thing. Joe felt if we got any closer, she might charge.

Quite a ways back, Joe handed me the .30-06 saying I could handle any possible situation better than he. I was amazed the bear knew we were that close. Our problem was, we had an alarmed bear that could charge at any moment. I can see her now – her legs and about half way up her body were the color of a woodchuck – from there up she was black. She paced back and forth a few times giving us the look over. While she was doing this, I took several pictures. All of a sudden she ran to the cubs and they all ran over the ridge out of sight. Joe and I hurried over the ridge to see where they went. With the rifle in my hand, we were ready for action but we never saw them again. No doubt that was a good thing. The whole encounter could have been just like Joe told about the other time. Later I saw another grizzly in the same area one day when three of us went by horseback to a lower camp to pick up some butter for the sheep camp. However, I didn't have the grizzly permit with me that day, so I didn't hunt him.

The lower camp was where Bob took his hunters grizzly bear hunting. I only got to actually see this camp from the air. The day we rode horseback to get the butter, I left the party before getting to the camp as I wanted to take some pictures of the moose and caribou that came to the salt lick. Later, Spider and I went straight back to the sheep camp. On the way back, I came close to losing the horse in a spot of quicksand. That was too close for comfort but we did manage to get through it. That finished this hunt in the Alaska Range. I forgot to mention, the day we flew in, the weather was clear – so I got a good look at Mt.McKinley which was quite a ways away but stood out sharp. It was solid snow and ice. The next day we loaded up the wagon and drove out to the airstrip. There was Alex Buzby, Bob's brother, Eddy, Joe, Bob and myself. At the airstrip Bob took the two boys with some other things and flew them out to the home base. After that, he was to fly Alex and me out. While he was gone, we broke out some G.I. rations that Bob carried on the plane. I never had any before or since – but I thought they were good. There were biscuits, chocolate bars and dried fruit of some kind.

As we sat on the ground eating, I noticed a wooden chute at the foot of the hill. Alex said it was a gold mining outfit so we went down to look it over. There was a small stream with a raised wooden chute above it where the miner would shovel the gold bearing gravel to have the water wash out the gold. I wish I had used this opportunity to try to pan out a little gold as we would have had plenty of time before Bob got back. On the way out we saw a huge bull moose that Bob tried to talk me into hunting, but I really didn't go for it as I intended to use the money to hunt for a brown bear. Soon, we were back to Bob's place and our car. This was the end of the sheep and caribou hunt. That is when I noticed Cole's note on my windshield. His full name was Lieutenant Cole McPhearson and he was stationed at the airbase at Fairbanks. He was a trapper and hunter and spent a couple of days at the sheep camp. He bagged his ram the same day I got mine. We shared two nights in sheep camp talking hunting and trapping until the wee hours of the morning. He was from Missoula, Montana. I had been there to visit one time, so we had that in common also. Time passed quickly but before he left, which was a couple of days before I left we half agreed to get together for a hunt. The note that he left invited me to come to his airbase and hunt ducks.

At the upper sheep camp, Bob's Mother-in-law had a cabin of her own to stay in. This cabin was built over a spring and that made it very convenient to get water for the needs of the camp. It was also used to keep meat fresh. While I was there, I would build a fire for her so when the evening chores were done it would be nice and warm. Well, at mealtime, she made sure I had plenty of food. I often think about her. No doubt she is long gone for it has been 30 years since I was up there and she was well along in years at that time. Every day after lunch, she would go picking cranberries and blueberries. One day, I said to her, "don't you fear the big bears going alone like you do – without a gun?" "No," she says, "I am so old and tough that no bear would want any part of me."

One day, I asked Bob, "how did you happen to acquire these buildings and campsite?" He was a man of few words and said he bought the whole outfit from a trapper – that's all he said about it. Several years later in one of the Alaska Sportsman magazines there was a story about a Game Warden by the name of Sam White that covered the area by airplane. He flew in one day to the camp to arrest and take out a trapper that was shooting Dall sheep to feed his dogs with. My guess is that Bob bought the camp sometime after that. While on location, I did find several 8 mm empty cases that no doubt the fellow used to shoot the sheep with. It must have been real handy to do the shooting as the sheep came down to the salt mine that was just across from the camp. According to the article in the magazine, the first thing the trapper asked the Warden was, "do you have any tobacco – I have been out for a long while." If I had known all this then, I would most certainly have gotten more of the story. The magazine said the trapper had some sort of ailment like asthma. He had two camps – one down low beside the river and the other one higher up in the mountains. I think this is the one that we hunted from.

Now it was time to pick up Ruth at the local motel and drive up to the airbase at Fairbanks to spend the night with Cole. At the entrance to the base, I checked with the guard that said, "state your business here." I said, "we would like to call on Lieutenant McPhearson." The guard said, "wait here." A few minutes later a fellow appeared with a Jeep saying, "follow me." He drove up to Cole's apartment, saluted and drove away. He was as polite as a basketful of chips. Anyway, it saved a lot of time as the base covered many acres. Cole and his wife were in the process of moving and had much of their belongings already packed. They had to unpack a few dishes so Ruth and I could have something to eat off of. Cole's wife was a real nice person – she didn't seem to mind the work involved by having extra guests. They had a little three-year old son and a Labrador dog by the name of Buckshot. I had a chance to see him in action the next day.

The next morning, Cole had a fellow officer alerted so the three of us with Buckshot went duck hunting. The rules of the base permitted hunting with shotguns but not with rifles. That morning we saw at least 30 moose and several had good racks. There were many ponds on the base that were caused by the huge amount of dirt taken out to make the runway. By going from one pond to the next we got quite of bit of shooting. As I recall, the bag limit was 8 ducks. It was getting close to noon, so we headed back to the apartment and lunch. Then, after a short visit, we expressed our thanks for the hospitality and were on our way once again, heading for Fairbanks to see the town.

CHAPTER 9   RON BOYDEN AND MIKE NISWENDER

Rich: What is the area basically – and does the camp have a name?

Ron: Well, the area is Spruce Lake located in the central Adirondacks and the camp is Camp Cortney.

Rich: That is the one French Louie stayed in?

Ron: Yes, it's mentioned in his book.

Mike: Cortney was another hunter, wasn't he?

Ron: Cortney was the boss of a logging camp, back in the '20s. We bought the camp originally from International Paper – they charged us $250.00

Mike: Who from our area originally got involved in this camp?

Ron: Well, it was back mostly when Donnie Young's father, Frank Young and Harry Young were involved in hunting up north – these were the first ones to use the camp. The original camp was located right on the edge of Spruce Lake. It was moved about 75 yards the first time. Before they acquired the camp, they tented on the far side of the lake – right straight across from the landing – where the Placid trail comes down to the lake.

Mike: When was that, in the '40s?

Ron: Yes.

Rich: Who are these individuals shown in the picture of the camp?

Ron: Harry Young and Ed Parker. In the other picture is Dewey Parker – they were brothers.

Rich: Well, I've heard those names, too.

Ron: Yeah, Dewey Parker and my Dad and I used to go up a lot, just the three of us. I remember one year we were up there and the woods were closed. The Ranger didn't come in – he said, "we'd been in there so many years he felt comfortable – didn't want the walk." The woods were closed after the season had opened that fall due to it's being extra dry. You used to have to sign in at Piseco at the Ranger Station when you went into the woods to hunt each fall. You had to show how many there were in your party and how long you planned to stay. This was so they would know where to look for you, I guess. We never had any problem. The Wardens used to stop at our camp once in awhile. It's just a bare spot in the woods now.

Mike: I've been back there a couple of times.

Ron: I've been back there just once – it was a heartbreaker. My wife and I hiked back in last year to Spruce Lake. We were going to stay there but the weather turned foul so we returned to our present hunting camp. The next morning we had two inches of snow and that was on the third of October. We plan to try that again sometime.

Rich: How did your Dad get involved in the camp?

Ron: Dewey Parker and my Dad were great friends. He was hunting out of Big Moose for a number of years. Eventually, that party just folded up. Different ones lost interest and several members got old and the camp just lacked the volume it needed to keep going. Dewey asked us to go up with him in the early '50s. I went up about 1952 but wasn't old enough to hunt then. The first time I hunted up there was in 1957. We were in the woods the year a bad windstorm hit the area. It took a tremendous amount of time to get out of there. The trails and roads were just full of trees that had blown down. The tops to the bottoms of the mountains were just blown flat and for years, you couldn't even think about hunting up near the top. Spruce Mountain was my favorite place to hunt. I would hunt down the length of that to Miller's camp on the other end of that mountain. Once in awhile, we'd meet someone from that camp while out hunting. We'd sit down and chew the fat for awhile – then realize it was time to head back to camp – it would be about three miles from there in order to make it back before dark.

Mike: One time Barry Warren and I were hunting on Spruce Mountain – we had split up and made plans to meet at a certain place mid-afternoon. That was when I found that old airplane. All that was left of it was the fuselage. I thought it was pretty neat seeing that old airplane sitting in the woods.

Rich: Was it a seaplane?

Ron: It was a pontoon plane – it was overloaded, so they claimed. They couldn't get enough lift off the lake to clear the trees.

Mike: So, they went down.

Ron: Yeah, they all walked away from it. They came back sometime later and took the engine out.

Rich: I don't think I ever would want to get involved in a bush pilot type of thing.

Ron: It's quite an experience to come in onto the water. When you come off the water and lift up between the mountains and then come out into the open range – it is very beautiful. I remember Ivan Gilbert. He was a big, heavy-set fellow and the pilot had him sit right up front next to the controls to kind of give him some extra ballast in the front. He would hang on so hard when he would do those lifts that the pilot said to him one time, "if you don't let go, you're going to pull the roof right in." It was a convenient way to get into camp – we still had a mile to walk.

Rich: When you moved this camp, did you move it as a unit or dismantle it?

Ron: We dismantled it.

Rich: Did you number the logs or something?

Ron: We used one horse. They had a way of laying the logs out so that when they got done, they would draw from the center of the pile. It was surprising how quickly it came down and went back up. They put a new tin roof on at that time – the old one was getting kind of ratty. Those old camps make for a nice atmosphere. That was what the old camp was about. Sleeping upstairs, it was like Snow White and the Seven Dwarfs, you know.

Mike: Well, when I started going back there about 1979 there were about twelve of us and it took the whole day just to get back into camp. We would park our vehicles back out by the old fellow's camp by Route 30. Then we'd unload and put all the gear on the tractor and trailer and go across by Carpenter's Hill and then back in by Tin Camp and then in to our camp. It was an all day ordeal. It was so cold the first night we were in camp even with both pot bellied stoves going full blast we were cold. You could lie on your bunk and look out thru the cracks in the logs right up at the stars. Donnie Young woke up during the night one time and noticed the stove at the far end of the camp was just cherry red. He yelled, "FIRE, FIRE." Everybody bailed out. They got that stove calmed down before it caused a problem – before the whole thing went up in flames.

Ron: There was only one time any of us drove all the way into camp. Ken Young did it out of "I can do it."

Mike: I think that was the year before I went up – I heard a lot of stories about that.

Ron: He beat his truck to death. He winched and pulled and got it back in there. When Ivan Gilbert used to go I recall one year we were sleeping upstairs. There was a little commotion on the steps. He rolled over and put his flashlight on and here was a porcupine sitting on the top step – looking at him. He just rolled over and went back to sleep. I've been up there a couple of times when it was only about 10 degrees. You'd have all the clothes you had with you on and still be barely comfortable. It was a great camp – we had a lot of fun. International Paper Company owned the land. They just closed their operation that makes paper bags – I just heard that on the news this morning.

Mike: In 1981 the paper company and the State traded the land where our old camp was. They made us burn down the old camp but at least we had an option to build a new camp on Paper Company land. They allowed us to do that. That's how our new camp evolved. We own the camp and lease the land that it sits on. There are fifteen of us in the club.

Ron: Just about eleven and a half miles back in.

Mike: We're fortunate – to be able to have that opportunity.

Ron: It's nice country where the camp is located now. There aren't the mountains in the new area we had in the old camp but we enjoy the new area.

Rich: Remember that old Route 30 that linked Speculator and Indian Lake Village? That used to go right by Mason Lake near the outlet of that lake. It was a dirt road and a good one. I assume that road is all gone and grown over now?

Mike: That road is opened back up again. It's now a fire trail and the loggers use it to go back in – it's all still there.

87

Ron: It's maintained and plowed by Speculator.

Rich: How far is it from that road to your camp?

Mike: It's ten miles from that road to our camp.

Ron: My wife was related to the Perkins' that were there and she has a picture of the cabin that was at Perkins Clearing. It was a postcard that was sent out advertising outfits.

Rich: Was it up in this region where your Dad got that big bear?

Ron: He got that bear on Moose Lake Mountain that is over towards the Big Moose area – over towards Twitchell. Between Eagle Bay and Big Moose Station. He went back on Twitchell Lake Road which dead ends at the lake and we hunted back in along the edge of the lake and in some of the hills in that area.

Mike: How big a bear was it?

Ron: It weighed over 600. We brought it out with two horses. We had quite a time with the horses – they could smell that bear and the blood and we had quite a time getting them anywhere near where they could get hooked on. They didn't have any trouble after they got hooked on. Dutch Casterline was hunting with him at the time. Dutch walked down one side of a little rise and Dad went the other side and the bear came right out on his side. Dad never aimed the gun – he was that close – he just swung around and fired – the bear did a flip and his hind feet hit Dad's boots. He hit him right in the temple. If it would have hit him anyplace else, that bear would have grabbed anything close by and it might have been Dad.

Mike: How many bears did your Dad shoot up in the woods?

Ron: Seven, I think. He was a very good still-hunter.

Rich: When you say a good still-hunter – did you ever hunt with your father to see how he operated in the woods?

Ron: He's the one that taught me.

Rich: Could you tell us a little about that?

Ron: He was very patient. He was agile, you know, and he picked out deer long before they got on the move. Traveling as he did, he studied everything. He shot some beautiful deer in the Adirondacks thru the years – his love was bear hunting, really. I remember one time, that he came onto three of them together. He taught me, "don't shoot unless you got a good shot. Don't waste the ammo by wounding the game and letting it get away." He knew the territory. He lived in the woods – he just loved it. You couldn't keep him home when it was deer season. We boys did the chores a good many times and he'd take off. That was good – that was his life.

Rich: A lot of people think that to be a good still-hunter you're simply out in the woods and luck has got an awful lot to do with anything good that happens. I think you make your own luck as far as that goes. I read someplace that if you're hunting downwind, you're not really hunting at all – you're just out for a hike. I really agree with that.

Ron: That's right.

Rich: Deer and bear have a very keen sense of smell. A still-hunter moving into or crosswind might take an hour to go a hundred yards or less.

Ron: It's not the distance that you cover - it's how you cover the distance.

Rich: That's true. My Dad's friend, Ray Williams, has a little different slant. It takes a lot of energy to go slow and to do all that careful looking. His idea was – you don't operate that way all the while – you go until you find where there's some sign to indicate that there are deer around. You can travel a long distance and be in an area where there simply aren't any deer there at all. What's the point in your pussyfoot thing if there's nothing to hunt? His idea was go until you see some sign and then pay attention and go slow and really look - and like you said, you have to depend on your eyes and it takes awhile to get used to what you are looking for.

Ron: Because they blend in so beautifully.
Rich: Somebody said, "horizontal is helpful to give you a clue that maybe an animal is there." Another friend of my Father's said what you're apt to see won't be a whole deer most times – it might be a tip of an antler or an eye or an ear or some movement of a leg or something. Still-hunting is a highly effective method but not very many people utilize it, I don't believe.

Ron: Well, I think the younger generation get impatient. So many of the younger ones that come up to camp lose the urge to go again because they don't see anything. You have to put more into it than just hunt. It helps to enjoy the wilds – just enjoy being in the woods. Deer are just a side part of it for me. I enjoy seeing how far I can go and seeing how many changes that have occurred over the years and seeing the old familiar areas – places you have been that really strike your heart.

Rich: When the paper company made you the offer to allow you to build a new camp your group had a limited period of time to decide. As I heard the story, you got together and decided if you wanted to kill a lot of deer you'd hunt the southern tier. There just had to be something special about that Adirondack country that was very appealing.

Ron: It's just the love of the wild. The camaraderie of camp and the old stories – that's what is great.

Mike: A lot of the old stories are disappearing every year. What I find hard to believe is we're not seeing a lot of the younger people really that interested in hunting. At the time Barry and I were young and planning on this new camp we were thinking, "down the road, we're going to have so many kids coming up from these people that are in here we're going to have too many people in the camp." That's not the case at all. What's happened, I believe, is the children of the people that are in the camp have other interests and things - and hunting is not as big as it used to be – twenty or thirty or forty years ago, I don't believe. It's important for me to go up there and I love getting away and going up there – I can't wait.

Rich: I believe there truly is something unique about deer camp. Whether it's a tent you set up at a spot or a cabin you can go back to each year, it's unique.

Mike: Here's some things I especially appreciate about deer camp. When we leave in the morning, every single person in that camp is on his own adventure. Basically, everybody in that camp hunts on their own – we don't do drives in our group. We usually all wind up hunting totally different areas and we take off. To me, the most exciting thing of the entire day is at 6 o'clock when everybody comes back to that camp and one by one – you go around and tell all the stories of all the things you've seen and you almost can't wait to hear. We sit there sometimes a couple of hours talking about what has happened that day. How much would you think you could see in the woods in one day? It's unlimited. There's so much stuff to talk about. This is one of the main reasons I enjoy going to deer camp every fall. This year was the first I missed being in camp with the usual group since I have been going up there because my wife and I were building a house. I did get to go on the last weekend. We feel the bigger the group the better.

Ron: It is.

Mike: You shot an eight-point this year?

Ron: Yes.

Rich: I figure any time someone kills a legal buck in the Adirondacks he's got a special bonus. An eight-point is pretty nice – what would he dress, would you guess?

Ron: I'd say he'd go around 140 – 145 pounds, dressed. Nice deer.

Rich: You didn't have any beechnuts either, in your area, did you?

Ron: Not this year. The year before was the first time in a long time we had a banner year.

Mike: There were so many beech nuts up on Blue Mountain where I hunt a lot, the bears had been in there feeding heavily. Everything was torn up from the bears digging around. They were still working heavily in the beech the last weekend of the season. This year, there were none.

Ron: We didn't see any bear sign this year, either.

Mike: I didn't either – they must have moved someplace else.

Rich: They move around – they have quite a large territory, I understand. I know you have coyotes in your area. Have you had any indication of any gray wolves being in your territory?

Mike: Not that I'm aware of.

Ron: You don't even see the coyotes. You see where they have been when the snow's on.

90

Mike: The last four or five years prior to the last couple of years, probably, I hiked back into the old camp a lot and hunted. I had a spot that I really liked near that old camp. There were a lot of deer back in there then. Two or three times while hiking in there early in the morning I'd hear the coyotes open right up. That would always put chills down the back of your neck. They didn't sound that far away – probably somewhere just to the left of the hog's trough. That's about where they always seemed to be.

Ron: That was back near Belden's Vly.

Mike: Yeah, towards Belden. You would most always see their tracks in that area.

Ron: You hunted over towards Balsam?

Mike: Yes – I'd turn right at the hog's trough and go over towards Balsam Lake and hunt back around the lake. It's gotten so thick over there – it's gotten harder and harder to hunt every year.

Ron: The beech died off. That took the canopy off and an awful lot of brush has sprung up. It certainly is a lot different from what it used to be.

Mike: A lot different.

Rich: My, how the woods change.

Mike: I barely can recognize that notch. The last time I walked over to that area I could hardly even recognize the area at all.

Ron: Speaking of Balsam, I remember one time it was cold and I was hunting along the backside of Balsam Mountain and you could look down at the lake and I could hear this funny sound – twing, twing you know. I worked my way down to the edge of the lake – and a bunch of our boys were out there on the ice, playing hockey with a stone and sticks. That's a real shallow lake – not much over six feet deep anywhere in it but it's a good-sized lake.

Mike: Being so shallow probably helps it freeze over early in the fall sometimes. One day I was learning the area between Little Moose and Otter Lake. I hunted all the way around Otter Lake - and wound up on the backside late in the afternoon. It was late enough I needed to be picking up the pace and heading down out. I came down by the lean-to on the end of Otter Lake and had just started down the trail heading towards camp when I met a fellow coming up the trail towards me. By now, it's getting around 4:30 and starting to get along towards dark. He appeared to be an older guy – he didn't have a rifle but did have a pistol packed under his shirt. Also, he was carrying a backpack. I asked him "where are you going right now? You're going the wrong way – you're going back into the" - - he interrupted me mid-sentence and said, "oh, I'll just sleep up there someplace by Otter Lake – I've got a trapline up there." I said, "no kidding?" It didn't look to me like he hardly had enough with him to keep warm. He said, "yeah, I don't mind staying out – I'll find a lean-to or something – I got a little blanket with me – I'll be warm enough." So then, he started telling me about his trapline. He asked me if it was my four-wheeler parked down at the bottom of the hill where the parking spot was and I said, "yeah." Then he told me, "I got a Honda three-wheeler there with a little box on the

91

back. When you get down to that Honda, open up that box and look in there – see what you can see." So I said, "ok."

I hiked on down and it was pitch black by the time I finally got to that parking area where my unit had been left. I even had to use my flashlight the last fifteen minutes on the trail to get there. There weren't any stars out or anything – one of those dark nights – a good night to be in camp. I found his rig and then took my flashlight and looked in that box and he had a bobcat that he had caught in his trap. He had it all skinned out and it really was a beautiful pelt. It had a little bitty round foot on it – it was gorgeous. The day before I had been over to DeWitt Pond and had shot a gray fox. He was about eighty yards away so I had a long shot at him – I just wanted to see if I could hit him – you don't get to shoot up there that often anyway. Well, when I fired my rifle, he dropped right into a heap. I took it into camp but the next day, I looked up this fellow's campsite. He had a neat little cabin. He happened to be there when I stopped in so I gave him that gray fox. He had pelts hanging all over the place – looked like a very successful trapper and appeared to be having a wonderful time – all alone there in the woods. I couldn't help but feel a little envious. I never saw him again.

Ron: Dad shot a bobcat on Spruce Mountain one time. It was on Big Spruce in 1973. I believe that was the only bobcat any of us ever killed while hunting out of our camp. Just about everyone has seen bobcat tracks at one time or another – it's always very special to identify them. They are a keen hunter and a lot of fun to follow their tracks for a ways to see where they travel in search of their prey.

Mike: I don't think any of us have ever shot a coyote in the woods, do you?

Ron: No, and I don't think any of us have actually even seen one up there.

Mike: I saw one while riding my snowmobile one time – a coyote – running. He ran across the trail in front of me up the hill just past our camp but I have never seen one while hunting that I remember.

Rich: Another story I would like you to share was the one where last fall, I believe, you and Barry were hunting back in somewhere and you found this new rock you utilized as a watch. A stranger came along and it really surprised you to see anyone outside your own party so far back in the woods.

Mike: Oh yeah, that one. Barry and I have a notch up on Blue Mountain and it's quite a job to get there and not many hunters go to all the bother.

Rich: Is this the Blue Mountain up from Blue Mountain Lake?

Mike: No, this is Blue Ridge – says Ridge on the map. It actually runs into Pillsbury Mountain where the fire tower is. It's within walking distance of our hunting camp. We've found a notch up in that area where we always see a lot of deer tracks and other sign – they travel in there a lot. We decided to set up a portable stand and would take turns spending time in that watch and then change off to give the other one a chance. It's difficult to still-hunt in that area due to being so steep. Some days, it's just better, we believe, to sit. We use the tree stand as our base and then probably a half-mile from there is this huge rock that we discovered we could climb up on and use that for a watch. It was

92

Barry's turn to go on the rock and I was up in the tree stand. Barry was on his way down there to that rock and not fifteen minutes after he left me, I heard a shot – sounded like it was right where he was, and I said, "boy, that's Barry." We had little radios with us so I radioed him – I said, "Barry, is that you – did you shoot?" He said, "you're not going to believe this – it wasn't me." I said, "you're kidding me here." It was so loud, it was right there. He said, "I'm going to go sit on my rock – after the guy shot, I heard deer running so I know there are other deer in this area." After another couple of hours, we switched again – he came over to me and I went over to the rock and I had no more than climbed up on that great big rock and I heard something coming – sounded like a deer walking – it was real crunchy that day.

It was a fellow all dressed in orange and he was walking back into our area – coming up from the edge of the lake. The way he was heading I couldn't imagine why he would be going there. I whistled and he turned and saw me up on that rock and he came running over. I asked "how are you doing?" He said, "aw, I'm lost – I am dead lost." It's about 1:30 in the afternoon. At the time he shot, it was around 11 a.m. For two and a half hours he had been walking around in a big circle. He said, "I shot this real nice eight-point buck somewhere in this area. I'm disorientated – I'm not certain where on my map I am." I said, "well, I know exactly where you are – I know this area really well. Let's get your map out and take a look – I'll show you." So, we get the map all out and then he says "an eight-point point came along right within good range so I shot him. He had several does running with him and shortly I saw another deer running behind those deer and you could have set my eight-point's rack inside the rack of that other deer – he was huge. He ran off and he's still running somewhere." When he shot, he was so close to Barry's location that he about jumped out of his skin, it surprised him so. I told him, "I bet we can find your deer," and I got the map out and showed him where he was. We hadn't gone very far down thru there and we picked up his trail where he had shot the deer, picked up the blood trail, and where he had dragged it and then we walked right to his deer. We got him orientated again, but even after I showed him which way was back to his camp, he had to keep looking at his compass. It just didn't seem right to him. He left his deer there. I gave him some orange ribbon and he marked his way back to where he was going and his buddies came and helped him. If it had been my deer, I couldn't have dragged him very far. It was a heavy deer. Probably would have weighed over 190. It was unusual for that area – and very nice – a real trophy. It would have been something to have laid eyes on that old buster that was traveling with him and those does that he saw. Barry and I thought we were the only hunters in the area. It was a surprise to have this strange guy shoot a deer right next to us. We had a real good time. The fellow was from the Albany area or Saratoga. I've got his address someplace.

Ron: I shot a nice twelve-point over on Stillwater on the backside of Spruce Mountain and a bunch of us went over there the next day to drag it back to camp. When we got it back to camp, there was no hair left on that one side. That was always a good mountain to hunt. One time I went down the north side of it – it was shadowed and the snow was crunchy. Bear tracks were in evidence up and down the mountain. It was one of the first good tracking snows that we had. I came around onto the south side and snow was starting to melt and it was slushy. You could see where the bear put his feet down – it made the snow splash with each step. I thought the track looked really fresh. Suddenly he came bolting out of one of those little draws on the side of that mountain – crossed a little stream and he ran across in front of me so fast, all I saw was a black blur. I never did get a shot at him – he went into the tall grass and I could see the grass going where he ran but it was so thick, I couldn't see the bear. Then I thought he might cross an area of open water that appeared ahead so I kept waiting – but

93

he didn't come out into the clear – he just stayed in that tall grass. They can really go when they're motivated.

Mike: When we were in the old camp, probably back in the eighties, Barry and I were hunting one day and it was snowing very hard. We were actually hunting together – it was snowing so hard it would have been easy to get disorientated. At that time we hadn't been hunting out of the camp a lot and we were both still learning the area. We walked over to Spruce Lake, down the trail a ways and then back over to Balsam. On our way over to Balsam Lake, we noticed a fresh bear track in the snow. We knew it had to be very fresh as it was still snowing very hard. There was no snow at all in the track – we figured this bear was right ahead of us. Barry is hot on the trail and I'm following right along - and we finally get half way around Balsam Mountain between Little Balsam Ridge and Balsam Lake. The track goes up to this great big old tree – and stops. There wasn't any track around it that we could find. We looked up the tree and couldn't figure how a bear could be hiding up there. Way up towards the top was a little hollow. Apparently the bear had climbed the tree and disappeared into that hollow. It was getting late so we had no choice but to head back to camp.

The next morning we got right up. The snow had stopped. We walked back to our tree and there was no evidence of the bear having left. About three other guys came back with us that morning. They got a little fire going and we beat on the tree some and did all this stuff to try to get that bear to show himself. Finally, the bear sticks his head up out of that little hollow and Barry pulls his rifle up and shoots. The bear pulled back into his hollow. After awhile, the bear finally did come out. Lewis Heath ended up shooting that bear down in the swamp. Barry made a rug out of it and still has it in his home today, on the floor. That whole ordeal was something else – those are the things you remember.

Ron: When you come down off Balsam Mountain, there's a sheer wall that goes right down to the lake.

Mike: I have been there.

Ron: That's just an ideal place for bear.

Mike: I've been there and noticed bear tracks and sign all over the place – they seem to use that area year after year.

Ron: I remember going back into camp probably in the early '50s and a fellow came in there that was lost. He came up from the lake on a trail and he had a dark Navy jacket on – the kind that hangs way down and he looked just like a bear. We gave him a tongue lashing for wearing such a thing in the woods during bear season. He was from Miller's camp so we gave him directions on how to get back there and he took off – and in about a half hour he came right back to our camp. Well finally, the Rangers who had been looking for him showed up at our camp to see if any of us had seen him. He was sitting right there at the table with us. When he got up to go out, he put on that black, Navy jacket. They almost took him into town rather than back to his camp. It's like some down home wear the Carharts – they think it is camouflage.

Mike: Yeah, it looks just like a deer, too.

Ron: I've had hunters come along – and I would just ease behind my tree – not wanting to break up that peacefulness with a conversation with someone I didn't know. I think a deer is reluctant to be pushed anywhere much. They'll stand perfectly still and let a driver walk right on by them. We put a drive on at Burnt Mountain one time. The drivers actually saw the deer in there – but nothing came thru. So, they turned around and drove it right back again and this time, they got a nice nine-point out of it. Later on I was hunting on Balsam and jumped a nice deer down in the lower end – I had a scope on my rifle. I couldn't find anything when the deer was running – that was the last time I used a scope on my rifle.

Mike: Sometimes they're nice – I put a tip-off on my rifle so that I can look thru the scope. Sometimes under the right conditions it's nice to have a little magnification just to look things over. There's other times when I like to be able to flip that scope right off and then can use my open sights on my .30-30. You just have iron sights on yours.

Ron: Yeah, .30-06. A couple of bucks ago, I got it over in back of Little Spruce. It turned out to be about a seventy-five yard shot and all I could see was his head. A doe came up there and stood and this nice buck came right up behind her. She must have been a little bit spirited because he was sniffing her over and all I could see was his head. I thought, when she bolts and runs, he's going to be right behind her – so, I didn't take any chance – I caught him right thru the ear. It dropped him right there. My brother Irwin and Charlie Poltz went back in to help drag it out. My brother wasn't too much oriented as far as hunting – he'd been up a few times but he hunted on the trail. He said he wanted to see the territory. So, I said, "follow me today – I need a dragger." We walked about a mile and got to the beaver pond and he says, "pretty near there?" I said, "oh, about half way." We cut down thru the other side of the outlet to the beaver pond, crossed the State Line and got into the State land and got on the backside. We must have walked another half mile or so and he says, "are we pretty near there now?" I says, "oh, about half way there." He got a little upset. Then he said, "I don't think you know where it is." So, we went over another little ridge and went down thru and pretty soon I pointed out thru the trees and said, "you see that orange hanging down there?" "Yeah, I can see something down there," he says. I said "the deer is fastened to the end of that orange."

Mike: I have hunted that area a few times. The last time, I got up on that mountain near where you were and could look right down and see Lake Pleasant. There's an open spot – you can practically look way down to Speculator. You guys go ahead now – I've got a couple of customers out in the shop looking for me.

Rich: Well, isn't it fun?

Ron: It is – it's the life. About the first of October until the season is over, I'm a nervous wreck. Not too good company for the wife, I think. I don't get to go up north very often – but when I do go, I try to take at least a week or ten days.

Rich: This past summer, Gerry Hines, a friend from our church took me up the Oswegatchie River – for old times sake. He had spent seventeen years taking youth groups from our church on canoe trips into the Adirondack Mountains. They basically had a good time – it was a mixed group of boys and girls – quite a challenge. Usually they camped on Dead Creek Flow on Cranberry Lake as their base camp. From there they would take day trips – sometimes they would hike up a mountain –

other times would trek in to High Falls – a great place to swim. As we get older it gets to be more of a challenge to share with and minister to young people. They've got so much energy, you know.

Gerry read my first book and I managed to get a copy of "Man Of The Woods" for him by Herbert Keith. Keith lived in Wanakena and personally knew most of the guides that worked the Oswegatchie River back in the days when the native brook trout fishing was real great. A three to five pound brookie was possible. You normally think of Quebec, Canada for trout of that size. He already had a copy of "French Louie." He also knew and loved the river so said, "let's go." Two summers ago we had our trip planned for four of us. I had to take that time to get my prostate problem taken care of so that ruled the trip out for that summer. Last year we tried for the same four guys – the other two backed out but Gerry said "regardless, you and I are going."

We planned a three-day trip and made our base camp below the falls a little ways. The second day, we went light – carried around the falls and headed upstream hoping to reach the old camp at Sand Creek at the head of the river. We had beautiful water for that trip – were able to paddle up thru every one of the rapids. Generally, in the summertime, you have to get out and line your canoe up thru some of the rapids. We noticed we were running short of energy. We both got very tired the previous day and when we reached the second big beaver dam above the falls, we decided to give up trying to make it up to the hunting camp and decided instead to do a little trout fishing. It was a disappointment, to say the least. However, we were wise to relax instead of pushing ourselves to the limit. We returned to camp mid-day and enjoyed sitting around the campfire and just listening to the woods sounds. Gerry saw a large buck mink running the bank the second morning as he was starting the fire. We had a wonderful time. The cardinal flowers were in full bloom. It was such a delight to once again be in the area – hear the sounds, smell the odors and see the sights – what a blessing. I appreciate Gerry taking the time to make it possible for me to enjoy that trip.

Ron: For me now, I appreciate seeing things a lot more than I did when I was younger. I was a dairy farmer and sold out but I kept about a hundred acres of land and the last few years, a friend that hunts with me all the while, used to work on our farm as a young lad. He went into the service in the Korean War. We plant Christmas trees. We planted about four hundred last year – not to sell, just for the wildlife. Like you say, your reward is just to put something back.

Rich: It sure is.

Ron: You spend your lifetime taking from – it's time to put back.

Rich: Your hunting camp that you have at the present time – is that log construction or stick frame?

Ron: No, that's board and batten. It's well insulated. It's 24 x 24 and has accommodations for twelve. We use double bunks and have six on a side.

Rich: Where's that – up in a loft?

Ron: No, it's on the outside wall – it's all one room. The place has a low ceiling – it's very comfortable in that camp. It's nice even in the summer. My wife and I enjoy doing some hiking – we

96

did it last year. We went back in to Pillsbury – it was about a six and a half mile hike one-way. We camped back in and then went to Spruce Lake. It's been an adventure for both of us.

Rich: I'd like to include some nice photos in this book – I appreciate your letting me borrow these to use. It says Camp Cortney right on the building.

Ron: One day, Donnie Young shot a nice deer – he sat on one side of the vly and the deer appeared on the other side. We went up to help him get it and he thought the only way he could get over there would be to strip down and swim across. Well, it was November and kind of frosty that morning so we talked him out of it. Instead, we made him go down below the beaver pond and cross down there and then come back up thru the thick stuff to where the deer was in a kind of little opening. He tied a rope on the deer and we drew it back thru the waterway. Donnie said he came out into that opening and was just looking around and he said it seemed like the deer just did the same thing.

Rich: We hear a lot about it's being attractive when there's an opening always to spend a little time looking around. I don't know what your experience has been but when it comes to openings, I have never ever seen anything. I think this story you just told about Donnie is very unusual.

Ron: It was a very beautiful deer.

Rich: By looking at the picture, it looks like he had lots of help to drag and haul it thru the waterway.

Ron: That was near Burnt Mountain – between Burnt and Little Spruce. When I read French Louie's book there was a mention of a camp that a hermit had in between that area near what we call Roundtop. Well, I went over there one day and I just did some scouting – back and forth along a little stream in the area. Pretty soon, I came upon an area that had a square mound so I dug up a whole pack basket full of old bottles. Malt liquor and Hollywood whiskey flasks with the big stars on them and ink wells that were cobalt blue and emerald green. There had to be a logging camp there too as I don't think the hermit himself would have ever used all that. The French Louie book is a very interesting book.

Rich: Isn't that a treasure. A few years ago I tried to order some additional copies and they told me it was out of print and none were available. Apparently the bookstore store at the Adirondack Museum had such an interest in the book that they were influential in getting an additional printing done so the book is available again. This thing rarely happens in my experience.

Ron: The fact that French Louie stayed in Camp Cortney has meant a lot from a historical standpoint to all of us. Louie always liked to sleep by himself downstairs by the kitchen stove. He wasn't a very talkative man.

Rich: He certainly wasn't unsociable – he was loved and admired by a lot of people and a tremendous guide. He could guide hunters as well as fishermen. I guess you made out best if you told him what you would like to do someday and just leave it up to him to suggest when and usually if he liked an individual he would come up with a suggestion as to when he would be able to take you. I got a chuckle over what the book said about his maple syrup business. It didn't matter whether the bottle was big or small, he charged $3.00 a bottle.

Ron: And then he collected the gum off the trees.

Rich: Spruce gum. Did you ever try any of that?

Ron: No, I never did.

Rich: My Dad introduced me to that when I was a youngster. He always brought me back a few pieces of nice clean spruce gum to enjoy. The trick to that gum was you had to warm it up. You'd stick one of those little gobs of spruce gum in your mouth and try to chew it right away and it would all get crumbly and just be a mess. You had to suck on it like you would on a gum drop or something for about fifteen minutes and then you could gently start to chew it and as it would warm up you could chew it just like regular gum. You'd have that spruce flavor and everything and it was kind of nice. Back then, there was quite a popular demand for it – they used it in the manufacture of chewing gum as a base and of course mixed a lot of other ingredients with it to make it readily chewable.

They had these long poles with a knife fastened to the end of each one so they could reach way up and harvest the gum beyond what they could reach by standing on the ground. They didn't score the tree or anything like that to make the gum grow – they just took it where and as they found it. The tree was not damaged a bit in the process. The little globs of gum appeared on the tree right on the bark and they would be in size from about a quarter to the size of a golf ball, though one that large probably would be rare. The whole deal would get a little sticky though sometimes, so they usually collected it in a cloth bag rather than just toss it into a pack basket. I got a kick out of what the book said about Louie selling deer hides. A lot of people would have been glad to accuse him of poaching or killing more than his legal limit of deer. Louie would find a dead deer in the swamp that maybe died of natural causes or perhaps had been wounded during the deer season by another hunter. He would check to see if the hair would slip and if not, would just skin the hide right off and add it to his collection. He traded a tall load of deer hides tied to his sled every time he came into town in the wintertime. The money he received helped buy some groceries.

Ron: Every time he headed into town, just at the edge of the Corners, now Speculator, he'd let out a war whoop and everybody knew he was coming. It was time for a big festival. He'd come in, sell his furs, get his supplies and stash them in his pack basket behind the bar – and then party until his money was gone or until he got rolled – whichever would happen first. Then he'd grab his pack basket and leave town and let loose with an owl hoot on top of the first ridge on his way back into Camp Cortney. That was his entertainment for the year.

Rich: It was a way of entertainment for a lot of the loggers that worked all winter in the area. A number of the men didn't seem to think they had a choice. They would work hard in the woods all year and then come out and spend their whole year's wages in some bar or in several bars and that procedure would only take a very few days and then they would be broke and the only hope they would have would be to go back into the woods and work another year and repeat the process all over again. I ran across a book that was about this fellow by the name of Frank Reed. The title of his book was, "Lumberjack Sky Pilot." He was a Presbyterian minister. Some Catholic Priest began this ministry to the men working in the logging camps. Mr. Reed got acquainted with him and was invited to accompany him on one of the Priest's visits to the logging camps. Mr. Reed was so impressed with that adventure he talked to his church about accepting this as a ministry. They accepted and he entered this ministry full time. He traveled to the camps to visit when possible and got there many times on snowshoes though sometimes he could hitch a ride on a sled loaded with groceries and supplies heading into the logging camp.

This ministry grew and didn't just include the northeast but extended clear into Michigan and Wisconsin – any place where they had logging camps. The Skypilots would never take an offering. The local congregations of the sponsoring churches provided their full support. They would share with the men, give a little talk in the bunkhouse after the main meal at night, distribute bibles and song books and eventually were asked to conduct weddings and funerals for the men of the camps. Mr. Reed spent his life ministering to these men. The way I heard about him was one night I received a phone call from Henry Stafford, a lay minister who was serving at a little Baptist Church up in Sempronius at the time. He knew about our boys program we had at our church in Homer so he called me up and said, "we've got this Skypilot coming to our church to give a talk and show some pictures – why don't you bring your boys and enjoy the evening?" Skypilot – I thought it would be about some guy flying an airplane. "No, it's a missionary – he speaks to lumberjacks." It sounded like it would be an interesting program. So, we brought a couple of cars full of the boys – probably had about fourteen kids. He showed 8 mm movies plus slides – the movies were especially of interest because he showed some of the old river drives of the logs – that was a piece of history. He gave a great talk – really was interesting. He loved the woods and of course, loved men and the Jesus he served.

There was a Jobber at South Lake lumber camp by the name of Sol Carnihan. He was a favorite Jobber that the men all really liked to work for as he treated them fair. They named the dam he had built on the South Branch of the Black after him. The following spring when the snow melted and the rains came and the water came up high, they floated the logs down that little river. You would wonder how – it had boulders the size of the average room and you would wonder how, under any circumstances, they would ever have enough water to float anything down that little river, to say nothing of huge logs. They would pile the logs right out on the ice of the pond created by his dam. In the spring when the water rose, they'd lift some boards on the sluice and let the logs down thru the gate.

His Brother was trying to break up a jam in the South Branch and somehow slipped off the log he was riding on. It was quite deep at that spot and the logs began to move and they closed over above him and he couldn't make it to the surface and drowned. This was very dangerous work. It was really interesting to hear him talk – he'd just written his book, "Lumberjack Skypilot" and just happened to have several boxes with him – probably fifty to the box. We took that up as a moneymaking project for our boys program and thought that some folks would surely be interested in finding out about this unusual ministry that had occurred.

Ron: Since then PBS has picked up on that and had a beautiful documentary on the whole thing. I've watched it several times.

Rich: Wasn't that interesting – the pictures he included of the Hudson River and that area where they used to move so many logs. Another thing of interest, his book was the first one published by North Country Books – he helped establish that business which today is very successful as a book publisher. They are located in Utica, New York.

Ron: I never go thru Speculator but what I go thru Charlie Johns' store. He carries quite a nice selection of books about the out-of-doors and the north-country. I have purchased several from that place.

Rich: Yeah, he even agreed to handle a half dozen or so of my first book. That was fun.

Ron: We even went fishing in Spruce Lake a couple of times.

Rich: Are there any lakers in there?

Ron: Yes, we used to catch some nice trout there. We used a copper line to troll with – that really got our spoon down deep.

Rich: Are there any smelt in that lake that you know of?

Ron: I don't think so – but we used to see brook trout spawning near shore on the sandbars in the fall. It's a very deep lake – we think it may be about 300 feet deep in places. Those big old lakers just hang right down on the bottom and it takes a good copper line to get down to them.

Rich: One of the stories about that Honedaga Lake where the Adirondack League had their big camp was quite interesting. The members wanted to help the brook trout out on their spawning venture as their opportunity was limited in that lake. So, they brought in a load of nice, clean gravel and dumped it off the mouth of one of the little streams that came down off the mountain. They spread the gravel within about a foot of the surface of the lake. I think they controlled the depth of the lake with a dam. Before they actually spread the gravel on the lake bottom, they went thru there with a pipe full of holes to allow the spring water from the little stream to bubble up thru the pipe. Then, of course, in the fall when the brook trout wanted to spawn, they were really attracted to that spot and it worked out beautifully. The brook trout came onto that pad to spawn like gangbusters. One day they looked out there and saw all this commotion and here were a pair of otters that were causing a big problem for the trout.

Ron: That must have been easy pickings for them. This fall when I was up in the woods hunting, I was on a stand at a spot where I had spent quite a lot of time and I spotted a little dark movement down in the pines below me and my heart picked up the beat a little bit – I thought it was a bear. I could only see little spots of black movement here and there – but pretty soon, out came a fisher. There were a couple of logs laying on the ground near where he was – one came parallel to me and the other came right up towards me. When the fisher came out, he came up the log that headed right towards me. He got to within about thirty yards from me and he sat right up just like a woodchuck and cocked his head a little. He just stood right up there looking around. He appeared to have a silvery sheen to his fur on his back.

Rich: No doubt with that coloration he was a male. The fur is quite coarse and has a silvery sheen to it generally. It has a beautiful pelt – but the female fisher is usually about half the size of the male and the fur is soft and silky and jet-black. There isn't any gray or silver on her fur at all. That fisher you saw, was he walking on the log or at one side of it?

Ron: He was walking along on the log.

Rich: I kind of like the new fiber optic sights – had a pair mounted on my .280 Remington.

Ron: Does it have a red dot?

Rich: It has two green ones for your rear sight and a red one on the front. Just like when you're using a peep sight, you automatically center that and bring the red one level with the green dots and center it in between. All that kind of happens automatic – you don't have to concentrate on it and best of all, you can track game with this kind of sighting arrangement and keep both eyes open. I asked the gunsmith at Arnold's for a peep sight and he said he could do that for me – then asked if I had ever seen fiber optic sights. I said, "no, I don't know what you are talking about." Then he said, "come on over and I'll show you." A number of turkey hunters I know have had these installed on their guns. So, when he showed it to me, that was all it took and I like it very much.

Ron: It makes it a lot easier to draw?

Rich: I think so – I can't operate with a scope anymore. Like Mike said, there are times when it does help you to see – but if that deer is moving – and he doesn't have to be running – for me it is bad news. For me, it got to be a mistake waiting to happen. I have killed a number of animals while using my scope sight including a bear, caribou and several white tailed deer. For now, and probably the rest of my life, I like open sights. My, this is a beautiful picture of your camp. When do you think the picture was taken?

Ron: This was taken in the early 1950's. Shown in this picture is Howard Parker and the other is his brother. One time Howard hunted back toward camp from being down on Spruce Mountain and got over in the Belden Vly. This is real flat and nondescript land. When in that area, you can't tell one knoll from the other. Well, he got lost in there that time. We went out in the woods after it got dark and tried firing some signals and we could hear him answering with a shot – so far away. So, Dewey Parker and Wayne Dimmick and myself decided we'd go get him. About a third of the way in we let Wayne Dimmick off. He was the oldest of the three of us. Dewey Parker stayed near the outlet of the lake and I went the rest of the way with a lantern and caught up with him and he was tickled to death – but he was all prepared for the night. He had gotten some wood and had a nice fire started and he was ready to hunker down for the night. He was really glad to see me. We shouted back and forth and got back up to the first guy and then back to the next man – and then, back to camp.

Rich: Well, that's a good way to do it. My, camp is a wonderful spot. I love being there – especially at night.

Ron: I stayed over on Spruce one night – I wasn't lost, I just wanted to see what it would be like. I figured if I ever did have a problem, I might not get quite so upset.

Rich: Does everybody utilize four wheelers for getting back into your camp now?

Ron: Yes – it's about three quarters of a mile from where we leave the trucks so in order to get the goods back in, it helps a lot. Just about everybody has one. Some used to come in with horses. The year of the big blow they spent a week cutting trees so they could get the horses back out.

101

Rich: Did they have deep snow, I wonder?

Ron: No, it was just the blow – there didn't any snow come with it. It was quite a warm, southerly storm.

Rich: A few years after that blow of 1950, the usual bunch were hunting out of my Dad's camp at the head of the Oswegatchie River. Ray Williams was one of the most successful still-hunters I have ever known. He was up on one of the ridges not too far from camp and so many trees were down, it was difficult to recognize anything. There were a lot of spruce blown down and also some huge white pine trees. He said he got up on this ridge and was ducking under trees and climbing over them – and suddenly he found this fresh set of bobcat tracks. It appeared to be a big animal, from the size of the sign. He started following the animal and right away he climbed up on this great big white pine log. He said the cat went right to where the branches started on what would have been the top end of the tree. He said he couldn't tell where the cat went from there – so he looked down and discovered he's about twelve feet above the ground. He thought he'd followed him far enough and turned himself around and backtracked off that log. Whew.

Ron: It was horrible – it just leveled the tops of the mountains. It has taken a long time for the woods to get back to anything like normal.

Rich: On our trip this last summer up the Oswegatchie we couldn't help but notice the results of another heavy blow they had in the summertime a few years ago. We could hardly recognize High Falls. On the west side of the river, there wasn't a tree left standing. It looked like a war zone. I discovered after I began to trap, I would pay attention to detail much more than ever before. That is a wonderful hobby.

Ron: Did you ever go to a trapper's convention?

Rich: No, I was always busy with the insurance business and never had the opportunity or time.

Ron: I think Daily was there at one of the meetings - that was quite an experience to see and hear him. He held it in Piseco for several years but then the meeting got too big for the Town so they asked him to take it somewhere else. Yes, John Daily was there. He became famous as a trapper and mentor and of course made it his business – sold supplies, traps and lure. He taught many young and old people how to properly handle a trapline, prepare their pelts for sale and every other aspect of the sport. For many, it was a part-time business.

Rich: When we sold our home in town before moving to the woods, I had so much stuff I decided to sell all my traps. I might better have given them away than try to sell them in an auction. I had a dozen #44 double under spring beaver traps and all types of smaller traps for fox, raccoon, mink, weasel, fisher and bobcat. I always made a drowning set for beaver and otter so had a one-inch piece of angle iron securely wired to the trap chain within about a foot of the trap where it attached to it. Using wire attached to a rock or pole out to deeper water, it was a safe, secure and very humane way of trapping the animal. I never had a beaver pull out or twist off. If he got into the trap, he was done. There was a hole in the angle iron slightly larger than the diameter of the wire I used and as soon as the beaver got into the trap, instinct would cause him to dive for deep water. The iron could go down the wire – but not back up. In no time, the animal is out of its misery and down at the bottom of the river or pond or whatever where he couldn't even be seen. Most people wouldn't recognize anything unusual if they paddled a canoe over the spot.

Ron: I got a bear in 1998. When I hit him, he let out the most bloodcurdling roar – I hit him right behind the front shoulder. He turned around and went back thru the woods from where he had come and went over the top of a little hill and out of sight. I was quite sure I had hit him good. As I got up there, I could see blood on the sides of the little saplings and stuff and he probably ran a good sixty yards. It got part of the heart and part of the lungs also – yet he still ran all that distance.

Rich: It missed the solid shoulder?

Ron: Yes.

Rich: You were hunting deer – so probably you were using a soft point bullet of some sort?

Ron: Yes. I was using 160 grain .30-06.

Rich: A .30-06 – that's a wonderful piece of medicine. That thing kicks, though.

Ron: Yeah, you sight it in and you get a few black and blue on your shoulder. I bought the gun in a garage sale down in Florida. The guy bought the gun brand new, went out west and got hurt apparently while riding horses. I got it for $100.00. It had a variable scope on it and a sling – it was a semi-automatic action. Before that I always hunted with a .30-30 Winchester model 94.

Rich: That caliber has killed a lot of game.

Ron: My Dad hunted with the .30-30 all the time. The first bear he killed he got with a double barrel shotgun.

Rich: My first rifle was a .35 Remington. That's an interesting caliber. I used a 200 grain Core-Lokt bullet made by Remington. That's got a definite limitation as to the range – anything over 100 yards, you're really stretching it. It's much better to be shooting within fifty yards. One of my Dad's friends used a .300 Savage – that turned out to be a great caliber for whitetails and bear. That .30-30 – that would reach out halfway decent. One hundred fifty yards wouldn't be stretching it too much with that unit, would it?

Ron: Right – nice and light and well balanced.

Rich: This .300 Savage had a lever action and open sights of course. Good thing he didn't notch his stock every time he killed a deer or bear as if he did he might not have had enough left to hold the gun together.

Ron: My Dad was a lot that way – he shot a lot of deer in the Adirondacks. He loved it up there – he killed a lot of them in the southern tier also. He used to tell about shooting this deer one

103

time and he went right down just like he'd been hit with a maul. He got up there and set his gun against a tree and he got his hunting knife out and got ready to gut the deer and he noticed the deer was blinking his eyes. Then, all of a sudden, he realized that what he had done was he shot one antler right off and just stunned him. He went back and got his gun and shot him. He said when he shot him the second time, the deer came right up on all fours – but he just dropped right back down. He came just that close to losing it.

Rich: This friend of my Dad's – Dick Armstrong – worked for a local sawmill over near Sempronius. He was woods-wise – to a point. He had just climbed to the top of a hogback ridge – up on top it was only about two feet wide at that spot. He looked down the other side and spotted this deer so he shot it and it dropped right in its tracks. He slid down there and like you said, leaned his gun up against a spruce tree, got out his knife and went to slit the throat. I don't know why he'd want to do that – but he was of the old school. He was straddling the animal probably because it was so steep at that spot. The moment his knife touched his hide, the deer came to and got up with Dick astraddle. He rode him down to the bottom and finally got his knife in him – that could have been a problem too.

Ron: Their hoofs can do about as much damage as their antlers – so I've heard. I'd like to share one final story. Lee and Rena Hollenbeck were friends of the family. She was the cook for the lumber camp in Nobleboro at one time and he was the game provider – the meat provider for the camp. Before he came into the United States, he worked in Canada. He said one of the big things up there were the professional gamblers that would come into the camp. He said if or when they got found out, they very often left the camp. Lee said he woke up one night and the gambler was rummaging around and getting ready and he put his hand up to his mouth and told him, "now, be quiet." He was a professional gambler and he was heading out of there before he got caught. He told him "they're getting suspicious of me." They said they never knew whether he made it back into the town or not. They were about thirty-two miles back in and the wolves were quite numerous. In the camp they had their own hogs and beefers – they raised them right in there and butchered them and everything. The bears would get after the pigs. He used to tell while in Nobleboro of hunting the deer with dogs. He also told of how numerous the partridge were. They put them up in barrels. I've been in the Adirondacks when there would be a lot of partridge – but it has been a long time.

Rich: I really appreciate your taking the time – it's been fun. I am glad we could get acquainted and I thank you for sharing all the wonderful stories.

CHAPTER 10   E. THOMAS CAIN

Rich: I'd like to introduce Tom Cain, a good friend who is also a hunter. He's had a number of experiences in a variety of places and I think what he has to share will be of interest. Well Tom, what would you like to tell us about first?

Tom: Let's talk about the State of Texas. I've had an opportunity to hunt in Texas on two occasions. My first trip was in 1990 in south Texas down below San Antonio on Tom Henderson's ranch. This is a working cattle ranch. Recently I hunted near George Bush's home in Midland, Texas in a little town called Garden City. I went on this particular trip alone and rented a car in Midland and it was about forty miles or so to Garden City where I found the Curry Ranch where I had a chance to hunt for three or four days and I thought I'd tell you about those two tales as they are rather similar. Those trips resulted in the two nicest whitetail bucks I have seen while hunting. I had the one mounted and just the antlers displayed of the other one.

Let's start with the one in San Antonio. In 1990 I flew down there with a friend during our Thanksgiving break from work at the college and took about six days for the trip. We made arrangements with a family from Kerrville, Texas to meet them at the San Antonio airport. They took us in a Jeep down to Tom Henderson's ranch that he called the Unimas Ranch in LaSalle County. This is a part of Texas that is known pretty much for its deer quality. We didn't realize when we first got there just how many deer there could possibly be on ten thousand acres and frankly, I have never seen anything like it – before or since. We drove for a very long time, it seemed, and finally got off the paved road onto a dirt road. We finally came to some locked gates and then came into a marvelous parkland-like compound of buildings – barns, stables and workshops. Then he drove us around to a ranch house which turned out to be our very own for three or four days and he said, "if you want to go hunting this afternoon, I'll come and get you in about an hour – that'll give you time to get your things unpacked and we can go – or if you're too tired and don't want to be bothered, we can go in the morning." Of course, we wanted to go this afternoon. He was back there in an hour and we stepped out on a little porch as he was parking his Jeep and waiting for us. Probably the largest buck I've ever seen on four feet moving proceeded to jump over the fence and he ran across this compound where we were to stay and he cleared the fence on the other side. I'm sure he was a twelve or fourteen point buck with a huge set of antlers. We were all excited and wanted to see if we could go find him. He said, "we can't go for that one – he's the ranch mascot – this particular buck is off limits."

There are a large number of closed ranches in Texas but this was a working cattle ranch. This was not a high fenced operation at all. It had not been hunted for several years, we were told. The family that owned it previously had sold it to Tom Henderson who had made his personal fortune in the plastics fabrication business. At the time, he was on sight with the ranch foreman. They took their meals with us at the cookhouse where we ate along with two or three other fellows who were there in attendance and preparing for future hunts. These were employees of the people who met us at the airport. There were two other hunters from Virginia that were scheduled to arrive within the next few days. Anyway, we went out that afternoon. The hunting in Texas is done for the most part from stands. You sit and wait for a buck to come your way. My partner and I were both put into stands at a spot where two sendoros crossed. A sendoro was a clearing in the cactus and trees and sometimes they would extend for literally miles and crossed themselves in all directions. The sendoros allow for cattle to be herded and also allows you to look for deer. You can see a deer a half-mile away sometimes.

It's pretty flat country. It does tend to sweep and gradually rise or decline in all directions depending upon the nature of the earth.

Tony, the guide, told me I ought to get up into this elevated blind and open up the shutters. They kept them closed when the blind was not in use to keep the birds out - particularly, the owls. After telling me he would come back and get me at dark, he left. So, I'm fiddling with the shutters – they swung inside and they each had little hooks that kept them open. I was working on probably my second or third shutter. There were six or eight on this stand. I just happened to look down at the ground and here was a gorgeous ten-point buck looking up at me. No doubt he was wondering what in the world was going on up there in this little building. He was about fifteen feet from where I was and he saw me at about the same time I saw him and he left – he was gone in a big hurry. I got all the shutters fastened and sat there and watched the deer until dark as Tony said I would be able to. There were Russian boars as well – and javelina. I lost track of how many I saw, but there must have been close to a hundred deer.

Those Russian boars I saw were big black critters and some of them had some white spots on them. We were told we could shoot those if we wanted to and the javelinas as well. I didn't want to shoot anything. I just wanted to see what I could see that first afternoon and get a sense of what was around. Tony came back to pick me up. Monty, my partner, didn't shoot anything either but he saw some deer. He didn't see any of the boars but he did see some javelinas. They are little pig-like creatures. They are throughout the southwest and weigh probably thirty-five or forty pounds at most. They generally travel in groups of up to a dozen and root around in the ground like little pigs. The Russian boars on the other hand are big – I ended up shooting one and I would estimate that he weighed around three hundred pounds. He was a very large boar. It was a treat to have the little ranch house all to ourselves. When you go on these trips you never know where they are going to put you or how many other guys there are going to be in there, snoring away. The food was much less a consideration for me but it was very, very good.

The next morning Tony met us again after we had our breakfast and when we climbed into his Jeep it was still dark. We were going to ride around the ranch and see what we could find that morning. We had drawn straws to determine who would take the first shot that morning and I had gotten the longest straw so it would be my turn to shoot if we saw a buck we might actually want to shoot. We hadn't been out there more than an hour and we came onto this very nice deer. The only one I had ever seen that was any nicer was the one that ran across the lawn. We drove beyond the deer and I eased out of the passenger side and then Tony parked the Jeep out of sight of the deer. We eased our way back and the deer was still there. After awhile, it did become time to shoot. I was using a .30-06 that had the old Mauser action with the kind of safety that swings around the end of the bolt towards the end of the action – the old fashioned kind. The deer got within shooting distance, I would say - well under two hundred yards. That safety got away from me and it clicked – and of course, the deer was gone - just like that.

Rich: Was it a military rifle?

Tom: I think it was an old Winchester. We hunted the rest of the day and saw a lot of deer but nothing we wanted to shoot at. During the three or four days we were on that ranch I saw two hundred bucks. I couldn't begin to tell you how many does I saw. They do try to keep the does in balance with the bucks. Probably I saw about four hundred deer total. It was not unusual to see a group of five or six – eight or nine or ten-point bucks all together. I said to Tony late in the day, "how about if you take me back over where I saw that big buck and scared him. You drop me off there and then come back and get me at dark. I'll see if I can't find him – see if I can't have another chance at him." He consented to do that, and that's kind of nice when you're on one of these so-called guided trips to get off on your own. I appreciated that. They didn't all let you do that, but he did. So he dropped me off and then he took Monty to another spot overlooking some sendoros. Tony told me about one of those elevated blinds in that area and I was able to find it – and climbed up in. There weren't any shutters on this one – it was wide open – not nearly as elaborate as the one I was in the day before.

I hadn't been up in that blind ten minutes when I spotted what I was certain was that same buck. He got right out in the middle of a sendoro and began to move right up towards where I was sitting. When I first saw him, he was several hundred yards away. I got myself in position and took the safe off well in advance of his arrival – this time he didn't hear me. He came to within about a hundred yards and I shot him. I looked down another sendoro which came in at side angles to the one where the deer lay, and here came this huge Russian boar, just as black as coal. I shot him too. I looked down beyond where the deer lay and probably about four hundred fifty to five hundred yards came a coyote. I shot at him – but missed. I looked down another sendoro and here came eight or ten of these javelinas and I shot one of those. So then I thought I'd better check to see about all the havoc that I had created. Everything was dead on its feet after the shot so there was no chance it would crawl off in to the woods. Tony heard all the shooting so he came with the Jeep. We loaded up the deer first and then the big old boar and then the javelina and then we went and got Monty and went back and had supper. The main reason I told this story is that you don't often get a second chance on a buck. A similar thing happened on the hunt in Midland, Texas.

From here I flew into Midland, Texas. When I went to get my baggage, my rifle didn't come thru on the conveyor belt –which is something that happened once before on one of these trips. I had my rifle end up in Berne, Switzerland one time coming back from an African safari. Fortunately, on that trip it happened on the way home and not on the way over. In that deal, we ended up with about a three-week effort on our part to track them down and get them back. Monty was along on that trip also and his rifle was lost as well. They did finally send them to New York and we had to go into Kennedy Airport and get them, which turned out okay – it ended well. We won't bother to talk about how hunters have been demonized and how their rifles seem to get re-routed to strange places.

Anyway, I went to get the rifle, the rifle wasn't there and I went to see some of the folks who were responsible for handling the baggage and they said, "we put that rifle there on the conveyor belt." I described my aluminum case to them and gave them its dimensions – but it was nowhere to be found. Two young chaps that were working there said "well, it had to have been picked up by someone other than yourself before it came to you on the conveyor belt." Well, that was a sad thing to be told. In any event, I reported it to the next level of authority there in the airport. The woman to whom I spoke said, "that's utter nonsense – I know that didn't happen. I know those two boys, who they are, they've been working for the airline (it was United) for less than two months and they frankly had no business telling you that and I am sure they are totally wrong in their assessment of what has taken place here. Your rifle will show up and when it does, we will bring it to your ranch where your hunt is to be held." Well, I thought, "ha, ha – I can well imagine that's going to happen." Anyway, I wasn't left with much choice – I went and got my car and packed up what baggage did come thru – my suitcase and a duffle bag.

That was one of those hunts where you took all your stuff with you except your food. They were going to feed me on this trip. I spent the night in a hotel and then the next morning drove out to the ranch. In the meantime, I had reported it to the police in Midland, Texas and also in Odessa, Texas. The police came to my hotel room and took depositions and they were really very helpful and they were going to check the pawnshops and so forth for me. I regretted losing the scope more than the rifle. It turned out the woman was right and the two boys were wrong. I drove out to the ranch and had quite a time finding it. I saw someone plowing a field quite a bit beyond where I thought I should turn off to go to the ranch. I pulled over and he drove his tractor over and we talked. I commented upon the likelihood of there being some big bucks in the area and he said there were some nice bucks in this country. I said, "I'm looking for the Curry Ranch." He said "well, which one are you looking for?" I said "I'm not sure which one I'm looking for – I'm looking for a fellow by the name of Gary Connor who is an outfitter and he's going to take me deer hunting." Then, he directed me to that ranch – I had driven right past the thing. So, I drove up to his place, parked my rental car and walked up to the little ranch house and I was greeted at the door by the outfitter and he said, "you know, you're over a day late for your hunt." He said "everybody is pretty much gone at this point." Well, I didn't know how that had happened – but a little later, I figured out how I had made the mistake – it was my error. In writing down an initial date on my calendar, I forgot to change it when the date was changed. So I, in my absentminded way, had bought my ticket to conform to the first date. So, I had no rifle and I had lost a good shotgun that was included in my case. I felt worse about the Browning shotgun than I did about the Zeis scope and the Weatherby rifle, which had turned out to be the best shooting rifle I have ever owned. Then I said, "I would hope I could hunt that afternoon and perhaps another day or two." He said I could but I would be in the camp alone. The other guests that were out already in the field were either leaving this afternoon or the next morning. Frankly, it was not a concern of mine that I would be on this ranch by myself. As it turned out, we had a very good time together. It was one of the more pleasant trips I had been on.

I hadn't been there more than two bites into a sandwich when the phone rang and it was the airline. They were coming with the rifle and the shotgun. Well! They asked where they could find the Curry ranch – I'd given them the phone number. Gary told them to drop them off at the general store in Garden City. So after lunch, we went down and picked up my rifle and my shotgun and he took me out to, again, an elevated blind. It was a marvelous spot – you could see forever there too. There weren't any sendoros. West Texas is very different from south Texas. It is not nearly as thick – much more open. It has a lot of mesquite and a lot of quail. By the way, there were a lot of quail in San Antonio too – just by the thousands. Texas is a great state for people who like to hunt – there's no question about it – and fish - it's just a sportsman's paradise. The problem with it is, it's all privately held. You have to pay an access fee – you really don't need a guide. You do need to get on these ranches to be able to take advantage of what's there and in order to do that you need a guide or a lease or to know somebody. He drove me right to this place in his pickup truck, dropped me off, and then parked his truck about two hundred yards away and walked back and he sat with me that afternoon and we watched the deer and the quail. I was never so cold in all my life. You go to Texas and you think it will be this nice balmy opportunity to kind of soak up some sun and get warmed up. This was about the first of December.

I'm retired at this point so could go whenever it was possible on the other end to get there. We watched several nice bucks in the course of the afternoon but they were very long distances away. They were so far away you really couldn't tell a whole lot about them except that they were very respectable deer. Again, this is not a fenced operation – it's free range – there were a lot of cows on this ranch. Tom Henderson's ranch had very few cows by comparison. He had just recently bought it and had taken the cows off. I'm not sure what Tom's intentions were on cattle but this place was a bona fide cattle ranch with cows everywhere. I had to be careful with all these cows around - they were so numerous. The deer were not nearly so plentiful on this ranch – in the course of three days, I might have seen a dozen buck. The next morning, I went out by myself right behind the little ranch house and climbed up in one of the elevated blinds. It was raining and the rain was freezing on the sliding windows on this thing and you couldn't see out of it. At one point during the course of the morning I got a sense there was motion off my left shoulder and I looked out thru this ice and glaze on the window and I saw this big animal running across the pasture around behind me. I finally was able to slide open the window and here was this horse – which shows how much distortion there was – I was certain this was a big buck. It was quite a distance away – it wasn't right under my nose.

Later that afternoon, I am watching a bunch of deer out in front of me and there are probably a dozen of them – they aren't out very far in front of me – they were all does, as I recall. Then I was conscious that in amongst these deer, there's a cat. That's not a deer's face – looking right at me – about a hundred yards away. It turned out to be a big old bobcat that was sneaking up thru the grass trying to catch one of these deer. Now, everybody in camp, and now we're down to the cook and the main guide – agreed there is no way a bobcat is going to kill a deer. Those deer out there aren't very big, by the way – and this bobcat was going to kill one of those deer if he could get his jaws and claws on one. Well, he finally sprang on the deer closest to him and he almost caught it – but he didn't. The deer all went out into the nearby woods and proceeded to stamp the ground with their front feet – as deer do – and this cat never made another appearance. About a half an hour later, some of those deer started to come back and there were probably five or six deer out in front of my blind in a kind of a cleared area. Suddenly, here came another cat from generally the same direction. It came and scared the deer but it didn't make any strenuous effort to catch one but sat down right where the deer had been, and I thought "that's not the same cat." It turned out there was a pair of them – they had been seen in that area before. Of course, when I told this story later on at supper, they wondered why I hadn't shot those but I didn't choose to shoot them and it was fun to see them. It was also fun to see all the quail that ran along the ground and all the deer that were in that area. I wasn't more than two hundred and fifty yards from the ranch house.

The other fellows that were in the camp were a father and son from Houston and they had each killed eight-pointers. Their deer were hanging on the meat pole in camp when I arrived. They were both nice racked deer – not great deer – but they were nice representative white-tailed deer. I couldn't get over how small they were in the bodies. They seemed to be very short in length and light in frame. That was something that I noticed. Stretched out on the meat pole, I don't think they weighed one hundred pounds apiece.

The next morning Gary, the outfitter, said "I appreciate the fact that you hunted all the previous day by yourself - today I'm going to drop you off by the west pasture and you can sit up in the owl blind, if you want to, or you can still-hunt or do whatever you want to do. I'm going to give you this radio and if you need me, you call me." I thought, "this is perfect – this is just what I'd like to do." He dropped me off at the owl blind. It was pitch black. He said, "why don't you start out here and see what you can see – right from here – but be careful when you go up into the owl blind – we call it that for a reason. This place really attracts the owls. They'll swoop down and scare the dickens out of you if you are not aware that they are going to be there. You have your flashlight, radio, rifle and binoculars – your lunch and some water to drink and so on." By now, the weather has warmed up somewhat but it was still chilly and a little wind was blowing. This was a wide-open blind. When I climbed up the ladder I really wasn't sure it wasn't going to fall down in a heap. The blind itself was very rickety which definitely was unlike the other two I had been in – those were really pretty sturdy. The cook and the outfitter had built them by themselves. He said "after you get up in the opening, shine your light around to be sure there isn't an owl." So, I did – and then called down to him and said, "no, there's no owls here." Well, just as I said that, out came the owls – and it was quite unsettling to have some owls flapping in your face – literally. He handed me the radio and then left – I sat down on a five-gallon pail up there in that open, enclosed space – more open than enclosed. I sat there quite a little while – it was a very dark morning. The owls were in the woods off to my right and they hooted back and forth.

I was conscious at some point that out in front of me a fair distance were some forms that hadn't been there before and I started watching them and they were moving. Clearly they were deer – they weren't big enough to be one of those cows that were plentiful. I watched them for some time but it was too dark to tell whether they were bucks or does. This went on for quite awhile - probably the better part of ten minutes. It was starting to become lighter and I could see they were definitely deer but I couldn't see antlers. Then it started to get even lighter and I could see antlers on one of the deer. His body appeared considerably larger than the other deer he was with and his antlers went out beyond his rib cage on each side. I thought, "that's gotta be a pretty nice one – but I didn't want to shoot one that I didn't want to shoot, and I held off on shooting it. I had the rifle up and the safe off – this wasn't buck fever. I've been doing this too long for it to be anything other than what I am telling you. I thought, "if its not a real fine deer, I'd rather not," so I didn't.

He hung around another minute or two and he was just gone – the other deer – and there were five or six of them – were still there. Probably ten minutes went by and he came back. By now, it's bright enough so I could really see the deer – and he was really a nice buck. I had my binoculars with me and made up my mind, "this is the deer I ought to shoot." So I brought the rifle up, got the safe off – and how in the world he knew I was there – but he knew – he really tensed up and looked right at me – and then I shot him. It turned out to be the largest buck they had taken off that ranch in three years. So, there were two bucks that I got two chances on in the same state. Texas has been really good to me. I would recommend it to anybody who likes to see deer and watch them – and be able to see nice bucks and lots of them. I have been to the neighboring state of New Mexico five or six times. I never had a good hunt there in terms of the outcome. In Texas I've been extremely lucky and the outcome is more than I deserve.

I have had some very good times hunting in New Mexico with the Indians but I have never really gotten a good trophy there. I've gotten three or four elk and while hunting in the northeast part of the state this fall got a pretty nice antelope near a little town called Wagon Mound. The coyotes have really decimated the antelope in the west.

The big deer I shot in San Antonio actually had thirteen points. He's a bona fide twelve-pointer – just has an extra fork out on the tip of his antler on one side so he's a seven by six. Both the deer I killed in Texas have twenty inch spreads and they have thirteen points on that first one I was telling you about and ten on the other. Both are nice long, beautifully conformed racks. The deer in Texas are really very pretty deer. The thirteen-pointer was unusually dark – he came across almost black. He had very unusual coloration on him. The ten-pointer from west Texas was the usual gray and very pretty racks on both of them. Both have long tines and long main beams as well – you don't have to

110

squint to see whether or not they are bucks. This was kind of a treat having been raised in New Jersey. I hunted for years down there before I shot a buck – and then, it wasn't very big. All those deer get killed when they are about a year and a half old in New Jersey. If they don't get run over, they get shot. That's much less the case now with the marvelous increase in the deer population and the increased resistance on the part of land owners to let people hunt. The Texans are all hunters. They will let you on if you are willing to pay the price. They really have the goods there and if you are selective in what you shoot and you're not in a big hurry to shoot anything you can really have a good time and see a lot of game. If you're lucky, like I have been, you can come away with an unusually nice deer.

I haven't seen any nicer deer here in New York State. I also hunted for a season in Vermont where I shot a perfectly nice eight-pointer – and there certainly are some magnificent deer here in New York and in New Jersey – but I haven't seen them and I suspect most people don't in the course of a hunting lifetime. The biggest deer I have seen since living here in New York was over in the Virgil area during bow and arrow season. He was a superb buck, no question about it – a ten-point buck. I've seen some mighty deer that other people have shot certainly and if we attend the State Fair in Syracuse, the DEC will have a display of humongous bucks. These deer that I shot in Texas are not as big as those. But they're the biggest ones I have been able to find and get a shot at.

Rich: White-tailed deer – there's just something special about them.

Tom: I couldn't agree with you more. I have had opportunity to hunt in Europe and Africa and throughout Canada and throughout much of the United States and I keep coming back to white-tailed deer. They are what I grew up with and what appears in my back yard right here from time to time – right here in Cortlandville. We had a nice buck in our yard again this fall. They do more to quicken my heart rate than anything else. I've been in the African bush and come onto bull elephants and cheetahs and you name it over there – there's lot's of game but it doesn't excite the way a whitetail does. I'm glad to have been able to look at some of those other critters and to hunt them on their own ground and to recognize the whitetail for what he is. He's a superb animal.

Rich: He's a worthy animal – he really is. He's a trophy – in every respect – something to be proud of and thankful for.

Tom: You bet – they're every man's quarry. That makes them all the more desirable to me – they're available to all of us. They're living right here with us, and what an adapter they are.

Rich: I was really interested to hear about your hunting trip for caribou this past fall. That was up in Quebec, Canada?

Tom: It was. A friend of mine whose name was Fred from New Jersey and I went on this trip. Fred drove – he had a diesel three-quarter ton Chevrolet truck that he had used to go back and forth in the past. This was to be Fred's third trip. Fred's a fellow I have known ever since I was very young. We grew up in New Jersey together – he's a little older than I am. He has been an extremely successful whitetail hunter – he's hunted them all his life in New Jersey. He's done far better than anyone else I have ever known. He has gone to Maine numerous times and always comes back with a nice buck. He invited me to go with him to northern Quebec this past fall and he made all the arrangements for us to go. He came by at the appointed time and spent the night here in Cortland and we left the next morning. We drove for two long days to get to the southernmost tip of the Ungava Peninsula. This was to be a do it yourself Caribou hunt. We drove up to Ottawa and up thru the province and entered into "the park" – which was the last place where you could buy gasoline or diesel and food - and signed in so that in the event we ever got lost or were waylaid or something happened to us or if we broke down – at least they would know we were in the so-called park – which is a huge piece of country.

I simply didn't know how pristine and beautiful Quebec is. I was very impressed with the stands of spruce, which don't get very large, but the lakes and rivers and the mountains and hills – and the lack of habitation there were impressive to me. There simply are very few people in that region. Maybe every fifty miles there would be an Indian dwelling. Martins and grouse run and fly across the road in front of you and after you get up into the area far enough, the ptarmigan are in the road and fly out of your way when you drive past. If you go beyond where the ptarmigan start to show up, you will begin to see caribou. They're in the road or alongside the road or on the hillsides or streaming across the frozen lakes or somewhere if you are in the right spot to see them. We drove up and towards the middle of the first day Fred started to lament the problems with the camp we were going to. He said that was the most awful place he'd ever been in his life. We even had to take our own water as you couldn't drink their water. So, he had a truck full of water and we took all our own food and bedding and towels and pillows and pack boots – we had a truckload of stuff. I didn't know where we were going to put the caribou if we were going to bring any home with us. He said, "we've just got to do something about where we're going." I said "well, where else can we go – we could stay in the truck, I suppose." He said, "you can't do that – it's going to go down below twenty below zero at night – you'd freeze to death in the truck." Well, okay. Who else would put us up? We'd already paid to be put up by these people. All he wanted to do was talk about what an awful place it was. I took that to heart and thought maybe we'd just drive to something else. In addition to that we were going to arrive a couple of days early. We're both retired and on our own. The hook in the whole thing is that they had our licenses. We really had to go to the camp and declare ourselves. So, all of this is being kicked around on this thousand mile journey to the north and finally, I said, "listen Fred, let me go into this Indian camp you have described, which was run by a group of Cree Indians, and I'll see if we can't get a room in one of their cabins." He had said what a nice camp it was – and they cook your food for you and they have running water and heated rooms – separate rooms, of all things. You don't have to sleep in a big old barracks arrangement. So I said, "let me go in there and see." So, he did – we finally got there – drove about two hundred miles off the main road on a gravel road and parked in front of this place.

It looked like it had a lodge and lakes frozen all around it and spruce trees and sleeping cabins were scattered throughout the area. They had a place where they sold diesel fuel, which was something we hadn't anticipated so we brought our own diesel with us in a tank in the back of the truck along with all this other paraphernalia and as luck would have it, the manager of the place and his son were in the office.

I introduced myself and told them a little about our situation and after they had spoken to one another in their native language for a moment or two said, "sure, we'll put you up." Then I thought, "one night isn't going to really be enough – we really need to do this for two nights. We're all the way in here and Fred didn't want to have to try to find accommodations at another place." So, I said, "what about the next night – could you put us up for two nights?" After further back and forth in Cree they said, "yeah, we'll put you up for two nights." I said, "how about meals – could we buy meals in your dining room?" He said, "sure – you can have supper and breakfast and we'll put up a lunch for you – or if you want, you can eat lunch here."

What I really wanted to do before we started to hunt these caribou was to hunt ptarmigan. I bought a bird license at the last stop along the way. So, we were all set up for the two days. Now we had to go down to the other camp and see if we couldn't get our licenses. Actually, we hoped, now that we had two nights at this other place, we might be able to negotiate more nights – but I didn't want to push it the first trip into the office. We drove the sixty-five miles down to this other place. They were every bit as difficult to deal with as Fred had said they would be and we went in together. I did negotiate the licenses – they did consent to hand them over to us. But when I asked if we could please be put into a no smoking cabin with some other hunters that Fred knew who were coming up from Virginia, they said, "absolutely not. The assignments had already been made and they weren't going to rearrange their schedule." We didn't take too kindly to that and when we got back into the truck, we decided we'd stay with the Indians as long as we could and we would forfeit the whole price of this room that we had rented. Once we had crossed the Polaris River we were in an area where we could hunt big game. We could hunt ptarmigan anywhere. The hunting on the west side of the river where the Cree Camp was located was reserved for the citizens of Quebec and Cree Indians. The area east of the river was available for non-resident hunting.

We hunted ptarmigan the rest of the day and saw a few caribou and went back and spent the night at the Cree camp. The next day we shot a few more ptarmigan and saw a few more caribou and then it became time to negotiate some additional nights of lodging with the Indians, which I did. They got to the point where they actually liked us at this camp. I talked to them in French. The people who worked there, especially those who worked in the kitchen were French-speaking people and that really did make a hit with them. Fred is a Frenchman. In fact, he's an Indian – but he has a French name – he's a Mohawk. He's from New Jersey. He's a Mohawk Indian and he has a French surname but he speaks no French and so he got a certain amount of razzing – to be with an English guy who spoke French, and here he is, a Frenchman, and he can't speak the language. That was kind of fun. We went around and around on that the entire trip. Throughout Quebec, they like it if you speak French.

I went back into the office at the camp and asked John, who was the manager, "how about if we just stay with you the rest of the hunt?" "Well," he said, "come back tonight and we'll talk about it some more – that will give me a chance to see what I can learn – we're booked pretty full." So, later I went back there and he said, "I've spoken to the cooks and they said they are willing to have you two guys move in with them – if you don't mind sleeping with our cooks. They'll let you move into their bunk house with them." Well, I thought that was pretty nice. You'd go a long way to find a group that would allow you to do that. They certainly didn't need to do that – they had plenty of money – plenty of other hunters coming in – they didn't need our two cents. The price was extremely reasonable – I can't recall how much it was but we hardly lost any money by staying with the Indians. The food was delicious. They'd hired these French cooks to come up there – being enterprising Indians. They knew their business and staying at that camp was a real fine experience. Then he said, "I think you can stay right in the room where you already are – but if push comes to shove, I'm going to put you in with the cooks, if you're agreeable." I said, "John, I couldn't ask you to do more than that – this is marvelous" – so we ended up staying where we were for the remainder of the hunt. We had a nice room at the end of the corridor – we had wash basins, hot and cold showers – the other place didn't have showers – didn't even have water you could drink. It did have running water – but no hot water. You had to do your own cooking and at twenty below zero you had to cook outside. It was a terrible situation for everyone who stayed there. Fred had tried to get reservations with another group of Cree Indians closer to where we were headed to do our big game hunting but was not able to do that.

The next morning we had made arrangements with Chris, John's son, to take us deep into the woods on a snowmobile and drop us off. In the meantime we had a chance to talk to some people to see about how you get one of these caribou. They all maintained you get them by getting back away from the road and you get back into the woods and sit yourself down and watch for them. They'll come thru if you get in the right place. The Indians will know where to put you. Well, that made good sense. So, we made arrangements to meet with Chris at noon at a particular spot out there, and of course, noon came and went – and there was no Chris. We then decided we'd work our way back to camp. We drove probably thirty-five or forty miles to the west. We had about one hundred fifty miles to go to be where we were going to sleep, at this Cree camp where we had our new arrangements. As we were driving along the highway, we looked out on this lake that was frozen and covered with snow. Here were streams of caribou going across this lake – there must have been hundreds of them. We parked the truck. There was another truck parked next to us. After we had sat there ten or fifteen minutes, Fred said, "you know, I think this is Chris's truck." About that time we looked out on the ice and we could see this snowmobile coming lickity-split across the lake and it was Chris. He pulled up alongside of us. He had told us he was going to take two hunters out in the morning, that he would be finished with them by noon and he would meet us and take us. Well, they hadn't begun to shoot a caribou by noon and he was still with them, which was perfectly understandable. So we chatted with him for a few minutes – he was an awfully nice kid. Fortunately, he was very large and very strong which helps when you got two old men on social security trying to hunt these caribou.

After we had chatted with him a few minutes, Fred said to him, "how about if you take us out there and drop us off on that lake?" I said to Fred before Chris even showed up – I said, "let's walk out there on that lake. It's only about a mile and a half out there at the most. The lake is frozen and the caribou are walking on it – it's got to be safe." Well, apparently, it's not a given that the lake is safe. He talked about hearing about people who fall thru the ice on those lakes. You know you're only going to fall thru once. He said "no - I don't want to take a chance." I didn't say anymore but after Chris had been there awhile, Fred said, "how about taking us out there on that lake and drop us off?" Chris said, "sure – hop on this snowmobile" – so we did – we went lickity-split out there and he dropped us off. He said, "sit right here on this little island." I told Fred, "I'm going to sit right here amongst these spruce trees and I'm going to walk up amongst these little islands." So, I did – I just had the best time I have had in a very long time – sneaking around these little one acre or two acre islands and of course, the lake is totally frozen.

There were caribou tracks everywhere and the wind had blown the snow off the lake. It was very easy walking and extremely pleasant and you were out of the wind because you had all these little islands to break it up. After awhile, here came these caribou right off the main shore right at me – right toward the island I was on at the time. I kind of melted into the trees the best I could – but they saw me and they turned and ran back the way they came. There were quite a few of them – probably eighteen or twenty of them, and one nice bull, I thought, in the bunch. Apparently, I scared them. I anticipated they would come out further in toward the main shoreline toward the road where we were parked. I walked over there and hid myself on a little island and sure enough, I assume it was the same bunch, they came out on the ice right in front of me – but the bull wasn't there. They were all cows and calves. I watched them a couple of minutes – then caught a movement out of my left eye and here came the bull. He was quite a ways behind them. They were out in front of me further down the lake

114

on the ice. I feel certain he saw me but he wanted to catch up with those cows. He jumped about three feet down on the ice off a steep bank and he didn't skid or fall down and he stood right there and threw his head back and I could see these great tops. Those were the ones out in my garage that you took the picture of. I haven't read a whole lot about caribou hunting but what I do know is that you hunt them for their tops. Where the number of inches accrue is in the tops of the antlers as opposed to the shovels and head.

I have a Harris bipod on my rifle and I sat down kind of all in one motion. I slipped down the Harris bipod and tried to get the legs out. I got the one leg out fine but the other leg was frozen. It was about twenty below zero. It had only slightly warmed up during that day but it was still mighty cold. I'm sitting there with one leg out and the other one half out so I propped the short leg against my knee while sitting on the ice and the caribou proceeds now to take off. He was running to try and catch up with those cows. They can move right along. My first shot missed him – it went in front of his nose – I could see it hit the ice and it went up into the spruce trees on beyond him. He's still running at this point and my next two shots both hit him in the lungs. He went down at the second shot and he was dead when I got up to him. It was a very thrilling experience and to do it without a guide – although, Chris did have a hand in getting me into position. He came back about an hour later. I just continued to have a good time walking in amongst these little islands. When Chris came back, he put a rope on the caribou and took me and the caribou to the truck. I said, "now Chris, how about giving us a hand in lifting this thing up into the truck?" – which he did. The animal weighed several hundred pounds and we weren't used to handling anything that heavy.

We both got two. Fred shot one out on the ice. He stayed where Chris dropped him off on that first island – he shot one out there. Each of us had shot one earlier in the day while hunting near the road. We had spotted these herds on our own. The herd I shot the bull out of came right along the edge of the road for a very long way and we parked the truck and we watched them and they paralleled the road and then they came up a hill and then across the road. I said, "that one bull looks like it has nice mass." A lot of them don't have much in the way of mass – they have kind of spindly antlers. The really big bulls, we were told, have lost their antlers by the time they get to their winter range. I did see one bull that didn't have any antlers. He was clearly a large bull – but no antlers. The really big ones had lost their antlers and the lesser bulls still had their antlers on them, if they have them at all. After that experience, we figured we would need to see about two hundred animals to see a mature bull.

Rich: Did you happen to spot any wolves or hear any?

Tom: We didn't hear any or see any but we knew they were there. We were told about the wolves and the Indians are the only ones allowed to shoot them. You've been up there before – did you go on a guided hunt?

Rich: Yes, it was a nice experience. It was a treat to see those little tamarack or larch and they couldn't have been more than eight or nine inches in diameter. They would have over a hundred growth rings. There was permafrost in that area. The ground was continually frozen. The trees grew really slow – but that was what they used for firewood.

Tom: Were you in the tundra or were you in the woods?

115

Rich: Mostly tundra as there was caribou moss covering much of the ground in open areas. There were some groups of these larch trees.

Tom: You could see forever, correct?

Rich: Yes. We were camped near the outlet of Lak Chompadore, pronounced, Chonderay. The outlet ran into the upper portion of the Whale River that eventually found it's way to the Ungava Bay.

Tom: I guess I'm not acquainted with that area. Where did you fly to – was it near Shefferville?

Rich: Yes.

Tom: Do you remember the outfitter's name?

Rich: It was Krim from the Watertown area. He had a couple of young men he had hired as guides from the Canadian east coast. The head guide was someone that I immediately recognized. He was a good friend of the outfitter and his name was Truman Keller. There was something about that man that just looked so familiar and when I met him I said, "I think I have seen you before." He said, "Oh, really, where?" I said, "were you ever up the Oswegatchie River?" He said, "yes – and I think I remember seeing you, too." He had some features that were outstanding. As a matter of fact, in the Second World War, he was assigned to a submarine and their duty was to go down below a Japanese ship and they would open up these gates and the ships would go into a harbor. The submarine would travel right underneath the ship – then they would shut the gate behind them. Sometimes they were to blow up targets and sometimes their orders were to do some reconnaissance but either way, it sounded like pretty dangerous duty to me. He was one rugged individual – but a wonderful guide – loved the out-of-doors, obviously.

Tom: It certainly sounds like his tour of duty was really something. It's great country up in that area – it's practically untouched. The only reason the area where we were hunting was accessible at all was because of the power plants that had been put in up in that region. The power plant employees need to be able to get around to do whatever power plant employees do. So, there's a road system up there. This is well maintained with road scrapers and snowplows and the roads really are in very good condition. The snow is largely at least ten feet deep much of the time. It's vast country – we're talking about hundreds of miles of snow plowing that takes place up there. We may see one of the employees driving along in his pickup truck almost every hour or so. There's even a little village within about forty miles of the camp where we stayed. The employees reside in large condominiums in the little town of Radison. It's a full-grown town in terms of having doctors and lawyers and grocery stores and whatever else you might need.

Rich: To my way of thinking, that country reminded me a good deal of the Adirondacks with the flora – what you'd expect to find in the northern reaches with the caribou moss and the little bushes. You could sit down on the ground just about any place and right within arm's reach there would be all kinds of fruit that you could pick off little short bushes. There were three kinds – blue berries, something that reminded me of a cranberry and then the most interesting of all, the item that the locals called baked apple. It grew on little short bushes about five or six inches tall and the fruit was shaped like a thimble. It was about the size of an average strawberry – and tasted like apple. It was bright pink in color.

Tom: Was it tasty?

Rich: Very much so. The locals picked it by the bushel. They jammed it and made pies – you could have yourself a nice snack just by reaching out and picking this stuff. It gave you something fun to do while waiting for a caribou to come along.

Tom: Did you fish at all?

Rich: Oh, yes. We caught lake trout, brook trout and landlocked salmon.

Tom: Did you see many caribou?

Rich: Not many. Everybody in our party killed one. We had good hunting and a lot of fun fishing – it was a grand experience in the out-of-doors. I should think the experiences of the trip you just told us about that you and Fred shared in the area where you hunted must have been so satisfying. It's great that the two of you old buddies got to go up there and to have all that fun.

Tom: It certainly was.

Rich: Thank you for sharing these stories.

CHAPTER 11   JEFF DE MANN

Rich: I'd like to introduce you to Jeff DeMann, a young friend who happens with his family to attend the same church I do. One Sunday after the service about four months ago Jeff greeted me and just happened to have a photo with him that he wanted me to see – of a real nice buck his bunch had collected on opening day of the hunting season the fall before. His is a story of a different style of "hunting camp" than what we generally think of – yet I believe in rural America, his style of doing it is rather common – especially among relatives and close friends. Jeff, please tell us a little of the background of this camp.

Jeff: I was raised as a child on my Uncle's dairy farm. My Uncle's Dad is an Irish farmer who had never hunted – but the Uncle got interested in hunting and we kids got interested as we were growing up so we became his "hunting group." There are two brothers, my cousin and myself plus a couple of my Uncle's friends. Usually opening day there are about five of us that actually show up. Generally no more than eight of us hunt the area at any given time.

Rich: What do you stay in – do you have a cabin?

Jeff: Fortunately, my Uncle's father has a huge farm and his house is right on the edge of it – so we stay at the farmhouse. Usually all of us travel back and forth to our homes at night as everyone lives in the immediate area. My friends Tim, Doug and I grew up together. We were walking those lands when we were about eight years old – we finally got the big pay off.

Rich: Wonderful. About how many acres are on the farm?

Jeff: On that farm there are about eight hundred – and then there is some additional land in another county that we can hunt. It's similar to the old days – my Uncle's last name is McCloy and the neighbor is Hatfield and they had a farm – and then there is Randolf and Sears and Davis. None of the owners of these farms were particular about who hunted where back then. That made it really nice – not like many other groups today where you must have posted signs to please everybody else. Everyone respected the land ownership and we all knew each other. We kids were all a part of the 4-H group as we were growing up and the dairy farmers were continually helping each other out. This made for a close knit friendship and trust among the owners of the land.

I grew up on my Uncle's farm – he took me in when I was younger. My Uncle had a brother. He said, "listen, you can have the farm – I'm going to be a tool and die maker." This was great as there weren't any battles over the family farm. We may not have owned it, but we did enough work on it. That is what you need to have land. When we were eight and twelve and fourteen and we were unloading hay, we were paying it forward for the use of that land when we got older.

Rich: How did your interest in hunting begin – who taught you how to shoot?

Jeff: It all started with my friends Tim and his brother Doug Murdock and I – our first hunt was for pheasants – using green apples. We chased a lot of deer looking for pheasants. That got us hooked.

Rich: On a stick or pitching them?

Jeff: Pitching them. When we weren't having apple fights we were hunting pheasants. We raised pheasants for 4-H. My Uncle taught us how to hunt – we got our license certification from a guy that lived over the hill, Bert Court. Back then it was a little more informal. The kids in the neighborhood came and the guy showed us gun safety and asked us how our families were doing and made sure we weren't some renegade – that was nice. We started out with .22's and then with bows. It seems archery around here has gotten popular within the past twenty years. When the bow craze came, we were a little bit behind but it wasn't long and we caught up. That was a whole lot of fun. My Uncle was the driving force for all of us.

Rich: What are your cooking arrangements when you all get together for your hunts?

Jeff: Ah – I have to bring the doughnuts in the morning. My Uncle will usually have a hindquarter of venison left over from the previous season so he will have the chili made up beforehand. We have a big eight-quart pot of chili going on the stove. We usually get a deer hanging and before long, we will start in on that. This whole experience is a lot of fun. My Uncle really likes to cook so the rest of us just kind of step out of the way.

Rich: Do you all stay there overnight or go to your own homes, as most of you live in the general area?

Jeff: We usually stay until late at night. We're there for supper after we've been out all day. We just touch base with our wives to make sure they still know who we are. Our group has traveled to Canada for bear and moose hunting. They also had a trip out west that I had to miss as our child was being born. On those times, of course, we just camped right out. We're planning another one of those trips soon. We did get a moose up in Canada, my Uncle and I – the first morning of our hunt – we called one right in. It's a lot of fun – and a lot of work. Have you ever shot a moose?

Rich: No, I never have had a chance to hunt them.

Jeff: Do you know where to shoot them – if you ever get a chance?

Rich: You tell me – I'd probably shoot them in the antler and stun them so they could fall into the lake and drown.

Jeff: Shoot them next to the road! Bringing them out of the bush – that's a lot of hard work. It took us about eight hours.

Rich: That's very similar to bear hunting.

Jeff: Even a bear isn't as big as a moose. My Uncle has killed a couple of bears – they were easy to drag out compared to that moose.

Rich: Were you able to bring home most of the meat from that moose?

Jeff: Yes. We brought it all home. What we did was, we rented land up there. They flew us in for $90.00 round trip for two people. We didn't have to get a guide – we just went on our own. We've done that on every trip we have been on.

Rich: With hunting deer in the southern tier, it probably isn't so important to have a large mast crop of acorns or beech due to the farm crops usually available to the deer. The location of your camp is the area off the McLean Road in the Town of Cortlandville. Is that anywhere near Dick Haines' farm?

Jeff: Right over the hill. Our place was just a little bit north of his property. We had plenty of invitations to hunt with Dick but even my best friend, Tim – we don't hunt together. We just stay in the same general area. We might run into each other sometime during the day, but we prefer to hunt alone.

Rich: What's your favorite method to hunt – do you put on small drives or still-hunt?
Jeff: Our preferred method to hunt whitetails now is to have a light snow or wet leaves, binoculars to our chest and still-hunt thru the woods. When you use binoculars and stalk the woods you'll see more game than you've ever seen in your life.

Rich: I'd appreciate it if you'd take just a little time and explain what you mean by still-hunting – how you conduct yourself in the woods. You're by yourself in the first place – you aren't twenty yards from someone else and you're probably working into the wind – I won't tell your story – but I'd like to hear how you prefer to do it.

Jeff: Our most preferred method is to have three or four people. We'll put one person out ahead – someplace where we know from experience the deer are apt to cross or run. The rest of us will attempt to stalk the woods in that direction – and that's how we got this big buck. We jumped the deer earlier in the morning while doing a small drive in some swampy area and the deer bolted across some open fields and went into some big woods. There were three of us driving – my uncle, David McCloy Sr., my Cousin, David McCloy (we call him Skip) and myself. We decided we'd do our stalking – one guy will go and sit where he thinks he should be and we say, "we'll bring the woods to him." It's a drive – but we go at a very slow pace. We always try to have a tree in front of us – nearby. Or, if we're coming out of an open field towards a woodlot, we first will sit down in the field and carefully scan the woods – and you can't believe the deer just inside the woods that will be looking back at you. Being in the open, and the deer inside the wooded area – they have no problem seeing you under those conditions and generally they just bolt and head out of the area – don't even slow down.

We have observed people walking towards a woodlot completely unaware that there were deer just inside the woods. In approaching a wooded area, we always try to walk in the brush if we can – try to keep ourselves hidden – that's the best thing you can do. Use your binoculars and scan that wooded area ahead of you. Then when you get into the woods, get yourself behind a tree – and scan some more. This seems to work really well when the woods are quiet but I've never seen anybody yet who could pull this off when there's even a little bit of a crunch. Those days you're better off just having a seat or trying to move them around.

One thing we have noticed – people have come into our woods and tried to put on a drive and then might say, "the woods are cleaned out." We have kicked up more deer after others have walked

120

thru our woods once. We have found that the deer many times will just lie there. If you're patient enough and quiet enough and willing to get into their brush – you'll be amazed what you can kick out of there. Our first few years of hunting we were just marchers. We'd march thru the woods, say there were no deer and get disappointed. Now, we go slower – maybe we're older – we just take our time now – and kick up deer. One good thing about this method is that you don't have to take every deer you see. You can pick your deer – why end the hunting season early?

Rich: You're not barking like dogs or making a lot of noise – you're going thru the woods quietly, right – when you're doing this still, quiet hunting?

Jeff: Yes. The only time I'll make noise is if I happen to see other hunters that I don't know – then I'll start barking like a dog. I'm wearing my orange fluorescent. Also, I think it helps to break up the pattern of the orange with a camo. This can be readily seen by other hunters but won't stand out like a beacon to the deer. I know the deer will pick up the beacon but I feel that with the red or orange in a camouflage pattern most deer are not so apt to pick you up with their vision – but some of them are so smart that they will. Probably the movement is what does it.

Rich: What attention do you pay to the direction of the wind – or aren't you too concerned?

Jeff: Definitely – if you can go into the wind and get it on your side, that's what you want to do. I kind of like going crosswind – it gives you a chance – but the deer will smell you. I remember bow hunting one time a deer smelled me over three hundred yards away that I observed.

Rich: Let's hear about this big buck that you just gave me a picture of. How many points did he have?

Jeff: It was entered in the New York State Big Buck Club. All he had was ten points but it scored him 157 and ¾. He only had three quarters of an inch deduction – that's how symmetrical it was. It measured eighteen and three quarters, inside, so that'll give you an idea of the mass. Most of them will measure twenty-three or twenty-four inches. This was an eighteen and three quarters that scored 157 and ¾. This deer was a perfect example of just taking your time thru the woods and a bigger example of a guy going to a place in the woods where he said he was going to be – and staying there – not giving up. Boredom can be a problem. You can fight boredom sometimes when you're sitting – but in this case, it was a trust we had built over a number of years – and that's what got him the deer. He trusted me to come out where I said I would and I trusted him to be there. Starting thru that piece of woods, I only saw one track and thought, "that isn't much." That deer was a good eight hundred yards ahead of me. Using my binoculars, I never saw him. But that deer must have smelled me. When I came out into the edge of the lot, I came right out where that deer did – right to Skip, so he knew I was there. What he did, he came all the way thru a nice big set of woods and thru some brush and he was running with a spike-horn. Skip said he saw the spike-horn and then saw a big-racked deer – and didn't look at the antlers anymore. He waited and when they got to that open field and decided to go they took off at full speed across that field. Skip said, "I thought they were going to walk – but that big guy must have done it before. It looked like they were scanning across the field like we do with our binoculars to see what was on the other side. They went right in the middle of a ten-acre field so if an enemy was on the end, they would be safe. Very smart deer. The spike-horn came out first and then the ten-point followed. He hit the deer four times."

Rich: Where was Skip located when he shot at the deer?

Jeff: He was on the edge of the woods in the middle of the field. He was sitting probably sixty yards away from where the deer hit the edge of the woodlot at that open field. He was using a rifled barrel with a four-power scope. The big deer was about sixty yards from him when he started to shoot – running full tilt. Fortunately he was running away so he could get into the shoulders. That's our policy – we don't stop shooting until the deer is down or the shot might become hazardous. If it's a killing shot, that's nice – we don't like having to chase deer – especially onto someone else's property. During the gun season it can get hazardous. My Uncle taught us, shoot them behind the shoulder – you're going to get the lungs or heart. Other people say shoot them in the head or neck – that's fine, but we know if we shoot them behind that front shoulder we're going to get that deer. We have hunted for twenty-four years and only one deer has gotten away. That was the time one of the hired hands shot a deer in the back leg.

Rich: That is wonderful – boy, that is some record – congratulations. That's not by accident, either, is it?

Jeff: No, it's not. And the one that got away bow hunting, I shot the deer that year and I could see the scar where he pulled the arrow off. We feel pretty good about our record.

Rich: Who was the person that shot this big buck you just told about?

Jeff: My Cousin, David McCloy. My Uncle is his father.

Rich: How old is David?

Jeff: At that time, he was twenty-six. He had gone into the Navy after High School and it was his first year back – he was happy to be home. He was a construction welder in the Navy and he has started with the Union up in Syracuse as a steel worker. We went out hunting and it was about one-thirty in the afternoon, a nice sunny day. There was a little snow on the ground and a perfect setting to get a deer. The place where he was hunting was out in the back lot where we used to unload hay and jump in the pond on our way back thru – it had the best blackberries out there. We had spent a lot of time in the area and knew it pretty well. The best thing about it – it was on un-posted property. No posted signs. There are deer out there if you hunt them.

Rich: It's getting rare to find prime deer hunting territory in the southern tier that isn't posted.

Jeff: The last few years it's getting even tougher. Many of the people around our area now are posting their property. Most of the signs apply to the road hunter – the guy that's not willing to tell you he's hunting on the land. The way the guns are shooting now, you need to know who's out there. Most use rifled barrels and shoot a hollow point sabot slug. You can sight them in at a hundred yards or more but I don't recommend it. Whatever you're using, you have to feel 100% secure with it. Do your bench shooting and practicing before hand and then you'll have a lot better time when the season opens. That's our hunt – we keep the group small, know where each other are and now we're using two way communication to assist with that. Presently, so not to allow hunting to take time away from my kids, I'm pretty apt to take my kids out in the woods early in the season and take along my video camera. They enjoy being out with me and we have a fine time together. After we jump a few deer they begin to ask, "how do we get closer so we can take better pictures?" Then it's the time to introduce them to tree stands or a ground blind. Let them see how well these methods work. I suggest that these are the precautions we need to take in order to get close to deer.

Rich: That's how you interest young people in the sport. It seems these days there is more anti-hunting. Time spent with kids in the woods camping, hiking and as you suggested, hunting with a camera are ways to interest them in the sport later on. But they have to have a way to feel included and be able to participate – now! It's only as fathers or uncles or somebody takes an interest in sons or daughters and introduces the sport that the thing will survive. I for one and a lot of my friends really believe that hunting is a worthy pastime and a wonderful hobby and a thing we look forward to every year. As long as we're able, we will.

Jeff: One thing a number of landowners in our area are involved in now is the Quality Deer Management program – they shoot only bucks with the antlers out beyond the ears. We don't enforce that on our property because we call that "buck management." For the still-hunter, stalking with binoculars and shooting a deer out of its bed has to be an ultimate challenge – a deer's a deer. I've gotten one out of its bed and my Uncle has killed two. You really have to have things go right to do that.

Rich: I have a friend who tells of the time he was still-hunting on his property one fall and managed to spot a deer in its bed. It appeared to be a yearling and he really wasn't interested in shooting it but just wanted to see how close he could actually come. Well, you know, the wind had to be right. He managed to get up within reach with the end of his gun barrel – and thought, "I wonder what would happen if I touched this cute little thing with the end of my barrel." Well, he did and guess what – he said that cute little critter virtually exploded from its bed and the feet went in all directions and fortunately for the hunter, he made his exit away from him – or he may have been injured.

Jeff: I know a couple of guys that can do that trick consistently.

Rich: I managed to kill a five-point an hour and a half into opening day of the season in the southern tier this fall. The weather was such that I could let it age for five days in our barn. We'd never been able to do that before – always had to cut it up within a day or two of when we shot the deer. So far, I like the results. The meat is tender and delicious. The previous fall, I killed a nice big dry doe. That meat was so tough we could hardly chew it. The steaks were better the next day – eating them cold. We finally wound up grinding up the remaining steaks and making burger. Do you let your deer age or try to cut it up right away?

Jeff: I shot a buck on opening day and cut up part of it that night and finished it up the next day. It was a very warm deer season this past fall.

Rich: This was the first time I had ever let a deer age. It never got above 42 degrees in our barn and most of the time it was in the mid thirties. A couple of nights it got down to the high twenties but in the barn I suppose it stayed up around 30 degrees or so.

Jeff: Mine was a scraggly eight-point – weighed one thirty-eight but it's been real good. My Cousin, Skip shot a one hundred sixty pound doe late in the season – that one certainly tasted good.

Rich: On your arrangement can you get near most deer with a tractor to help drag them or at your age, isn't that a problem?

Jeff: Yeah, this year we got one right in the cornfield. Four wheel drive right to it. The deer Skip got was handy because we could get near to it right on the road. Two years ago, I dragged one about a half mile across a wooded area and that was far enough for me. We try to limit our motor vehicle use as much as possible. We will park a pickup on the hill and hunt around it and then come back to it but normally we prefer to walk to our areas where we hunt. If you really want to kill a piece of land, just give people permission to drive. They'll drive four wheelers thru the woods, use them to run down deer and chase the deer right out. If you can't walk, I have no problem. But if you have the ability to walk – do it.

Rich: I never take a vehicle out in my woods to hunt but when one is down and gutted, if I can get within reach with my tractor I surely do use it. I usually take my wife along – stick a couple of boat cushions in the bucket, you know. She's had to give up hunting due to health reasons and this gives her a chance to get in on the deal a little bit and we have fun. In all the excitement we usually forget to take our camera back to the kill site – but we've made up our mind to try and include that in the future. I think we'll make up a list of gear items for the wife to include in future episodes.

Jeff: I have no problem with that. It's just the guys that show up on your trail – thirty years of age, riding their four-wheelers into the deer woods.

Rich: One February, shortly after we moved in to our remote home, one blustery afternoon I was on my way to the barn to get a shovel or something and here comes this guy on a powerful snowmobile. He waved – and then proceeded to rip out thru a hay field, across the hedge and then out into the next hay field. Midway out in the middle of that second field I had observed five deer slowly making their way single file heading towards the big woods after having fed awhile in a standing cornfield. Well, that character on the snowmobile gunned the machine and must have had a great time ripping after those deer. I have an idea that for the animals to have had to expend the energy to avoid that machine while heading for the relative safety of the hardwoods may have been a real strain on their systems. It had been a real hard winter and with the deep snow, the deer already had about all the stress they could stand. Coyotes are a natural predator and I know they take a deer once in awhile as well as clean up the gut piles during the hunting season. They are doing what they must to survive. I find it a stretch to excuse the behavior of that snowmobiler, however. He even had the audacity to wave at me as he tore back on his own trail and headed back down my trail from whence he had come. My land is posted and will remain so.

Jeff: We've noticed a tendency of some after having shot at a deer, if they don't observe the animal falling immediately, they won't even bother to go to the area where the animal was, to see if they have made a hit. They'd rather rip to another area and try another shot. That's not the way I plan to teach and train my kids. Responsible etiquette requires that a hunter carefully check the area where the animal was at the time of being shot at. Deer are too valuable a resource to waste. It's a strange mentality that some seem to have regarding hunting. They just pull up at a flash and try a quick shot – blam at one running thru the brush and don't even have a clear opportunity – it seems spooky. It's best to make sure you have a good shot – a high percentage shot.

Rich: A friend was telling me one time he was hunting out in some State Land. It was near dark and he was heading for the road and his vehicle. Suddenly a car came along, stopped, and some guy got out apparently to unload his shotgun. The way he did it was to shoot all five shells right down into the woods. My friend said he couldn't see the car or the individual but when the gun first went off, he was shocked to realize the guy was shooting right down towards him. It scared him so that he flattened himself right down onto the ground. There was a large blow down there and he dropped right behind it until the barrage was ended. I think if that individual had come toward him, one way or the other, he would have let him know he was there. I admire our present hunter-training program put on by the Conservation Department and sponsored by many of our local gun clubs. When my daughter took her class I attended just to see what this program was all about. I was greatly impressed with the quality of the teaching and the booklet they passed out to everyone in attendance.

Back when I was young and itching to get my first license, I had my Father and his friends to tutor and train me. Believe me, if a young person was to accompany that bunch you needed to be on your best behavior and handle your gun safely. Any violation of safety or etiquette was immediately noted and sternly dealt with. My Dad and I did a lot of competition shooting. At first, we started out with a BB gun. Then I graduated to a .22 rifle. Then we had a lot of fun and further instruction in the safe handling with my Dad's Colt Woodsman in the .22 caliber. Next, we bought a case of clay birds and a thrower and took turns shooting with the 12 gauge. All this resulted in quality time spent together and that was the best part. For me, it was quite a challenge to get so I could outshoot my Dad. It took awhile but I managed to improve.

Well, I guess we have pretty well covered it. I appreciate your interview. It's always a thrill to harvest an unusually big and beautiful deer like the one in the photo that Skip got. I thank you for sharing these interesting stories and for your valuable insight into so many of the fine points of our sport. I wish the best of success to you and your group.

CHAPTER 12   PETER YOUNG

Rich: I don't feel any compilation of hunting stories would be complete without including some about elk hunting. I have a friend who has been involved in elk hunting and also has worked as a guide with an outfitter that his brother works for out west – his name is Peter Young and his brother's name is Brent.

Well, Pete, I appreciate your sharing some stories about elk hunting. Many of us who have enjoyed deer hunting for whitetails for a number of years have nursed a dream of someday going on a guided elk hunt. Your brother must really love the west in order for him to be a dedicated guide. I understand he not only helps the outfitter with elk hunts in the fall but also organizes and leads packing trips for fishermen who want to visit lakes in the high country.

Pete: Due to some back problems he pretty much is confined now to doing ranch hunting where he doesn't have to pack and handle the horses much. A lot of times we would ride in the night sometimes three or four hours. We'd pack in the dark with lights on our heads - that would leave our hands free for tying the knots in the rope – it's rugged.

Rich: It's tough, hard work, isn't it?

Pete: You're right out there with the elements. I first went out west before Brent did. My first trip was to Utah. We have hunted in Utah, Idaho and Montana. I first started hunting elk in the fall of 1978. Since then there has only been five years that I haven't been out. I've been pretty active with the Rocky Mountain Elk Foundation – I've helped run some shows and booked hunts for outfitters and have worked with potential clients. I've really enjoyed working with the people. I met a Christian friend, Chad Shear – he had just started up Central Montana Outfitters. I was working with Christian Bow Hunters at the time and Keith Rush was aware of his outfit and directed me to him and we became really good friends. Chad's Dad was a Baptist minister in Great Falls, Montana. Recently Chad came out east and was working for an outfit in Tennessee doing a film for turkey hunting and he met this nice Baptist girl and he sent me an announcement of his wedding. Well, I booked a flight and went down there – walked into the church and I thought he was going to have a kitten – these are really nice people. He's doing well in his business now.

Rich: I've got a question for you. These people that you guide and play nursemaid to on these wild trips – are these people for the most part apt to be ranchers or other folks that are already horse savvy or are a large percentage of them still greenhorns when it comes to handling horses and being around them – like I would be?

Pete: I would say seventy-five to eighty percent have never ridden a horse. You'll hear them talking to themselves – usually they don't divulge their unfamiliarity with handling horses to a guide. They'll go somewhere that they have horse rides, maybe a week or so before they arrive, just to get toughened in. Just by watching the clients you can tell – like a dog can tell – if you're afraid of them or not. You can tell if they are comfortable or uneasy and then when you get into rough terrain you really have to talk to them and work with them to gain their confidence so there isn't an accident. You try to avoid an accident as much as possible. If you can settle them and gain their trust, they are more apt not to have a conflict. A few clients will have had real experience hunting with outfitters previously. Most will get a hook onto that horn, you know, and they'll start to talk – "whoa, whoa" –

and then they'll lean into the mountain – as on the other side you've got a sheer drop of several hundred feet. The trail may not be over two feet wide. When you lean, it offsets your horse a little. They'll try to overcompensate and then it offsets the horse's balance – so you really have to stay centered.

A lot of times if we're pulling a pack string, we've got the lead. Sometimes the guides will have lighter packs on our horses so they will shift away so they don't hit the mountain. It's almost like they can feel – they don't look back but they'll just scooch over. Same way with the pack animals – they will get away from the rocks – so that means you might have a foot on some of those trails – especially in Idaho – you've got a foot before there's a three hundred foot or more vertical drop. Sometimes the horses are slipping if the trails are iced up – sometimes that's when you have a wreck. Brent was real fortunate to get off his horse when he did. That was in Riggins, Idaho one time. He'd gone back in to set up camp for bear season. Dennis Kirk from Cooperstown was coming to do a video. Well, they had a horse there – a Belgian – they used to use him to pull a wagon for steak dinners and rides at the ranch and he had a large growth on his head. They did all they could for it. We took it back into the mountains to use for bear bait. We walked it back in and shot it. We cut it open and then put logs and brush all over it and then began to watch it from a distance using our binoculars.

Once a bear starts working on the bait he'll have pulled the trees off. He'll gorge himself and go maybe a hundred yards away where there's some cover and water and then he comes back to the bait. We can watch all this from three or four hundred yards away. When it looks right, we put a client down wind within range. Our party killed a couple of nice bears and then I had to leave. They were coming out during the spring runoff in April. Well, Brent had just gotten his feet out of the stirrups. When you get in trouble you at least take your downhill boot out of the stirrup so you can bail to the uphill side. The moment he got both boots out, the horse slipped on its shoes and went downhill over into the rocks and then it got into the Rapid River and went across. This was on the Seven Devils Range. Somehow the horse got up the bank on the other side of that river. Down below there was a bridge but it had washed out. They tied a rope around Brent's waist and he waded in that ice cold water up to his chest and got over to that horse. He got a lead on it and led it back across and they got it back to the ranch. The injuries were too severe so they couldn't help the horse. It was a really great animal – a good dude horse for clients. Reluctantly they had to take it to the auction for dog food.

In my times out west I learned a lot about nature. I discovered how awesome the force of water is while rafting the Teton, Snake and Salmon rivers. While fishing for trout here in the east in our small streams, I had never gotten around that kind of power. Our Creator gives us things for a challenge. A visit to wild country gives us a much needed retreat and rest from the challenges of every day life. I experience His presence in a very strong way in a wilderness setting. I can look at pictures with mountains with snow on them or with clouds around and it's just like they are alive.

Rich: I know how you feel. In the fall or any other time we might happen to be there, we always enjoy soaking in the beauty of our little hills and lakes in the Adirondacks where we hunt. Most of our hills in the north woods aren't very big compared to the mountains out west – but we believe our little hills are very beautiful. We've tried to capture some scenes on our small camera but it doesn't do it justice. Howard Henry made a comment to Martin Knobel this past fall – he said, "I've got three complaints about that hill in back of camp. Number one is that you've made the hill a lot steeper than it used to be. Number two is that Spike Rock watch is a lot further up the hill than it ever

127

used to be – and I can't recall what complaint number three is. Let's see now, with elk hunting, many times you have to travel quite a ways from your camp to where you can hunt. What determines this – mostly the weather?

Pete: We usually try to have a base – we try to stay within an hour of where the animals will be located. There's cooking and of course noise. A number of people come to elk camp and don't give it a thought. They are there for vacation. They're talking and visiting and hooting and hollering and just enjoying themselves. Even so, sometimes we've had elk within fifty yards of camp. Some mornings, with a fresh snow, we might see where elk have traveled real close to camp. During the early part of the season when some hunters move in, many times, the elk move out – and go to higher elevations. At about ten thousand five hundred or so, not many hunters will go that high and the elk seem to know it. Also there's usually a lot of food at that timberline – the grass is protected by the small trees. Even if you're in on an earlier hunt, sometimes the elk aren't where you expect them to be, and you have to travel a lot to locate them. Generally we'd set up base camp at a trailhead and then go to a dropcamp from three to eight miles in from there. Normally there would be some canned goods left at that location. Later on a packer would come in with some perishable foods that I'd cook up for the clients. We'd tell him how long we planned to be there so he would keep us in good shape from that standpoint.

A good outfitter has to be flexible so he can move with the game. Many outfitters are situated in a certain area and if the animals aren't there it's a problem. Many outfitters bring in clients and know full well the elk aren't there. They are coming in full of optimism – there may be signs – the wallows are fairly fresh, the trees are all rubbed. Maybe the elk have been pushed out from a previous hunt. Or perhaps they have moved to where they have found some other feed. So, you just have to go out as far as you can to try to locate them. Sometimes hunters may come into camp with a hard attitude. If things don't shape up about like they expect, they can be so negative that it spoils the hunt for everyone. There's more to an elk hunt than just killing an animal.

Rich: Up in the Adirondacks, you don't have that problem. About everyone that goes up there for just a weekend thinks he probably won't see anything to shoot at anyway. If you do, that's just a bonus – like frosting on the cake. A member of camp, Bob Schoenfeld, has been coming for twenty-nine years and in that period of time, has killed eleven Adirondack bucks. I think that is a super record and so does he.

Pete: You must have remembered Art Rutan, don't you?

Rich: Oh, yes, he was a part of the Knobel camp. For years he hunted out of some other camp. I never did know what happened – whether the camp broke up, members got old or could no longer go – but Art loved to hunt and he had a lot of stories to share. He was working at the Thompson Boat Company. That was where Bob Knobel worked. Bob found out he was a deer hunter and he invited him up to camp one fall. He became part of the regular gang in no time. Martin tells about him along towards the end of his hunting career. He hated to give it up. He had arthritis in his hands so bad he could hardly carry a gun, to say nothing about shoot the thing, you know. He enjoyed being in camp and getting out in the woods too – he just loved it.

128

Pete: Some of the older fellows had a bunch of antlers they had collected and I took them over to Art and he did a really nice job of mounting them. He put them on a plaque and put felt or something on the base – did a really nice job.

Rich: He did the same thing for Bob Schoenfeld on the last buck he killed while hunting up to camp. Well, that's got a lot to do with why this present book was written. Howard Henry and Art were great friends. We all felt pretty bad when Art dropped out of the picture. Howard said, "look, I'm eighty – and when I depart this world, there go all the stories. We really need to preserve a few of these." Did you just guide or did you get a chance to hunt elk yourself?

Pete: When we didn't have clients, I had the run of the place and could hunt. It was great to be able to hunt that private ranch of nine thousand acres. Clients were paying $3,400.00 to hunt that for five days. I was able to hunt there and to spend time with my brother, Brent – which was very special. I went to town – the nearest place was twenty-seven miles. If you didn't catch the mailman at the KOA campground, you had to go twenty-seven miles to mail a letter.

Another time I went to Steamboat – I wanted to see Brent who was working for some construction firm at that time and also wanted to shop for my daughter Kendra's birthday present. I had been to Steamboat previously a few times. This was just after September eleventh. There were a lot of tourists and the town had gotten a lot busier – kind of a hustle – so I did my shopping and then I tried to locate Brent but couldn't find him. So, I left him a message. I had been there about two hours and I wrote, "Brent, I have had about all I can handle – I've got to get back to the mountains." I left without having had supper with him. The next week, he took a week off and we hunted together during the archery season. I had a Superintendent I worked for in the late seventies. He had retired. He had worked the last four years on I-17 – they put in another lane getting ready for the winter Olympics. He came over and hunted with us for three days. He had an injury and also an operation on his knee. His knees were real bad – he used to rodeo a lot – rode bulls mostly. We were hunting some rugged stuff. We had a real nice time. He had never hunted elk with a bow or where they were called in and he got really excited.

Rich: When you hunt elk with a bow, are you watching active trails in the hopes some will come along or are you attempting to call them in or just how do you go about it?

Pete: Well, there are different strategies of hunting elk with archery or a primitive weapon. Elk wallows in the early part of the season are good to watch. It's a lot like a buck whitetail when he makes a scrape to have doe come in. Elk will use a wallow – it could be anywhere that there's a spring or like a swamp. Their body temperature elevates when they are in the rut. It's pretty apt to be warm then so they use that wallow some to cool down. They are urinating in the wallow in a dominant area and then they will go. The cows will come in to check those wallows and they do similar to what a doe deer does when it comes in to check that buck scrape.

About now, the bull is starting to form a herd and he comes back in and checks these areas. When we find a hot wallow, a tree stand within range is good or if you have been in that area long enough to define a good bedding area or feeding areas or a good dominant trail, with patience and a properly positioned tree stand – it can be very effective. This method can be especially effective for those hunters who haven't gotten into the calling. We like to use calling as it's the time of the rut. When the calls first came out we didn't have a lot of trouble as there wasn't that much competition in the woods. When you'd call, a bull would hear that and maybe think another bull was coming in to try to take over his cows. This causes a fight or aggression. They come in to investigate and they're wired – they're mad – they are tearing trees up and tearing the ground up and urinating on themselves and bugling and squealing. I could make a call and hear a bull answer sometimes three quarters of a mile or more away. So then you just go in and get set up downwind and just be careful.

Now that there is a lot more hunting pressure with the bugling, the elk have responded. It's breeding right back in just like anything else – once they are exposed – it feels like it goes right into the genes and they're taught to be less vocal because of the danger. So, lately, using a cow call has been real helpful. A bull may not even respond to a bull call at all but is very apt to come in when you give a cow call. It's much less aggressive than a bull call. With the cow calling, you really have to be on guard because you don't know where that bull's coming from. You're always watching your upwind area because a lot of times they'll come right in silent. All of a sudden, they're just there. Ninety percent of the times you aren't going to get a chance to get set up to get a shot. With the size of the elk you try to get a double lung shot. That's the most lethal and humane – you're less apt to lose the animal.

One time I stuck a five by five bull two days before clients came in. When the bull came in, he was just at about fourteen paces and I had come to a full draw on my knees under the pine boughs and he was coming up thru the high grass in the quakies. When he stopped, he only had a little more ways to go and I had vitals. It seems like they know. He stopped with two or three quakies right in his vital area. Here I am, full drawn and he turns right around and looks right in at me. This is the first bull that I killed with a bow. I'm trying to hold things together and just tickled to be this close to that kind of an animal. After he made me, I started to shake a little and I had to let it down. So, I let it down as slow as I could. A lot of times they'll snap and turn right around on a quarter and they're gone. He just rolled around and started to go back the same way. I redrew and I had to lie down because he was moving out. I caught him in the liver and one lung and he still went a hundred and eighty yards. He ran deep into dark timber. I had my pack and all my gear on and I was pretty excited – it was quite warm. I was dropping this pack off and this jacket and that sweater off – finally, I told myself, "I've got to slow down." One way of doing this was to go back on my trail and see if I could locate all my gear and get it together. This way it'll give the animal time to lie down and die. I got all my stuff gathered and checked again the direction he was moving in and finally found him. I went back to camp and got another wrangler. We only had one spare horse in camp at that time. Everything else was out with other hunters in a different area. We sent someone out to KOA and got out a message for Brent. We got out the hinds and antlers and cape – we left the front quarters. About that time Brent showed up – he had come back in with another horse. We didn't have ropes with us so we couldn't get the front quarters off the ground. It was getting late and we thought it would be okay. In the pines, when you cover it with pine boughs so that the birds and other predators don't get at the meat, the fronts took on a smell of pine. It was mostly burger but you could smell it in the burger so it's important to try to get your game out or try to get it hung and get it aired out and cooled off.

Rich: Do they recommend skinning it – getting the hide off as soon as possible?

Pete: We usually quarter it. That alone helps the heat escape. We leave the hide on primarily for protection of the meat – to keep it clean. Then, when we get back to camp, the hide comes off and we put it in game bags and cover with cheesecloth and if it's warm, we pepper it to keep the flies off. Then, as soon as possible, we get a wrangler to take the meat out the eight or ten miles to the meat

130

packer. The client will write a list of how he wants his meat cut up and sends it right along with the meat to the packing outfit and by the time they get there, it's all cut up and frozen according to their preference.

If I had known you were going to take my picture, I'd have brought my cowboy hat. The packers will even make jerky, salami, pepperoni, sausages – hot or sweet – they really cater to the hunters because sixty or seventy percent of the western state's budget is generated by the hunters – and primarily, non-resident hunters. The various organizations and groups that are supported by hunters have been trying to get the Federal Government to control some of the lands out west. The issue has really gotten heated. Hunters from all over the country go there and pay a high price for a non-resident tag. Montana just went up to $1,000.00 for elk and deer. Iowa is big on deer – their non-resident tag just went up to over $300.00 and they limit non-resident hunting to less than 20% of the licenses available.

Some neighboring states say, "come on, your hunters are coming into our state and our license fees are still in the $100.00 class. Can't we work something out?" Iowa says, "no." Colorado has raised their cow tags up to $430.00 last year, which was the same as they charged for their bull tag. With the open weather, and the raise in fees, the number of non-resident hunters just wasn't there. They had the lowest take since the seventies. They've got a population problem with the herds now. They are considering dropping the cow tags down to $235.00 but they've raised the bull tags up to $470.00   The higher fees is kind of cutting out the blue collar – he's not going to be able to go. The cost of flights and everything else has increased. The government doesn't own the animals. They are capitalizing on that resource and it seems they are depriving people that have just as much right to hunt as the rich fellow.

Rich: That's one beautiful thing about the whitetail – he's every man's quarry. I discovered recently, however, that a buck is a much better eating animal than a doe. I love a rib roast – the flavor. A doe is so fat and tallowy it's much harder to get to that sweet meat. A buck most times has run off the fat and you can get right into his ribs without a concern for any fat – it just isn't there.

With elk hunting, you're calling or maybe setting up near a trail or near a wallow or a feed area or water hole. Still hunting, like you might pussy foot around for a whitetail, in the thick areas where an elk would be bedded – would be impossible for a hunter to get within range of an animal. It might not be possible for a hunter to work thru those areas and get within range of an elk. He would see you or hear you and be gone, at a distance, so you might not even see the animal.

Pete: That's a good point. I've hunted a whitetail buck since I have been twelve and elk for the past twenty years and it's harder to kill a buck deer, one on one, than it is a trophy bull elk. It's hard to beat a buck deer as far as sharpness, awareness and everything. What you said about still-hunting elk is right. They usually bed on a north-facing slope – it's cooler there and by that time, they have begun to put on their winter coat and they like it where it's cool. So, elk will stay in that dark timber. The bulls will generally separate a little from the rest of the herd but the cows are the brains of that outfit. The cows are more alert – the bulls are depending on the cows. If you get into a right area, you can bust thru the thick stuff provided you can crawl up over the downed timber that will be in there. And if you do, you surely will bust animals out of there. There is almost always a movement of the air and their nose and ears are incredible – just like a whitetail. Most likely, all you will do is alarm those animals and the cows and calves will bust out of there – you most likely won't even see the bulls. We seldom will hunt during the mid day – we don't want to push those animals out of their bedding

131

area. If you jump a whitetail buck, he might circle two miles – in the rut, they hang pretty tight. He'll be back to that same general area in a day or so. If you bust elk and push them hard, sometimes they won't stop for five miles. Your chance of locating those elk again in a five to ten-day hunt is fairly limited. Unless you know the area real well – even then there are no guarantees. You can't say, they'll go here or there – they go where they want to. Another thing, if you go to hunt dark timber – it's a lot harder to count the points to make certain you have a shootable bull. We just like to stay away during mid-day.

Rich: When Jani and I had that vacation out in Idaho and got to fish with our guide for those huge rainbow trout – he had a slightly different approach to elk hunting. He always hunted alone. He'd come onto some elk part way up one of those steep mountains and start them running around the mountain on a main trail. He was quite familiar with the area. He'd shout and yell and run right after them and then after he had gotten them started good, would cut out and cross over the top of the mountain. Sometimes he would barely make it back to the trail on the other side before that troop would come along – still running. They'd go right by him – with the bull bringing up the rear in most cases. I thought that was quite creative a method – it worked for him.

Pete: We've done something similar to that – on horses. We would put the clients out on watch and then start something moving to them but in the greater percent of the time, you're only going to hurt yourself by running the game right out of the area. Being an outfitter, you've only got a certain area that you can hunt. You want to maintain as many animals in that area as you can – you've got other clients coming in – and if you go in there and drive them out, well, you're not going to have hunting for awhile.

The natives in the area, lots of times, would wait to fill their freezer with the winter's supply of meat until late in the season. Then the elk would be heading out of the deep snow in the high country. They'd have their radios and be driving their pickups and just go along the roads and find out where the elk were moving and simply cut them off. It's legal. A great percent of them won't even shoot bulls. They'll shoot a cow or even calves – because they're the most tender. It's always a possibility that a bull would be strong. They don't care for antlers – they've got their antlers. The antlers are on the barn and ranch buildings – they're doing it for the eating.

I've been around some bad outfitters and you hear a lot of stories but generally a good outfitter is very naturally related and in touch with the animals and the preservation of the animals. They aren't going to step on their nose to spite their face. If they do something out of line, then they got the forester and the wardens always checking their camp. Checking their fires, checking their outhouses, coming in and checking tags. Also, they've got a responsibility to their license. If you get busted, you can lose your privilege to guide. You're done – plus big fines. So, the good ones, they keep it pretty clean.

We have to talk with the clients – if there's a good bull in with some cows – we have to hold them back because if you hit a cow, the first thing we do when we get out is we got to call the game warden to come in there and deal with it. There may be a fine or they may rule it a mistake. Generally there is always a ticket issued because it was an illegally taken animal. You as a guide have the responsibility to preserve things. We always have clients that want to get game. They're here for a short while. There's money shown, quite often. A few seem to take the attitude, what do they care? If they break the law, it doesn't matter to them. In most cases, they won't be back again. We're here from year to year and we have to deal with the forest service and game wardens. In some of the National Forest areas, they regulate numbers in there by heartbeat. If there's two dogs in camp, that's one heartbeat. Each horse counts for one. They even insist the hay we bring in to feed the horses be certified. This controls the weeds coming in to an area and it prevents the spread of undesirable weeds. You've got to have proper paper work – if they come in and check you and you don't have certified hay, you're in trouble. It's very easy for a growth to begin that they can't control. They've come a long ways.

Rich: It's getting to be really sticky, isn't it?

Pete: It's a good thing. It's just like trying to clean up pollution around here – trying to clean up the environment. All some companies seem to be able to see is the money. They can't see what their pollution has done to things. I'm glad to see we have begun to make some progress so that our children will have something to enjoy in the out-of-doors. If you tie a horse to a tree – you can't tie a line on a tree. You need a special wrap like a pad – sometimes we use a double inner tube. We wrap that around a tree so it doesn't wear the bark off the tree. I've been in areas where people have come in and tied their horses up with a rope. After being in an area for a few days, the tree is girdled – the bark is worn right off – and that kills the tree. There are a lot of regulations – it's a good thing. It's easy to do things that are not right and a lot of people are not aware of it or they don't take that into consideration. If they are not really in to nature – have a respect for that – some of the people are pretty bad – they just leave their trash. I really got a good experience with that when I floated with those fellows in Idaho on the Snake and the Salmon Rivers. The guides were Native Americans. Anything you took in, you brought out. On one of the trips, one of the clients smoked cigarettes. After he had his smoke, he put it out and had a plastic bag right in his pocket – he put the filter tip right into that bag – so there was no track for the environment.

There's nothing that makes you want to cry more - than to go ten or fifteen or twenty miles back into the wilderness and find somebody's candy wrapper, or a pack of cigarettes. It's good they're doing that. It makes me mad when I'm driving behind somebody and they toss their empty papers from McDonald's or Burger King – right out the window and it ends up on the shoulder – waiting for somebody to come along and pick it up. The other day right where I live along Dillon Road – I picked up a whole trash bag full of cans and bottles and trash – a cup from one fast food and some other trash from some pizza place. I come home from working in the city or on the road someplace – I don't want to have to come home to something that looks like a dump. I don't say anything – I just pick it up.

Rich: Right here on Long Road, they toss out their used Christmas trees, bags of trash and left over pumpkins from Halloween – it's there for the rest of us to look at every time we drive by.

Pete: You know, the deer really like the pumpkins. They take the seeds first – then they eat the meat of the item. I put mine out on purpose in a nearby field right back of my house – I take a big knife and cut them in half to make it easier for them to get into them. The skin is really tough, you know. Years when we used to raise pumpkins, the ones we'd have left over in the field – I'd take a big knife and split them open to make it easier for the deer and turkeys to utilize them. Then in the spring I go back and pick up the skins as it takes quite awhile for them to break down. I've had a lot of fun watching them – our winters sometimes are tough on them and they need all the help they can get. I throw out an apple once in a while and you know what – they go after that first. They can smell an apple thru about three feet of snow.

133

Rich: Well, when we have a good wild apple crop around home the squirrels, partridge, turkeys and deer – the whole works really utilize them, don't they? There generally aren't any apples at all in the Adirondack area, at least in areas where we have been hunting. I have seen some wild apples along the roadside in certain areas of the north woods but it's nothing like what we have available for the wild game here around home. I always enjoy seeing a full head mount of a big bull elk – they really are beautiful and impressive. We saw one recently, didn't we – that was a nice mount. I never saw one before that was so dark in the mane area.

Pete: They are certainly majestic animals. They're strong – their will to live is incredible. I'm in awe of the amount of punishment they can take and keep going. That's why it's critical for shot placement – especially with archery and also with a rifle. Some guys think because they have big caliber guns, and all they got is a hindquarter to shoot at, they're going to kill the elk. Well, if they don't break a bone – I've tracked them for three days when they've been shot in the butt. Then you can just see them starting to go downhill – but they just keep on trying to heal up – they start feeding and doing all they can to gain strength. Usually we have been lucky in recovering wounded animals and have been able to save them. One time Brent and I were on the Peterson Ranch – he was a commercial airlines pilot and his wife and his son ran the outfitting business. I would say his money probably subsidized the business. Sometimes he'd get snowed out of his north camp and when that would happen, we'd go up in there, on the front side of it on our line.

We'd get up at three-thirty in the morning, wrangle our horses and get them saddled. Get the fires started in the client's tents, and then I'd go and help the cook. She'd usually be working getting the fires going and I'd finish starting the fires and lighting the lamps. She'd start cooking the breakfast and I'd go and get the clients up. They'd stay in bed, you know, until the fires burned down and their tent was nice and warm. Get them breakfast, make a lunch, and head out. Three hours on a horse to the bottom of the sheep trail. The grade in that area is probably eight or ten percent. It's just a narrow trail and there are a lot of rocks up there – up towards the top. You're climbing in the rocks, iced over rocks and snow. Clients are getting nervous, horses are going down, clients are jumping off the horses. We never had any real trouble the year I was there. We had two clients from Reno, Nevada. One was a fireman – he was on search and rescue and the other fellow worked for the power company. He had experienced an accident on a motorcycle – he was kind of a wild bird. These are two I especially remember having shared with them before we left camp the first day – I always shared and had prayer.

We usually have two fellows on that type of a hunt and we will have them decide beforehand who gets the first shot – either by a flip of a coin or a verbal agreement between themselves so we don't have to get into the middle of that. Brent would take us up there and then he was going to bring the horses back. Then I was going to go on thru the timberline and back to camp. We were up there first light and there was this big basin – probably about two miles in size. It was just a big steep bowl with nothing in it. There were some small trees on that south face, where we were looking into it. We got up in there and the wind was blowing and it was cold. We were lying in about two feet of snow and began to glass the area and spotted a dominant trail coming out of that timber. It wasn't long and we saw a bull. The bull had gotten up and came out of the timber. We're probably seven hundred yards from the animal and I'm lying there with the glasses and here's this crazy one lying right next to me. His name was Todd – I heard this click. I said, "what are you doing?" He says, "I can take him – I can take him." We've probably got forty mile an hour winds coming up out of the bottom – thermals, you know. He thinks he can take him. At that range I can't count all the points on the bull. He's all excited and he's pumped up and I said "put that safe back on – you aren't taking that animal from here." He kept trying to get me to let him shoot. Here he's lying right next to me and the muzzle of the rifle isn't over twenty inches from my ear. I said, "just relax – we'll start a stalk up – put the safe back on." So, I got thru that. Then I figured, they'd had their coin toss and he was going to take the first shot. I crawled up and talked to Brent. He said, "I want you to drop right down off the face – get into the timber and swing right back up around and get in where you can get a decent shot at around three hundred yards or so." So, we dropped down, came back up thru and I kept an eye on him – he was going to let me know if the bull went into the timber. We got up there and it was a little over two hundred and fifty yards. Todd says, "piece of cake – I've got a 7 mag." I fixed a good rest for him and had him lie right down. I told him "now, take your time – compensate for that wind coming out of the bottom. You're going to have to pull south on that bull. Powwwww – the bull never moved. Powwwww. "What are you doing – where are you holding it?" He says, "I'm holding it on his shoulders." I said, "you ought to be holding it on his tail – and about a foot high." The third shot, the bull finally turned and it looked like the hindquarters were hit. I said "you ass-ended him." I was really mad then, because, he was supposed to be such a great shot, you know. So I says, "well, come on." He had trouble with that one leg. The grade we were on was all iced up and quite steep. Even the ice was iced over slippery – the rocks were slippery.

Well, I was pumped up so I started down there and when I got into the timber there were rocks all iced up as big as this room so I was jumping from rock to rock just trying to get there as quickly as I could. I got down there and Brent said "he's still in there – just moving." So, I wasn't even sure if he was even hit. Then I came to a place where it really was steep – Brent was pointing to a place ahead where apparently the bull had gone – into the dark timber. I was looking and trying to find him – and finally I saw a dark mane and the bull was coming right towards us at probably about a hundred yards – just coming right thru there. I said to my client, "come on, come on – there's this window – you got to get up here so you can shoot." He's down behind me quite a ways at this point, having trouble. He's struggling to get up there – with his injuries – he's having quite a time. Finally, he got up where I wanted him to be. I said "do you see that window – that's where he is coming thru – get ready. You see that window?" "Yeah, I see it." About that time the bull stepped into that window and – bang – the bull went down. I said, "good shot." The client is still lying there and he's still looking at the animal thru his scope. About then Todd said "he's getting up." I said, "you want to get right behind that tree there – he's coming right to us." Actually, the elk was dead on his feet but with the momentum, he rolled once and because it was so steep he came flying down thru there and he hit a tree about twenty feet from us and that stopped him – otherwise, he would have gone down into that basin and we'd really would have had some time getting the horses down there to pack him out.

Brent came down to help with the care of the animal – we told the other client to go up to the ridgeline and just sit there. We told him it probably would take about two hours to get the elk ready to pack. On a previous hunt, Brent had two clients up there in the same general area hunting – both from Lake Tahoe. Brent had this one client he was guiding at the time – two bulls got up and were running away from them at about forty yards. Brent is lying there with his glasses trying to see which one is the better bull to make certain it's legal to shoot. Well, the client gets excited – he's got a .338 mag – he pulls up right by Brent's ear and shoots and ass-ends that big bull. Thought it would kill him. Well, I'll tell you, camp was quiet that night. Brent about lost his hearing on that shot – and then he hit him in the hindquarters.

This bull that Todd just killed was the same bull that was wounded in the hindquarters the previous week on that other hunt – so we were glad we got that bull. After we got that animal butchered, I went to pick up Wade and he wasn't where I had told him to stay. So, here I am – right out on the Continental Divide – looking right into Wyoming. He's down into another outfitter's area and found animals. It's a good thing there wasn't a bull there in that bunch – because he was going to shoot. I had talked to him and told him to get in among the rocks and get out of the wind and to wait for me and just be patient. He was kind of disappointed – he wanted to kill something. I had a little chat with him – not too bad – so we headed south on the timberline. We got pretty close to another basin where I knew there were elk holed up.

It was noon and we were going to stop and have a sandwich. I could only see the top part of that basin but not the good part where the smaller trees and the feed and the protection was – where they'd be lying. I tried to get him to move with me. He says, "no, I'm going to have my lunch and I like it right here." I said, "okay, stay right here – I'm going to slide down below a ways and see what I can see." I had belly crawled down thru there seventy-five or a hundred yards. There were cows and calves lying right there on the edge of the timberline. They're just lying around so I belly crawled back up and got him and got him down in there.

The wind was swirling and wasn't really pronounced. I said, "we've got to be really patient because if this wind changes we aren't going to get a look at where those bulls are and the bulls are tucked back in here somewhere. We moved around some but basically stayed away. There was one bull in the bunch we saw that was a legal bull – he was a four by four. There were some snag bulls and cows and calves – I said, "the third animal coming thru that window will be a shootable bull – if you want, shoot him." He had his Grandfather's pre sixty-four Winchester .30-06 using a hundred and twenty grain silvertip. It was his tenth anniversary and he'd been on three previous elk hunts and never killed an elk. The bull came thru and I said, "there he is." About that time we had a forty-five or fifty mile an hour burst come up thru there with snow and wind. It blew his gun right up – that bull went thru his window and he didn't even get a shot. I said "don't worry about it – don't get excited – we'll get a look at him again."

About that time, I caught something over in the corner of my eye. Here comes a coyote – about fifteen yards – beautiful winter-haired coyote. We let those animals move out ahead of us. We slid down thru there. We had elk very close to us several times – cows and calves and smaller bulls. I said, "I know there are some good bulls in here – we just got to be patient." He's starting to get a little antsy – trying to push me to get where the big bulls are. I kept trying to tell him, "you gotta realize the situation here – it can be win or lose real easy without our making a mistake – if the wind changes and once one of those cows gets our wind, she's going to bark and everything's over." So, we worked our way down thru behind the group of elk that were headed for the basin and I thought that was good. We came to a little neck and I checked it out – came back and told him, "the bulls aren't there."

Then we entered an area of down timber and dark timber and were crawling over and under blowdowns and stuff. Out on the edge of this little neck where it came thru was a downed tree and we both just sat right down on it. I said "right there is a legal bull – a good bull." Here's a bull right down in this kind of a ravine and he's feeding in some grass. He's sort of corner turned to us – he's a big, beautiful five by five. I said, "take your time – it's about a sixty-five yard shot – pull it right behind his front shoulder. Just breathe – and squeeze it." Bang – and the bull went right down. It was a good shot and I was excited for him. In the area where the bull went down, there were a number of trees and

136

rocks and pretty soon, all I could see was tines coming up. I said, "he's up – we gotta get up there – we got to cut him off." I started sprinting up there and I blew a calf muscle in my leg. It was just like someone threw a brick at me. It brought me right down. I said "you gotta get up there."

So, he got up there – and then looked back at me and said, "which one do I shoot – which one do I shoot?" Well, I can't see anything as there are pines up there. When he got up there, four big bulls stood side by side at forty yards – he didn't know which one he had shot at. Finally, he figures this must be the right bull and pulls down on the head at about twenty yards. He goes, bang, bang – a broadside shot – so I hobble up and I'm looking up there and here comes another big bull in front of him – one of those four – he comes around the pines and I say, "there he is – there he is – shoot him!" It's really a nice brown animal with grayish antlers with white tips – a good five by five. He says "no, he's over here." I look over "here" and there he is – down. He hit that bull once – the first shot. He was so excited – all he could see was those antlers – he missed those first two shots at twenty yards. I had to cape it – he wanted it mounted – quartered it – and while I was doing all the skinning and stuff, he was looking for a crutch for me. I pulled the inside tenderloins and the hinds – the top tenderloins – and he wouldn't leave those antlers there. I didn't have a saw and I already had a cape. So, it was the skull and the antlers, a load of forty-five to fifty pounds, anyway. I figured I had sixty to seventy pounds of meat in my pack – his pack was full of meat.

I says, "we got to get going – we must hit this certain point while we still have daylight which should put us within about an hour of camp and then we'll have to climb another divide." This long basin we were in was a big wash – when we were going down thru there, we were climbing off rocks eight feet high, with snow and ice. The "cane" he found me had a kind of swoop on the end of it and it worked pretty well. We had to be careful that we didn't break a leg going down thru there – and it was getting dark. We just kept going and going – finally I hit that point – within five hundred yards of where I could pick up the light from that divide. Well, it was dark and I couldn't read it. We ended up heading for Muddy Park.

At this time, here he is – he's a search and rescue and he's got nervous. It was cold – with all our exercise, I didn't feel there was any hypothermia setting in – he wanted to stay – he was scared. I said, "there isn't any need to – I know where we're headed." I had to sit down and let him relax and I rested and I got his confidence back up to where we could continue. We finally got down into Muddy Park – there was a camp down there and we wanted some water. All they had to offer was beer – or drink from the creek. I decided I didn't want to take a chance on giardia – I said, "thanks." So, we headed out and got back into camp at twelve-thirty that night.

The next morning – I had iced my leg all night with snow – put it in plastic bags and put them inside my sleeping bag and held them right over my leg to help control the swelling. When I got back to camp, my hide had come right over my boot with the swelling, you know. Six o'clock the next morning I was right up and wanted to take out some of the other guests. There was an artist in camp and I wanted to help him get some action. I brought the horses and away we went. We had another storm before we left during the night. The trail was tough – snowed in – we had a young mare and she kept going down. We had some time. We got out thru there – he was keeping tight and started going down thru the rocks – I wanted to go a little higher in the basin. I wasn't going to argue with him. We came to this point and he says, "I doubt we can get out thru there – we got to go back out" – so I backed out. He got off his horse and led it back. We were going to drop down thru another area but it was much steeper. We thought it would be better at this point, to head toward the timber.

137

We brought his horse around and he slipped on the ice and his hinds went down and those horses were all roped together and the next horse went down and that pulled this next horse down and then the last one – she was a mare – a big old pack horse – she went down. Here I am, sitting on my horse. I could see his orange vest in the snow and stuff snapping and cracking and he's sliding down this grade – must have gone about seventy-five yards before he could stop. All the time I'm thinking, "I don't have a gun with me to shoot a horse – how am I going to pack him out?" When I got down there, we both sat on a rock for about ten minutes looking at each other and looking at those horses and just thanking the Lord that everybody was okay. We re-did the horses and cobbled everything up the best we could with bailer twine. We got over and got the elk packed and headed up and ran right into seventy-five to eighty mile an hour winds. I was bringing up the tail and the rear horse had the hinds on it. The force of that wind was blowing that horse eight to ten yards out of line – that horse plus the weight of the hindquarters of that elk. The temperature was incredible – I'm beginning to worry, "we're going to freeze up here."

About this time, his hat goes off. We're in about three feet of snow. I says, "I'll go get your hat." He says, "no, another bound or two and it'll be in Wyoming – don't do it." Sure enough, the next time it hit, it bounded up and sailed right off that face – right over into Wyoming. We finally got up thru there and got into some rocks – we're both cold by this time. We had drover jackets – it's a good thing I had my fleece lined drover jacket on. We're right into a critical situation – with seventy-five to eighty mile an hour thermals coming right out of the bottom – right out of the Continental Divide – looking right into Wyoming. We get into the rocks and get out of the wind for awhile and kind of regrouped. We decided we can't back-track to get to the trail we came up on because of the snow and severity of the trail and the icing. We elected to go three hours out of our way north, to come into a protected trail. We did that – and we got back to camp that afternoon at three-thirty. I was working for a hundred dollars a day plus room and board plus tips. That was one of the experiences in the Rocky Mountains.

Rich: I thank you very much for sharing these exciting adventures. I could really imagine I was on this trip with you – this is the kind of story I truly enjoy.

CHAPTER 13   DAVID FLAVIN

Rich: I'd like you to meet David Flavin – a friend who loves to hunt and loves the out-of-doors. Dave, I know you enjoy hunting with a gun but I believe your major interest is in the area of bow hunting. I also am aware that you have been involved in competition archery. Please tell us a little about that if you would and how it impacts your hunting ability.

Dave: I've shot competitive archery for a number of years and really love it. It used to be that I played with all types of bows and setups and tested all kinds of broad heads and other kinds of testing and did a lot of competition shooting. Early on, even though I did some hunting, I put my emphasis on the competition shooting. I got prepared real well so far as being able to shoot but my hunting skills were lacking a little bit. I'm far from being a great hunter, I believe, but I have improved from what I was. Recently the number of animals I have taken with my bow has compared favorably with the hunting results of my early years. Now it is very common for me to get at least one deer each season with my bow.

Rich: Some people who are not acquainted with the weapon, think it is bogus so far as a hunting weapon is concerned, and all you're doing is sticking deer in the hide and hurting them and wounding them – tell us a little about what you understand about the effectiveness of the broad head hunting arrow – properly placed within the kill zone of an animal.

Dave: To be honest with you, I'm not just saying this because it is my opinion – I have searched this out because early on I believed when I first started hunting with a gun that what you said was true – that people were just sticking deer and whatever. What I have found out since, is that any well-placed broad head is just as effective on any game in the world as a rifle – it just doesn't have the shocking power – it generally won't knock the animals down as quick. A killing shot on any animal in the world – whether you're using a high-powered rifle or a bow – the results are the same. It's really all about shot placement with either weapon.

A sharp broad head kills by causing the animal to bleed to death. This occurs very rapidly and sometimes the animal expires within yards of the place where the arrow struck the animal. Many deer I have gotten have gone down within thirty to fifty yards – that's how quickly they die. When you think about that, when a deer starts to run – it doesn't take it very long to cover the thirty to fifty yards – that's how quickly it can happen. I believe as long as an archer prepares himself and can shoot under pressure somewhat he can kill game successfully. The same applies to a gun hunter. He's got to shoot many times under pressure too. If the hunter lacks preparation to shoot any weapon accurately, then wounded game may result. With bow hunting the animals are a lot closer normally – most game is killed within twenty yards or less.

Rich: Still-hunting with a bow usually requires you to get closer to the game for making an effective shot than when you are hunting with a gun.

Dave: I think still-hunting requires a lot more skill whether you are hunting with a gun or with the bow. With my bow, I shoot very effectively at long ranges when I am shooting at a target – but that doesn't transfer over to hunting situations most of the time. The distance to the animal with archery is very important. If you don't know the distance and if you're off by four or five yards when you judge that distance either you miss and you feel bad or you wound and you feel even worse. So, with the bow, the animals have to be very close – probably thirty yards or less. Then you have to be able to shoot thirty yards effectively or that's not even a possibility. Or, you're taking risks at the expense of some animal and that's something we really don't want to do. Wounding an animal for most bow hunters is a dreadful occurrence.

Rich: Un-recovered game is a disappointment and a waste. It is small consolation to figure, well, the animal might have been hit by somebody's car or the coyotes will get it. Dave, I've been in your home and I have seen a mammoth, beautiful mounted set of antlers from an elk you had mounted on a plaque and fastened to your living room wall. It isn't just white tailed deer that are effectively hunted with a bow – it's animals like elk apparently.

Dave: Exactly. Elk hunting is probably one of the most exciting hunts that you can do with a bow. Elk season runs to coincide with the rut in most states where you can hunt them. You're hunting at the most exciting time of the year and calling elk is a real possibility during those times, either with a bugle or cow calls. At the present time, cow calls are probably even more effective than bugles even though bugles get most of the press. It's a wonderful opportunity. You get to go to the Rocky Mountains and to see what God has created – it's just amazing.

I was successful in getting a six by six elk with my bow. The range to that animal when I shot was around twenty-five yards. I had a fellow call it in like you would call in a turkey. It was a wonderful trip. I had a friend in church that moved to Kansas and he had always dreamed about going on an elk hunt. Something fell thru with the guy he was going to go with so he called me to see if I would want to go. At that time my Dad was dying of pancreatic cancer and he was in a nursing home. He had to be fed thru tubes and stuff so he couldn't be at home. I told my friend I couldn't go as I needed to be with my Dad – I didn't know how much longer he was going to live. My wife talked me into going for the ten days. Really, it was such a blessing – she said she would go and visit my Dad and tell him what's going on and that he would understand.

Even though I knew something about bow hunting and I knew a lot about accuracy in archery I knew nothing about elk other than watching a few videos. The fellow I went on the trip with didn't know anything about elk either – it was his first trip too. I really believed God intervened on the trip. This was kind of beginner's luck – the shot wasn't – but just to be that close to a magnificent elk on my first day. We had walked in the dark for about three hours. The first ten minutes of our hunt is hard to describe. There were three bulls and a tremendous amount of cows that were calling and bugling to each other. We could see only shadows. It was a great experience – God was good – by ten minutes after first shooting light that morning I had killed a six by six elk. The events leading up to this were incredible. I believe the Lord intervened – I had been under a lot of pressure about my Dad. You could hunt your whole life and not get an elk like this. I just felt it was something He had given me. It was a thrill of a lifetime.

Rich: The other day we talked briefly – you mentioned something about your deer hunting adventure around home here this last fall. Please share that story with us.

Dave: I was hunting down near Hornell – at a place called Canisteo. I went on this trip with my Stepson. He's really a terrific guy to go with. We had gotten a late start from home. It was about a two and a half hour drive to get to where we were going to hunt. I had permission to hunt the area myself with the bow but I didn't have permission from the landowner for my Stepson to hunt so I took him to some State Land up the road and dropped him off. Later on that morning I was going to try to get permission from the landowner for him to hunt too. I had never hunted this area before but I had scouted it a little bit. I really got there later than I had wanted. I got my gear together and started walking in.

I was carrying on my back one of those climbing tree stands. On my way in I spotted this large buck walking right toward me. It was just after daylight and the buck was coming toward me with a large bunch of does. The does were all in back of the buck – normally, it doesn't happen this way. The buck was in the lead and he had a beautiful rack. The does and I saw each other at the same time. They took off – kind of ran a ways, then stopped and looked – then kept going. The buck just kept coming – and he was coming close. I was looking for a place to shoot him because we were close enough but there was brush in the way. When I stuck out my arm, trying to draw my bow, I got into some little saplings that caused my arrow to go off the rest. I had put some padding down on the shelf so the arrow didn't make any noise. The buck just didn't seem to be paying attention to anything. This seemed out of character in a way. He didn't even notice me putting the arrow back on and continued to go across in front of me. It came to an area where I thought I would have a clear opportunity for a shot. I came to a full draw but now there are saplings in front of the deer. I had decided if I had another chance at a walking buck I would try to stop it. Two years before I had killed a nice buck with my bow but hit it further back than I had planned. It was a liver shot so I got the deer but I thought this was irresponsible. A walking deer over twenty yards – even if someone has prepared – is not a good shot

Well, I did a buck grunt with my voice to stop it and I was very disappointed because when the buck heard me grunt, he ran down the hill. Normally, this doesn't happen. Usually it will stop them. It must have felt some kind of a challenge or else my grunt was so bad - but, whatever it was the buck departed. It didn't go far but it was out of range and it was over.

I thought about this for a bit and decided maybe I shouldn't have tried to stop the buck. This one was much closer than the other incident I told about that happened before. The deer wasn't traveling nearly as fast. I felt I could have made the shot – I just wanted to be responsible. I did it the way I did it – and it didn't work out. It was the way it was supposed to be, probably. The buck went towards the does, I picked up my stand and continued on.

Shortly I arrived at the tree I had planned to use my stand on. But then I got to looking at another tree and I thought it looked better. I laid my bow down and carried the stand over to the other tree. I got down on my knees and was putting the cable around the tree. I looked up and here's another buck. He's not fifteen yards away. Then, he proceeded to come closer to me – got within five yards of me, and looked the other way. This wasn't as big a buck as the one before but it still was a decent buck and one I would have loved to have gotten. Then, he turned and looked right at me – he even put his front hoof into the ground a couple of times – trying to get me to move. He wasn't sure what I was. We were eye ball to eye ball. If I'd had my bow when he had looked the other way at five yards – it would have been over. So then, he bounces away. I said, "wow – this is not turning out to be a very good day." Finally, I got up in the tree and sat for hours and nothing happened. I didn't see anything. I thought, "well, maybe it's all over for today." I had thought about staying longer but I had promised I would pick up my Stepson at the State Land. I wouldn't leave him up there too long – but I didn't have any other place for him to go. I felt bad about just dropping him off. I knew I had about twenty more minutes to go before needing to get down and go visit with him.

After about fifteen minutes went by, I suddenly saw these two large does coming thru. The owner of this land I was hunting on had a lot of deer damage and he had given me two doe permits that were given to him by the DEC. These were for people like me that could help cut the population down. These were large does and they kept coming closer. They appeared to be feeding – nibbling on some browse. The lead doe came walking thru and stopped at about fifteen yards, broadside. It looked like a good opportunity – but there was a little sapling there. I waited until I was sure that wouldn't come into the picture. I made the shot and knew at once I had a good hit. The arrow went completely thru – the deer took off and went about fifty yards and just fell over.

The other deer didn't know what had happened. It heard the bow and saw the other deer take off but didn't make any turn or run away for some reason. The deer kept coming towards me. It got about twenty-five yards from me and stood broadside. I double lunged that one too. It ran down the hill and didn't go more than fifty yards and just raised up with its front feet and fell over backwards. So, within a period of time of no more than forty-five seconds, I had killed two deer.

From the time they were struck by my arrows, neither deer lived more than three seconds. Considering all that had happened that day I was very pleased with those two deer. It was the first time I had ever killed two deer in the same day with my bow. I was pleased that my arrow hit exactly where I had wanted it to hit. Also, it was great to have both deer go down so quickly. Things worked out nicely and it was a thrilling day. Many times success is not just about taking game. What counts is being able to see game and experience the hunt. Also, I had some help dragging them. I went up and got Michael and he came back and gave me a hand.

Does tend to be very wary. After all, they are the one's responsible for raising and training the fawns and teaching them how to survive. They must be taught how to avoid not only hunters but also coyotes and other predators. Bucks tend to be encumbered. They've got their mind on other things some of the time and they may let their guard down. A nice part about bow hunting is that you can try to figure out things through most of the season. With gun hunting, after the first day or so, the deer are not doing what they normally do every day and it makes it a little more difficult.

Rich: You shoot a compound bow for hunting, don't you?

Dave: I have hunted with both. I used to use a recurve a lot but in recent years I hunt almost exclusively with a compound bow.

Rich: Let's say something happened to your compound and you couldn't get it repaired right away and you had made plans to go hunting. Would you be apt to pick up your recurve and go or would you prefer to wait until you could get your compound fixed?

Dave: I absolutely would not go with the recurve unless I had spent months preparing and shooting and getting in shape. The recurve requires a lot more time to be proficient. Today, with some of the mechanics and stuff in the compound bow, especially the release aids, generally bow hunters can become proficient comparatively easy. Becoming proficient with a recurve normally requires a lot more time and practice. I have friends that are just traditional people and I have nothing against that. It's the way I started and if you're prepared and you do all your homework and get very efficient with it, you're very capable of taking animals at close range. Most people don't want to put that kind of time into things – even though I do. I'm shooting all the time – even with a compound.

Rich: I used to hunt a bit with a recurve bow. After having used my compound, I personally would not want to have to go back to the recurve. Having sights on a compound helps with accurate shooting at known distances. For example, I mark somehow distances from my tree stand so I have a fairly accurate indication of how far away a deer might be when it shows up at my stand area. The biggest problem I have is judging distances in the woods when hunting.

Dave: That is certainly true. They have even got people in the military that are specifically trained in judging distances and they have put them on 3D courses. These are courses that we shoot where the targets are simulated animals at certain ranges. Those people, when it got beyond thirty-five yards, might be plus or minus three or four yards. That can be very critical on real animals. Keep in mind those people were trained in it – most of our hunters aren't. Lots of times in a hunting situation you're not taking the time you would on a target situation. You will be excited and the deer may walk away and you won't get an opportunity for a shot. Even though I shoot great distances – many times, up to eighty yards – I would never – ever – shoot at a deer over my self-imposed limit which would be under thirty yards. An exception might be if I were elk hunting and had the range finders and items they have today. I do have forty and fifty yard pins on my bow sight for that type of hunting. However, to attempt a shot at an animal at about fifty yards would be totally irresponsible, even if I could shoot accurately at fifty yards, if I didn't know how far away that animal was. Especially with elk, being such a big animal, they appear to be a lot closer than what they actually are.

I know traditional people and they shoot without sights on their bow. They kind of just shoot where they are looking. I believe that most of them that are very responsible at getting game in very close and they work constantly at making shots. Most people with recurves ought to have a sight on their bow – but that's just my opinion. I guess I'm entitled to it as I have been in this game a long time and given lessons in shooting recurve bows. The same thing applies to shooting a compound. Some would disagree with that. To shoot a compound bow without a sight requires a lot of work. Some people can really do it – but it requires a lot of work. Most people need a sight regardless which kind of a bow they shoot.

Beyond that, they need to pick a small spot on a deer – because otherwise, they end up aiming at the whole thing generally and that's how I believe they get into trouble. With the excitement – hurrying to get off a shot – by not picking a small spot or a "couple of hairs on the deer" – where you want your arrow to hit – is the difference between making a good shot and making a poor shot. That should be done, probably, with every weapon – where you pick a small spot. With a bow, it's probably best to make the area where you want to hit primary. The sight pin is a secondary thing. Where you want to hit is the primary thing. Some people do it the other way around – but most of the time it's done where you concentrate on where you want it to hit. The sight pin kind of gets you in the ballpark but you are actually seeing the arrow go in where you want it to go – before the shot happens. That's concentration.

Rich: another thing I have noticed is how very effective the camouflage you are wearing during that early bow season really is. When you are hunting with a shotgun or rifle you get used to the idea that you are apt to be seen by the deer. During the bow season, when most hunters tend to wear camouflage clothing, if you're wearing yours – be prepared in the deer woods to be practically run over by deer sometimes. It is just as though they don't see you – and they actually don't under most conditions. After a few episodes of practically being run over by deer within three to five yards, you wonder, "what's going on – how come that animal is so close. It doesn't seem to even know I'm here." Then, all of a sudden, it catches my scent and then it knows I'm there and then it runs for maybe fifteen yards and stops and stands and looks, like, "what was that?" you know. Camouflage must help a stand hunter immensely. A person hunting with a bow and wearing camouflage is really invisible to deer much of the time. If the wind is right and the movement is not detected by the deer, for all intents and purposes the hunter won't be seen or identified. I know some hunters who toss their clothing in a plastic bag with some pine boughs and bathe with special no-scent soap to eliminate as much odor as possible. They wear rubber hunting packs so not to leave their scent on the trail thru their feet.

Dave: I do most of those things. I know you have been a stalker of deer and that's the most challenging kind of hunting – for whitetail deer especially. Even with a gun, still-hunting requires a lot of skill. This is especially true when hunting with a bow due to the need to get in really close to the deer or other animal you may be hunting. Here, camouflage really comes into it. Most times we would really like for the deer not to detect us and maybe even come towards us. This is where camouflage helps. Movement of a hunter that might be detected by the deer is a main problem. Scent is also a major problem. You simply aren't going to get close to a deer if it can smell you. Normally, it just won't happen. Most people that hunt with a bow believe that getting a game animal close enough to you so you can make a clean kill is what bow hunting is all about.

Suppose I had a range finder and I shot an elk or something at sixty yards. Suppose I knew to the foot that it was sixty yards. Even then, it's somewhat risky because if the elk takes a step or something, the time that it takes for the arrow to get there can be a problem. I practice a lot at long distances and being able to kill an elk at sixty yards would be very satisfying. But, to call one in to five or seven yards like many people do every year is even more satisfying. These animals are huge and magnificent.

Rich: One concern that seems to come out in these interviews is a concern about how this hunting sport is going to continue. This is a concern all of us have. Members of some of the deer camps I have talked to kind of give a sad, woeful story of how the old guys are dying off, and some are getting sick and just simply can't go any more and then there's nobody to take the place of the missing members. My question at this point is, what have the individuals done to encourage a young person to take up the sport of hunting? In another camp that I have been a part of, recently they fed seventeen on a Saturday night and there were only three of us in camp at that time that were over age fifty. Now, that's something. In fact, there was a fifteen-year-old son of one of the members in camp that weekend. He wasn't old enough to hunt. The next day his Dad took him with him and they spent the day in the woods together exploring an area where neither of them had ever been before. They worked together with map and compass, found some great deer sign – fresh rubs and scrapes. They had a wonderful time. What's your opinion on how to encourage young people – what to do about that?

Dave: In my own case, my Dad was a hunter and he always wanted to include me even at a very young age when I couldn't carry a gun. He encouraged me to be in the woods and to see wildlife. Many times we didn't collect any game – it wasn't about success. It was about enjoying the outdoors – about enjoying the woods and learning things about trees and animals. A lot of it is enjoying what God has made and the wonderful sport of hunting. I think a lot of times today that is not being passed along like it used to be from father to sons – I think that is part of the problem. There has been a drop off recently in young people becoming involved.

Rich: They seem to have an interest in other things.

Dave: Right. Exactly – the world is moving awful fast and a lot of times we're caught up in things in a fast-paced society.

Rich: Right. You know, these days, a lot of single-parent Moms have got their hands full. How are they going to be able to take the time even to go on a picnic to say nothing about a camping trip with the family. That's asking a lot. These are the kind of activities traditionally handled by Dads. If Dad isn't around or available, or doesn't exist in the relationship, that might have something to do with some of this. For those of us that are able to enjoy the hunting aspect or just plain enjoy being out in the woods, that is marvelous, isn't it?

Dave: Another point on that – I think because of some of the reasons you just mentioned like the importance of families staying together - I'm fifty-four years old now and when I was young, divorce didn't seem near as prevalent. People stayed together and weren't so quick to leave the family situation. A father figure is important and the outdoors is a great place to develop strong relationships. Hunting or fishing are great activities to share. Uncles or close friends can fill in the gap where it exists. Youth programs like Scouting or Brigade used to be more prevalent than they appear to be today.

Rich: The bow is a marvelous tool and marvelous weapon, isn't it?

Dave: Yes, it really is.

Rich: There are people right now living in the world – bushmen or whatever – native peoples of the earth even today that hand make a bow and some arrows and then they must practice a lot because they get really good at it. They can shoot monkeys out of treetops and fish out of pools and do all kinds of outstanding things. The Bible tells about the bow being a weapon of war – it's been around a long time. It's also very effective. The mechanics of the modern day compound bow are awesome. Just for the record, please give us a little rundown on how a compound bow works – what the principal is.

Dave: What it does is it allows somebody to shoot a certain weight, perhaps a greater weight than if you were to use a different type of bow, like a recurve. This happens as a result of the pulley system inherent in a compound bow. Suppose you're able to pull a bow weight somewhere around sixty pounds. In the process of drawing the bow, it will begin to tip-over and actually reduce the weight of the draw. Most of the modern compound bows available today are letting off from sixty-five to eighty percent. So, the final holding weight when you have come to a full draw of the bow is almost nothing compared to the weight you are pulling at the start of your draw. You begin in this example to have to pull the full sixty pounds and when the draw has been completed you're only holding twelve or fourteen pounds. This makes it so that you can hold the bow at full draw very steadily. It's not like you have to hold that thing back with the full weight. Actually, you can come to a full draw and then wait for a deer to come into an opening allowing a clear shot opportunity or even for it to come into range. You can plan this necessary part of shooting a bow ahead of time so they don't see you drawing and then you can hold very steady for long periods of time. Actually it makes hunting a little easier with the modern compound. If you had drawn a sixty-pound recurve bow or a long bow, the type Robin Hood used to use, you wouldn't be able to physically remain at the full draw position for a very lengthy period of time. The strength required to hold the bow at the full draw position would impose a limit for remaining in this position.

A number of traditional people are actually snapshooting with their weapons. They just draw kind of all in one motion, hit their anchor and it's gone. It doesn't give you an opportunity to hold and wait for something. The compound innovation has helped so far as accuracy is concerned. I certainly don't want to brag about abilities – mine or anyone else's – but we've had several people that are good shooters in this state – some of the top – that went to competition shoots where they have competed with their bows against shooters using shotguns with rifled barrels and shooting Sabot bullets. This type of competition uses a known fifty-yard range. It is amazing to me to realize that the archers come out on top, at fifty yards. It is not at all uncommon for good archery shooters to be able to do that.

When shooting indoors at twenty yards, even though we have a three inch bulls eye, when the results are being decided, it's being decided by the inside little ring inside the three inch bull's eye. That is not much bigger than a quarter. I have won several tournaments and in order to win, I have to shoot sixty shots and I need to have fifty-eight of them inside that little ring within that three inch circle. Even at that range, it would be difficult to shoot your shotgun any better than that. In fact, it kicks – so you probably wouldn't want to have to shoot it sixty times, but if you did, it would be very difficult off-handed to do any better than that. Another comparison we could make between a gun and a bow would be the fact that when using the bow, we have to know the distance. With a gun, if a deer is forty or fifty or sixty or even seventy yards, if your gun was sighted in at fifty yards, you would be okay for all of those distances. Maybe if you got out to around a hundred yards, it would begin to drop quite severely. Using a bow, if you're off five yards in your estimation of the distance, it is serious business. Anything beyond twenty-five yards, it's real serious.

The accuracy available with a compound with the release aids and the sights is an incredible thing. Some of us that shoot in the upper levels have even shot arrows inside of arrows at sixty yards. That's kind of an accident when it happens but it means that you're grouping real tight or you wouldn't be doing that. At a fifty-yard target, it's not uncommon for archers today with compound bows and mechanical releases to shoot four-inch groups with all their arrows. I'm not talking about your backyard shooters who are getting ready for the season. A lot of times they don't have the form or the knowledge to shoot them like that – but they still shoot them very, very well.

Rich: If we can put them inside an eight-inch paper plate at twenty yards on a consistent basis, we feel we're ready to go hunting – we'll be within the kill zone on the deer.

Dave: Most guys have no trouble in doing a six-inch group at twenty yards with today's equipment. If you're shooting traditional stuff, that wouldn't be true. You would really have to work hard at it – to get those kinds of groups.

Rich: What's the difference between a double pulley and a single pulley on a compound bow – does one or the other let off more weight?

Dave: This is a rather complicated subject. There's a number of people today shooting with one-cam bows which means that the bow has a round wheel on one end and a cam on the other. The advantage of this system is several things. If you have a bow with two-cams, they must be timed. In other words when you are pulling it back, both those cams have to come over in unison. With the one-cam bow, because it has a round wheel on one end and a cam on the other, generally they don't go out of time. This is one of the advantages. The other main advantage of the one-cam bow is that it is very, very quiet. When hunting, if you have a bow that does not make much noise when it is being fired, you have a real advantage. Normally when you pull the bow back, the cam just turns over and kind of stays there so you can even be steadier when holding at full draw. Most of the manufacturers are pushing them right now, but they aren't telling all the truth. Mostly they are concerned about selling the product and I don't blame them – I know they want to stay in business. There are however, some disadvantages with a one-cam bow.

After you've come to full draw, there's what, for lack of a better term, we call a wall. There isn't much valley with a one-cam bow. If you're in – like – the front of it, there simply is very little there. If you are not in exactly the same place each time you have come to that "full draw" you can have trouble. Specifically, if you're too hard into it one time and too soft into it the next and you're not consistent, it will make small differences at the other end.

With a two-cam bow, it's pretty easy to get them in time if they need some adjustment. They have cables on them so you can twist one or the other and get it right back in time. Comparing the one-cam bow with the two-cam – most of the one-cam bows have a continuous string which is over a hundred inches long. It used to be strings were forty, fifty, or sixty inches long. With the longer string, string stretch can move your nocking point – which also makes your sights off. They are coming out now with better materials which have less stretch – but that's another of the disadvantages of the one-cam bow. You don't hear a lot about that because all the manufacturers claim they have level nock travel but in my opinion, again, I don't think that some of them that claim it have it.

I've shot a lot of bows in the one and two-cam styles. I don't prefer one over the other – I'm just looking at it with an honest approach and appraisal. I'm not a salesman for either one. I am just trying to understand the advantages and disadvantages because everything you do in archery effects the results at the animal or target. If you get a fast bow, it's harder to shoot. If you get a slow bow, you've got to be more accurate with your range estimation. I believe a person ought to get the most accurate item they can possibly come up with. The forgiving bow, even though it might not be as fast at deer hunting ranges, the biggest thing is to be able to hit your animal exactly where you want to hit it. Speed is geared more to the 3D archery where you are guessing distances. Many people that are shooting speed today don't have the form in archery. Perhaps no one has worked with them so they can develop the ability to shoot very well and with a lot of speed. If a person is getting into archery today I would recommend he or she get into the middle somewhere.

Rich: Boy, it's complicated, isn't it? That's what helps to make it a sport.

Dave: There are a lot of different opinions out there and a number of people wouldn't agree with me I am certain. I can give you my experience and try to be as honest and impartial as possible.

Rich: I recall back in the days of Fred Bear – he started out with just a long bow. It wasn't even a recurve. The push at that time seemed to be that they were just as happy to sell you the materials so you could make your own arrows. I recall trying some of that stuff. It turned out pretty good. It was fun and a challenge. Also, it's hard to explain the personal satisfaction I received just from the process of "making my own." We didn't have machines to hold the fletchings – we held them by hand and used good glue. It's truly amazing what they have got to do with today. I have a question. Maybe not top of the line or the cheapest – but what should anyone anticipate having to spend for a suitable compound bow that they could use for hunting today?

Dave: Well, it's all over the ballpark – it can even be as high as seven to nine hundred dollars. Actually for someone to get into a good bow – either one or two-cam – many times now the companies offer packages that include a lot of the stuff you will need to buy to go with the bow already on it. Today, if you spend three or four hundred dollars you can get a decent bow. A lot of the other stuff that will be included with the purchase won't be the most expensive but it will suffice and be very serviceable. When you buy a sight – a sight's a sight. If I put a matchstick on my bow and taped it on there and it didn't move and I had it adjusted or sighted in for a certain distance, it would work. Many times, it's the adjustability of the sight that makes it more expensive. You need solid stuff like sights to hunt with. You don't want things moving around or changing on you. Generally the items you will get in a package deal will be fairly good. Even then, it won't cover everything as you still will have to buy a release or if you decide to shoot with your fingers, you'll have to buy a tab. You'll also need to buy some arrows although some might be included with the package deal.

Rich: It seems to me that a number of people should be able to afford to purchase a quality bow-hunting outfit. It might be a good idea for an individual to check things out at a local bow shop. Usually the owner or someone would be available to encourage and assist with this whole process. Many of these people are highly qualified to help. Most people that get involved in archery today shoot both target and hunt. In my experience every pro-shop has several bow hunters on hand and they have all been willing to share information and like in your own situation, will even assist with tuning a bow.

Dave: Another thing, if you bought a .30-06 or .280 or whatever to hunt with, to practice with that unit, you'd have to keep on buying ammunition. If you get good arrows and take good care, you can shoot those things for years. The practice doesn't cost you other than a little maintenance on your bow – the cost is minimal and the fun is great without spending a lot of money.

I've asked a number of gun hunters that do both – "if you had to quit one, which one would you quit?" Most of them wouldn't want to quit either, but what they'll say is, "if I had to, I would quit the gun." The reasons usually given are that the bow occurs before the gun season, the animals are not spooked and you're dealing with them more on their own natural terms. It's easier to figure them out – it's thrilling to get so close to your quarry, and then of course, you have the opportunity to hunt in the pre-rut season that normally coincides with the opening of the bow season. These are a lot of the reasons – and there are others – it is just so rewarding to get one with a bow. Any whitetail for most people, be it a buck or a doe, is really a trophy to be mighty proud of. Small game provides an extra bonus for the bow hunter. Of course you can kill a squirrel, grouse, or duck with a shotgun but when you pull that off with a bow, you have a reason to be especially proud and satisfied. I haven't shot a turkey – yet. They always seem to catch me in the act of drawing. To get a turkey with a bow and arrow is a real accomplishment. I know some guys that have done it and I just haven't put the effort in it, I guess. That remains a real challenge.

Rich: Dave, we thank you for all your input. I can hardly wait to share all this with the ones that will read this book. Good luck to you in your enjoyment of the woods and of bow or gun hunting – hope you get that turkey with your bow real soon.

CHAPTER 14   JOHN S. MACNEILL, JR.

Rich: We're going to talk about a trip you and I enjoyed a few years ago. We went caribou hunting and fishing up in northern Quebec, Canada in the fall of 1974. John, how did this trip come about?

John: I first met Ivan Greenfield at our son Allen's wedding in July of 1974. Allen married Lorrie Penfield in the garden behind her father's house in Vestal, New York. It was to be a Quaker wedding but Lorrie's father, Bob Penfield wanted his long time friend Ivan Greenfield, a minister from a Presbyterian church in Sandy Creek, New York to sanctify the wedding. It was after the wedding that a group of us began to talk about hunting and fishing. Bob Penfield and Ivan had been fishing buddies since they had met each other in college. Bob had a fishing camp in Ontario, Canada and they had spent considerable time there so the talking centered about fishing. Bob said he had seen some pictures of a fishing trip that Ivan had taken to northern Quebec and asked Ivan about that trip.

Ivan said he had gone with a group of friends and guides to the area north of Shefferville, Quebec to fish for lake trout, ouananiche – or land locked salmon and Quebec red trout - which was a species of large brook trout. The outfitter that supplied the guides and the camp equipment came from Pulaski, New York and was licensed by the Province of Quebec to operate a hunting and fishing camp on Lac Champdore in northern Quebec.

He said that the fishing had been unbelievable and that everyone in the party had caught their limit of large, almost trophy fish. Some of the lake trout ran over forty pounds. The Quebec red trout ran between five and ten pounds and the salmon between ten and twenty pounds. I was accustomed to catching brown and brook trout in our local streams and thought if I caught one ten to twelve inches long I was doing good. My immediate reaction to this information was to tell Ivan that if he was planning another trip and needed someone to fill in the party to please be sure to give me a call. Ivan said he was going there again that fall on a combined fishing and caribou-hunting trip but that the party was full. He would keep me in mind for future trips, however.

Two weeks later, Ivan called me and said that two of the party had cancelled out. It was a father and son team and the father had just been diagnosed with cancer. He asked if I'd like to go and if I knew a friend that would be interested also. I asked how much the trip would cost and he said $1,000.00 and that included the cost of the license to fish and hunt caribou. Without hesitation, I said I'd be interested and would call a friend of mine, and would let him know the next day. I called Rich Davis, a hunting and fishing buddy of mine, and told him the deal and extended Ivan's invitation to him. He said he'd let me know the next day. He called the first thing the next morning and said he would like to go. I called Ivan and said we'd take him up on his offer. Ivan said they were planning to show some movies of the area in Fulton the following Saturday night. If we could attend, we could bring our $1,000.00 apiece and get to meet the outfitter. I told him "we'll be there."

Rich and I attended the meeting the following Saturday night and saw the movies and met the group of fishermen that caught the fish as well as several of the people who were planning on our trip that fall. The outfitter's name was Robert Krim. He took our money and gave us a written itinerary of the trip and a list of things to bring and the name of the motel where we were to meet on the day after Labor Day, September 1st in Sept-Isles on the north shore of the Gulf of Saint Lawrence. There were ten of us paying customers, five guides, a cook and Krim himself that would make up the trip. They would provide wall tents all set up on wooden platforms – each with a wood stove and cots for us to sleep on. The camp also boasted a large cook tent and one for dining and another for storage. We would fly from Sept-Isles to Shefferville on a commercial jet. There are no roads to Shefferville. It lies on the northern boundary of Labrador. The only access is by daily commercial flights or by a passenger train that goes up to Shefferville one day and returns to Sept-Isles three days later. The railroad trip takes eight hours. We would stay at the camp a week, fly back to Shefferville and then take the train back to Sept-Isles with whatever game and fish we had. The hunting license would let us hunt moose, bear, wolves, deer, small game as well as caribou. The only big game in the area where we were going was caribou and the wolves that followed the caribou herds. Small game consisted of ptarmigan, Canada geese and snowshoe rabbits.

I was going to take my .30-40 Kraig rifle that a friend, Bruce Merkur had customized for me and installed a five-power scope. I bought some ammunition and Rich and I went out to a local shooting range and sighted in our rifles. I decided to take along my wife's Ithaca Featherlight .20 gauge shotgun in case I had the opportunity to hunt ptarmigan.

On the night we left, Rich stayed at our house as we were planning to start early – about 4:30 – I left a note for Betty, my wife, saying I would call her as soon as we got to Sept-Isles and we headed out. It was a lovely cool, clear night and it seemed that all the stars in the heavens were out to wish us on our way.

We had breakfast at a popular diner in Watertown. It was a lovely day for travel and we managed to get thru Canadian Customs in under a half hour. They told us that the ferry at Tadoussac was not operating as the crew was on strike so we would have to cross the Saguenay River at Chicoutimi. It wasn't long and we were in the city of Quebec. We were slowed down when we came to a traffic light that was not working at an intersection of four lanes of traffic going in all directions. There were no police present and there was one grand traffic jam. It seemed like hours before we got through the mess and headed north toward the Laurentian Mountains and Chicoutimi. The drive through the mountains was beautiful and there was no traffic. We stopped alongside a rushing mountain stream and ate the sandwiches Rich had brought along for lunch. It was late in the afternoon when we reached the city and crossed the Saguenay River and headed toward Tadoussac.

The ride along the river was through wild and beautiful country and we were glad that the ferry wasn't operating and had forced us to take the alternate route. We reached the Queen's Highway just at dusk and headed northeast along the north shore of the Saint Lawrence River toward Sept-Isles. We soon came to the little village of Petites Bergeronnes and saw a sign that said there was a hotel in the town. We decided that our best bet was to take a room at the hotel, get a good night's sleep, and get up early in the morning and continue on to Sept-Isles.

We found the hotel without any trouble. It was a newly constructed two-story structure that looked in good shape. We went in the front door and up to the registration desk – and right into our first trouble with the French language. This part of Quebec is strictly French speaking and neither Rich nor I could speak French. The woman behind the counter gestured that we should wait and she went away from her desk. After a few minutes, she returned with a young lady who could speak English. We told her we were looking for a room for the night. She said we were lucky – their busy season was over and they had an empty room for us. We asked if they had a restaurant and she said, "yes, but it had just closed for the night." She suggested we put our bags in our room while she checked to see if we could still get dinner.

Our room was on the first floor and she met us there after we dropped our bags off and led us downstairs to a large ballroom where several people were setting tables and preparing for some sort of festival. We walked across the floor to a person who seemed to be the Maitre d'. He was carrying a large tray of silverware. She said something to him in French and he looked at her for a second and then threw the whole tray of silver up in the air. It went all over the ballroom floor. She turned to us and apologized for his behavior, said that there was to be a Labor Day celebration that night and to follow her to another small coffee room and introduced us to a cook, an older woman, who also could not speak English. After talking to the cook, she turned to us and said "the cook would make us a dinner of broiled fish, string beans and boiled potatoes." We said, "fine," and thanked her for the help and then she left us. The cook soon brought in the dinner, we said, "thank you," and began to eat. The fish was very oily and the veggies tasted like they had been boiled for hours. Neither of us could finish the meal and we left a small tip and headed back to the lobby. We told the young lady, who was at the desk by then, that we would like to pay that night in advance. We wanted to get an early start in the morning.

The room appeared to be okay. It had two single beds, a bureau, a clothes closet and a bathroom with a shower. When I went into the bathroom to take a shower and pushed the switch to turn on the light, I found that there must have been a leak in the water system on the second floor. Water was running down in the partition and through the light switch and the switch was red hot. I don't know why I wasn't electrocuted. We decided to turn off the light and used a piece of wood to do so. We went to bed without having taken a shower.

It was nine o'clock and just as we got into bed a rock band started playing in the ballroom right underneath our room. The noise was deafening and everything in our room began to vibrate. This went on until four o'clock in the morning and we both found it impossible to sleep until the noise quit. At six o'clock in the morning our alarm clock went off and we dragged ourselves out of bed and got dressed. We packed our bags and left the room, locking the door behind us and headed for the lobby and the main entrance. The lobby was empty and when I went to hang up our key, I found out that there were only two others missing besides ours. It sure wasn't a full house with only three rooms out of about thirty occupied. When we went to the main door to leave, we found it was locked. We returned to the registration desk but couldn't find any key to the entrance door. We tried all the other exit doors on the first floor and they were locked also. We went up to the second floor and tried exit doors and finally found one that would open. We had to carry our bags down a long, steep set of wooden stairs to get to the ground at the back side of the building. We were both thankful that we didn't have a fire during the night.

It was a cold and foggy morning when we threw our bags in the back end of the truck and headed out to find a place to eat breakfast. We couldn't find any place open in Petites Bergerones and we didn't find any place until we reached Les Escoumins about ten miles down the road. We saw several vehicles parked in front of a small restaurant and so pulled in. We took a table in the corner of the room and waited – to be waited on. In a few minutes, a very pretty young blonde waitress – wearing the shortest miniskirt either of us had ever seen came to wait on us. We were quite taken aback by short miniskirts for breakfast and when she asked us, we assumed, what we wanted – in French – we both looked at each other with a helpless, dumbfounded look. It took us a long time to "order" but with the help of two other guys who were sitting at the counter who also spoke mostly French – were able to order scrambled eggs, bacon, toast, coffee and orange juice – partly in sign language. When our order arrived it sure tasted good – we were mighty hungry.

The remainder of our road trip was without further incident except that the scenery was spectacular and awesome in the extreme. We arrived in Sept-Isles late in the afternoon and met the rest of our party at the motel. Our party consisted of ten men. There were three Doctors in the group and the teenage son of one of the Doctors who had taken a week off from college to go on the trip. There was a Dentist, a Mechanical Engineer, a General Contractor, Reverend Greenfield, Rich and myself.

Ivan said he knew of a great restaurant not too far from our motel and suggested we eat there. So, after taking a shower we all met in the lobby and walked to the restaurant. When we arrived we noticed quite a few motorcycles parked out front and the restaurant was full of people, most of them were wearing black leather jackets. It appeared to be kind of a rough crowd and we were all a little uneasy, being foreigners and because we could not understand a word they were saying. We sat at two tables in the corner and waited for a waitress to come and take our order. We had the same old problem of not being able to communicate but Ivan said that he had seen the menu before and so he pointed out what the different items were and we all ordered steaks. They did not serve water with the meal and I was very thirsty. I asked Ivan if he could get the waitress to bring me a glass of water. He got the message across to the waitress who acted like she couldn't believe anyone would want a glass of water. She shrugged her shoulders and then took a pitcher of water off the top shelf and poured a glass. She brought me the glass and when I took a mouth full I knew I had made a mistake. That pitcher of water must have been standing on that shelf for quite a long time. I did not know what to do with the mouthful, so I swallowed it. It was awful – it tasted downright polluted. I quickly got a cup of coffee to change the taste in my mouth.

The steaks were okay and after dinner, we walked back to the motel. I was quite tired so I went right to bed. I awoke in the middle of the night and just made it to the bathroom before I threw up. Before the night was over I had a bad case of "Montezuma's revenge" – and I thought, "what a great way to start a trip." Luckily, by the time morning came around, my stomach had calmed down and I was able to eat some breakfast. We all went to a diner for breakfast and several of us ordered scrambled eggs. Rich and I were able to get that across due to our previous experience the morning before but when someone ordered donuts, we had a real problem. Somebody drew a picture – but it looked obscene, so they changed their order to a Danish.

After breakfast we all got to the airport in a taxicab that made several trips to transport all of us plus our luggage. We bought our one-way ticket for the flight to Shefferville. The plane we boarded was a forty- passenger Air Canada jet and it made one stop at Labrador City, in central Labrador. Then it continued on to Shefferville. After landing we picked up our bags and took a taxi to the bush pilot landing port. There were two floatplanes tied up to the dock – an Otter and a Beaver. The Otter is a high wing, two-engine prop plane that has a capacity of about ten people plus the pilot and copilot. We loaded most of our gear into the Beaver and the Doctor's son sat in the copilot's seat and Rich and I crawled on top of the luggage. The outfitter sat in the copilot's seat of the Otter. They loaded the rest of the gear and the remaining seven guys climbed in the back. The planes taxied out between several other planes into a large lake and faced into the wind to take off.

Due to the weight we were carrying, our plane required quite a distance to get off the water and into the air. Once in the air the pilot took the plane up to about two thousand feet and headed north. The Otter was a British World War II surplus plane. It had seen lots of use. The Beaver was about the same age as the Otter but appeared to be in better shape.

It was a beautiful day with a bright blue sky and white puffy clouds. We were flying just beneath the clouds and could see for many miles in every direction. The land beneath us seemed to be more than half made up of lakes. The pattern of the lakes was long and thin with the striations running in a north-south direction. The sides of the mountains and the narrow valleys were covered with spruce trees. The tops of the mountains were treeless and covered with low-lying brush. They appeared to have snow on them but the pilot told us it was caribou moss. The countryside was wild and appeared endless in every direction. At this latitude there were no signs of civilization. There is only one village far to the north of us, Fort Chimo on Ungava Bay, near the Arctic Circle. We could see many trails along the hilltops. The pilot said that the trails were made by the caribou as they migrate across the territory.

Lac Champdore lies approximately one hundred miles northeast of Shefferville in the midst of a vast wilderness. From the air it is possible to get a feel for this immense lake that is approximately forty miles long and one mile wide. It is bow shaped with the rise of the bow to the north. It lies mostly in an east-west configuration, which is contrary to most of the other lakes in the area and forms a portion of the headwaters of the Whale River which runs north into Ungava Bay. Its waters were clear and sky blue on this beautiful day as we approached the western end of the lake where the Outfitter had his camp set up. The camp was located on a little bay about one half mile from the rapids where the lake discharges into the Whale River. Our plane landed smoothly and taxied toward the shore where the other plane was already unloading. The members of the party and the gear were transported to shore in large cargo canoes.

Once ashore, we were introduced to the four guides and the cook. The Outfitter, Bob Krim, was to be the fourth guide. Each guide was assigned to two members of the party. My guide was Truman Keller and my partner was Chuck Livingston, the son of one of the Doctors in the party. Truman came from the Village of Parish, just north of Syracuse. One of the other guides was a Frenchman from Quebec City and the other two were younger men from a village along the north shore of the Gulf of Saint Lawrence east of Sept-Isles and accessible only by boat. They were fishermen and only spoke a little English. The cook came from the Village of Pulaski just north of Syracuse where he ran a bakery shop. He was on a working vacation and had been a cook for the Outfitter on previous trips.

We were assigned to one of the sleeping tents and spent a few minutes stowing our gear away and unrolling our sleeping bags. There was a short wave radio in the dining tent with which the Outfitter kept in touch with Shefferville in case of emergencies. Rich and I and Chuck Livingston got to share one tent together. It was fun to get to know Chuck – he must have kept things at his college humming. Oh, to have all that energy again. Rich and I put our fishing rods together and thought we'd try our luck right off shore for something to do while waiting for dinner. On Rich's second cast he tied into a nice lake trout and soon after I had one on also. We were both using our spinning rods with bright copper colored spoons. Those fish were hungry. It seemed that almost every cast brought us a strike. Bob Krim came over to where we were and took some of the fish we had caught to have the cook fix for dinner.

The dinner bell rang and I was hard put to lay down the rod and go eat. We were all hungry though and it wasn't long before we were bellied up to the table. What a wonderful meal – the cook had put on caribou steaks, cut from a caribou they had killed for camp meat. There was lake trout, ouananiche, mashed potatoes and gravy, string beans, fresh baked rolls and warm fresh baked apple pies. Everything was cooked to perfection and there seemed to be an unlimited supply. I could see that this was going to be a memorable trip if only for the food. During dinner, Ivan said the best plan was to go after your caribou first and when you got that, then go fishing. The Outfitter said that because of a late warm season the caribou had not started to herd up and migrate south and so there were only those in the area that had spent the summer months there. We all turned in early because we would be up at the crack of dawn for our first day of hunting. Rich got the fire going in the wood stove. Chuck said he would tend it during the night and it wasn't long before we were all sound asleep.

It was still dark when I awoke. The cook had breakfast going and offered me a cup of coffee – it sure tasted great. The morning air was cool and there was some fog out over the lake. Breakfast was just as grand as dinner had been with fried eggs, bacon, deep fried fish, hash brown potatoes with sliced onions mixed in with them, pancakes with maple syrup, orange juice and lots of great coffee. What a way to begin a day in the north woods.

After breakfast, three parties loaded their rifles and some sandwiches into three large cargo canoes. Rich and Ivan, who was his partner, were going to hunt close to camp. The other two canoes headed toward the highest mountain on the other side of the lake about a mile and a half away. The canoes were propelled by large fifteen horse motors and soon had us ashore on the other side of the lake near where a little stream came in at the base of the mountain. At this point, there was a notch dividing two sections of the highest mountain in our area. We later named this ravine, Krim's Notch.

Two of the groups decided to hunt near that ravine. There was a large territory there so that they wouldn't crowd each other. Truman said he would take Chuck and me over the top of the mountain and we would hunt along the west side of the ridge. We found our way up thru the forested side of the mountain to its broad open top. As we neared the top the spruce trees thinned out until at the very top, there were none at all. The top of the mountain was covered with the same brush that filled the woods plus lots of blueberry bushes. The caribou trails here paralleled the clear mountaintop and we followed them southward toward the ravine. We each carried a pair of binoculars and Truman said that in addition to watching the area of the ridge ahead of us we should scan the ridge of the mountain to the west of us. He explained that the caribou grazed the open tops of the mountains in small herds and could usually be seen silhouetted against the sky.

We had probably traveled about a quarter of a mile when Truman said there was a herd of caribou on the ridge of the other mountain. He saw them with his naked eye and I had trouble finding them even with the binoculars. We could see about fifteen or twenty animals and at least one big bull with an enormous set of antlers. Truman said that one of us would cross the valley with him and the other one would stay behind and keep an eye on the herd. If the herd started to move north the watcher was to shoot once and if it moved south he was to shoot twice. Truman got out a coin and I called for heads – he tossed it – and it came up tails. So, I was left behind to be the watcher. Truman took a compass bearing on the herd and he and Chuck started down the mountain.

I found a good-sized boulder that I could sit on and started my vigil. It was a clear sunny day with white puffy clouds that were so low it seemed that I could reach up and touch them. The wind was out of the west. Where I sat, I was sheltered by some bushes and it was not cold. There were a few black flies but they didn't seem to bother. As I looked west across that vast wilderness I thought to myself, "there probably isn't a village or a living soul in that direction all the way to the Pacific Ocean three thousand miles away." I sat for what seemed like a very long time and did not see my partners come up the other mountainside. After a long time, the big bull on the other mountaintop stood up and started walking north. The whole herd of cows got up and followed him. I watched him for a while and when I was sure he was headed north I took my rifle and touched off the one signal shot. The bull didn't seem to pay any attention to my rifle shot – he just continued grazing.

I still hadn't been able to spot my partners on the other mountain so I got out my lunch and started eating. After about a half hour I noticed that the bull had turned around and was headed south. He kept coming until he reached his original resting place and lay down. I did not know what to do. How could I let the other guys know that they should ignore my first signal? I sat and watched for a while and suddenly I noticed out of the corner of my eye, far to the south on the other mountain, a red spot that moved. It was Chuck's red hat. They both were about a mile away and were working their way north along the ridge. I watched the unfolding of the saga through my binoculars as if I were watching on television. I could see them walking side by side along parallel caribou trails. When they got within fifty yards the bull got up and started to run westward down the other mountainside. There were three quick shots – followed after a few minutes by one lone shot.

After what seemed like an hour, Truman came up the mountainside in front of me. He said that he had dressed the animal out and left Chuck beside it while he came back after me. As we started down the mountain toward Chuck I could see that he was quite a bit upset. He said when the big bull had jumped up Chuck had taken a snapshot at him and the bullet had clipped off both antlers several inches above the head. The next two shots were taken at the bull as he was running straight away from Chuck. One shot had gone through the right hindquarter and the next through the left. That had dropped the bull and the final shot I had heard was the coup de grace. Truman said that with the long distances we had to haul a carcass back to camp and since everything had to be flown out, all they took from the carcass was the two hind quarters, the tenderloin, the antlers without the head and the hide. He said that Chuck's two shots into the hindquarters had about destroyed the meat. He said he was sorry that I had not gotten a chance to go on the hunt but if I would bear with him, he would help me find a good bull before the week was over.

When we got back to Chuck we picked up the two hindquarters, the tenderloin, the antlers and we left the hide high up in a spruce tree. Truman said he and I would pick it up the next day when we returned to hunt the area. Truman put the two hindquarters, or what was left of them, in a backpack. Chuck took the antlers (both of them) and I carried the tenderloins. Truman said that the remainder of the carcass would be cleaned up by wolves in the next day or so. On the way back over the top of the mountain we put up a flock of ptarmigan. They were pretty in their brown and white plumage for they had already started to change to their white winter color. They circled out in front of us and would have made an easy shot if I had been carrying my shotgun. By the time we got back to the canoe, it had gotten close to being dark.

We headed across the lake guided by the lights of the camp. At dinner that night we learned that Ivan had hunted along the shore of the lake near camp with Bob Krim that day and shot a nice caribou cow. We also learned that two of the Doctors had killed young bulls with immature antlers.

156

Two of the other guys, the Dentist and the other Doctor, had shot cows. That left Rich, the Engineer, the Contractor and myself that had not gotten our caribou. One of the guys had killed a Canada goose and one of the Doctors had gone ptarmigan hunting and shot two of those birds. The dinner that night was even better than the one before, if that was possible – and included roast goose and ptarmigan. After listening to a little of the chatter on the two-way radio I went off to bed early.

Up before daybreak, same super breakfast as previous day, Truman and I made sandwiches for lunch. Soon we were off to the previous day's hunting area – just Truman and I. The sky was cloudless and the lake as calm as a millpond. We put ashore in the same place that we had the day before and started up the caribou trail toward Chuck's caribou hide. It was about three quarters of a mile to the tree where we had stashed the hide and it was still there. Truman suggested we leave it there and continue on south – we could pick that up on the way back. We hiked south on well-traveled caribou trails. I was in one trail and Truman was in another parallel one – we were separated by about thirty feet. We traveled through the forested valley floors where the trees were so thick we could not see each other. Soon after, we would be traveling over open mountaintops where there were no trees at all. This was pristine wilderness with spiky, greenish blue spruce trees silhouetted against an azure blue sky. We drank in mountaintop vistas that probably had not been seen by any human being. This was truly God's county.

We walked for several miles and were passing through a forested valley floor. Up to this point we hadn't seen any game. Suddenly I looked up and just ahead of me was a wolf sitting in the center of my caribou trail looking directly at me. How beautiful he was, a silvery gray animal with his ears pricked up and not making a sound. The moment he knew I had seen him he vanished from the trail like a ghost. I stood there dumbfounded and mesmerized by the sight of the wolf – which burned itself into my mind. It seemed like minutes had gone by when Truman hollered, "hey, why didn't you shoot the wolf?" Actually, it had only been a few seconds after I had seen him that he crossed Truman's caribou trail. I didn't know how to answer Truman for I could no more have shot that beautiful animal than tried to jump over the moon. He'll always be my symbol of the true wilderness and I thought I was the luckiest man in the world. Truman said that in all the years he had been guiding in the area, this was the first time he had seen a wolf. We continued walking the trails and finally stopped on the top of a mountain to eat lunch and enjoy the beautiful day. After lunch Truman said we had better head back because it would be late when we picked up Chuck's caribou hide and got back to the lake. Back in camp during dinner that night we found out that Rich, the Contractor and the Engineer had each shot a cow and so I was the only one who still had not filled his quota.

The guys who had gotten their caribou the day before had spent the day fishing for lake trout and had some great fish stories to tell. Two of the Doctors and their guide had gone up the lake where the water was very deep and had trolled with spoons on eighty-pound test line. Twice they had tied into fish that towed the twenty-foot cargo canoe with the guide and two Doctors aboard for what seemed like miles around the lake before the fish broke the line. They never did see the fish but were very impressed with the strength of them. The rest of the crew that had been fishing in shallower water had caught legal sized lake trout with about every cast. The largest fish caught weighed thirty-five pounds. A lot of other great fish stories came out during dinner and we sat around the wood stove in the dining tent talking until quite late in the evening.

The next morning Truman said he would like to try a new area to hunt that was quite a long ways down the lake. We ate breakfast and packed a lunch and got ready to leave. Rich asked if we

157

minded if he came along. Truman said, "come along." Rich, Truman and I headed down the lake toward a place that Truman said he had seen caribou before. It was about fifteen miles down the lake and on the opposite shore. We had to cross the widest part of the lake and it gave us a wide panoramic view of the countryside. The lake was calm so we made good time in reaching our destination. We put in to shore at a rocky cove and headed up a mountainside. We came out into the open on the mountaintop and spent some time glassing the tops of other mountains that surrounded us. We headed out in a westerly direction down a caribou trail on the opposite side of the mountain. We had dropped Rich off at a place where he could glass the area. Truman and I went on ahead, crossed a valley and started up the mountain on the other side.

When we reached the open mountaintop we stopped for a breather and scanned the surrounding areas with our binoculars while we rested. Truman said that the next day would be our last to hunt before the plane came in to pick us up for our return to civilization and that he hoped I would get a chance at killing my caribou today.

We started out again walking along the open top of the mountain and we hadn't gone more than a thousand yards when two cow caribou stood up about one hundred fifty feet in front of us. The two cows just stood there and looked at us as if they had never seen a human before, and they probably hadn't. Truman said softly to me that I would have to make a decision. He said that he could not guarantee that we would see a bull that day nor the next day either. If I did not shoot one of the cows we might not see another caribou in the next two days. I could gamble and hope that we would see a bull – but I must decide – right now. I thought about it for a moment and then drew a bead with my scope on the chest of the largest of the cows and pulled the trigger. After all, I hadn't even had a chance to go fishing away from the camp area yet and if I passed up this opportunity and we did not see another caribou in the remaining time we had to hunt, I would wind up without a caribou and no fish either.

Just as I pulled the trigger, the cow started to put her head down. The bullet entered her jaw and went on into her brain – she dropped instantly. She was dead when she hit the ground. Truman dressed her out. We all had something to carry when heading back to our canoe. She had nice antlers – cows do have antlers though not as large ones as the bulls have. I was very satisfied with that animal. The bulls were scarce in that area that fall so far – besides, now I could go fishing.

The weather had been deteriorating all day and when we got back to the canoe the wind was mounting four-foot waves on the lake – and it had started to rain. We all put on ponchos, which we carried in our daypacks. Rich sat in the bow of that canoe and I sat in the center. Rich put the front of his poncho up over the bow of the canoe so that water coming over the bow ran off the side of the canoe instead of into his lap. Even so, we both had to bail for all we were worth and water came in with every wave we hit. Truman had all he could do to keep the canoe heading into the direction we wanted to go, and to keep us from becoming swamped. The canoe would ride up the face of a wave, cut through the crest and zoom down the other side with the prow diving into the base of the next wave. I thought to myself, "what a terrible place to die – to drown in the middle of a lake in the middle of nowhere."

We struggled and fought the elements for hours before we got close enough to the opposite shore to be sheltered from the wind. We pulled into shore for a rest and to quiet our nerves. While we were resting we heard the roar of outboard motors. Out on the lake we saw the two young guides racing each other at top speed. They were alone in their canoes and they were flying from the top of one wave to the top of the next. This was their kind of sea and they were enjoying every moment of it. This seemed to contrast sharply with the terror at least Rich and I felt as we had battled and bailed our way thru the same area only a few minutes before.

After a short rest we got back into the canoe and headed for the point that was at the start of the large bay where the camp was located. We landed and unloaded our gear, washed up and got into some dry clothes as we were all soaking wet and were just in time for dinner. The talk around the table that night was about fishing. Everybody by now had gotten his caribou. Tomorrow would be our last day at camp and I would get my one-day of fishing in. The talk on the short wave radio was about how the weather was deteriorating to the west of us and there was some chance that the area may see some snow in the near future. All the meat and fish that had been gotten so far was packed in plastic foam iceboxes. With the permafrost in the ground, a foam cooler would keep meat in good shape just by sitting on the ground in a shaded area. The caribou moss that was abundant made an excellent material to pack around the meat and fish. Where the outlet of the lake began there was an area of about three hundred yards or so of very heavy rapids. We had some good luck catching brook trout and salmon in that area. The Outfitter told us he had a seventeen foot Grumman aluminum canoe stashed at the foot of those rapids and that there were several flat water pond-like areas between there and where that outlet actually dumped into the Whale River. We planned to check all this out the next day and hit the sack early.

The next morning arrived before we knew it but we were ready for our fishing adventure. I packed my rifle and shotgun so that I would not have to do it later on. At breakfast, the cook said he had just enough eggs and bacon left for one more meal. Soon we headed for the end of the lake. Much of the time while hunting we had worn our hip boots because we were constantly walking through waist high wet brush. When we got to where the canoe was to have been stashed, there was a small Piper Cub type floatplane there and the canoe was gone. Since the Outfitter's territory was exclusively his for the use of his guests and clients we returned to the camp and reported to Bob the fact that someone was fishing with his canoe. Rich and I went down to the outflow rapids and fished off the rocks for landlocked salmon. Later on, Bob came by and said that the plane was gone and the canoe had been returned. We immediately headed back down the river.

The area where we fished downstream from the lake was about two hundred feet wide and flowed gently for about a half mile toward the next set of rapids. The river was pretty deep and as we drifted down the center toward the rapids we were able to cast our spinning lures in both directions. Almost every cast we got a hit and caught some nice lake trout. As we neared the second set of rapids, we began to catch salmon. The fish ranged from two to about five pounds and were beautiful to see.

The moment you hooked one he would come right out of the water doing cartwheels back and forth across the surface of the outlet. I have never before caught a fish that provided so much fight and action. We paddled upstream several times to drift over that same section and each time saw fresh action and kept catching the salmon. We both hated to quit even to eat lunch but decided we should take a break. We beached our canoe within about thirty yards of where this outlet we had been fishing in actually dumped into the Whale River. After tumbling down over one final rapids area the outlet entered a huge hole on one side of the River.

I grabbed my spinning rod out of the beached canoe and went a short distance downstream and cast my lure out into the big pool. On my very first cast, I tied into a good-sized fish – it looked like a lake trout about two feet in length. He fought hard so it took me awhile to tire him and begin to work him in toward the shore. It was kind of sandy at one spot and I thought I could beach him easily. Suddenly he made a powerful and frantic run right towards me and I saw this humongous fish chasing him. I stood amazed and wound up with only half of my twenty-four inch trout. I thought to myself, "I am glad that I was not out there swimming or I might have been that big trout's dinner."

Off to the northwest we saw a storm brewing so Rich and I put our gear back into our canoe and started paddling as fast as we could trying to get back to where the rapids entered the Stillwater area below the lake before the storm broke. We had a mile to go and could see it was going to be a close race to make it there before the storm caught up to us. We almost made it ashore when the storm hit with a roaring wind that immediately turned the previously calm outlet into crashing four-foot waves. It was snowing so hard we could barely see our hand in front of our face let alone the shore and with the help of God got there safely. We pulled the canoe out of the water and crouched behind the canoe and a clump of young spruce trees to wait the storm out.

Just as soon as it began, the storm suddenly quit but left the ground covered with snow. We collected our gear, stashed our canoe in its hiding place and headed back to camp. On the way, while I was hopping along the lakeshore from boulder to boulder, I slipped on a snowy one and fell with my right leg slipping between several boulders at a peculiar angle. It hurt and at first I thought I had broken it. I managed to get up with Rich's help and decided I was still in one piece. I limped back to camp and lay down on my bed until dinner-time. Soon the call came for dinner but I could not get up on that leg and walk to the dining tent so a couple of the Doctors came to look at the leg. One of the Doctors is a surgeon and the other an obstetrician. The leg was pretty badly swollen by then. The surgeon said jokingly, after checking it over, he guessed he would not have to amputate. The obstetrician said it was not his kind of medicine but he recommended that I see my Family Doctor after we got home. The surgeon agreed and they brought me something to eat in my tent.

When I awoke in the morning the swelling in my leg had gone down and I was able to limp around and get dressed. I stuck my head out the door of the tent to find a winter wonderland. It had snowed again during the night and the clouds had settled down so that we could not see the tops of the mountains. While we were eating breakfast we heard over the radio that all bush planes were grounded because of the bad weather. I was going to get another day of fishing in, albeit on a sore leg. They would try to fly us out the next day. We had plenty of caribou meat and fish to eat so we weren't worried. However, the surgeon was scheduled to do some major operations on the next day and the obstetrician was concerned about several of his patients. We got word that one of the pilots, flying a Grumman Goose seaplane, would try to pick them up the next day.

The weather continued stormy all day alternating between driving sleet and snow. We spent most of the day in the dining tent listening to the saga of those stranded in the wilds of northern Quebec and the stories of pilots flying above the clouds trying to get down and get them out. We played cards, talked about hunting and fishing and got to enjoy more of the cook's great snacks. Besides the regular meals we were treated to a steaming bowl of delicious soup anytime we had the urge. I went to bed early hoping that I could get out and do some fishing the next day. When we awoke in the morning the weather was pretty much the same. It looked like my wish was going to

160

come true. The radio at breakfast confirmed the weather report. However the Goose would try and get the Doctors out. All other planes were still grounded.

A little later, Rich and I walked along the shore south of camp and tried fishing for lake trout. We made a good effort but could not get a single strike. It seemed that the fish didn't like the weather either, so we returned to the dining tent in time for lunch. Sure enough, after lunch, the Goose came in and took the two Doctors out. We heard from them when they arrived back in Shefferville on our radio. They found the place to be totally jammed with people trying to get out of the area. Most had missed the train and the commercial jets to Sept-Isles and other locations were simply not flying. Every room in the hotel and private boarding houses was filled. They finally were able to get a room at the hotel and were trying to arrange for a private plane to fly them out to Montreal.

The following morning, the weather began to break. We had a call on our radio that they were going to try to fly us out that afternoon. We got everything packed and ready to go including the meat and fish. The Outfitter and his crew would remain behind to clean up camp, work up another week's supply of firewood and get ready for the next group of hunters who would be flying in the very next day.

The planes arrived on schedule right after lunch and we loaded our gear aboard and went bouncing along down the lake for a takeoff. On this trip Rich and I flew aboard the Otter. I sat up front in the copilot's seat. The weather consisted of a partially blue sky filled with large ominous clouds – each of the clouds trailed a long plume of snow. There were two small sliding windows in the windshield of that plane – one on the pilot's side and one on the copilot's side. They opened by sliding downwards and were held closed by a friction catch. The catch on the pilot's side worked but the one on my side held for a little while and then the window would fall open. On the way back to Shefferville the pilot skirted around the snow clouds in a circuitous route trying to keep in the open blue sky patches. However there were times that he had to fly through the snow and my sliding window would keep falling open and I would get a great blast of snow in my face. Aside from that inconvenience, the trip back was uneventful.

We landed and transferred our gear, meat and fish to the railroad station where they put our meat and fish in a refrigeration car. Our gear, except what we needed for the night, was placed in a baggage car. We headed for the hotel to see if the Doctors were still there. When we arrived, we found them waiting to confirm a flight out that night on a chartered plane to Montreal. We checked with the desk and found out there was a long list of people waiting for rooms and we would have to find other quarters for the night. We went back and talked with the Doctors who said that they had rented their room for that night and if they flew out we could have it – provided they did not check out of the hotel. If they did check out, their room would be given to some other party on the list ahead of us. The room held two single beds – and there were eight of us. We said, "great – six of us can sleep on the floor – at least we'll have a roof over our heads." With that problem solved we all went to dinner and it was then we discovered how costly it was to live in Shefferville. We all were craving a green salad and so we all ordered one plus of course, the regular entrée. We discovered that a single tomato cost several dollars. It was an expensive dinner but a good one. We returned to the hotel to await the call that the chartered plane was ready. It was quite late when word finally did come. We said good-bye to the Doctors. Rich and I agreed to take their gear, meat and fish back to New York and drop it all off in Watertown on our way through.

161

We enjoyed our sleep on the hotel room floor. After breakfast the next morning we went to see what a Hudson's Bay Company store was like. It was a very large store and we found it to be much like a department store at home except it was a grocery store also. You could buy anything from a ladies nightgown to a string of beaver traps. We did a little sight seeing around town and then boarded the train at ten o'clock for what was to be an eight-hour ride to Sept-Isles. The train was pulled by a modern diesel engine and consisted of five passenger cars, a dining car, two baggage cars, a refrigeration car and several freight cars. The passenger cars were very comfortable and every seat was filled. We were very glad we had purchased our tickets in Sept-Isles before we came up to Shefferville. Almost all the passengers were caribou hunters. We got acquainted with an attractive young couple in our end of the car that were returning from a hunting trip. We learned that he was the chief of police of the City of Quebec. He and his wife had spent a month alone on a very remote lake north of Shefferville. They had been flown in by a bush pilot and dropped off at a lake they had chosen and told the pilot to pick them up in a month. They had no radio with them and we asked how they felt about being left alone for a whole month with no way of asking for help if something happened. They said it was a concern but they just had to be very careful and not make any serious mistakes, like to break a leg or cut themselves with the axe, etc. We all agreed that this took a lot of self-confidence. Both of them had shot a nice bull caribou and she was proud that the antlers of her bull were the biggest. They said this was their vacation and they did something like this every year.

The train travels through some very spectacular and beautiful country, through miles of virgin forest and along the shores of large beautiful lakes. When we boarded the train we noticed that the windows were so dirty we could hardly see through them and so a couple of the guys got out and cleaned the windows where we were sitting before the train started. We were thankful they did or we would have missed some of the most beautiful scenery we have ever seen. It snowed on and off during the whole trip which added an extra degree of beauty to the countryside. We passed an Indian village with about ten large white tents that were in stark contrast to the dark spruce forest around them.

We went to lunch in the dining car at two o'clock. The food was delicious and a lot less expensive than the food in Shefferville. The train stopped several times along the way apparently in the middle of nowhere. If an Indian appeared alongside the tracks and was standing beside a small fire the train would stop. Usually just one or two people would board one of the baggage cars though sometimes they would have a pack-basket or maybe even a canoe to load. At one place the tracks ran parallel to a beautiful mountain river. Suddenly the area opened up and the river split in two and ran around a large island. We noticed a beautiful setting of buildings and manicured lawns and someone said, "well, there's Bing Crosby's salmon fishing camp." I had always appreciated Bingo's singing but now I liked the guy even more.

We arrived in Sept-Isles at around six o'clock, picked up our truck and loaded in our gear. Ivan asked us if we would carry all the meat, fish and guns in our pickup while he and the other five guys loaded their gear in the other two vehicles. We would meet in Watertown and sort all that stuff out when we got there. We said, "sure," and since it was still early and we had some daylight left, we decided to start driving for home rather than spend the night in Sept-Isles. We got something to eat before we left town – told Ivan we'd see him in Watertown and then were on our way. Just about dark we saw what looked like a very nice, new motel. We pulled in and when we stopped at the office they said that they had just one room left. We said, "good – we would take it." It had been almost two weeks since we had taken a shower and slept in a real bed. However, when we got into the room we discovered that the beds had not been made up after the previous occupants left and the room was in a pretty messy condition. We got our sleeping bags out of the truck, spread them out on the bed and spent the night in our clothes. It didn't bother us at all – we both slept like a rock.

We were up at daybreak and on the road. We stopped and had breakfast again at the little restaurant in Les Escoumins but the waitress with the mini skirt was not there. On the road to Tadousac after breakfast, we were passed by a Volkswagen "Beetle" which had the antlers of a caribou fastened to a rack on its roof. It was very comical because the antlers appeared to be larger than the car. As the vehicle passed us we noticed that it contained the Chief of Police from Quebec and his wife that we had met on the train. They waved and she indicated that it was her caribou antlers that were on the roof of the car.

When we arrived in Tadousac we found that the strike of the ferry boat people had been settled and we took the ferry across the Saguenay River rather than the road to Chicoutimi. We ate lunch somewhere along the way and when we arrived at the U.S. Customs, it was about nine p.m. As we started into Customs, we realized that we had brought only three guns into Canada but we were returning with eleven guns, ten boxes of meat and ten boxes of fish. We were only allowed a certain number of fish and one caribou apiece to say nothing about the extra eight guns. We were sure we were going to get into trouble but we sailed right through without any problem at all. Rich said he felt like getting down on his knees and kissing the U.S. soil.

We continued on to Watertown where we met with Ivan and had dinner. After dinner we sorted out all the stuff and then took off for home. It was after midnight when we arrived and after dropping Rich off, I headed home for a quick shower and my own bed. We decided to sort our stuff out early the next day.

The next morning Rich and I sorted out our gear and split up the meat and fish. The meat kept in beautiful shape. Unfortunately, due to being marooned for several extra days by the weather at Lac Champdore, the fish were all spoiled. We were glad we had gotten to enjoy eating some fresh fish at camp while we were there. We did enjoy sharing the caribou meat with some friends and family. It tasted quite similar to venison but was a little milder and very delicious. We would have a lot of exciting and we hoped interesting stories to tell. It had been an adventure of a lifetime for both of us and we are indebted to Ivan Greenfield for making it possible. We learned the following year that the cost of the hunting license went up from $150.00 to $1,000.00 dollars. I had hoped one day to be able to return with my wife to Shefferville to share with her how beautiful and wild that area really is.

CHAPTER 15   TODD KNOBEL AND MIKE FEINT

Rich: Please welcome Todd Knobel and Mike Feint. Todd is the youngest of the Knobel boys and Mike has been his best buddy since these guys were toddlers at about the age of three. These boys are an important part of the Knobel Deer Camp each fall. Though they probably don't have the interest in deer-hunting as some of the other members of the camp seem to have, nevertheless they greatly enjoy getting out into the woods and make a point of spending some time hunting every day they are in camp. Todd has a greater interest, it seems, in engines and motors and anything that you can ride on that goes fast. Likewise, his buddy Mike enjoys a fast ride but his primary interest is in aviation. Specifically, he has built his own airplane. He invited Howard Henry to ride up to camp with him this last fall – looking, I suppose, for somebody to keep him company on the trip. Howard informed Mike that he thought that the weather was too changeable in that north-country to suit him and he didn't want to chance it. Mike doesn't have any problem bringing the plane down onto the lake and greets the challenges of flying with great enthusiasm. He has plans for building at least one more aircraft and perhaps two.

Todd: We've been hunting about twenty years and haven't shot or killed a deer yet.

Rich: Think of all the fun you have had being in the woods.

Todd: Yeah, that's the whole idea.

Mike: Killing a deer is a distinct possibility – but that's not the reason we go to camp. We enjoy the fellowship and seeing all the old guys.

Rich: That's right, Howard and Norm are both about eighty.

Mike: We don't know for sure how old Frank Underwood is, but he's getting right up there.

Todd: He's having some health problems now – been diagnosed with cancer of the brain and lung. He's on a chemo treatment course now – we're all hoping he comes along okay.

Mike: Last fall he was helping clean out some trails. He was carrying the chain saw – and working his way up the hill. He's always been a very active outdoor person.

Rich: You weren't there the time he came dragging in the iron sleigh runners from the old lumber camp, were you?

Mike: No, I guess I missed that.

Rich: Now, Todd, I have heard that you have a great interest in snowmobiles and dirt bikes and about anything else that goes fast.

Todd: Yeah, and Mike, here – built an airplane.

Rich: You did! How did you do that?

Mike: I built it from scratch, all by myself.

Rich: What kind of a plane is it – what do you call it?

Mike: It's an amphibian – it's called the Aventura – a two-seat plane.
Todd: It's a pusher plane.

Mike: The engine's on the top.

Rich: Where do you fly out of?

Mike: I built a landing strip up in Truxton – put in a runway and put up a hangar – I fly right out of there. I've flown in the Catskills and also up in Canada some but my favorite place is in the Adirondacks.

Todd: He's got some beautiful video footage.

Mike: I've strapped the camera inside the plane to the passenger seat and of course wherever the plane points, that's where the pictures are taken.

Todd: You got to realize he's flying the plane also.

Rich: Have you ever landed on South Lake?

Mike: Oh, yes.

Rich: There's something about that place – it just catches the wind.

Mike: There aren't mountains around the lake to protect from the wind.

Todd: Over on North Lake, we've got the mountains – but also another problem – downdraft. You can be climbing and all of a sudden hit a down draft and fall about fifty feet in no time.

Mike: On North Lake, we come in under the turbulence. Sugarloaf, being the highest mountain near the lake, creates the most downdraft. Coming in from the north end of the lake, usually you can just get right under it and not be effected by it at all but you have to be constantly wary. If you are going to fly in the north-country you have to expect that kind of thing. I love to fly – I wouldn't give it up for anything.

Rich: How long does it take to get to camp from Truxton?

Mike: About an hour is all. It depends on which way the wind is blowing. Every two years you have to take all the tests all over again. You get a written test for about an hour and they take you up in an airplane and you fly about an hour – you have to prove yourself all over again.

Rich: Well, Todd, I'd like to hear something about your involvement at the deer camp.

165

Todd: Okay. Years ago, I used to attend all the clambakes at the Atwell Fish and Game Club with my Dad and brothers. Dad would always put in raffle tickets for us kids. I'd win all sorts of stuff – hunting gear mostly – but I never got to see any of that. It somehow disappeared. When you've got three older brothers that hunt – that kind of stuff just disappears. I was only about eight at that time. Then one time, a young friend and I were out in our rowboat using my Dad's three-horse outboard. We were probably whipping the thing around more than necessary – and apparently didn't get the motor properly fastened to the boat and the first thing we knew, it just hopped off the transom and headed for the bottom. We never saw that motor again. Several years ago after I took up scuba diving, I thought maybe I'd be able to locate that engine but we never found it.

A few years later, I was able to use our aluminum boat with the eighteen-horse outboard. That unit would move the light aluminum boat right along. It would plane in just no time at all – it would hop right up on top. In fact, that summer I would give high-speed rides to people on the lake. That boat just scooted right across the water – it handled really well. I would only take one or two passengers at a time – to keep it light. I would just follow the contour of the shore and run as close to the shoreline as I could. Everyone, me included, thought that was a lot of fun.

Rich: I seem to recall – maybe it was you telling us at hunting camp one evening – about you riding on a high-powered snowmobile one time and you hit something –

Todd: I didn't hit anything – there wasn't much snow on the lake at the time. It was my brother, Martin's sled – he had just bought it – it was only about two weeks old. We were all riding in a group – and came down off the Sand Lake Road. Being on a trail thru the woods, we were all going kind of slow but when we got back to the lake we all zoomed out onto the ice right at the campsite where the old fireplace used to be just across the lake from the State House. We all just opened our sleds right up. I looked down and I'm doing about 85 miles an hour. Just then, my sled started to slide – sideways. I realized I wasn't going straight anymore and that I needed to turn around so I'm gassing the engine and turning the skis and I spun it around real quick. Then, it straightened out – but then started doing it again. I spun it around like that about three times. Finally, one time as the sled was spinning sideways, the skis hit a hard spot of snow on the ice and the skis caught and flipped the sled right over.

I ended up face down on the ice with the sled upside down on top of me. Here I am, scooting along probably doing about seventy miles an hour. I remember saying to myself to the sled, "get off me." All of a sudden, it just came off almost right after I said that. I'm still sliding at a high rate of speed. So then, I thought I ought to flip over – so I did – and I was kind of going down the lake spread-eagled - sliding along. I lifted my head up to see if I could see where the sled was – and at that time it was just going end-over-end – coming right at me. I remember thinking, "I hope I'm going faster than the sled." I finally skidded to a stop right by the island near Spellicy's camp so I probably slid a thousand yards. I got up and walked over to the sled and flipped it over. It was all smashed, gas was pouring out of it, tools were scattered all over the place. I was kind of in a daze – walking around in circles at that point. We put it back together the best we could. We put the hose back onto the gas tank and bent the skis back straight and I drove it back to camp.

Rich: Just a couple of days ago a friend told me about her Dad and some friends who were snowmobiling up near Stillwater beyond Big Moose a ways. They had four sleds and her Dad was in the lead. For some reason, he kind of swung around on the ice so he avoided the hole where the

166

following three sleds all went thru. He was out in front and noticed that the other sleds weren't following him anymore so he turned around and went back – and he also went thru the ice. It is a wonder they all didn't drown. There happened to be some other guys in the area that saw it all happen so they're right there trying to conduct a rescue. They got everybody out of the water. The sleds of course are on the bottom of the lake. Now the thing to do is get these people who are sopping wet someplace where they can get out of their clothes. It's cold – down around zero and the wind is blowing so you know what that means. They got them into a warm camp – everybody got out of their wet clothes and they got dried off. Nobody had any real problem at all.

Todd: Weren't they lucky! I only went thru the ice once – on North Lake. My friend and I were cross-country skiing. We're just skiing across the lake heading towards the next bay. This was early in April and it was probably 65 degrees out. The ice was soft on top but there was still snow everywhere. I recall stopping and turning around to see how my friend was doing and all of a sudden, I heard a crack – then splash – I only dropped about a foot. I'm now half way up to my knees in ice-cold water. Apparently I fell thru the first layer. I was able to get back up on the ice so we headed to shore and went down the road back to camp. That was the only time I ever had this kind of a problem. When I went thru, my first reaction was – both arms came right out straight to my side. I had hold of ski poles in both hands – I got everything out as far as it would go. When I hit that second layer of ice underneath – that was a great relief.

Rich: This past January, a friend's brother-in-law fell thru the ice over on Whitney Point Reservoir while ice fishing. There was about eight inches of ice at the time. He's a big guy. Would there be springs coming up that maybe could make the ice thinner in spots?

Todd: There's a current that runs right thru the middle of that body of water – maybe that's what he hit.

Rich: Jim was down the lake cutting more holes so he didn't see this happen. Fortunately some other guys were in the area and they saw him go thru. If they hadn't seen him go thru the ice, he would have been in big trouble. He couldn't get up onto the ice all by himself. I think the guys took quite a chance in helping him. I used to be quite enthused about ice fishing but the older I get the less it seems to appeal to me.

Todd: I live quite close to the Erie Canal. I drive right by the Canal each day – you know how this winter's been – quite open. The other day I observed as I was driving along, open water on both sides of a large ice patch. I'm not even sure how the guy got out onto the ice. Our area is at least 10 degrees warmer than it would be around here in Cortland County. I could not believe that this fellow would be out there – fishing. He was on a floating patch of ice. He's out there – with water surrounding him and I know very well, it's not very safe. The chances some of these people take just to go fishing – it's unbelievable.

Another exciting snowmobile event we had up to camp was the year my son Mike was big enough to begin riding the sled. He'd been riding on his own most of the day, and seemed quite comfortable with what he was doing. This one time I'm riding on the back of the sled and he's driving. We had come up the lake on the ice and were about to run up an incline to get up onto the beach by our camp down by the lake. The sleds these days are pretty powerful. He gave it some gas and we came up over the beach in the air. About that time I figured, we're okay – we're staying on the

167

sled and I figured when we would land he'd let off on the gas and we would come to a stop in front of the cabin there.   When we landed, I'm not sure what happened – but he just stabbed the gas again – the skis just picked right up and we're headed straight for the cabin – just as fast as the thing will go. I kind let go of him – as I had been hanging on to him – I hit his hand off the gas, reached back and stuck my arm in the snow and hung onto him and pulled us both off of the sled. It slammed into the pole that holds up the right front corner of the porch. We kind of came to an abrupt stop and he shot out of my hands and went head first into the railing. We both had a full-face helmet on.

I pulled him back and stood him up and pulled the helmet off of him and I'm looking at him and asked "are you okay?" He says, "yeah." "Does your neck hurt or anything?" "No." That was one of those scarey moments. He kind of took a back seat to riding snowmobiles for the whole next year.

It was about two years ago when he actually got back on the machine himself. He started out slow – and you could tell he was mighty gun shy. He's fifteen now – I just bought a sled – one of Martin's old ones. He had a lot of fun with that.

My daughter just turned thirteen. She had been riding with someone else on the sleds but this last winter was the first time she wanted to drive. I'm riding on the back and we were traveling down the road toward the north end of the lake from camp. She turned around and we were coming back. When she got to the driveway, she could have turned either way or gone straight. She decided to go straight. We got practically back to the other end of the lake and I said, "don't you think we ought to turn around?" She said, "why?" I said "well, camp is back that way." She apparently was having so much fun driving she simply didn't notice when she came by our driveway. She was happy to drive us right back to camp.

We stayed at the lean-to out at the end of the Sand Lake Road on purpose one night last winter.

Rich: Was that the lean-to that Howard's Grandson, Skeeter spent the night in that time?

Todd: Probably. When we stayed there, we each had a snowmobile and a dog sled that we pulled behind to carry all our gear. We had a Coleman heater and cots and stayed there overnight. We had been there before – it looked like the lean-to was pretty well chinked and airtight. We hung a tarp over the front and enclosed it all in and the Coleman heater was doing its thing. We didn't have any problem that night with having adequate ventilation. What appeared to be well chinked up logs turned out to be pretty drafty. There were large holes between some of the logs. Apparently the mice or squirrels had removed a lot of the chinking. It might have gotten up to forty or fifty degrees inside. We were nice and warm when we stood up but down at the level of the cots it was a different story. We tried that another time in the lean-to across the lake. Mike went up there first and got the camp set up and I couldn't get away until later. I thought on the way up there he'd be freezing. When I got there, he was in his shorts and T-shirt cooking chicken wings keeping plenty warm. It was about 80 degrees in that camp – very comfortable compared to several degrees below zero outside.

We abandoned the idea and packed everything up the next day and returned to camp. Martin was staying in the small cabin down by the lake so that place was all heated up. We went down and kept him company. I went up a couple of weeks after that with a couple of cans of that expanding foam, and I sealed the whole place up at that lean-to. It was fairly warm that weekend – up to around forty so the foam applied fairly well. It didn't work nearly as well as if it had been seventy or eighty.

It came out of the can quite slow and it took awhile for it to expand. We had no problem with the sleds operating on that trail at all. We had a battery-powered winch with us as well so if we had gotten stuck we would have had some help on hand. It was much better than having a come-along. The winch was good for about fifteen hundred pounds so it could have pulled the sled and loaded dog sled out of most anything but we never had to use it on that trip.

Mike: Yeah, other times we didn't have the winch and needed it and wished we had it. This time we went prepared. Without a winch, it takes a couple of people to get a stuck sled unstuck. When did you talk to Martin – did he tell you about his excursion up over a tree with his new snowmobile?

Rich: I don't think so.

Todd: It was the first weekend with his brand new sled. He's got the track all studded with spikes for running on the ice and the sled is real powerful. We were going down the trail and we came across a few trees we either had to work our way around or under because there wasn't enough snow on them. We came upon this one when we were on one of the old log roads on the other side of the lake. He tries to climb over this one log and blips the throttle. The sled kind of stands right up on its end and then flops down over the bank. There were a couple of trees angling down from the bank and the sled kind of just crashed against them. Without those trees being there, the sled could have gone down into the valley. It was all the three of us could do to haul that thing up out of there. That would have been a real good time to have had the winch with us. We had several cameras with us that weekend but with all that was going on, none thought to get his camera out so we could get some pictures.

We've noticed quite a bit of ice fishing going on at the lake recently. They had stocked some tiger muskies in the lake about four years ago. We saw a couple of guys fishing to the right of the State House. It appeared they had about twenty holes drilled in the ice. They made all their holes about a foot in diameter.

Rich: Do they have an engine on their auger?

Todd: No, they just use hand power. Larry's got one he bought recently. It's a foot in diameter. It goes right down thru the ice real easy.

Rich: How about sharing a first hunting experience – were you alone?

Todd: The second time I had gone up the hill I was with everybody but I had gone out hunting by myself. The first time I went up I was age fifteen so I couldn't big game hunt yet. Dad was going to just take me out in the woods and show me the places to walk and sit. But, sure enough, it snowed eighteen inches Friday night. It took us about four hours to get in to camp. We had to stop a couple of times on the way in. It was snowing so hard we couldn't even see the road. Larry was driving a big car and we were all together.

Over the years Mike and I have kind of played with the whole idea of what kind of lunch are we going to have? Dad mixed up peanut butter and cheese and gave me an apple and a box of raisins. He said, "head out that way." It was Saturday morning and there were eighteen inches of fresh snow that we received the night before. I didn't seem to know how to dress or even what gear to take with me. Well, Dad dropped me off and said, "stand here for about two hours – I'm going over there. After awhile, come and get me and we'll go somewhere else. Go slow." He was telling me the whole thing. I froze to death. I thought it was the worst experience I have ever had. After about an hour I was just shivering – and gave up on my watch. I headed off in the direction he had gone – following his footprints in the snow. I probably left my watch sooner than I should have. He probably expected it. I actually took a break from hunting a few weekends after that.

Later in the season when I tried it again, there wasn't quite as much snow and I could walk around pretty easily. I had been going up there a long time so I thought I knew my way around pretty good anyway. I went up over the top and passed the swamp and wound up way out there – somewhere. I had two compasses with me. I was using my compass and going in a direction away from camp and walking in what seemed to be about a straight line. I'd look at my compass and I'd pick a tree and I'd walk to it and I just kept doing that.

It got to the point where I thought it would be good to head back to camp. Back to camp was in a totally opposite direction from what I thought it was going to be. So, I got out my other compass and was looking at it – and sure enough, they're both the same. I just totally didn't believe that compass. I followed it anyway and got off of the trail and ended up in the swamp and started stepping from log to log – still trying to follow the compass. Well, I was lost. There's a difference between being lost and not knowing where you are. I came close enough to genuine panic that I could identify that feeling but resisted the thought and that seemed to work for me. Then I realized all I need to do is walk "this way," following my compass still. I was able to T-bone the trail about by Spike Rock just above camp. At that point I was once again on familiar territory and was able to recognize and identify my location from the landmarks I had become accustomed to. I really gained a lot of confidence with this initial experience of trying to orient myself around in the woods. With practice, this whole routine not only became easier but also became fun.

Mike: always believe that compass.

Todd: Yeah. I had a hard time believing it. It told me to go "that way" – and I just didn't want to believe it. I thought, "this can't be" – but I followed it and sure enough, it was right. Another time, Rich, was the day you wounded that big deer. We followed it and came so close at least four times. We were as careful as we could be but it would jump up and we could hear it go. That deer took us for a ride. We wound up way over in Grindstone. It would probably have been shorter in distance to use our compass and follow a straight line back to camp. We opted at that point to just follow the Sand Lake Road. Even though it would be a much longer distance, the going would be easier. By then we were all tired.

Rich: I felt real bad about that deal. I had hunted with that scope on my rifle for a number of years. I'd killed a bear, a caribou and several deer. Apparently my eyes had changed enough that I couldn't use the scope like I used to be able to. It was just terrible. That was the only time in my whole hunting career that I had wounded a big game animal and had it get away. I got rid of my scope – traded it in for a set of fiber optic sights. I like them very much. You can leave both eyes open. It's easy to follow and shoot at moving game. You automatically center the sights very similar to how you use a peep sight arrangement.

Todd: I bought Norm Bahnsen's rifle. It's a Marlin lever action in .35 Remington caliber. It's just like Grandpa's gun. It's got a two to eight power scope on it. It's sitting up on these circular mounts. I can choose to either look thru the iron sights or thru the scope. The iron sights are fully in view – underneath the scope. I like that a lot. I take it out for a walk at least once a year. Mike and I aren't much in the way of being mighty hunters – our biggest thing is we wake up in the morning and we spend about two hours deciding what we're going to eat. We've taken some pretty interesting stuff out and cooked it out in the woods. We had shrimp and steak kabobs one year. Another time we had some buffalo that was real good. We'll take Howard's beans out with us and scalloped potatoes and ham. We usually have enough food for about six people – but who knows, maybe someone will come along and join us for lunch.

One day, Jim, Norm's son came along about lunchtime. We were out by the cannon watch. That's a great place to see deer. He came along and smelled what we were cooking and said, "what are you guys doing – this smells great!" So, we invited him to stay for lunch. We certainly had a great plenty. We called them our MRE packs. We'd put the stuff in an aluminum pouch and put it on some nice hardwood coals there and it would heat thru in no time at all. We'd have appetizers – start out with cheese and crackers and maybe sardines. We generally hunt from the camp to where we eat. Then we eat about two or three hours and hunt back. If something stands broadside to us in the woods or runs by like with Larry's deer, then we'll feel obligated to shoot it. We don't actually go out looking for them. If we see one and the opportunity is there we might act on it.

Rich: The important thing is that you guys both can enjoy being in the woods and are able to get out and have fun. With all your adventures and camping and the activities you share it sounds to me like you have a very active life in the out-of-doors. Save the serious deer hunting for the serious deer hunters. I know you're available to help drag whenever someone manages to kill a deer. That's pretty important too. Thank you for sharing and for your contributions to this book. I wish you success in your ventures.

CHAPTER 16   BARRY WARREN

Rich: Barry Warren is a young friend that enjoys the woods and hunting. He and my Nephew, Mike Niswender, are partners in a real estate business. They lease a number of residential apartments and houses and this project keeps them both busy in their spare time. Barry is a member of Camp Cortney that we talk about in Chapter Nine of this book. Barry, when did you and Mike first join the hunting camp?

Barry: It was about twenty years ago this last fall. At that time, it was an all day event to get there. We used a tractor and hauled a trailer behind that. A lot of the way we traveled on truck trails thru the woods. Sometimes, we'd have to winch the tractor out of the mud holes. After that, we tried motorcycles for the majority of the people and then we used three wheelers for a little while. We've all got some great memories of the original camp. It was of log construction and let the air and mice in quite freely. At night after the fires went out, it really got cold in that camp.

I've got a wonderful memory of a ten-point buck I killed in that area and I'd like to share that story. We used to go in for a week at a time. The very first day I got in to camp was on a Tuesday. I went out on a scouting trip just to see what things looked like over toward Balsam Lake. On my way over to the lake that morning I found a scrape line and filings on some trees where a buck had been thru there and I followed that line for quite a ways. The trees he was filing on were about six inches in diameter. I figured he might be a pretty good buck. On my way over there I found a couple of other scrapes and filings of smaller deer, but when I found this one, I decided that he was the one I wanted to pursue and hunt. On Tuesday afternoon I spent a couple of hours sitting near this scrape line but nothing showed up. Wednesday morning I hurried right over there and still, nothing happened. I told one of the other fellows about the smaller buck's scrape line I'd seen on the way over to where "my" big buck had been working. I took him over there and set him up on the smaller buck's scrape line and he killed that deer.

Twice a day beginning Tuesday afternoon I spent some time on that big buck's scrape line. All during that period of time, I hadn't seen a single deer on that line. It's awfully hard to keep your enthusiasm up if you're not seeing anything, but I stuck with it. On Friday morning, I'd been there since daybreak and at 9 o'clock that morning I saw a doe coming. I began watching very intently hoping there was something coming along with her. She came out right thru to where I had set up. I kept watching and kept watching – and sure enough, I could see the antlers of this big buck that was with her. He came towards me parallel and then turned right toward me. She did the exact same thing ahead of him first. When she got about twenty yards away, she turned and went broadside away from me – never knew I was there. I figured at that point he would do the same thing – and sure enough, when he got to about twenty yards away from me he made that turn and I shot him. He bolted out of there of course – I hit him right thru the lungs. Actually I was so excited with him running – I shot again, and missed the second shot. He ran only about seventy yards and fell. I went over there and counted those points. He was a nice ten-point buck. His rack was only about seventeen inches wide but he had nice tall tines and was perfectly symmetrical. What an honor to take a deer like that. I counted those points and let out a "yahoo" – I bet everybody heard me.

I had heard somebody say, if you get a big deer the best way to get him out of the woods is to make a pack out of him. So, I put a cut thru the hind hocks and slid the front hooves thru there and put a stick thru them to lock them in place and made a pack out of the deer. There was no snow on the ground and I had a couple of miles to go to get him back to camp so I decided I'd give it a try. I had tried dragging him a ways – he was a big-bodied deer and I couldn't do it – I couldn't drag him. So, I made this pack out of him. I leaned him up against a tree and I sat down. The problem was, I had to get awfully close to the ground to get my arms into the pack. I just couldn't do it. I couldn't pick him up off the ground. I finally decided I better go back to camp and get some help.

Four or five of us came back and dragged that deer out. It turned out, it weighed 188 pounds and that's one reason why I couldn't drag the thing. That was the dressed weight. The live weight was over 200 pounds for sure. I did my own taxidermy on that deer and did a head mount. My taxidermy doesn't turn out like it might if I had paid a professional to do it. However, the price was right – and I don't hear any complaints from me. It's very meaningful to me to be able to see that deer mounted and hanging on my wall in our home. This was the nicest buck I have ever killed. I think this goes to prove persistence pays.

Rich: Apparently a buck makes quite a wide swing after laying out his scrape line – in fact, I believe a buck will make several of these thru the woods.

Barry: I think what happens is that a doe is attracted to the scrape line. Once the buck finds a doe that is about ready to come into heat he'll stick with her until that particular doe has been bred. My theory is why he didn't show up all week was because he was with this doe. I think the only reason why the buck came into the area at that time where his scrape line was – was simply because he was following this doe. She's the one that led him back thru the area and what allowed me to get a glimpse of him. Probably during the pre-rut would be a better time to watch a scrape line. Later on when the rut is in full swing they're normally with does. I think a doe is attracted to the scrape line. A buck might pick up his first doe or two by checking his scrape lines.

The law of averages is not as good so far as success in killing a deer is concerned to hunt in the Adirondacks compared with hunting in the southern tier. That's not the main reason most of us go up there. We go to camp in the Adirondacks for the fun and fellowship around camp and the atmosphere – the quietness and peacefulness and maybe the chance to get that one monster buck that could have survived for six or eight years.

One time I was hunting out of the new camp after we had moved our location. I actually started hunting right from the camp. I hunted down along to where we had parked our vehicles and then went across the road down by the river bottom of the Jessup River. I'd seen some good sign down in that area before so thought I'd hunt my way thru that section. I did a slow walk and still-hunt thru the morning and hunted down along the Jessup until I came to where the road crosses the river on a bridge. Then I headed over toward Little Moose and Otter Lake area. I knew that area fairly well so I hunted up the side of the mountain to that area.

There was a crust on the snow so it was noisy walking. It was difficult still-hunting under those conditions. I guess my main goal then was to use the snow to see what sign was in the area and check for tracks and see what the activity was in that area. All morning I walked basically without stopping to rest. My goal was to keep going until I reached an area that at least looked like it mighty be productive. When I got up to Little Moose and Otter, I finally came across some fresh tracks. It was nine-thirty in the morning so I had spent a few hours just hiking.

When I found these tracks I could see where they had been digging in the ferns a little bit and the deer had fed their way thru sometime that morning. The sign was very fresh. So I thought, "well, it looks promising enough so I'll at least sit down and catch my breath and relax." I picked this downed tree and sat next to the roots that were sticking up and sat on the edge of it. I hadn't been there five minutes when I heard – crunch, crunch, crunch – a deer was coming – I could hear it quite plainly. Sometimes it can catch you off guard – it's difficult to tell from what direction that noise is coming from. So, I had to turn my head and try to focus on which direction the noise was coming from. I spotted a deer about a hundred yards away from me – it came up thru toward me somewhat but I never did see the head – I couldn't tell what it was. I was tempted to get up and travel along in the direction the deer had gone but I felt that if I did try that, the deer would definitely hear me – so I decided to stay right there.

Another five minutes and what appeared to be the same deer came back on those same tracks and this time he headed right towards me. I turned around this time – and once again I had a hard time of focusing on what direction the noise was coming from. As I turned I could see a nice set of antlers – it was a very impressive deer.

When he went behind a blowdown, I swung around off my log and laid my rifle on top of that log and waited. I remember distinctly that he had his nose right down in those tracks of a doe. When his vitals came into a little opening in the blowdown I pulled the trigger. He bolted out of there doing a hundred miles an hour. He was dead on his feet. He went about forty yards and ran right into a big tree.

Rich: Was it a heart shot?

Barry: It was a heart shot – he was dead on his feet and didn't even know it. He hit the tree so hard he broke his front teeth. My concern was, don't hit the antlers. He was a pretty deer – he had seven points and a nice wide rack – heavy beamed and again, a big-bodied deer. I went about the task of getting him gutted and prepared. We had good snow on the ground so I could drag him. He weighed one eighty-three. I dragged him for about two hours down the trail heading generally in the direction of camp. I still had a long drag ahead of me – at least another four miles or so. I'd go for a ways, stop and catch my breath, and then would carry my gun ahead and set it down and go back and use both hands to drag. I kept this up for another two hours. Right from this same area I had just come from, I heard another shot. I wondered, "who's up in here – who might I know that would be hunting?" The only one I could think of that would be hunting in this same area would be my Father. I thought for his best interests, I'd leave my deer right here and I'll walk up and see if I can intercept him. So, back up my trail I went. I felt like it was time to eat my lunch so I sat down and was about half way into my sandwich when I noticed a movement – and here he comes – it's my Dad and he's dragging a deer too. He killed his deer close to the same general area where I got mine. This was going to work out great. When we came to a little grade or a difficult part, we could team up and the two of us would drag which made it a lot easier.

Rich: Was his deer anywhere near as large as yours?

Barry: Nope – his wasn't – he had shot a spike-horn.

Rich: Now, couldn't you offer to drag his spike and let him handle your seven-point?

174

Barry: That was what I was thinking. He seemed to have had the more experience. He didn't see it that way – he said, "you're young and youthful – drag your own deer." We did team up when we would come to a creek bottom. It helped a lot to have the two of us on one deer getting thru a stream and then up the other side which of course would be somewhat of a grade. He was glad to see me and I was glad to see him.

Rich: You bet – what a time of companionship. Wasn't that a wonderful experience?

Barry: With the success ratio being what it is for that north country, it was pretty amazing that two people out of the same camp would get two deer in the same area at about the same time of the day. He wasn't all that far from me when I shot. He wondered at that time who might be up there in that same area. I really didn't have a destination in mind when I left the camp that morning. I guess it pays to wait until you find some fresh tracks before starting to do your hunting.

Rich: I'll just bet that this was a high point in both your hunting careers.

Barry: It was neat to see the two of them hanging on the meat pole. Usually the meat pole doesn't get used or abused much in that north-country, as a rule.

Rich: I love the Adirondacks, for hunting. If the Lord gives me strength to go up there and tromp around in the woods or even sit in front of the fire in camp for another season – or even another ten or twenty years or whatever – and if I don't happen to see and kill another thing – I don't care. It absolutely does not matter. Mike and Ron were sharing – and especially, Mike was saying, the thing that means the most to him about deer camp is when the guys all get back to camp after having been out hunting all day and he gets to hear what everybody else has seen – and he gets to tell his story too.

Barry: We've had a little bit of luck hunting the migration trails. Did any of the other hunters mention that?

Rich: I've heard the story from Mike before – he may have made some brief mention of that method in his interview but I don't think he said anything very specific about it. I'd like to hear what you have to say. It's kind of a concept I have known about a long time – that when the heavy snows come the deer get out of the high country and head for their winter yarding areas. I've always known about that. When hunting up the Oswegatchie River area of the woods, the yarding area would be down near the river. Up at North Lake, the yarding area would be down near Forestport where the year-round residents feed the deer. What have been your findings about this phenomenon?

Barry: When we go up to camp at the end of the season, two things happen. Weather permitting and if we've had some snow we'll find trails that are beaten right down. All the tracks are going the same way. We've found that year after year the trails are in the same area. The trails are completely packed down – they get a lot of use. From different places in the higher elevation, they'll branch together into one main trail – almost like a creek does. We've followed them backwards. One year I went up to camp the last weekend of the season. Two things were happening – the migration was occurring – they were beginning to move to lower country – and the rut was still on. The bucks were still chasing does.

175

I followed one of those migration trails backwards until I came to a place where I had a good watch. There were two heavily used trails that came together right there. I climbed up on a large rock and sat there. I had been there on that rock probably an hour and a half and saw a movement. Another fellow in our camp had already taken the biggest buck of the season so far – it was a nice spike-horn. We have a little friendly contest in our camp each year to see what the biggest deer taken will be. I thought, "what a shame that just a little spike-horn will take top honors this year." Two does were coming down this migration trail. Always when you're sitting on a watch – especially when overlooking a trail – you begin to wonder when it will be that the next animal will come along on that trail. It might be within a few minutes or in a day or two.

Well, here came two does – but they kept looking behind them. I started doing the same thing and pretty soon here comes a spike-horn. Well, somebody else already gotten one of those for a trophy – so I just kept watching and sure enough, here came a six point. He came right along on that migration trail following along behind those other deer. So, from up on my rock, I shot him and then I had another one of those long drags to get back to camp – in deep snow. On one hand the snow always helps in dragging because the deer kind of slides along when you pull. But, on the other hand, when the snow is several inches deep it can make the task difficult. It's not an easy job no matter and I had about two miles to go to get him back to the roadway. It took about four hours to make that drag. I kept looking at my watch and thinking, "let's see – what time does it get dark?" When I got back to the corner and the road I hid the deer underneath a tree and then sat down and waited for Mike to come along – he was going to be my ride back to camp that night.

When he finally pulled up along the road, I walked out and asked him how his day was and if he'd seen anything. He had seen a couple of deer – then asked how my day was. I told him, "well, I saw quite a lot of sign – as a matter of fact, there's a large track right over here – come on over and take a peek at it." So, he followed me over to where I was looking underneath this tree – he thought what he saw there was pretty good sign. That weekend turned out to be very good hunting. Mike got a shot at a big buck on a migration trail but he hit a sapling and missed the deer. Lew had been hunting in the same general area and figured he got a crack at the same buck that Mike shot at – and he missed him too.

When I returned to camp that night I said, "looks to me like that migration trail is the place to hunt." I put another one of our fellows on that same watch. I told him about that rock – he said he knew exactly which one I was referring to and he would stick it out on that spot for most of the day. I made a big loop that morning in search for new tracks. The tops of the mountain were pretty barren of sign so it appeared that a lot of deer had already moved out.

I slowly worked my way back to the trail where I had put that fellow on watch and there he was – sitting – patiently waiting. I climbed up on that rock with him and we chatted a little bit and we had a cookie or brownie together and right while we were sitting there I said, "look there – don't move – here comes another deer." I had already gotten my deer – so this fellow pulls up and got a nice eight-point with a seventeen-inch spread – right on that same trail. This all happened on that same weekend. I said, "I've got to get going now – congratulations." No, of course I helped him drag that deer into camp. This trail paid big dividends for us that weekend.

We believe timing is everything when it comes to hunting migration trails. Every season doesn't allow that. The migration doesn't have to be at any set time – but is the result of a combination of events and how deep the snow is. The snow depth turns out to be one of the things that cause the deer to move out of the high country and head toward their wintering areas. We learned a lot that weekend and in the future made it a point to try to go up to camp to hunt the very end of the season. A lot of the years when we tried this, the timing didn't turn out to be right so we didn't have the success that we had hoped for. That's the chance you take.

Rich: As a general rule in the area where you hunt, you don't get that lake-effect snow, do you? We get the results of that phenomenon in the North Lake area very heavily – from Lake Ontario.

Barry: I think we're far enough east that we probably are not affected by that.

Rich: You probably get weather coming down from Canada that affects the snowfall in your area.

Barry: Another item that may affect the amount of snowfall in our area is our elevation. We notice and wonder at the increase in snowfall – on our drive into our area where we hunt. In that ten or twelve miles we can't help but notice the further back and higher we go the snow just seems to be getting deeper and deeper. We have found that we can't judge it by the Speculator area – there is often more than five inches difference in the amount of snow between Speculator and when we get back into our camp. Also there's another additional difference in elevation from where our camp is located to the tops of the mountains where we hunt. We believe most of the deer that migrate out of our hunting area actually winter close to Speculator – mostly due to their being less depth of snow. It would not be unusual for a deer to travel fifteen to twenty miles to reach its favored wintering area.

Rich: In the wintertime when you go back in snowmobiling – what kind of depth of snow do you find then?

Barry: One year we traveled back in mostly out of concern for the depth of snow and especially the snow load on our camp. We started in one day with snowmobiles and on anything that was not already a packed trail the snow was too deep to travel. We tried and tried all afternoon to make it to our camp. We took turns breaking trail. By that I mean one man would drive his sled down the trail we were making and go just as fast as he possibly could to go as far as he could until he got stuck. Then he'd have to turn his sled around and ride back to where he had started from and then the next man would go down that freshly made trail until he got stuck. We went about half the distance to our camp but we could not make it in all the way that day. We went back and stayed in a motel in town. We were able to borrow some snowshoes from the people that owned the motel. We finally got in to camp and found about five feet of hard packed snow on top of the roof. There was so much weight from all that snow that we could see that the rafters were bowing. We had to unload the snow off the roof before we really dared spend much time in the camp. It came off in big chunks. It had snowed some and frozen – then thawed – and frozen again. It took us a couple of hours to get all that snow shoveled off. Our roof on that building has a twelve-twelve pitch – it's a steep thing. Normally we could get the snow to unload by itself just by starting a fire in the wood stove. As soon as it would warm up in the camp, the snow would just slide right off. But this time, the load was so heavy that it caused the stovepipe to disconnect so we had to do it the hard way. Once we had removed the snow, the stovepipe lined up again and we could get the fire started safely.

177

We learned a good lesson that year. We since have beefed up the interior considerably to better hold and support the snow and resultant weight when it does accumulate. We added a second crossbeam half way up to help withstand a greater snow load. We probably did the right thing that year by checking on our camp when we did. Are you limiting the stories for your book to basically Adirondack hunting?

Rich: No, I discovered that almost everybody that hunts New York eventually hunts somewhere else if even for only one trip. It could be Montana, Colorado, Texas or Alaska. I know, for instance, that you have hunted elk with your bow out west. Several others that have participated in this book have had hunting experiences for a variety of game animals and in a variety of places. Just about everyone I have talked to have concluded that there is no finer quarry or challenge in hunting than the white tailed deer. They're sharp and they're worthy and they're wonderful.

Barry: They'll test the wits of any hunter, I'll tell you that.

Rich: Before you get into a story about hunting out west, would you just give us a little input regards your participating in still-hunting?

Barry: I'll begin by saying that I don't consider myself to be a very good still-hunter. The reason is I have a hard time slowing down. My life-style in general seems to be at a fast pace. I simply can't slow down when I go into the woods for a weekend. Maybe if I had a whole week at a time to hunt like I used to be able to do, it would be different. Much of the time, what I call still-hunting – is my desire to get from point A to point B in the woods. Usually I have in mind visiting an area in the woods where I have been successful on previous hunts. I don't go as slowly in the woods as I should and I know I miss seeing game because of that – or if I do see it, normally it's the tail-end of the animal that I notice when it is making its speedy departure. I always have a destination in mind – a place I want to visit that I know about – and I realize I try to get there too quickly. There are skills involved and a knack to being a successful still-hunter and I'm still working on that. I think Lewis Heath is an excellent still-hunter and he's been successful in doing that. There's no better teacher than success itself. It can reinforce that what you are doing is right and will encourage you to do it that way the next time.

When hunting, I like to see what the sign looks like in a lot of different areas. That's another reason why I perhaps hunt a little faster than I should. However, when I get to an area that I think looks really good and the sign is very heavy there – then I'll slow down and spend some time – perhaps sit on watch for a little while. It's awfully hard to beat a situation where the deer are on the move and you're not. They've got such keen eyes that even while still-hunting you have a hard time beating them if they're not on the move too. I'm still working on my techniques, to be honest with you. I do a lot of hiking and cover a lot of miles in a day's time and enjoy searching a vast area of the woods. I enjoy this method and I guess that's mostly what it's all about. In the meantime, I still manage to kill my fair share of the deer that wind up on the meat pole in our camp so I don't feel too badly about my method.

Rich: The day may come when you may want to experiment with something else. And that something else may come as a result of hearing or reading about someone else's success and you might want to give it a try – but you might want to just keep on doing what you're doing – nothing wrong with that. You have my admiration about the way you conduct yourself in the woods, that's for certain. I can imagine your Dad is very proud of you. I just completed my interview with Lewis Heath

178

last evening. He loaned us a couple of photo albums to look over when we got a chance. Those photos made me feel like I was actually there and taking part in the building of your new camp and in the many hunting adventures and stories you and your friends have so graciously shared. I count this as a blessing in my life – thank you.

Barry: Killing a deer far from camp gets me those nice long hauls. But, I usually don't have any trouble sleeping at night when I do get back to camp.

Rich: Bob Knobel would have some advise for you. He'd say, "now look, Barry, when you get beyond a certain point, take the shells out of your gun. I don't even want you to be tempted to kill a deer so far away from camp."

Barry: There have been times, I will admit, when I was kind of glad I didn't see anything to shoot because I was a long ways from camp. It's fun to explore and go see new areas where you have never been before and learn a little something new or just to see what the sign looks like in an area that you are already acquainted with. Sometimes it takes a day or two – or even three to cover your complete hunting area to see where it looks like the hunting will be the best. I enjoy noticing where the scrape lines and filings appear and sometimes I can determine how big a buck actually might be by paying attention to these kinds of signs. I truly enjoy just spending my day in the woods observing signs and tracks. I can tell how many deer there may be in a given area and how large they are apt to be. I can tell what they did and where they were – the size of the deer and how many there are. We've even seen, in recent years, moose signs and tracks. One of our hunters was traveling thru a thick area by the end of one of the ponds not too far from our camp and he heard a large animal go crashing out thru the woods but didn't actually see the animal. He went over there and sure enough, he found fresh moose tracks – they are really big. The State began by relocating a few pair of moose into our area and they seem to be really doing well and the population is getting better and better. It would be wonderful to think that eventually the numbers would get to be such that someday they could open a limited moose season.

I've been out to Colorado and Montana at least eight times now. Everything I do out there is with a bow and arrow so my success is of course limited. I've had some great experiences. One in particular was in Colorado where I was hunting one time with two other friends. Every day I would go out and hunt by myself. On this particular morning I hiked to the top of a mountain. We stayed in a tent at the bottom of the valley. We did all our own cooking and hunted on our own without the assistance of a guide. During the bow season for elk, the rut is generally in full swing so it can be compared somewhat to turkey hunting. I use a mouth diaphragm and a tube and also might cow call a little bit and even bugle once in awhile to see if I can get a response.

At about nine-thirty in the morning, I was at the top of this ridge. There was a sizeable bowl down below me so I bugled into that bowl and I immediately got a response from down in there. The bull bugled back. My heart started pumping and I got all excited so I called again and whenever I talked to him he would respond. I'd bugle to him and he'd bugle back. After about fifteen minutes of this, I realized I wasn't about to call him out of this bowl. I would need to go in there and see if I couldn't step in on his territory. It was fairly steep going into this bowl – I remember I sat down on my rear end and let myself slide down one step at a time so I didn't get sliding and once I got to the bottom I was concerned that I didn't expose myself to where he could see me and if that happened, the whole hunt would be over.

I worked my way in slowly and when I got to the bottom I called again and he responded again and I kept working on him. When he wouldn't come any closer to me I would go a little closer to him. Every time I would move, there was a fear in the back of my mind, "I'll be seen and could lose my opportunity." I do recall at one point I called and he responded and he was a couple of hundred yards away. In just a few minutes, I heard him coming. He's walking in the rocks and sounded like a horse coming, he's so big, you know. So, I got ready – and sure enough, I spotted him coming. I could see the antlers – here comes the bull – and it appeared he would come in between two trees that were about thirty yards away and I thought that would be my perfect opportunity.

I got my bow up and I'm ready to draw and just before he went between those two trees I saw his nose go in the air and he caught a whiff of me. The wind had circled a little bit and away he goes. Just about then I heard him bugle again but he was still two hundred yards away – this wasn't the bull I was after. The bull that came in so close wasn't the one that was talking to me. The other bull came in silent – came in to my call and caught wind of me. So, once again I moved another time – moved in closer. I think I made two more moves.

This ordeal started at nine-thirty in the morning. At twelve o'clock I made my final move. I got on my knees in front of a pine tree and made my call. I knew I was getting fairly close to his area this time so I took my grunt tube and put it behind me to make it sound like it was further away. As soon as I called, he bugled and then I could see him – he's coming right in to me so I got everything ready. He went behind a group of trees while he was probably fifty yards away. I didn't make another peep but came to full draw. I held for quite a bit of time – waiting for him to get close enough and he finally came in to within eighteen paces – eighteen yards – and I released the arrow. He was quartering towards me so it wasn't as good a shot opportunity that I had hoped for. It had begun to sprinkle rain on and off and I was concerned I might lose my blood trail if he took off. I could see my arrow – it got great penetration – right up to the fletches. He started to do a half circle on a run around me.

I had recently read a story in a magazine that suggested you might calm them down sometimes by calling again. So, that's exactly what I did. I cow called to him while he was running and he came to a stop. Now, he's only twenty yards away from me – a nice bull – and here I am, on my knees, trying to make a decision. Shall I try to knock another arrow and shoot him again – or – do I stay right here nice and quiet – and allow him to stay calm. He's looking around and can't find me – doesn't see me and the wind is right so he doesn't smell me. I remember at one point, an airplane went overhead and that bull looked up at that airplane while he's standing there with that arrow in him. That was kind of an interesting thing – something that happened that stuck with me, you know.

I decided not to do anything that would spook him. He finally went and laid down. He was down behind a log but his head is still up and I can see his antlers going back and forth. Once again, I didn't do anything to stir him or scare him out of there. A couple of times I saw him try to get up and he couldn't do it. The third time he finally got to his feet and then he tipped upside down and that was when I realized, "he's my bull!" It's pretty exciting to do this one-on-one – no guide. To do the calling and do the work all yourself and everything you did was apparently right because it ended with success. That was a hunting story that will stick with me a long time.

Rich: Congratulations!

180

Barry: Now the work begins. They're big animals. Every part of the gutting operation is similar to what you do with a white tail but about four times in proportion bigger. I never knew exactly what the body weight was but I'm going to guess somewhere between six and eight hundred pounds. He was a large-bodied animal. I took the head and the cape out with my first trip and then went and got help to bone the meat and carry that all out. I used ribbon to mark my way down thru to make sure I wouldn't have any problem of finding him when we went back after the meat.

Rich: You haven't had any problem, have you, with bears being attracted to the area where you have made kills?

Barry: There certainly are black bears in the area where we hunt. It's always a concern because they are omnivorous. We've been fortunate whenever we have made kills out west – we didn't have to leave the kill for any length of time. One concern in the Rocky Mountains is the blowflies will lay their eggs – and they'll lay them so quickly, you can't believe. I was with a fellow that killed a cow elk. He came back to get us and within a three hour period we all made it back to where his cow was. He had covered the animal with pine boughs to prevent the blowflies from getting into the cavity but he had gotten some blood on the fanny pack he was carrying. I looked on his fanny pack and thought it was a fat deposit or something. It was a quarter of an inch thick and still growing when we got there – with blowfly eggs that had been laid in that three-hour period. It was hard to believe they could do that so quickly. I have a special love for the Rocky Mountains. It's quite similar to the Adirondack Mountains in many ways. The Rockies have their own atmosphere and their own type and style of hunting and I have a special love for that. What an honor – to take a bull – the one and only one I have taken with a bow. I've had other opportunities – but they just didn't pan out. It is extremely difficult with a bow to get within shooting range. I've often said if we even had black powder, we'd have them piled up like cord wood – with a bullet, it changes things.

Rich: One thing that I couldn't help but become aware of in talking to people about this Rocky Mountain hunting experience is, here you are with a bow – that's all fine and good – we know that it's a marvelous killing weapon and the broadhead will do its thing if you make a good hit. However, if a black bear wanders in within range for whatever reason – that's got to be a special cause for concern, I would think.

Barry: It is. I think the black bear's nature is not to be aggressive necessarily – but I got to tell you, encounters happen and cubs can be a factor – and you can't help but think about it when you're hunting in the mountains. Another concern, perhaps more than about bears, is mountain lions. I think that mountain lions do have a tendency to be aggressive sometimes. They'll pursue a hunter whereas a bear would normally avoid a hunter especially if they had been downwind and caught his scent. Hunting with primitive weapons gives us cause for concern when it comes to the issue of protecting ourselves. We do read about some pretty scary situations but we try to take into consideration the number of hunters that are out there and very few do actually have a problem.

Rich: The mountain lion that you mention – a number of states are beginning to have a serious problem. They have closed all hunting opportunities. It doesn't matter whether it is black powder, archery, rifle or what – they just think that animal is so beautiful and wonderful – which he truly is – but – he doesn't seem to have an innate fear of human beings like a lot of animals do. Joggers, for example, have had numerous confrontations with lions – there have actually been several cases where cougars have killed people. It isn't just children – they have killed several adults.

Barry: More and more houses are being built in what was their own natural domain and they are losing their territory because of it. That puts the humans and the animals closer to each other all the time. We've been fortunate in the fact we have never seen a mountain lion or come across any confrontations while we have been hunting out west. I do know they are in this area where we like to hunt. Fortunately they don't expose themselves very often – they are very elusive. Black bears are actually quite prevalent in the area where we hunt.

Rich: Normally when a black bear gets a whiff of a human – he's gone. But according to what I have read and heard – occasionally, you will get a bear that doesn't know he's supposed to be afraid of a human being and many times, that is where the trouble begins. I read somewhere recently – and I believe it – that when a black bear does attack, he has every intention of eating you. They recommend that you play dead if attacked by a grizzly. But, if you are so unfortunate as to be attacked by a black bear – regardless of the size of that animal – you better forget about playing dead and make up your mind to fight for your life. Literally, that is what you must do if you plan to survive. Someone told me recently if he saw a black bear he'd just climb a tree. Actually, that would be no protection against a black bear at all. They can climb the straightest tree that ever grew – and grab you by the foot and haul you out of there too.

Barry: Grizzlies don't climb trees – but black bears do. The evidence is very apparent in the Adirondacks. A lot of the big beech trees in the areas where we hunt bear the scars of bears having climbed them over a period of years. A beech is a shiny barked tree too. If a bear can readily climb them he can climb any of the others – and more quickly. Some of the old beech in our area bear the marks over the years where the bears have just climbed right up. Their claws leave little holes in the bark of the trees and look like so many lineman's spur marks on a telephone pole. They reach out and pull the upper branches in and then eat the beechnuts off the branches. Sometimes it looks almost like a crow's nest where they pull the branches in like that. I've been in areas up north where while sitting on a watch, I look around me and almost every beech tree within view have those dots going up and down where the bears have climbed them.

Rich: A friend of mine recently told me while hunting in the Adirondacks years ago, one day he was in an area where he noticed a lot of activity where the bears had been feeding on the beechnuts that were on the ground. Then, all of a sudden, he could hear a bear actually feeding in the beech because he was snuffling up the beechnuts and scuffing them up with his paws. This sign is really rather strange – but once you identify it, you will always recognize it when you see it. When a bear is in an area of leaves with no or very little snow on the ground, where he has been working in the beech – it looks just like he took a barn shovel and dragged it backwards and it doesn't go straight – it goes in S curves – left and then right thru the area. I don't know if you've ever noticed that – but the next time you see it, you can know for sure that it is bear sign.

Barry: They're raking the leaves away looking for the beechnuts underneath.

Rich: In this case, the bear actually came out in the open where he could see it and he was able to kill that bear. Another thing I thought was interesting that I heard recently was a story about a fellow who was hunting white tails and he heard click, click, click, click. It turned out to be the sound

182

of the big antlers of a deer going thru the woods. I have never heard that sound while in the woods – and I have hundreds of books in my library and I have bought and read thousands of magazines over the years and I had never heard of anybody else hearing that sound to identify it either – of a large buck going thru a thick brushy area of the woods and of his antlers making a clicking sound while he was traveling thru bushes. Isn't that unique? Doing this book I've gotten into more stuff that is interesting and it's been more fun.

Barry: I could listen to hours and hours of this kind of stuff. I wish you success with your book.

Rich: Thanks. I'm in hopes it will just be a delight to everybody – that they'll find something in here that will be of great enjoyment and provide some interesting and helpful information and woods lore too.

Barry: In my experience, when I look thru my magazines, the thing I enjoy most is reading about success that other hunters have had. This educates as well as entertains and I enjoy it greatly. There's nothing like a mess of fresh fish when we are in our camp out west. We always take a little breakdown fish pole and there are some beaver dams on the little stream that runs right by the place where we camp in the mountains. We try our luck and have been quite successful. The fish in those little clear pools become educated quite quickly. All you need to do is catch the lip of one and whether you catch him or not, the rest of them are immediately educated.

We have always managed to catch more than enough so everybody could enjoy a wonderful fish fry around the campfire. One year the only thing we had to roll them in before cooking them in a frying pan, was part of our blueberry pancake mix. We'll sneak up to a large pool and just sit there awhile until we begin to see a little action. Then by using a small fly or small worm of some sort can usually have some good luck. We've found it interesting that in a little bitty stream that isn't more than two feet wide we've been able to catch a trout fourteen inches or better. They seem to do well – they're nice and fat. One time I snuck up to a beaver pond and noticed this nice trout laying over on it's side and it appeared to be dead. I went over there and looked at that thing and noticed that it had a large mouse stuck in his mouth that apparently he wasn't able to swallow and so they both met their demise. That was something I had never seen before.

Rich: I think the woods are wonderful. It's really great to get away from this computer and stress and all this junk. What a blessing to have the privilege to spend some quality time in the woods just soaking in the atmosphere. The fellowship and camaraderie in the camp is always a real joy too. How thankful I am that our Creator has made all this possible.

Barry: Sometimes while hunting in the southern tier here around home you realize when sitting on watch and waiting for a deer to come thru, it's awful hard to get away from what would be noise that's from the main roads. Sometimes on a clear day even if you're back in the woods a few miles, you can still hear traffic. Somehow it takes away from the pleasure of hunting when you have to listen to big trucks or road noise – trains or horns blowing. I enjoy this about the Adirondacks – we can get away from the road noise. Once in awhile we will hear or see the occasional airplane but other than that, it is so peaceful. That's one of the true pluses of hunting the north-country.

Rich: You bet. One day I was up on a ridge and a fighter jet came over and the noise was so loud that it actually hurt my head – almost brought me down to my knees. Thank you for the wonderful stories. You are an excellent storyteller. I can hardly wait to share these with friends.

CHAPTER 17   WAYNE MATTESON

Rich: Please welcome my friend, Wayne Matteson. Wayne, I know from the experiences that we have shared together that you own a shotgun and a nice deer rifle. What has caused you to become interested in black powder?

Wayne: A couple of things – first of all, my love of reading about the Civil War. It was always intriguing to me that these guys were shooting at each other with a muzzle loader using black-powder – the only kind of powder available at that time. I guess the main reason I got interested was due to the late season that was available after the close of the regular gun season here locally. I had always just gone hunting in that cold weather with my bow. It was in 1996 and 1997 that I spent considerable time hunting during that late season and I saw a lot of deer. They're all out of range of the bow and I kept thinking, "man, if I had a gun in my hand – maybe I should get into this muzzle loading thing." I like to hunt extensively during the regular early archery season and if I could hunt with the muzzleloader during the late season that would extend my ability to get out and enjoy my favorite sport for a lengthier time each fall.

So, the quest is on. I decided I would do some serious shopping for a muzzleloader and I would investigate the whole thing because I was essentially clueless about how it all worked. I did my homework and eventually bought a muzzleloader in April of 1998 at a gun show up in Syracuse. I recall that you gave me some powder to start with. I shopped carefully for all the possibles I would require for using the muzzleloader and came up with all that – without totally breaking the bank.

I spent the summer of 1998 getting familiar with the muzzleloader. I really enjoyed learning to shoot that thing – it was just like shooting a mini cannon to me. I just loved it and found it to be a tremendous amount of fun. Just going out and shooting that rifle was so satisfying and after awhile I decided I was going to leave my shotgun at home even for the regular gun season and use my muzzleloader. It's legal to use it during the regular gun season if you preferred. I decided I'm going to take it out and see what I can do. So, the very first day of the 1998 gun season I decided I would load up. I had to accept a little bit of harassment from my family because I was out there with the "one shot" and they're loading up their guns in about three seconds and it takes me a couple of minutes to get myself ready to just get one shot down the barrel and head up the hill after getting all my toys together. That rifle weighes about three pounds more than my shotgun does.

I had talked to my Dad – we're hunting on his property over in the Georgetown area – he had seen a pretty decent buck running around in a field the day before chasing does. I had killed a nice eight-point buck in that same area the year before and since this buck had been running the same area I thought I'd just go and try that spot again. Well, I lugged the muzzleloader up there and got set. That rifle is so long and heavy you can't really stand there holding it like you can a shotgun so I leaned it up against my tree. It was a perfect morning – crispy in the upper twenties temperature and nice and clear. I had a twelve-acre field behind me and the woods and a swamp in front of me. I stayed right there for over four hours and did not see a deer.

I began to get really cold but you know how it is, especially on the first day of hunting season, you keep telling yourself that something may come right along. I looked out behind me in that field – I was constantly scanning and hoped I might hear or see something. Well, I looked to my right like I had done hundreds of times before and then I looked to my left – and here's a deer – and he's not even twenty yards away from me. Where did he come from? He hadn't made a sound. At this point I couldn't tell what it was. My view was blocked by some trees. All I could see was his legs basically – but he was close. The muzzleloader at this point is leaning up against the opposite side of the tree I'm standing beside. I had to reach around to get the rifle.

One little thing with the muzzleloader is when you pull the hammer back – mine is a percussion rifle – it makes a clicking sound. At the time I wasn't proficient to know that there is a little trick you can do to keep that click from happening. If you pull the trigger at the same time you cock the hammer, it keeps the clicking sound from happening. Well, I didn't know that until later – I had talked to another muzzleloader about that problem. I was planning that if I saw a deer hopefully I would see it far enough away that I could cock the hammer and get ready so that the deer wouldn't hear the noise. Somehow the deer appeared to be just frozen in place – I couldn't tell what he was doing because I still couldn't see his head or much of his body. I had a doe permit so I figured, either way, I'm going to try to get a whack at this thing – it's really a big deer – I can tell that much about it.

I decided I better get my rifle up and moved extremely slow as the deer is just right on top of me. Then I thought, "here's the moment of truth – the first one anyway" – I cocked the hammer back to see what's going to happen. I pull it back and it goes, click. The resulting sound didn't even seem to phase the deer. In fact about the moment I cocked the hammer, he stepped into the woods and walked parallel to me. I picked a small opening that appeared in front of him and when he reached that opening I picked my spot and fired the rifle – BAROOOM -. I knew I hit him pretty good because I actually saw where the bullet hit him when I shot – right in the heart area. He ran just out of sight about thirty yards or so away. I reloaded just to make sure I'd be prepared in case I had more shooting to do. Right about then I was really starting to get excited because it wasn't until he had stepped into the woods that I could tell that it was a buck. He died under the same tree as the buck did that I had killed the year before. It turned out to be a very nice six-point with a seventeen inch spread and the longest tine was about eight inches long. I dragged him out to the tractor path and gutted him out and then went back to hunting as I still had my doe permit.

This all happened about ten-thirty and at noon I decided to go talk to my Dad. He had heard me shoot. I told him I had killed a pretty nice six-point. He usually thought of a six-point as a rather small deer. When he got back to where my deer was he said, "oh, this is a nice six-point." The best part was later when he brought the tractor with the trailer. When we got it loaded on the trailer you could see the antlers sticking up over the sides of the trailer. You know you really have a good buck when the antlers stick up over the sides of the trailer. That was a lot of fun.

So far, that is the only deer I have gotten with the muzzleloader. A couple of years ago on opening day, I missed one that was a little bigger than the one I got. I've had some other good opportunities and managed to mess them up. One time I shot at a doe. After I fired my rifle she ran right by me within ten yards – I knew that I had missed her when I shot. She was about forty yards away when I fired the gun – then ran right towards me and went right on by. So, while I'm standing there trying to reload, here comes a whole herd of deer. They just stand there and watch me trying to reload. I couldn't get it done fast enough and just before I finished, they all took off. They have these "speedy reloaders" and I've used them some – but to be honest, there's nothing speedy about reloading a muzzleloader, even with those things because I did have them. It just takes time and you might as well figure you're going to get one shot and one shot only and you better make it good.

186

I had my orange coat with me. The last few years it has been quite mild so I usually take it off when I reach my stand. That coat just adds a lot of bulk so if I can hunt without having to wear it I do. I seem to have more freedom of movement without having to wear that bulky thing. I'm really looking forward to this coming season and plan to hunt with my muzzleloader. I think it is a lifelong thing I have been bitten by and I love the smell of the powder and enjoy shooting it. Already it's been a lot of fun and even if I don't get anything with it I prefer to use that rather than my shotgun. I haven't had a lot of experience – only have hunted three seasons but look forward to many more.

Rich: For the benefit of the majority of us who have had very little or for the most part no experience with a muzzleloader, would you be willing to just go thru the steps of loading the rifle?

Wayne: Sure. Basically the way to do it is first, you have to make certain the barrel is cleaned out so generally after I fire the rifle and again before I reload, I run a swab down the barrel to remove any excess powder that there might be left in the barrel. There are several different grades of powder you can use. I happen to use 3-F. There's 1,2,3 & 4 F and presently I use 3-F. Depending on what kind of a projectile you're shooting – for example if you're using a round ball there's a little different procedure for loading than if you're shooting a conical. If you're using a round ball the general procedure is to measure out the powder with a powder measure. Generally anywhere from 85 to 100 grains of powder is fine. Dump it down the barrel – tap the side of the barrel so that the powder settles in there good. With the round ball you must also use a patch. You try to center the ball in the middle of the patch and place it on the end of the barrel. There are a couple of tools you use to get the ball down there. The first is a ball starter that serves to get the ball just past the lip of the end of the barrel. You use the short end of that tool to do that and then you use the long end – which might be six inches long to get it part way down the barrel and then you use your ramrod to get it seated at the bottom of the barrel next to the powder.

There are different tricks of the trade – depending upon how much powder you like to use, you can make a mark on your ramrod so that you know when you push it down the barrel that the bullet is seated on the powder correctly. When you reach that mark on your ramrod you know you've got it properly seated. You don't want to have a gap in there that could cause an explosion that you don't want. You always need to use a lubricated patch – not a dry one. Now you have the shot in place. My rifle is a percussion cap rifle. There's a little cap that goes on the nipple at the bottom of the hammer. When the rifle is fired, the hammer strikes the cap which is very similar to the primer in a modern center fire shell. When the cap is struck by the hammer the special powder contained within the cap explodes and this in turn ignites the powder within the rifle barrel and of course this explosion causes the bullet to leave the barrel with a degree of force. When placing the cap on the nipple you generally would not want to use your fingers – they have a cap holder that can be used for this purpose of placing the cap. Actually, the caps come in a holder of about six or eight caps and the holder is a part of that unit.

Generally you have your hammer in half-cock position when carrying the rifle. Then, before you can shoot, you must pull the hammer back to the full-cock position. You don't want the hammer actually resting on the cap because if you were to stumble, it might be enough to cause the gun to fire. So, that's why we carry the rifle with the hammer in the half-cock position. This way, it's not going to go anywhere. Now, you are ready to fire the rifle. That is the general procedure for loading. Finally, you need to be certain that your ramrod is out of the barrel and been replaced into the proper location on the under portion of the rifle barrel. Once in awhile someone will actually shoot a ramrod down the range when target shooting. That is something you definitely do by accident – or best don't do at all.

Rich: There no doubt have been numerous cases where the "enemy" has been killed by the ramrod rather than by a bullet. Well, thanks – that is very interesting. It certainly is more involved than merely loading a shell into the action or chamber of a modern rifle and using smokeless powder.

Wayne: You don't use smokeless powder in a black powder rifle. It's way too high powered compared to black powder.

Rich: Also, there's a cleaning procedure you must do every time you take your muzzleloader out and load it – because to unload it the rifle must be fired. The only legal way to transport the rifle in your vehicle is to unload it – so it must be fired at the end of each day. So, due to the extra corrosive properties of black powder, you must also clean the rifle after each time it has been used. Otherwise, residue will build up in the barrel and will harden and pretty soon, you won't be able to get a bullet down the barrel and accuracy will be affected adversely.

Wayne: I've never used soap and hot water. I've always used solvent to clean my barrel. I soak my cleaning patches with the solvent. There's a little patch holder that can screw into the end of your ramrod which will hold a patch. I usually use two or three patches and run them up and down the barrel to be sure it is very clean each time. You can unscrew the nipple and I take care to clean that area good each time. You need an open passage in order for the percussion cap explosion to be able to reach the powder charge in the bottom of the barrel. I normally will use a toothbrush in that area around where the nipple goes. It gets pretty fouled up in that area – there's sometimes a little blowback that occurs when the rifle is fired each time. The explosion comes out behind the bullet in the front of the barrel but also a little bit comes out the hole to the nipple. I've never had a problem with it coming in my face at all – it just seems to come thru that area just enough to get the nipple fouled up so that it requires cleaning each time. It's necessary to use the hole cleaner in the process to make certain that the touchhole is clean and not fouled.

As you clean the barrel a lot of that stuff will blow out. I feel there isn't such as big a mess involved in cleaning the gun when using solvent as compared to using soap and water. At least that is what I have decided on for now. I figure I can shoot the rifle about four times before I have to give it a cleaning again. I don't always clean it after every shot. My present preference is to use the maxi-hunter and it is a 350 grain bullet. The maxi ball is in the range of 435 to 485 grains of weight. It's a pretty hefty item. When you use that maxi hunter type it doesn't require the use of a patch. The bullet already comes pre-lubricated and when you drop it in the barrel it sits directly on the powder.

Rich: Then, don't you need a different mark on your ramrod to indicate when using that type of bullet that it is properly seated on your powder?

Wayne: Yes. You will have at least two marks on your ramrod. If you use the maxi-hunter like I do, that's shorter than the maxi-ball. I feel that the round ball is a little less accurate than the conical. When that bullet is made it has a little protrusion attached which makes it not perfectly round and that effects accuracy. They appear to be out of round or not balanced like the other types of bullets available now. In my experience the round balls do not expand but in the deer I shot, that conical just perfectly mushroomed. That bullet went thru the heart and didn't exit the animal – it wound up against the opposite shoulder.

188

Rich: I'd like to take a moment and tell the little story about the time recently when you brought your muzzleloader to our woods one day and we hunted together. I placed you on watch early in the hunt at a spot where I previously had good luck hunting by myself. I made a large circle in the hopes of stirring up some game. You had stood on that watch for quite a period and suddenly you had a funny feeling so you turned carefully and looked behind you and noticed a large doe standing directly behind you not twenty yards away just looking at you. You didn't have a doe permit at that time so didn't shoot at the deer. Then, towards the end of the afternoon I suggested another watch and told you the exact time I would be coming thru to you. So, you stayed on that watch and remained alert. I kept track of my own wristwatch and about two minutes prior to the time I said I would come thru – made the final push of seventy yards or so thru some extra thick cover. A few minutes after that, I came out to where you were still standing on your watch and you told me you had just made the most difficult decision of your whole hunting career. At precisely the time I had said I'd be coming thru to where you were on watch, you noticed a string of does being followed by a large eight-point buck coming along just slightly uphill from your position. The buck was standing broadside to you and just uphill from your position at about forty yards. You said you had raised your rifle and were going to take your shot – but noticed all you could see behind the deer was clear sky and didn't know for certain where our home was located in relation to your position so didn't shoot. I told you I thought there wouldn't have been a problem – but thanked you for being so considerate and taking the extra precaution.

Have you had opportunity to take part in any sort of competitive shooting or be involved in any of the groups that have common interests in muzzleloader shooting? I understand there are all kinds of groups out there that have good fellowship and share the learning experiences and fun.

Wayne: There are opportunities but I haven't been able to take advantage of them mostly because of family. With raising four kids, we don't have any extra time. I guess I'll just have to compete against myself for now.

Rich: Has your Dad gotten involved yet in black-powder?

Wayne: Not yet – he's mentioned I really had a dinosaur in my hand there. But, you know, they're talking about changing the season. They're thinking of having the two weeks after Christmas open for black- powder. This would really expand the opportunity for hunting and give more people a chance to be involved.

Rich: I've got the idea that there's still some of the rut business going on then – all the does aren't bred. The bucks may not have the enthusiasm they seem to have for that procedure that they do earlier in the year but there's a late rut type of thing too.

Wayne: This year in the middle of February I was out partridge hunting. When I got thru I returned to my car and was traveling toward home when I noticed out in this field a group of deer and a large buck running with them. He still had both antlers and he was running deer all over the place. I've also noticed fawns in late August with their spots still on. They must have been bred in that January-February time frame in order to have been born that late in the season.

Rich: How's your turkey hunting been?

189

Wayne: I'm not one of those trophy hunters – I just shoot whatever comes along – as long as it's wearing a beard it's fair game so far as I am concerned. I don't have a lot of time and I get out whenever I can and put my effort in and generally am not going to pass up a turkey that comes in to my call and gives me an opportunity. I've been pretty successful – I've shot a lot of turkeys – not a whole lot of big ones but I do have a couple of interesting stories. It took me five years before I finally got a turkey.

Rich: I don't feel so bad then.

Wayne: I started when I was fourteen. It really wasn't until I started to hunt on my own by myself that I began to have some success in killing birds and not relying on my Dad or someone else to do the calling. When I began to rely on myself I soon discovered I really could call in birds. I made a lot of mistakes and still do. One of my biggest problems was the one of position. You know the turkeys are out there but it's important to get yourself in the right spot, and hopefully being able to invite him to come over to you.

The year I killed my first bird they had a split open season. It must have been around the 18th of May when I was able to get back out there again. I called this turkey that I heard gobbling early in the morning while he was still on his roost. I heard him fly down and could hear the bird coming to me in response to my calling. I wasn't in a good spot at all – I was sitting in the middle of a berry patch. I could hear him gobble and he gobbles right by me. I couldn't believe I couldn't see him but I was in a terrible spot. I finally got myself up and walked about seventy yards in the direction he had been going. The last time I had heard him he seemed to be about two hundred yards away – still gobbling.

It was sheer frustration. I was just standing there with the butt plate of my gun on my foot. I made a long lost hen call and in just a few seconds flat that turkey ran right to me. He ran and stopped less than ten feet away from me. I'm standing there with the gun on my foot like I'm having my picture taken. I thought, "this is a fine situation – here's this gobbler less than ten feet away from me – wondering where I am – the only chance I've got is if he turns and walks behind that little tree over there." Well, he went behind that little forked tree – I raised my shotgun – but right then he took off running. At first, he went diagonally away from me and then for some unknown reason, he made a ninety degree turn to his right – which put him at about twenty yards running full tilt and that's how he died. If he'd kept going straight and not made his right turn he'd have made it. Lesson learned was if you're going to call – be ready – because they can be on you pretty quick.

The tendency is to say, "there's no turkeys around here" – and you just stand and call. Well, you can't do that because it's going to happen often enough when something's right there and you are not ready or in position. I remember another time I was standing and thinking nothing was around and gave a couple of yelps and two gobblers came right over. They both saw me and walked away.

The biggest turkey I ever got was a twenty-two pound bird with a nine and a quarter inch beard. That was on opening day and I had gone up to my Dad's and hunted hard the whole morning. I was on one ridge and all of a sudden, two gobblers opened up on the far ridge. It was on our property, across the road and probably four hundred yards away. I thought I'd just sit there and talk to them a little bit. They were gobbling to each other and they were gobbling at me and it was a lot of fun to hear them – but after awhile I thought it was apparent they were not going to come over, or so I thought. I took off and made a little loop thru a swamp and didn't really think much about it until I came back around again to the place where I first called to the birds and a bird gobbled right from the place where I first had called. I don't know whether they flew or ran but there they were. This was about thirty minutes after I had initially called to them.

I went and plopped myself down and the bird probably wasn't seventy-five yards away from me when he gobbled so I got all set up – facing where he is and here he comes – off to my right – in full strut, ninety degrees from where I was hoping he would come in. I had enough presence of mind not to do something foolish and try to make a quick turn on him or whatever – I've never really had any success with that. So, I let him walk by and he gobbled a few more times. I wanted to get up and move way around and try to get in front of him again. I made the move – about two hundred yards – he had just gone on down the ridge. About then I lost track of him. I made a gobble and he wasn't fifty yards away from me so I threw myself down in front of a tree and gave a couple of clucks on a box call and he came right in and I killed him at about twenty yards. It all worked out in the end – I was in exactly the right spot – it was a lot of fun. It seems to work out for me about one in five times when it comes to killing turkeys.

Rich: What has been your experience – when a gobbler comes in will he come thru more or less open spots or will he tend to stick to the thick stuff and appear to utilize cover?

Wayne: My experience has been he'll try to find the thickest stuff to come thru. It's nice to think they'll come straight to you – but ninety percent of the time they'll take diversions and won't really come in straight. A lot of times you just have to make the best of where you are. Another difficult thing for me to decide is how far away to shoot. Things look different from when you're standing and when you're sitting. You really should pick a tree and say, "I'm not going to shoot at that bird until he gets on this side of that tree." I've had to let some pretty nice birds go because they were just on the other side of that tree.

Last spring a turkey spotted me. I was in full camouflage and sitting in front of a tree but he still spotted my outline or something. I needed for him to keep coming another couple of steps but apparently he could tell that something just wasn't right. The more open it is sometimes, the harder it is to get them. I think it is helpful to have a little bit of ground cover. Last year a bird came thru and got to a downed log. I had to wait until he popped his head up high enough so when I shot I lost about half my pattern to the log but the rest of it was able to get him in the head.

Rich: Are you using magnum three-inch stuff now?

Wayne: I just use two and three quarter inch – generally fours – the special turkey loads. They definitely give you a larger number of shot in your pattern. I used to use just high base fours but by experimenting with my gun I discovered that the turkey loads really are superior in the pattern. After making that discovery I would wonder how you could ever come home with anything using just regular shells. The pattern is much more dense in the turkey loads.

Rich: Do you run over there right away and step on their neck after you have shot them?

Wayne: I'd say only about a quarter of them are dead right away.

Rich: Have you ever had one fly off on you?

Wayne: Oh, yeah. A couple of years ago I had to run one down. That same year I had to run after two of them. In both cases it was very thick. The range I was shooting from was fine – but the area was just extra thick. Well, the race was on. I had to chase one – I never lost sight of him and thought if I could get within range of him, I'd shoot him again. I knew he was hurt because otherwise he'd have been long gone. I was finally able to get up to where he gave me another shot opportunity and that finished him. The first one wasn't so bad but it still was about a three hundred yard run thru the woods by the time it was all over. Believe me, you don't want to do that. With that hunting outfit on and all your toys in your pockets – I was pretty well whipped. It was exciting but it's not what I want to do again. Some of that run was uphill.

Rich: What actual range do you feel you can confidently kill a turkey at?

Wayne: I will not shoot at a bird over thirty-five yards. Generally, I want him at twenty-five yards. I have killed a number of birds at the thirty-five yard range but I don't enjoy those experiences where I have to chase them thru the woods. The closer you can get to them the better and the less chance you'll have to try to run them down.

Rich: Did you ever kill one that you had flushed and was flying and you would have to shoot him out of the sky?

Wayne: Nope, I have never shot at a flying turkey.

Rich: I flushed a big gobbler once and never did take a shot at him. He surprised me so when he took off that I forgot all about my gun. He was a huge gobbler and most beautifully colored. He was only twenty yards ahead of me when he flushed in the open in a hay field. It was fun seeing him take off. Being able to see him that close and watching him fly – it was awesome.

Well, Wayne, I appreciate your time and participation. It won't be very many more years and your boys will be right out there hunting with you. You were telling me a short time ago about you and your older son, Curtis going partridge hunting. You said you came up with three birds. That was really great. I haven't seen three birds during one outing in a number of years. Sounds like they may be making a real comeback in some areas.

CHAPTER 18   LARRY KNOBEL

Rich: We tried to get together to do our interview but our schedules just didn't match. Larry works as an inventor for a company over in Ithaca. His wife, Sara, loves animals and recently accepted a fulltime job as director of the local S.P.C.A. in Cortland. For the most part this has been a very fulfilling job for her.

One weekend a couple of years ago Jani and I were invited to the deer camp one weekend early in the season. There were just the two couples of us at the camp that weekend with Martin. It was a totally delightful weekend. I was able to get out on Saturday and hunt the forenoon but didn't happen to see any game. On Sunday, Jani and I took an extended hike in the woods and explored several trails near camp that we hadn't run onto before. One in particular took us to a summer campsite situated on North Lake near a small island at the northern narrows. That was the spot where the big buck came down off from Sugarloaf Mountain that time searching out some does that were just across the lake. He swam right over there in pursuit of them. Ah, love!

The following fall, Larry and Sara were up in camp and decided they'd take a stroll. Larry has hunted using his sidearm for several years. Since his involvement in the Military a number of years ago he has made it a point to keep his shooting ability sharpened and enjoys using and carrying his revolver. Well, this particular afternoon they swung around the base and then came over the top of Sugarloaf Mountain heading in the general direction back toward camp. It was a lovely day to just be in the woods. They were sauntering along and carrying on a conversation when all of a sudden Sara said, "there's a deer." Sure enough there was a deer – Larry noticed it was carrying a nice rack of antlers – and it was even walking right toward them. About then Larry thought, "if I kill this thing that'll mean we will have to gut it and drag it into camp – but if it comes much closer I think I will try."

There wasn't any snow on the ground at the time so they couldn't tell if the buck had been following the trail of a doe but that is a distinct possibility. Anyhow, Larry drew his revolver, took careful aim and let drive – at about twenty yards it wasn't too much of a challenge to make a perfect heart shot. The buck ran a short distance and collapsed in a heap. Normally when you kill a deer the fun ends and the work begins. They continued to have an enjoyable time as they shared together the dressing of the deer and they even dragged him into camp. I think they were glad for some assistance to get it hauled up onto the meat pole. This past season Larry brought the mount of his deer to camp and hung it up on the wall. However, at the end of the season it went back home and I presume it graces the wall in their living room. It is a very beautiful mount. I believe it is a special challenge to hunt while using a revolver, especially if you meet a bear!

One evening we were sitting around the fireplace in camp. Larry said he was going down on the beach and see if he would get his cell phone to work. Well, at that time, I hadn't had any opportunity to see how one of these items worked so I asked if I could go along. He said, "sure." Then he explained there was only one spot down on the beach – if you stood in the middle of a four foot square next to the lake you could get real good reception. He tried making his call – but the line was busy. Then he asked, "is there anybody you would like to talk to?" I thought, "why not – I'd like to call my wife and surprise her." So he showed me how to dial the number with that unit and I was amazed at the clear reception and had a nice conversation with my wife.

Sara owns a horse and loves to ride. Well, the only way they can enjoy this sport is for Larry to own a horse too. One day Jani and I were shopping in the local Tops Market. We saw Sara and greeted her and asked how Larry was doing. She said, "why don't you ask him?" He was coming along in the aisle and wearing a big beautiful cowboy hat – we didn't even recognize him with that hat on. Then he told us about his learning to ride and how much they were enjoying this activity. He indicated that any day he didn't get thrown off was a good day.

CHAPTER 19   LEWIS HEATH

Rich: Please welcome Lewis Heath. Lew has been a personal friend for many years – also, he is an electrician and has helped us with our needs in that area both at home and at our business. His annual deer hunting vacations to the Adirondack Mountains have brought the much-needed respite from stress and strain of business. Lew, when did the new young gang of members join the Camp Cortney deer camp and did that group get to enjoy a season or two at the old site? (See chapter #9 for information about Camp Cortney.)

Lew: We went up in the summer of 1977. We reconditioned the camp and took it over. Also, the fall of '77 was our first hunting season at that location. In 1980 we were informed we would have to move the camp location so we got to hunt out of that locale and enjoy the camp for three years. The time we were able to be there was very special – I don't think anybody really wanted to move closer to Town. Hunting back in that area, we rarely ever saw another hunter. Actually, we rarely saw even the other hunters from our own camp as the area was so large and remote. I would say at least half of us had never hunted the Adirondack Mountains previously and had no experience with the north-country.

I killed a bear my first year hunting the Adirondacks. My very first afternoon out, Barry and I were hunting together. We wound up near Balsam Lake just before dark. We'd gotten to the point where we realized we had to go thru the notch, stay high and then go to the lake. I found what I thought looked like a good watch about three hundred yards up from the lake. After a few minutes, I saw this black thing coming thru the woods. My first impression was – it was a coyote. The animal was heading toward the lake and the longer I looked at it, I said, "no, that's a bear." So, I just pulled up and shot and it went about fifteen yards and dropped dead. I went over there to take a look at it and thought to myself, "that's quite a big animal." The closer I got I realized it stank something terrible. It was really rank. Some of the older members of the camp said that an older male bear might be strong smelling.

Anyway, I rolled it over and proceeded to gut it out and checked its stomach and he was just full of grass. He had apparently been feeding in an area down by the lake. Then I discovered, "I don't have a rope." Luckily, I had a knife. There isn't any flashlight. Meantime, Barry came along so we hooked our belts together, fastened one around the neck of the bear and headed for the notch back towards camp. We were traveling more of less downgrade but soon discovered this bear was like a suction cup. Everything you went over, the bear just seemed to grab hold of. We broke our belts and had to square knot those together so we'd have something to take hold of in order to pull.

About then I looked around and from the draw where we had stopped to rest, noticed it was straight up on about every side around. I took a look at my compass and told Barry, "I think we've taken a wrong turn." We really had to go south to cut the trail that leads to camp. So, now it's getting really dark. We used our compass to get our bearings and then headed up over the ridge and headed back to camp.

The next day we went back with about four other guys and realized then we had slid down the hill with the bear and hadn't stayed up high enough. We built a stretcher for him, piled him on that stretcher and carried him out. That was my first experience with hunting in the Adirondacks. He dressed 249 pounds. We hunted another four days. We had the tractor in there with the wagon and the bear went on top of the gear on the way out of the woods. When we got out to the highway, we drove the tractor up on the large trailer we had hauled it in on. Somebody got the bright idea, "let's put this bear on the seat of the tractor and fasten his paws to the steering wheel on our way back out." So, this bear's going to be sitting on the tractor seat as we're going down Route 8 thru Utica, and back to Homer.

The first thing we ran into was a State Highway construction site. There was an elderly man there directing traffic with a flag and he had a pipe in his mouth. He was motioning traffic thru the construction site and when he saw the bear on the tractor, he opened his mouth and the pipe fell onto the ground and he dropped his flag and he just stood there looking – like he couldn't believe what he was seeing. We arrived in Speculator and turned the corner onto Main Street and started heading out of town on Route 8 towards Piseco. We saw two hunters that had a camp right near the road and they are unloading their gear from a car. One hunter is standing next to the trunk and the other one has his head in the trunk getting his duffle out. The guy standing next to the trunk sees the bear and he cannot believe what he is seeing. He grabs his friend by the back of the shirt, yanks him out from underneath the trunk, the guy's head hits right smack into the latch on the trunk lid and he's all folded up – the other guy is still watching this bear go by on the tractor. I don't think the guy that had his head in the trunk of that car ever did see the bear.

Rich: Probably all he ever saw were stars.

Lew: Well, we had a few other frights on the way home – the bear sat up there in the seat really well and we finally got him home. I took the animal up to Doug's and he didn't dare cut into it – thought there was too much smell to it to want to take a chance. He thought it was spoiled. I caped the bear out and took it to Clearfield, Pennsylvania and had a mount made out of it. To this day I have no desire to shoot another bear. I called ahead down to the Taxidermist and he told me how to prepare the head. When I got it all down there, they said it was in perfect condition to make a mount out of it. At first they were a little afraid when I talked to them on the telephone that with the bear hanging in camp so long, maybe the hair would slip. In fact, they gave me $150.00 for the rest of the hide that they didn't use to make up my mount so at least the hide was really great. Barry lost his camera on that deal. I think he put it in his pocket and maybe one time when we stopped it might have fallen out. If you're ever hunting in that area and run across that camera, never mind the camera – just bring out the film.

Rich: I really like to still-hunt. I don't consider myself extremely good at it but I truly enjoy doing it. My Dad had some friends that were really excellent still-hunters. I've heard from other members of your camp this is one of your favorite methods that you use when you hunt. I wonder if you'd fill us in a little on some details.

Lew: That's the only thing I ever do. Before dark I can go and take a watch some place for a half an hour or so and be there. I will still-hunt up to that point. During the day, I might find a place and sit down and stay there a little while and just think over in my mind where I would like to go next. I probably don't cover as much ground or territory as I should – not nearly as much as most of the other hunters in our camp. Deer up north are like the turkeys down home. They may be in an area one day but then they'll be gone for the next two or three days or longer. I find that heavy beechnut years provide the worst hunting conditions that there are. Deer can be wherever there are beechnuts. They certainly don't have to go any distance to find cover where they can lay down. They can spend the whole day there and then late in the afternoon, get up, go to water, and then return to feed in the beech.

I think these are the most difficult hunting conditions that there are. Years when there are few or no beechnuts, you can check out the wet areas where there are lots of ferns and usually get an eye on them after a day or two when you discover where they are feeding. Those conditions are normally found on the north side where it's damp and then when you find feeding sign you can concentrate your efforts in that area. I just can't sit for more than fifteen or twenty minutes and be able to concentrate on what I'm doing.

Rich: Now, you don't do the slow, pussyfoot thing all the while, do you? Don't you go until you find some good sign and then really slow down and do your careful still-hunt?

Lew: Yes. If I'm in the open hardwoods, I'm moving – because there's nothing there. If I must travel thru an area of open hardwoods, I try to drop off the edge because the deer don't walk on these tops either. They go down over the bank about fifteen yards and they'll run parallel with that ridge until they want to cross over or drop down. I take the same path that they do. Normally when they get into an area where there are a lot of small evergreen such as spruce or some other and that patch is six to ten feet wide and interspersed thru the hardwoods, I expect to spend a lot of time in an area like that. I might go three hundred yards the other side and turn right around and come right back thru again. Not only is there a possibility of finding deer feeding or bedded in such an area but they will move into that type of area most any time during the day. They like to bed where there is some kind of cover – unless you go into a swamp – and I've had very little luck hunting in a swamp, or creek bottom. But if you get on the side of a mountain where there are these areas of spruce interspersed in the hardwood with some washes and small creek areas – I like that type of terrain for hunting.

Rich: You're never far from water there either. That's what they are looking for some of the time.

Lew: Just about anyplace where you go up in that country you're not over a maximum of five hundred yards from water – more like one or two hundred yards from water. Whether you're on top of the ridge or down on the side – there's always creeks going down off on the side. The first buck I got over at the old camp – that was a nice one. I had hunted all day in the rain. It was just a nice steady rain – I hunted down low – along the lake – next to the hardwoods – where the hardwoods and the spruce meet. I just followed the edge of the lake around. I saw a lot of sign. This was the first week in November and I did see a number of fresh scrapes. I crossed up over toward Balsam again and I was hunting over thru there around one o'clock or so and I came onto another scrape that looked really fresh.

I left it and went back to camp and decided I'd rest up a bit and then go back around 3 o'clock and sit on a watch. I went back and sat near the last scrape I had seen. There was a log just perfect to sit on – but it was only fifteen yards from that scrape. I went over there and sat down and thought, "this isn't that bad – the deer will probably work his way up out of the swamp – and the wind is blowing into my face." I felt comfortable there – I could see seventy to eighty yards at the most and I thought I probably would be able to see anything that is coming. I hadn't been there twenty minutes. I caught a movement out of the corner of my eye and here comes this buck – right off the end of the log I was sitting on – his head is close to the ground and he's walking right up towards this scrape.

He comes from behind me and walks along the end of my log – he's not more than ten feet away. He's just off to my right and he came right around the end of the log I'm sitting on. He walked right over to that scrape and started sniffing the scrape and I just lifted up my rifle and shot. I was beginning to form an opinion about hunting in the Adirondacks. I thought, "this isn't bad at all – I get a bear one year and a nice eight-point buck the next – what more could I want?" It was a good experience.

Rich: How many years went by before you collected something else?

Lew: You know, I've really had good luck hunting up there – I've killed seven bucks since I've begun to hunt up north. I'm very satisfied with my results. In 1981 we went up north and looked to see where the sight of our new camp was going to be. This area was a place they had just logged off and it was really crawling with deer. I was hunting with two other fellows – they had both shot at bucks but had missed. I had killed a small spike-horn. We about devoured that deer – we had a large bunch in camp that fall.

In 1983 three of us went up the last weekend. We had about eighteen inches of snow on the ground. Other years, if we had that much snow the deer would have migrated out of there. That fall, the deer were still there. Doug Gilbert got a nice buck down in the swamp Saturday morning. He came back to camp for some help and we got it back into camp about three o'clock that afternoon. I decided to go down the log road that we come in on and to go up in on the left hand side. There's a bunch of log roads and timbered area near there and I thought I could just stand there until dark. I was standing there and beginning to get so cold – I don't think I had been there half an hour. I was just getting ready to leave and I happened to look up and here stands this beautiful buck – broadside. Just above me on the side of the mountain was what reminded me of a fire lane and it was just loaded with berry briars. Just where that briar patch started to go up the mountain was where he stood – probably a hundred and fifty yards from me. So, I swung around and he just stood there, broadside. I pulled up my rifle and fired. Apparently between helping to drag Doug's deer and having my rifle in camp, I'd never put a new shell in the chamber when I left camp. So, the rifle goes click. I pulled the action back – there was no shell in the chamber, so I dropped one in. He wasn't close enough apparently so he didn't hear anything and he just walked into the briars in front of me. About then, I'm thinking, "I'm on a log road – if he comes all the way down and crosses, maybe I'll get a shot at him. If he crosses in front of me, I'll get a shot but if he goes the other way, I'll be able to see him going thru the hardwoods."

I stood there and kept watching – watching – down the trail and up the briar patch – no deer. It got just about dark and I thought, "he had to go someplace." As I'm walking out, down the log road that I'm standing on the edge of, I come right up to a beech with the leaves still on it – the tree had fallen across the log road. I stepped over that log and looked down – and here's these fresh tracks – and I thought, "those weren't there when I came in." That pondered me all night long. I went back there the next morning. I went right up to where I had first seen the deer. He had been lying there and he had just stood up and then he moved down into the hardwoods on the edge of that opening and he had worked his way thru the hardwoods down to where that log was about twenty yards below me. He stopped – behind the beech branches that still had the leaves on and walked across behind that fallen tree down into the swamp, across the trail that goes to camp and right on down. We picked up his trail that morning but it started snowing real bad and we decided it was time to leave. He was a beauty – we didn't get that one.

Rich: Well, we don't get them all – it's fun to see them.

Lew: You bet – it was a great experience. It didn't take a rocket scientist to unravel what he had done – it was really fun to have good tracking snow so we could tell for certain what had happened. The next deer I got was the last weekend. Odie Young and I went up. It was in 1985. We were in our new camp by then. There was a little snow on the ground but not a lot. In the higher elevations we had five inches or so of good tracking snow. Up in back there were a lot of tracks and a lot of scrapes still. I have always noted that the last weekend of the season in the Adirondacks there is still a lot of rutting activity going on. I don't know whether it's the fact that some does weren't bred the first time around or the fact that some were just first coming into heat but it's always been very active that last weekend of deer season. Usually that's the first weekend of December.

We both hunted in an area up in back of camp – there's a large beaver pond up there. I had seen the tracks of where a deer had crossed by the end of the pond – good and fresh. He then worked his way up into a real thick witch hobble, spruce that were about eight or nine feet high and other brush – just a mess. So I pulled off to the side of those tracks and paralleled them and got up into that area and got up on to a little lip and turned around and looked – and I could not believe my eyes. There was a buck back down there. He was tremendous – heavy-antlered and he had a doe down there – all by himself. He was chasing her in and out. Before I knew it, he disappeared. Then I caught a movement out of the corner of my eye and then noticed another nice buck standing there – he's watching me. Apparently, he had been kicked out from below by the bigger one and I thought, "boy, this is a dilemma." I turned around again and looked back to where I had observed the big buck and apparently he's back in the bushes someplace but the doe is standing there – looking. I look up the hill a little ways and there he is – the big boy – he's got me arrowed – if I make the wrong move instead of having a bird in the hand I'm going to have no birds. I turned around and made my shot and dropped him – this was the smaller buck - hit him right in the neck. The deer I had just shot started flopping around like a chicken with his head cut off. Then, all at once, he quieted down and apparently died. The big one was a tremendous buck.

Rich: All this shooting and everything didn't seem to phase the doe.

Lew: No – she was in lala land I think. As soon as I fired the rifle I turned around and looked and she's just standing there looking into the bushes. I believe the deer up north are spookier than they are down home. I believe they run farther once you spook them. I've jumped deer up north and had them run down the hill, cross the creek, dash around the end of the mountain – and when you get up there they haven't quit yet. Down home many times, a deer that you have put out maybe won't go two hundred yards and then he'll settle down again. In the Adirondacks, if the next county line is thirty miles away, that's where they are headed, I think. It's amazing.

Another thing I have noticed – and I guess learned – once the bucks have made fresh scrapes in the snow – it doesn't matter if they're a week old or two weeks old – that buck is going to parallel those scrape lines downwind. He's not going to visit them unless a doe has been there and left her sign. It probably took me three years to figure that out. When you run into does and there are no bucks around you know they aren't breeding – the does aren't in heat at that time. When you move about forty or fifty yards parallel with those scrapes you'll find deer trails in the snow. The tracks appear to be several days old and some will be fresher than others. This means that a buck has been back and forth thru that area. He's not going to visit the scrapes until he has evidence that a doe has been there ahead of him. A buck may have several lines of scrapes. He'll just keep checking them until a doe shows up. Hopefully he'll be there about the same time she's been there so he doesn't miss his opportunity. When he finds the sign of a doe that's about to come into heat he won't leave her trail until he has caught up with her – and he'll stay right with her until she comes in and is receptive to his advances.

Rich: I saw a video recently taken by the owner of a Bed-And-Breakfast that Jani and I stayed in one time. The video was taken right thru his picture window looking out onto his backyard. A beautiful eight-point buck was "courting" a large doe. He was tickling her with his antlers and spending a lot of time doing what appeared like "foreplay" before he finally mounted her. It was truly a beautiful but unusual series that he had captured on film.

Lew: That's interesting. I've found that if the wind is right when a buck merely runs by his scrape line he gets a B-line on a doe and he's in business. I think it is different in that north-country than it is around home. A buck needs to cover a lot more territory because the population of the herd is not so dense as it is around the southern tier.

Back in the old camp, Ron's Dad had killed several bear over the years. He would stay behind and do the breakfast dishes and probably leave camp around 10 a.m. He might not get to his watch until around noon. He was able to stick with it on his watch though and most of the time he'd be back in camp by 4 p.m. Even so, he'd kill his bear because he had the ability once he got to his watch to be able to stick it out at that location for several hours. He always managed to kill his bear at that one particular spot. It was at the top of the mountain near Balsam Lake overlooking the green stuff on the steep side overlooking the lake. There was a hogsback and creek and that was just a natural place for bear to travel. If someone got back to camp around 4 o'clock and Fred wasn't there he would begin to worry because normally – like clockwork – he was always back.

In the old camp, probably the second year we were in there – Donnie Young took us across the lake in a boat. There was Dave Bush, Donnie and myself. There was some snow on the ground and it was windy. Also it was raining at the time but not too hard. We were going to hunt Burnt Mountain which was a real long mountain. It wasn't real high – but quite long. We were going to hunt down thru the length of it and meet someplace on the top at the other end. As we began to hunt down thru, a fog came in. It started really raining hard and the wind blew. We kept going and going and got to what seemed to be the end of the way Donnie described it. I cut off toward the side that he was coming up on and Dave was on the far side – on the south side of the mountain. He would have to come all the way over from the other side.

The wind was just howling. The fog came in suddenly and was like pea soup and appeared to be going by at about twenty miles an hour. After awhile I got over there and picked up Donnie's track where he had gone down thru – so I followed it a little ways and finally I bumped into him and he says, "boy, we're in trouble." I said, "what do you mean? You're the old hunter." He said, "this fog – this is bad. We'll hang around until Dave comes over and the three of us will see if we can get ourselves out of here." I said, "doesn't this ridge run the same direction as we came in?" He said, "yes, but it changes directions through the middle." He got his map out and was showing me. He said, "we can take a compass reading and get ourselves back to the lake." About then, Dave came plodding over the hill – he's got his boots on and he's been in the lake somehow. Both feet were soaking wet. He said, "I got to get my socks dried out before I go anywhere."

It's raining – wind's blowing – so we tried our woodsmanship. If we have to spend the night out here, let's at least get a fire going. Everything was wet. We had one candle between the three of us. We had three books of cardboard matches. We scrounged up some birch bark and squeezed the water out of a few leaves. Well, it took us all of twenty minutes – we had gone thru most of our matches and the candle was about gone. We had maybe one or two matches left and we finally got a fire going. We got some sticks put out to dry his socks on and we just sat there having some damp conversation waiting for his socks to dry. Meanwhile, the weather did not improve at all.

When we finally got going, it took us about two hours to work our way back to the lake. Since Hazel had come thru it had cleaned out all the big spruce near the lake. So, all the growth around the lake now is about four inches in diameter, twenty feet into the air and about eight inches apart. It's so thick – you can walk up to the lake edge and not know you are there. You can be within five feet of the water and not know it. We finally found the boat and got back across safely. That was my first eye-opening experience that you go well equipped on the hunt. Carry a day pack and all the matches and candles and all the other stuff you might require in order to spend the night out in the woods – just in case.

I determined that even if I just left the camp to go out on a little night watch – within that hour you could hit one and he could take you to some place you're not familiar with or you're not paying attention to where you are going and the next thing you know – there you are – in the dark. You might better stay there instead of floundering around and maybe put a stick into your eye or worse. Sometimes if you're familiar with the area you're in, you could compass your way out – provided it isn't too dark to travel safely.

Rich: Or have your buddies come and get you like that one night –

Lew: Doug Gilbert? That was quite an experience.

Rich: We got that story from Ron.

Lew: Barry ran into a hunter one year that was fifty yards off the road – and lost – petrified. Barry told him, "just follow this trail south – you'll hit the road. You're not over fifty yards from the road." The guy would not move. Barry walked him back to the road. One year back at the old camp I came near getting confused – near Spring Mountain. Russ shot his first buck over there. We had a real wet, heavy snow – wind blowing forty miles an hour, trees were falling down – it was terrible. All the snow was sticking right flat against the trees. It dumped about six inches of snow. We thought we'd be smart and put on a drive that day thru the swamp – but we had a few trees come down close so we all bailed out and decided the best place to be would be back at camp.

The next morning, it's perfectly clear – but you can't see because of the snow on the limbs and the trees. You had no idea where you were. We've been hunting this area now for four years. I took the trail down to Spring Mountain and the cut-off. There's a notch between sections of the mountain. I went thru the notch and was planning to hunt down along the backside. I probably wasn't gone more than half an hour and I came across these tracks – I looked at them – and they're mine. I said, "how can this be?" So, I followed them a little ways – and they took me right thru that notch. I said, "I don't believe I did this" and decided I would hunt the opposite direction thru the notch. I was gone a couple of hours and I came across my same track again. I said, "this is crazy – I'm going back to camp."

I took my compass out and said, "I've got to go north to hit the trail." I took off – heading north – and I had gone probably half an hour or forty-five minutes and said, "I should have come to the trail by now." I kept going and pretty soon I came to the creek. I said, "I don't believe this." I knew the creek – I could tell which way it was flowing – I knew where it was – it was going right down thru the hogsback. So, I turned around and backtracked myself ever so slowly. The limbs were hanging over the trail so heavy that it had completely camouflaged the trail. This trail was wide enough that you could get a tractor and a wagon thru with no problem. All the branches just hung down – and some of them, especially the beech, still had leaves on them. I was just going in circles and didn't even know it. This was another chapter of education of when you attempt to hunt in the Adirondacks. I also found you cannot dwell on that and hunt up there. If you're going to do that, you might better stay home.

Rich: Things can change a lot in a day. After a heavy wet snow like that, give it a day and generally, most of it will come off and then the deer will be apt to be up and moving.

Lew: Friends have said, "how can you hunt up there?" Well, if you really get in trouble, there's always the road. That's a last resort. If you take the compass heading for the road, that will take you on a long trip.

Rich: I wonder if you'd talk a little more about some of your chosen methods of still-hunting. Let's say you're in an area where you have observed some good sign and so you think it's pretty apt to be productive – how do you operate?

Lew: If I find an area that I like I'll travel with caution – and go right thru it and I'll probably go a half mile beyond it and turn around and hunt back diagonally thru it again. This way, it seems I can get a better handle on what has been going on rather than just making only one pass thru the area. I would prefer to go thru an area rather than to stay there. You can be within sixty yards of deer that are bedded and they will let you pass them and not even get up out of their beds. Or, they might even not know you're there. But if you get into their area and start monkeying around and doing a lot of concentrated tramping around where it looks good, whether it is a feeding area or a bedding area – when the wind is in their favor you may not make out too good. I'd rather come in at an angle where you're really not coming in from downwind from them – but you're coming in at an angle where they must turn their head to see you – that will give you a movement which you might pick up – and that would be in your favor. Does that work every time? Not very often – but even if it works a couple of times you're ahead of the game. Otherwise, just go on over the ridge to the next desirable area.

Try to keep expanding your own hunting territory every year. We've been going up there since 1983 – you have a natural tendency to go where you've always gone before and if you don't expand out it kind of limits you. I think this is what has happened to me in the last couple of years. I've got a couple of areas where I haven't killed a deer in yet but I believe I can – but I haven't – yet. That's why I think I should develop that area and work on it a little more – but it hasn't happened yet. Also, I haven't been able to spend the time up there that I would like to. I figure it takes at least two days to find out what the deer are doing in any particular season. You might not even see a deer for two days. But that two days can normally give you a pretty good idea of what's going on and then you can concentrate on hunting. Otherwise, you'll just cover a lot of territory and go from last year's memories as to what's going on – or two or three years ago and go from there.

Rich: It takes awhile to locate them. You hunt where you have found the sign.

Lew: That's why when you have a good mast crop – I don't care where you go there are signs. Maybe they're feeding during the night. You can go back there day after day and just not run into deer. It's a challenge. I don't think there is a better challenge, is there?

Rich: It's fun.

Lew: It is. I haven't heard the phone ring once up there in those woods.

Rich: Me either.

Lew: I have found that after the second day, you don't know what day it is and you really don't care. I think as time goes by it becomes less important as to what day it is. I hope to spend more time up there.

Rich: I hope you can.

Lew: Everybody says, "it's getting harder to cover the territory you have covered in the past." Also, we're all pretty much in the same boat – we normally travel an hour and a half from camp before we even start hunting. The last couple of years we haven't gone back to where the old camp was. We've gone just half way back. I killed a crotch-horn on Sunday. Everybody else wanted to go home – leave in the morning. This was at the new camp. I had been hunting back at the old camp – Balsam Lake area quite regularly. There was a little snow on the ground and I decided to stay. That's not a good idea because you're the only one up there. I took the trail back that morning and I just got off the hogsback and was heading down toward the swamp.

It was a kind of thick and swampy area – and I had seen several deer feeding nearby. There were seven or eight deer that I observed which was unusual for Adirondack hunting. All of a sudden I noticed about a hundred yards from me a deer climbing up out of the creek – a little crotch-horn. So I watched him. This deer appeared like he was coming along all alone. He'd turn and watch the other deer once in awhile. He was just standing there feeding.

I was checking over the other deer that I could see but if there was another buck in that area he was probably back in the brush. I looked over at the little deer again and thought, "that's a big gully he just came up out of – I'm going to lay one right on his front shoulder and he's going to stay right up on top of the hill." I touched the trigger and it was just like I didn't even hit him. He went off that rise and down into the creek below and I could hear a crash. He's clear down into the bottom. So, I went over to where I shot and there was a little bit of hair and no blood. I followed the tracks a ways and found a couple of little spots of blood. I thought, "this isn't good." I followed him further – and there are a few more spots. Then I heard another crash and I looked down in the creek – but of course – I can't see all the way down there. Well, I heard another crash and it sounded like he was going down the creek. I just started following the tracks down the creek and the blood sign isn't increasing at all. There's a spot here and there.

Then I found where he tried to jump up over a pine limb that was about three feet up and he got tangled up and went head first into the creek and then went up the other side. Well, there's a little more blood there now – but not much. About then I started talking to myself – "here you are – up here all by yourself – I don't even know where I hit him – I thought I had a perfect shot." So, anyway, I got onto his trail and he's losing a little more blood and when he gets to a treetop he just bulldozed thru it and then he climbed the bank on the other side of that creek and it's probably a couple hundred feet from the bottom to the top. Then he crossed the logging road. There was a lot of four foot high spruce on a rock ledge. Well, the rock ledge dropped off about fifteen feet. He went right off the end of that. By now there's blood all over the place. He went on down to another rock ledge and he jumped off that another three or four feet and he goes right back down to the creek and open hardwoods. Well, I follow his tracks down and I can see out the other side – but I couldn't see him anywhere and I couldn't see any tracks where he had gone beyond – and I'm standing there in the creek and just looking.

Suddenly I could hear this breathing. There's a birch tree on the edge of the creek about three feet in diameter and I peek around on the other side – he'd gotten across the creek and there he lay – still alive. So, I shot him again. Then I thought, "where am I now?" I had to think awhile. I looked him over and found that I hit him in his shoulder okay – the bullet went thru his heart, both lungs were practically destroyed and it came out in his hindquarters. He went, probably, five hundred yards. He weighed a hundred and six pounds when I got him home – soaking wet. I had about a two-mile drag to get him out of there. That was an experience.

Rich: I guess so. Probably you were lucky he wasn't a hundred and eighty pound deer.

Lew: I thought he weighed two hundred pounds when I got him back to the trail – by then the snow was all gone in the trail and with that gravel – it was just like three people jumped on the back of him.

Rich: I've been in the woods by myself and I know – it's kind of a little different feeling. I've always enjoyed those times. I have never been terribly uneasy about it but I haven't done it in awhile either. I don't know if I'd want to tackle that right now – I almost don't think I would – of being alone in the woods right now – with my situation. I wouldn't mind going anywhere with another individual that was compatible and we were hunting but as far as heading there by myself for an overnight or more than one – I don't think I would attempt it. It probably wouldn't be wise. I have – plenty of times – gone up that river and stayed there four or five days all by myself and had a real good time. You need to be a little extra cautious.

Lew: You need to have a lot of common sense.

Rich: Yes, you do.

Lew: That will take you thru just about everything or help you get thru just about everything. Back at the time of hurricane Hazel they were camped on the west side of Spruce Lake. They had gone in there with horses that time. They were camped on the west side and had gone over there in a boat. This was spruce park. Huge – Donnie said they were twenty-four to thirty inches in diameter, fifty to sixty feet tall spruce trees. Hazel came thru and leveled them. He said they were lucky to get out alive, because all they had was a tent.

204

They came back across the lake. They did have chain saws with them but it still took them two and a half days to get out – to clear a path large enough so that the horses could travel thru that mess of downed timber. It was just a little under four miles. Donnie said they got it figured where to cut a tree off so they wouldn't have to cut it more than once – the roots would pull the stump back out of the way. It's a wonder they didn't run out of gas or something. There must have been a lot of them to cut. He said you couldn't imagine what it was like – being in that tent and having that whole park just go flat around you.

Rich: I would not have wanted to have been at High Falls a few years ago when that wind hit the area on the Oswegatchie River. There were two lean-tos there and they both were occupied at the time but neither of them were hit by a tree.

Lew: A friend of mine and his son went up after that storm hit. They had been up there a couple of other times and they wanted to see what it looked like after the storm. They said that a camper at the falls was hit by a tree and killed during that storm.

We used to lock the door of the camp but they kept trying to break in so we just left it unlocked. The trappers would stretch their beaver skins on our table – we would see the little nail marks where they stretched each pelt into a round shape. They always cleaned everything up and left it in good shape. Quite often there would be a note left – "thanks for the firewood and leaving the place unlocked – we appreciated it." The Northway Trail went right by our camp – about ten feet from it. Some that used the trail in the late fall or wintertime seemed to appreciate it that the camp was left open. They'd leave a little note there.

Rich: It might have saved somebody's life.

Lew: Could very well be. Before we left the place unlocked, we used to have a big Master padlock. Somebody tried opening it by shooting into it. Two bullets went right thru the logs next to the padlock. One bullet hit the place dead center where the pin was – I don't know who was holding it for him. The slug was in there against the pin. It appeared to be a .30 caliber bullet. Even that didn't open the lock. When we got there we took our key – wiggled it a little bit and –pop- we still have the lock and it still works but we don't use it anymore. They must have used a rifle. I would think the metal coming off that lock would have sprayed back at him.

Rich: There's nothing like those north woods.

Lew: Every trip up there we feel like a little kid – we get about half way up there and we can't wait until we get there. There's nothing like it – for some people – I guess.

Rich: Some people just aren't acclimated or haven't had the background or the encouragement – just will never get involved – and that's okay.

Lew: I have always been amazed when we were at the old camp by the number of people that used that Northway Trail in the late fall and early winter. They'll park at Piseco and hike in to use the lean-to. They were coming up for the weekend. Our camp was right next to the lean-to. Our camp was about an eighth of a mile from the lake and that's where the lean-to was. Once in awhile hunters would hike in and use the lean-to as a base and hunt out of there. But generally, it would be young people that would hike in there. They would be driving four or five hours and then they're hiking in to get in to the lean-to.

Rich: I would dare say, that probably ninety percent of them or better would be unarmed.

Lew: Oh, yeah.

Rich: Well, there isn't any way I'd go into an area where there are black bears unarmed.

Lew: I've been in there in the summertime and it's been pathetic – with the amount of trash that has been left there – right by the path.

Rich: That's bad news. You know, though – I've been into a lot of areas and where there have been lean-tos in use and just the opposite has been the case – other camp sites too. The area has been left without even a gum wrapper or cigarette butt in evidence. Perhaps the message is getting out – "if you carry it in – carry it out." Has anyone seen any moose in your area?

Lew: Ralph had seen one over near Otter Lake. The Forester hunting out of another camp had seen a cow and a calf and a bull together – he had gotten pictures of them. Other hunters have seen moose in the area. Two years ago Ronnie saw where they had ripped the bark off tiger maple. The sign looks like they have been rubbing their antlers. What they're doing is they are eating the bark. They'll cut their teeth into the base of those little trees and then yank on the bark and the whole strip that they pull off with one bite is probably five feet long. Where they grab it with their teeth on the tree starts at about chest high. You can see the teeth marks. They just rip that and pull it right up and then they snap it off. He said he's run onto a whole group of these little trees and maybe forty or fifty of them and the moose have taken bark off the whole bunch. Most people when they find this sign think they have been rubbing their antlers on them.

They discovered that a moose had been killed up near Mason Lake. Another hunter discovered the animal that someone had shot and killed and he reported it. When we went out they had the road blocked – they had a check station set up and they were checking firearms. They knew what caliber they were looking for. They knew what had been used to kill the moose. Whether they ever found the violator or not we never did know.

Rich: They ought to be able to tell a moose from a deer – seems as though.

Lew: Oh, yeah.

Rich: Jani and I were camping on the east end of Mason Lake one spring and were certain we had heard an elk. We called the Conservation Department and the guy said hang on – let me check something. Pretty soon, he came back to the phone and said, "well, we haven't released any in the area but some guy has a high fence with a bunch of different animals and his collection includes a few elk – maybe one of them got loose." They didn't act too surprised that we thought we heard one in the area.

Lew: A couple of years ago I saw a number of fawns in the woods. This last fall I don't think I saw any. I think the coyotes get a lot of them. Bears will take a few fawns each spring – their noses are so keen they can pick up on them.

Recently they have discovered that the turkeys in that area will bud it just like a partridge. They have documented the whole deal. They have found that a turkey will eat beech and maple buds and will stay up in a treetop for a couple of weeks at a time. They seem to know if they land in deep snow they may not be able to take off so they stay right up in the trees. If they come down to feed on the ground they pick an area around a spring where they have access to solid ground so they can take off with ease. At first they wondered how they could ever survive in that deep snow area of the woods. They certainly seem to do okay. Well, I've got to be going down the road.

Rich: Well, thank you for this very interesting and entertaining interview.

CHAPTER 20   FRANK MC NEAL

Rich: Please welcome Frank McNeal. We met at a local diner a few years ago and discovered shortly that we both had extensive interests in the out-of-doors – and especially in the area of animal trapping. I had trapped ever since I was about age ten. I began locally and my first experience was with trapping skunks. That's a whole other story. Then I trapped muskrats and mink with a high school buddy locally in the river and other streams. When my Dad and I began to take our fall vacations up north and the deer population was way low due to heavy winter kill in our area, I decided to trap for something to do and to add a little extra excitement to our adventure. Well, I had no idea of just how much enjoyment there might be with the hobby of trapping. Up north, we could expand our trapline to include beaver, otter, fox, raccoon, bobcat, mink, weasel and muskrat. Also it didn't take me very long to discover this was no snap. To be able to run a successful trapline – you needed to learn to read sign. I learned more about the woods and animals and nature on the trapline than I had ever known before. My trapping was an interesting hobby. Frank McNeal's trapline was the way he earned his living for a portion of each year that he owned the rights to trap. His line was located in British Columbia, Canada. Frank McNeal – were you born and raised in British Columbia?

Frank: No. We lived in New York State. My father liked to hunt and fish and trap and started looking for a place where he could settle down and enjoy the out-of-doors to a greater degree. He got serious about his quest in about 1952 – I was age seventeen at that time. At first he thought he might be interested in the Amazon River basin down in Columbia, South America. Dad wanted to make this big change while he was still able. Somehow he found out about British Columbia, Canada and that's where he decided to go. He bought three quarter sections and part of another one – we wound up owning around seven hundred acres. The area was heavily forested at that time and there was a lot of old growth timber. I have an old photo of my mother and Dad and I standing at the butt of a fir tree that we had cut and the fir tree is still up above our heads.

Rich: Had that Conibear trap been introduced yet?

Frank: No. Frank Conibear came out with his trap in about 1954. I recall that he had Eric Collier who lived down on Riske Creek test the traps that he had made. Collier was one of the officers of the B.C. Trappers Association. They sent furs every year to Vancouver. The furs were graded and then sold at the auction. There might be a couple of grades sold at the first auction and then the balance would be held over and then at the next auction more were sold. You'd receive checks all summer – normally all the fur wasn't sold at any one time. The Association helped with this and usually managed to get us better prices for our furs. This was an important service that they offered. I had finished high school by the time we moved out there.   The kids in that area all took correspondence courses for the first seven grades. Then, for high school they went into McBride – it was just like kids going to college. They had to stay right there the whole week. Bob Hahn and his brother had the next sawmill over from us and when I was home and going out on a Friday night or something usually I would return home afterwards. They'd always try to look me up so they could arrange to ride home with me. I remember one night I had both boys in the truck with me – the heater had quit in my truck. It was about sixty below. The windows would steam up inside the truck so fast that we had to drive with the windows open. I drove with my head out the window so I could see and I didn't realize I had frozen my ears. I had my ear floppers down but the wind still got under there and froze them stiff. After I dropped them off at their place, I still had about three quarters of a mile that I had to walk from where I could park the truck. I had to walk down the steep hill to get to our place down by the river.

Rich: Did your Dad trap?

Frank: He never did get time to. He ran a couple of sawmills and was busy with that so he never did actually get to run a line himself. I was allowed to have one assistant on my trapline and Dad would go with me once in awhile just for something different to do and he definitely was interested – so, we had fun. Every spring I trapped beaver primarily and of course the other furbearing animals as we went along. I purchased my line from Shorty. He had left a lot of traps right in the woods. For example, when you'd make a set for martin or fisher, you'd normally make the set on the top of a pole you would lean up against a tree. I'd put some bait at the top of that pole and the trap would go right up there too. I'd fasten the little nail that was hooked to the ring of the trap to the pole and when the animal would get in, he'd just dangle there off that pole and soon freeze to death.

Shorty accompanied me back on that trapline the first time or two and then we'd go hunting afterward. He had two cabins on King Creek and one on Baker Creek. These were at opposite ends of my trapline so that worked out quite well. There was another trapper that also used the cabin at Baker Creek as that was near the end of his line – so once in awhile I'd get there and I would have company. My trapline included two main streams and the entire watershed in between. This would include various ponds and streams that eventually ran into the Frazer River. It was quite a large piece of territory – about all I could handle running the line by myself. He got into a post business on the side onetime back up on the mountain. He got out electric and fence posts which gave him a nice extra income. He had just entered the cabin one day and was getting a fire started. We didn't have glass in the windows – we just had a dried skin called a babiche. It would let in some light but you couldn't see out thru it. He heard something and looked over there at the window and he saw what looked like teeth making a tear right thru that babiche. So he went outside and looked and here's this sow grizzly with two cubs that probably weighed around five hundred pounds apiece. He yelled at them but she wouldn't go. She made a lunge toward him so he closed the door. He went and got his rifle and eventually had to shoot her. He also had to shoot the cubs because they wouldn't leave the area and they became dangerously aggressive. So, now he's got another problem. The weather was quite warm and he had to decide what to do with them all. He had a lot of scrap left over from where he had cut out the fence posts so he covered them all up with that stuff and then set the whole works on fire. He had to keep the fire going on them about a week before he got that job done. He didn't want to attract other bears to the area as he was living there so he had no other choice. After a few days the odor would have been atrocious.

I killed a black bear near my Dad's sawmill one spring – not too far back in the woods from his mill. One day I was over there and my Dad says, "say, you recall you shot a bear out in the woods somewhere – I think you better do something about it." So, I had to go out and take a shovel and bury him. After digging down thru the shallow soil and roots, the hole, such as it was, began to fill in with water. What a time I had getting him covered up so we wouldn't have to contend with that horrible smell. I was a lot more careful of where I shot a bear after that episode. Maybe I could have gotten a horse and dragged him away from the area but he stunk so bad I just wanted to get this taken care of.

Trapping was definitely an important part of my yearly income because in the spring we got laid off from our job at the sawmill. They didn't log in the summertime out there and by the middle of

March it was soft enough that you couldn't work in the area with heavy equipment back in on the muskeg. One of the sawmills was over across the river by the railroad siding that was on the south side of the Frazer River. To get across we used a ferry – we would drive right up on it and operated it ourselves – we could go across right on the current. In the wintertime it was much easier and faster when there was ice on the river – we could just drive right across. As soon as it got really cold we'd take pumps and pump water on top of the ice and then we'd put slabs from the sawmill on top of that and we'd have an iced corduroy road. We'd have men out there all night building that ice up and then you could drive a D-8 across. In the spring of 1957 it was about the 15th of March that we got laid off. It warmed up and we came out – the frost was going out of the ground. Beaver season in that country didn't close until the end of May, so that gave me a couple of months I could trap. There would still be lots of snow back up in those mountains.

Rich: Would you trap muskrats as well as the beaver?

Frank: There were not a lot of muskrats in that area. I don't know why. There were very few muskrats. There always seemed to be a good quantity of top grade mink.

Rich: Was the mink fur that time of year still good?

Frank: There was still ice and snow up in the mountains and it got cold nights so the fur was still prime. The first year I went out on that line I did a bit of trapping in the fall. I'd go back up in the mountains all by myself at that time – it got progressively colder each day it seemed. I liked trapping in the spring. You couldn't trap beaver in the winter. When it first got cold in the fall you could make a few sets but a little later on there got to be so much snow up on top of the ice you would have to try to find open water but then when you did find it, the beaver didn't bother coming out all that much. With the temperature at 40 below zero – they stayed in. They could keep warm and in good condition in their houses.

Rich: In that spring season could you still trap for animals like martin and fisher?

Frank: Yeah – we trapped everything at that time. There were a few wolverines but there weren't a lot of foxes. There were a few cross-foxes but not a lot. Canadian lynx were rather numerous but their pelts weren't worth very much so it didn't pay us to try to trap them. Their fur was certainly very beautiful. There are some funny things about fashion.

Rich: What about coyotes – did you make an effort to get them?

Frank: No.

Rich: They didn't have enough fur value then probably.

Frank: There were a few wolves around the area and where there are wolves generally the coyotes just aren't there. The wolves will run the coyotes right out of the territory. There was still a small bounty on the wolves. The Game Wardens poisoned the coyotes and wolves both – they almost got a couple of siwash Indians. They threw a haunch of horse or moose or something out of an airplane and they had it laced with poison and the Indians came along back up in the mountains. It didn't kill them but they got real sick on it. They would usually come around and tell you they were planning to poison a certain area. I've seen coyotes in the spring lying up on top of the willows where the snow had been four feet deep and that was where they had died after eating the poison. The coyotes would start yapping at night – pretty soon an old wolf would howl and then you wouldn't hear the coyote after that. It got real quiet.

Rich: The out-of-doors is very interesting and unique and a challenge. Most of my book is about deer hunting and different kinds of deer hunters and different types of camps but then we discovered that just about everybody that hunts Adirondacks or anywhere else in New York State eventually has a dream of going somewhere else to hunt big game like Montana or Colorado or Alaska or Canada or someplace so we tried to include some of those stories. I think trapping is a unique hobby. I used to do quite a bit of trapping, many years ago. There definitely was a learning curve connected with that sport. I believe I honestly learned more about the woods and wildlife thru trapping than I ever knew before and it stuck with me. It's just like opening your eyes to the woods and to be able to read the sign of animals and to be able to tell what they have done, where they've been and where they're heading lots of times. Tell us a little about trapping the other kinds of animals – would the area where you'd trap for the martin and fisher – would that be in conjunction with where you'd be trapping beaver?

Frank: Yes – many times the areas would overlap. Being an area where there was a quantity of virgin timber the martin and fisher would be available just back in the mountain a little ways from the areas where we'd be trapping beaver. There was one Sitka spruce just below my first cabin. The Conservation Department went up there and taped the tree and measured the height of it. They suggested back then you could build about five ranch houses from just that one tree.

All the animal's territory overlapped. I was able to trap mountain lions, lynx and other animals. They all pretty much would travel the trails. When I got laid off I'd begin by trapping the beaver close by. Then as the snow receded back up into the mountains I'd progress up the watersheds and that would get me into the higher elevations which would make the other type of furbearers available as I moved up into their territory. Eventually I'd work my way back up into the beaver meadows that would be at the beginning of the streams. There were so many small streams coming down from the ice fields in higher country, the beaver would make dams to allow them to create a waterway which would enable them to get back in to get to the poplar which of course was a main food source for them. The only time the Game Warden came back in was if someone made a complaint.

You pretty much did your own conservation. If you trapped an area out then you were the one to ultimately suffer. It was important to leave seed in each area so that the animals could multiply and restock the area. You weren't supposed to trap on a dam or in a house but occasionally those things happened. I thought that when they extended their season to the end of May they really overdid it as some of the beaver females would be about ready to give birth to their kits about then. The streams were so cold – there would be ice floating in them all most of the time. Snow-slides were constantly coming down off the mountains and dam up the streams – this would effect the temperature in a stream for a period of time.

Rich: Did you ever happen to use any of the Conibear traps for beaver?

Frank: Not out there.

Rich: What kind of a set would you prefer to use for catching a beaver?

Frank: Frequently we'd use a thin slice from a beaver castor as lure. This would always be very effective. They made runs that would go back to where they could get at the poplar and willows. We'd pick a place that was fairly shallow where they would be swimming back up their channel. I'd put a stick across that run on both sides of the trap. No matter which way they'd be swimming as soon as their chest would hit that stick they'd put their feet down. Otherwise, they would swim right over the trap. I found that it helped a lot in really shallow water areas to use snares. It wouldn't be possible to make a drowning set in a shallow area.

Rich: Did you like to make a drowning set where you could?

Frank: Always – we'd make a drowning set if possible.

Rich: How did you set up for that – did you use angle iron on a wire or how would you rig it?

Frank: Generally we would use snare locks right there. That will allow the beaver to pull the lock down but it won't come back up. We made our own snares so we used the same locks in making a drowning set. We'd fasten one end of the wire to a rock and throw it out in deeper water or use a log or trunk of a small tree and drive it in to the bottom where it was deep. I had a large female beaver in my trap one time – she was right up on top of the bank. I thought that was funny – there was lots of water there when I made the set. What happened was upstream one of those snow slides came down off the mountain and landed in the creek bed and that effectively formed a dam. It would take some time for the force of the water that was being dammed up to cut a new channel thru that snow slide. Well, this big beaver made a dive for the channel leading back to her pond and as she did, I got caught up in the wire so we both went into that little narrow ditch and we both got quite wet. I got her out of there. We had a lot of fun sometimes. It was a nice warm spring day – but that water was ice cold.

Rich: People who read that Eric Collier story found out that at the time he moved into his area on Riske Creek, the fur bearers were just about non existent at that time. The locals had over-trapped the area. The beaver were gone, the dams were in total disrepair and they no longer held any water back so that the farmers downstream didn't have enough water to water their stock to say nothing of having water for irrigation of their crops. Well, Collier got the bright idea that if he could just repair a couple of those dams and impound the water, that would provide plenty for his purpose of encouraging animals to come back into his region as well as waterfowl, etc. – and also would provide plenty of water for the neighboring ranchers downstream. This was an idea he had – wasn't really sure it would work – but thought it would. He checked with the ranchers downstream and they all said, "it can't possibly be any worse than it is right now – go ahead – give it a try." It turned out to be a success. Well, give it water and the muskrats and mink come back – ducks and geese – the whole works – except they didn't have any beaver – until one day, here comes the D.E.C. or whatever it was and they had two pair of beaver they had live trapped from some other area and they let them out at his new ponds. That was the beginning of the restocking of the beaver in that whole area.

Frank: I couldn't buy the trapline – I had to buy the trapper's rights – I had to be approved by the government before they would put it in my name. I wound up getting the cabins and traps and other items that he had left there connected with his trapline. Collier's efforts, though they were good and had fine results in getting fur bearing animals established again in his own area – really didn't have any direct effect on the fur bearers in our area as it was too far away. His area on Riske Creek was up

212

over a large range of mountains – it was the Caribou Mountain Range. That's the reason they had to bring beaver in down there where he was. There wasn't any way that beaver could naturally migrate into that area and if they didn't have some help probably there never would have been beaver in that area at all. Eventually, maybe, a few might work their way up into that region from the waterways but they would have had to run the gauntlet of all the native trappers and the possibility of their getting back into that area would be slim.

Rich: They will migrate quite a distance – the young get kicked out each year. That's asking a lot for them to have to travel over the top of a high mountain range. If any would try it, they likely would be picked off by natural predators such as bears, wolves or lions. Even a bobcat would consider a beaver, especially a young one, as being fair game and a good meal.

Frank: There's a two lane super highway thru the area now where my Dad had his homestead and sawmills. We had a huge cedar stump left from where I had cut one of those virgin trees. The stump was so big we couldn't drive the bulldozer around it. The bulldozer couldn't push it out so we took it out with dynamite. We put a couple cases of dynamite in there and it barely shook it. So, we dug around it some more and put in about six boxes of dynamite and afterwards we never found the stump. Now it's right where highway 16 goes thru there. The last year I was there was the spring of 1957. I worked at Harstead Lumber Camp. There were four of us staying in that bunkhouse which was about ten foot wide and eighteen foot long and it had one big stove right in the center – what we called airtight – it was just made out of a piece of tin. We had three cases of dynamite right near where my bunk was. When we came in at night we took turns cutting firewood.

This new guy came in and he was throwing those pieces of firewood into our bunkhouse and bouncing them right off those cases of dynamite. I stood there watching him for a while and finally I says, "hey, uh, you wouldn't mind throwing that a little lighter or in a different direction there, would you?" He said, "well, if you don't like it – cut it yourself." I replied, "I don't mind it but somebody's going to get a bang out of it pretty quick." He says, "what do you mean?" I said, "bouncing them off those cases of dynamite there – it isn't going to help you by being outside that door any." He didn't throw any more in after that. Around here, they'd have had a heart attack if anybody had that much dynamite.

Rich: Dynamite was something they used extensively in the Adirondacks on their river drives. If they had a log jam that they couldn't get apart with men using their pike poles and other efforts, they would tie two or three sticks of dynamite to a round flat rock – and swing it straight arm – like you'd toss a discus at a track meet. They'd light the fuse and make a wide swing and let it go – when it hit the surface of the water they hoped it would drop into the river on the right side of that jam. Meanwhile, you'd better be heading for some tree or something to hide behind.

Frank: Dynamite blows down and out. Stumping powder blows up. There's a specific stumping powder – a different kind of stuff. It's pretty stable to handle – unless it starts getting sweaty on the outside – that's nitro glycerin coming out of it and you'd better handle that carefully. Back east a friend used to supply us with dynamite. He'd pay us a visit and toss four or five sticks right over onto the couch we were sitting on. We'd take that and cut it into pieces – and use it to fish with. We'd ignite it by touching the fuse wires to opposite ends of a flashlight battery. We'd toss it in the hole and then wait awhile until the fish would come back to that area and then touch it off.

Rich: They really did used to fish using dynamite then?

Frank: Oh, yes – for trout.

Rich: I think it is a bit more sporting if you use a judo point on your arrow. That way you're looking at one at a time.

Frank: With dynamite – you're sure. The furbearers that were in the mountains usually didn't gravitate to other places. The beaver normally wouldn't go that high. The mountain lions would pick them off. The Frazier valley up thru there was so vast there really wasn't much necessity for any animals to totally leave it.

When we'd trap beaver in the Frazier River we'd make our sets where we'd find a beaver scent mound. This would be a place where the beaver would mound up a little pile of mud and leave their scent on it – their way of communicating to other beaver I suppose. We'd add a little fresh scent – use a thin slice from a castor – and then we'd put in some sticks and make a fence on each side. This would encourage the beaver to come in and have some effect on where they would put their feet down. We'd dig down a little in the mud to make a place to put the trap and would put a stick down in that area which would again cause the beaver to put its feet down. We'd always make a drowning set as we knew the beaver would be caught by its front foot.

Rich: Would you be bothered by the rise in the water level of the areas where you'd be trapping after a rainstorm for example?

Frank: No, generally not in the upper meadows. Downstream, near the mouth of the stream you would sometimes notice a rise or lowering of the water level but normally not enough to be a bother. Except for the times when a snow slide up in the mountains would dam up the creek for a time – that would make all sorts of changes in a hurry. One time I was trapping near the mouth of a creek and it split and ran around a little island. I had traps on both sides of that island. One day I was checking my traps and couldn't figure why my traps were right up on top – high and dry. All of a sudden I heard a roar and then noticed the water level beginning to rise very rapidly. Now my traps were covered by water and the level was continuing to rise. One of those snowslide dams upstream had given away and the whole accumulation was coming down fast. My little island was suddenly getting littler. I took my rifle and swung it way over onto the bank of the river. I removed my shoes and all the rest right down to my shorts and wound that all up and made a bundle and then took a stick and made it like a whip and I whipped them all over onto the bank and then I jumped in. There was a curve there right around that island and the current carried me over onto the other bank where I crawled out. When there's ice floating around your ears it's mighty cold. I wiped myself off with my undershirt and got the rest of my clothes on. Day by day it's a lot of fun sometimes on the trapline – it's a challenge.

Rich: Did you normally work your trapline by yourself or did you have a companion or helper some of the time?

Frank: Normally I went by myself. The old fellow I bought the line from did go with me several times. He didn't trap but just wanted to come along and lend me a hand. He was a wealth of information and I learned a lot from him and greatly enjoyed his company. I missed him when he wasn't along. Leo was a good old guy. He didn't own a car and would walk everywhere he wanted to go – probably would put in seven or eight miles every day just walking. He had been a guide for a number of years in the area. He always wore cowboy boots and a large cowboy hat. He even named a local mountain up at the head of Pine Creek after a wealthy dude from Wyoming that he had guided several times. He named it Harmon Mountain. Leo's last name was German sounding so the Canadians took all his guns away from him during the Second World War. Here he is – making his living trapping and being a big game guide – but he had guns stashed back on the trapline that they didn't know about to survive.

Before I moved away from that country I had been a wrangler for a couple of years with an outfitter. That was one thing I was really very interested in doing myself – I would only have to work as a wrangler one more year and then I would be able to apply for my guide's license. On one of our trips we had to hunt two days on foot because all the horses had wandered out of the area and it took us that long to find them. We were primarily hunting bear, moose, goats and sheep. Moose would be back in the valleys – anyplace where there were willows and that kind of growth. When they'd be feeding in the ponds, they'd dive right down out of sight and then come up all covered with mud and with a mouthful of aquatic plants of some sort. They'd feed heavily on the willow buds – they were great browsers.

Rich: How did you happen to leave that part of the country and come out to the east here?

Frank: In the spring of 1957 when I got laid off, another friend and I were planning to come out to Edmonton and get a job on the pipeline and run a bulldozer all summer. He worked a few days longer than I did but then when he got laid off, we took his car and fastened it down onto a flatcar. We pulled the springs down and tied it off with wire. He and I rode in his car on the flatcar on the train out to Jasper National Park. When we got out there we got his car unloaded and drove to the Union Hall and we got our jobs running bulldozer clearing right of way. However, there was a real cold spell that came in so the ground was still frozen.

Louie was born in Italy and raised in Yugoslavia and he and four other guys had escaped out of there during World War II. Mussolini killed all their relatives and friends – mothers and fathers and everything and those five guys escaped over the mountains. They were really close. When one got married the others bought him a house and paid for the wedding – they were closer than brothers ever were. Well, Louie and I were really good friends. He wanted to come to the United States – I was still a U.S. Citizen. I said, "well, let's see what we can do." We went to the immigration hall but we went to the wrong one. That was back when all the Hungarians were escaping in 1957 and they were shipping them by the trainload from Halifax all across Canada. These folks were stripped of all their possessions. Men, women and kids – just what they had on was all they had.

Finally we went to the American Consulate and they informed us that he had to be sponsored from the United States end. We returned to the Union Hall and they told us it would be at least three weeks or more before we'd be able to go to work. My brother was still living in Greene, New York. I said, "I'll fly back there and see if I can't get you sponsored from that end." He'd let me know then what he would decide and I'd fly back to Winnepeg because I had my job all lined up there. I went to the Post Office in Greene and told them that any letters that came for me to please hold them. A month later my Dad called my brother and told him that my job was gone. I'd left my rifle and clothes and everything in Louie's car and he shipped them all back to my Dad. He was a great guy – but I never saw him again. In 1957 I worked in the States but then returned in the fall to Canada. In 1958 my Dad decided to return to the States so I drove the truck with all the belongings and back we came. I didn't realize at the time what a wonderful place that really was out there. When you're young, there are so many things that you're interested in. My wife and I visited that area where we lived a couple of years ago and noted all the changes. There was a new highway right thru the area where we used to trap. They changed the names of most of the streams and the area is all built up with very expensive homes and what a change. All the old growth timber is long gone.

Rich: You lived out there and enjoyed that country at the best time.

Frank: Right.

Rich: So you can remember that and recall it very fondly and appreciate the time you actually did spend there.

Frank: There were great quantities of game of every kind back then. I've got the antlers of a huge moose that I shot while leaning against the corner of our cabin. He was in our garden. We had black bears in the backroom. A friend's wife used to do a lot of baking and made pastries. She wouldn't use anything but bear fat. Her husband was a butcher. When she needed more bear fat, she'd tell him and he'd get word to me that she needed some more. I'd get a nice fat black bear and take it to him and he'd cut it up and save all the fat for his wife. There was a full-blooded Indian that was head starter at one of the mills where I worked and I got invited one time to eat dinner at his place. Jack Walker was his name. He said, "well, how'd you like the meat tonight, Frank?" I said, "real good." He then said, "mountain lion."

One time some young friends went hunting and killed a nice moose. They came back to the ranch for a horse and when they got back to the kill a big grizzly bear had taken over the carcass. Well, they killed that bear and dragged him to the ranch and hung him up in the barn – his hind feed were just touching the floor. One of the boys was six foot six – he walked up and stood beside the bear and when he raised his arm he could just get his hand up to the bear's shoulder. He must have been able to reach up at least nine feet. They skinned him and they had his hide hanging on the side of the barn there for years.

I think it is a dangerous practice they seem to be following now days. They develop all these nice park areas in the wilderness and then turn the people loose. In areas where there are lots of bear I think they are making a mistake to allow people to go in there – but they aren't allowed to have any weapon or any way to protect themselves if they do get attacked. I want something besides a little bell to ring or stones in a tin can to rattle or a spray can of pepper or something to defend myself with. They aren't doing people much of a favor by just telling them to play dead if they get attacked by a bear.

I've been up in the Adirondacks and seen people take their little kid and sit him on the back of a black bear that was feeding there in a dump. That's just asking for trouble. After I left the west, up in Jasper National Park some woman took her little five year old daughter and tried to sit her up on the bear's back – of course the bear killed the little girl. It wasn't the bear that got the girl killed – it was the stupidity of the woman that did it. They shouldn't have the bears in the town – this was right in a park in the middle of town where it happened.

216

There was another woman out there recently that made the press – she would shoot any bear that came around with her gun using rubber bullets and then she'd sick her dogs on them. After awhile the bears will get the idea that man is nothing to trifle with and teach her cubs to fear man too. There was a couple we knew that killed a sow one time and it turned out she had two cubs. They thought, "aren't they cute" and decided to raise them. The little male cub was quite aggressive. One day he swatted the other cub when she was trying to drink some milk out of a saucer. Well, the fellow hauled off and gave him a hard swat on his little behind – but he never got his hand back. That animal turned so quick – he set his teeth into his hand and scratched his arm with both front feet and claws. He shook him loose, grabbed his .30-30 rifle and said, "I'll take care of this" – and turned them both out in the back yard and killed them right then and there.

One time a friend and I went goat hunting. We managed to kill a goat. It had been very mild but then it started to rain. Pretty soon it got cold and began snowing. He had a large coat he had been carrying but all I had was just the clothes I had on and not very warm. We got up by a sort of cave and got a fire going. I stepped out on some willows to get a pine tree that was lying there and pulled it in and used that for firewood. In the morning I looked out there where I had picked that tree up and all there was underneath those willows was a drop of about a thousand feet. They were all bent over from the heavy weight of previous snows. That night it had snowed about six inches. We had logging shoes and couldn't climb as the snow balled right up under our shoes. So, there we were with the goat. By mid-afternoon it had thawed enough so we could climb back onto the top of the mountain. We eventually got out of there with our meat. The change in the weather can happen very quickly and if you are not properly dressed it can be a big problem.

The people that bought the land right down behind where we used to live raise grain there now. They have about three hundred acres they have cleared that I used to trap on. A couple of years ago my wife and I went back for a visit. I was riding down there with a young lad in his vehicle right where I used to have to walk. We got out to take a look at the river and he had a little white dog with him. His mother really loved that little dog. Pretty soon that dog got out of sight and he says, "oh, oh – where'd that little dog go?" We stopped and he came running out of the bushes and I got him in my arms and put him back in the car. Then he said, "I'm sure glad you put him in the car. Recently we were down in here with his brother and a mountain lion got him" - so, they're still there. They don't show themselves – very often. When I was a boy I would park our car at the top of that same little hill just above our house. I'd have to walk down there in the dark as I seldom had a flashlight with me. As I'd walk down to the house I could hear a mountain lion growling – I knew he was following me. When I got down the hill toward the meadow and near where the house was, he'd quit. The game is still in that area though I don't believe the moose are quite as numerous as they once were, which you'd have to expect.

CHAPTER 21   THOUGHTS, THANKS AND ENDINGS

In Memoriam. . . FRANKLIN G. UNDERWOOD

Franklin G. Underwood, 72, of NYS Route 41, McGraw, N.Y., passed away April 12, 2002, at his home after a brief illness.

Mr. Underwood was born in the Town of Freetown, the son of Reuben and Mildred Underwood.

He owned and operated a dairy farm in the Town of Solon for 22 years, retiring in 1979. Prior to that he worked for Thompson Boat Co. for 10 years. He was an Army Veteran of the Korean War, an avid hunter, fisherman, and maple syrup producer.

Mr. Underwood was a member of the McGrawville Baptist Church and served as trustee. He was a former member of the McGraw Central School Board and Solon Town Board.

Surviving are his wife of 51 years, Mabel Kruger Underwood of McGraw; three daughters, Cynthia (Gerald) Craig, Cathy (Raymond) Salisbury, both of McGraw, and Christine (Robert) Buerkle of Cortland; four grandchildren, Gerald L. Craig, Julie Craig, Loretta Buerkle and Wayne Buerkle; two sisters, Margaret Dolly of Zephyrhills, Fla. and Eva Gabriel of Cortland; and several nieces, nephews and cousins.

He was predeceased by a son, Stephen in 1956; and a sister, Sarah Smith in 2001.

Services will be Monday at 11 a.m. in the McGrawville Baptist Church with the Rev. Alvin Mosher officiating. Internment is in Marathon Cemetery.

Friends may call Sunday from 4 to 7 p.m. at the Barth Funeral Home, McGraw.

Contributions may be made to the McGrawville Baptist Church Memorial Fund, P.O. Box 517, McGraw, N.Y. 13101 or Hospice of Cortland County, 11 Kennedy Pkwy., Cortland, N.Y. 13045.

It is better for a man to attend a funeral than to be honored or to have a party with his friends. We alike will all die – don't we owe it to ourselves to prepare for the reality of this eventuality?

Revelation 4:11   NIV "You are worthy, our Lord and God, to receive glory and honor and power, for you created all things, and by your will they were created and have their being."

Psalm 96 NIV "Sing to the Lord a new song; sing to the Lord, all the earth. Sing to the Lord, praise his name; proclaim his salvation day after day. Declare his glory among the nations, his marvelous deeds among all peoples. For great is the Lord and most worthy of praise; he is to be feared above all gods. For all the gods of the nations are idols, but the Lord made the heavens. Splendor and majesty are before him; strength and glory are in his sanctuary. Ascribe to the Lord, O families of nations, ascribe to the Lord glory and strength. Ascribe to the Lord the glory due his name; bring an offering and come into his courts. Worship the Lord in the splendor of his holiness; tremble before him, all the earth. Say among the nations, "The Lord reigns." The world is firmly established, it cannot be moved; he will judge the peoples with equity. Let the heavens rejoice, let the earth be glad; let the sea resound, and all that is in it; let the fields be jubilant, and everything in them. Then all the trees of the forest will sing for joy; they will sing before the Lord, for he comes, he comes to judge the earth. He will judge the world in righteousness and the peoples in his truth."

Inspirational Quote:

"You can read all the manuals on prayer and listen to other people pray, but until you begin to pray yourself you will never understand prayer. It's like riding a bicycle or swimming: you learn by doing." --- Evangelist Luis Palau

HOW DO I EVER GIVE THANKS to all of you that have helped me put this book together and make a dream come true! THANK YOU!

First of all to those of you that purchased a copy of my first effort at writing a book about the out-of-doors about five years ago, a big "thank you." The title was "Deer Camp – Oswegatchie River And Other Places" (currently out of print). The interest that was shown in my first effort encouraged me to try this writing business one more time.

Secondly – I owe a special debt of gratitude to each and every one of you that allowed me to interview you with my tape recorder in hand. I have always enjoyed to the limit the wonderful stories shared around the evening campfire or next to the woodstove in deer camps in a variety of locations over the past sixty years or so. However, I never expected these incredible results – you people are all great! Thanks for your making this book a possibility. Please all take a bow – and buy some books – I've got to recoup the expenses I've accumulated with this project in the over four and a half months that it has taken to complete.

It's been over five years since I've even looked at a computer, and I never did know anything about Windows. Without the special assistance, help and infinite patience of Gerald and Janet Hines, Lori at the Community Technology Center (Computer Lab) located at J.M. Murray Center, Inc., and my Great Nephew, Jeff Niswender who works for Best Buy over in Ithaca I would never have been able to do this project in the first place. My first book was submitted to the publisher on typewritten pages. Presently the manuscript must be submitted in a "camera ready" format and printed with a laser printer. I must give special thanks to Pastor Brian Rice, Ann Nafziger and Mary Dunham of Homer Baptist Church. These folks made the very difficult and technical problem of printing this manuscript onto laser paper via a laser printer seem like a snap. Thanks so much for your help! It isn't easy to learn all this high tech stuff at my age. I also give special thanks to my Lord and Saviour, Jesus Christ (Father God's only Son) who has given me strength and stamina to do far and above all I ever have been required to do – with joy! If I have left anyone out please accept my thanks and forgive me. My favorite scripture: John 3:16.

Special thanks also are extended to my precious wife, Janice. It's one thing to read a book – but quite another to read a book for the express purpose of discovering typos, glitches, misspelled words and whatever other problems might crop up – it's a huge job and takes a bundle of energy. Thanks, Jani – I love you!

I was a bit discouraged when I found out that the publisher was going to limit the number of photos that would be allowed. I believe black and white make very impressive pictures for a book on hunting and deer camp and story telling. If the pictures aren't what you expected or hoped they would be (me too) – then we can revert to the pictures in our minds. Even as we recall the events of a successful hunt - (and many successful hunts don't involve killing anything) – isn't it an incredible blessing to able to recall so vividly in our mind's eye various scenes and events? Numerous mentions have been made throughout this book of how much we all appreciate and enjoy the real benefits of

219

deer camp – the fellowship and camaraderie – especially that which is closely connected with story telling. In my own mind, I believe these blessings and benefits are all the more meaningful to me having been privileged to share these items with all of you. Story telling is a means of communicating that will never die out or disappear so long as deer camp and God's great world of creation still exists. Enjoy!

You may order a copy of "Deer Camp – An American Tradition" by Robert C. Mills thru Davis Book Store, P.O. Box 317, Homer, NY 13077-0317 phone (607) 423-5063 and the price is $12.95 plus tax. If you prefer to order an Autographed copy, send the $12.95 direct to: Mr. Robert Mills, 576 Hiawatha Drive, Mt. Pleasant, Mi 48858

As promised – here's the recipe for pickled deer (or bear) heart. Par-boil in a covered saucepan for about one-half hour or until tender (you can stick a dinner fork into it easily) – I like to add about 1/2 teaspoon of salt while boiling. When tender, drain and let cool to room temperature – about one hour or so. When preparing, a large deer heart will generally fit into two pint canning jars. Slice the heart about one quarter inch thick, trim off the obvious fat and cut in large chunks to just fit inside the glass jars. Slice a large sweet onion. Pack into the jars in layers – start with a slice of onion, then deer heart – salt and pepper quite heavily as you go – pack right up to the top. Fill with equal parts of apple cider vinegar and cold water. Apply lid tightly. Shake slowly to mix well the ingredients. Place in refrigerator after affixing a label identifying the contents – also include the date prepared. Let jars sit in refrigerator for TWO WEEKS! Now enjoy! Discard the onion – that was added for flavor. If you want some onion on your sandwich, please cut a fresh slice. The best way to build the sandwich (you don't really need to be told I am certain) – however, I merely like to put a little butter on a slice of favorite kind of bread – add one thickness of the deer heart – a couple of fresh slices of sweet onion, then some mayonnaise or Miracle Whip – some salt and pepper (nothing else) – and now of course the second slice of bread – and enjoy the best sandwich you ever did have. If you don't really like this please give the heart to me – or some friend that will appreciate it – or make up this sandwich meat and trade a couple of jars for some tickets to your favorite movie or basketball game.

A year or so ago I received at Christmas a book from my Step-Daughter Becci Kuske who lives out in Michigan. The title of the book was "The Education Of A Bear Hunter" by Ralph Flowers. Mr. Flowers told about his job working for a large lumber company in the State of Washington. He was hired to kill bears. The best way to do this was to catch them in snares and then he had to find the bear and kill it with his rifle. The whole purpose in killing bears was that one bear could kill as many as about 173 trees a day in the spring when he had first left his den. He would be hungry and there wasn't much else to eat at first other than the bark of a tree – even the grass hadn't begun to grow. This was a very expensive problem for the lumber company. In fact, he was the second bear man to be hired by the lumber company. The other bear man was an individual by the name of Bill Hulet. He had been hired to kill bears first – in fact he had worked for the lumber company for about fifty years.

Included in this delightful book was a poem that Mr. Flowers had written to honor his friend, Bill Hulet. He also included a photo of the man and when I saw the picture, it reminded me so much of my own father, Lester J. Davis, I could hardly believe it – right down to the cigar. I contacted Mr. Flowers and received permission to include the poem in this book for your enjoyment.

ODE TO BILL HULET

Up at the end of the Wishkah Road
And right at the foot of the hill,
   Across the river
   And close to the dam
There lives a fellow named Bill.
Tall timber surrounds his humble domain;
The river runs right by his door,
   And at night when the rain
   Rattles on the pane
Bill learns what an easy chair's for.
For fifty-odd years he stomped through the brush
To the north, the west, south and east;
   Chasing the hounds
   He covered the ground
Just like an old timber-beast.
When springtime arrived and the salt grass turned green
He'd shape up his whole pack of dogs;
   And any ol' bear
   A-wandering 'round there
Wouldn't even be safe in his log.
He loved those old dogs and treated them well
He saw good ones come and go;
   But old Iron Mike
   He especially liked
And another he called old Bozo.
Over three thousand bears fell to his gun,
He learned all their habits, and so
   When his dogs struck
   A bear track in the muck
Bill could tell you just where it would go.
Bill saw the old-growth go to the mill
He watched the second growth grow
   He knows all the land
   Like the back of his hand
But time has dealt him a blow.
The legs that tramped over all of these hills
And followed the dogs to the tree
   No longer respond
   To the urge to go on
And there's an occasional kink in the knee.
So Bill has hung up his .348
And sold all his dogs, you see;
   But his heart, it is still
   'way out on the hill
Listening to Mike at the tree.
I could sit and listen, hour after hour
To his tales of days gone by;

I'll learn from this man
    All that I can
So I can give it a try.
And now when the moon comes over the ridge
And the grass is covered with frost,
    He's without a care
    In his old easy chair
No worry for a dog that is lost.
He just kicks off his shoes and winks at Irene
With that bright little twinkle in his eye
    And there's nothing to fear
    As he strokes from his beard
The crumbs from a big apple pie.

Rich Davis
Chapter 1, Page 1

Howard Henry
Chapter 2, Page 10

Martin Knobel
Chapter 3, Page 21

Ginny Knobel
Chapter 4, Page 31

I

John & Robert Knobel
Chapter 5, Page 36

Robert Schoenfeld
Chapter 6, Page 52

John Davis
Chapter 7, Page 58

Ruth & Sam Mrosz
Chapter 8, Page 69

Mike Niswender & Ron Boyden
Chapter 9, Page 85

Tom Cain
Chapter 10, Page 105

Jeff DeMann
Chapter 11, Page 118

Peter Young
Chapter 12, Page 126

David Flavin
Chapter 13, Page 139

John MacNeill
Chapter 14, Page 150

Todd Knobel & Mike Feint
Chapter 15, Page 164

Barry Warren
Chapter 16, Page 172

IV

Wayne Matteson
Chapter 17, Page 185

Lew Heath
Chapter 19, Page 195

Larry Knobel, Chapter 18, Page 193 - No Photo

Charlotte & Frank McNeal
Chapter 20, Page 208

Camp Knobel
Chapter 3, Page 21

Tom Cain's Texas Whitetails

Tom Cain
See Chapter 10, Page 105

John Davis
Chapter 7, Page 58

Sam Mrosz
Chapter 8, Page 69

David McCloy's Trophy Buck
Chapter 11, Page 118

Robert Knobel
About November, 1982

Author, Rich Davis

Sam Mrosz - A few years ago - Gave us Gas